PRINCIPLES OF HINDU JURISPRUDENCE

First Published 1996

ISBN : 81-85616-41-8 (Set)

Published by :
B.L. Bansal for Sharada Publishing House,
40, Anand Nagar, Inderlok,
DELHI-110035. Ph. 5117390, 5116768.

Printed at :
Santosh Offset, DELHI-110035.

PRINCIPLES OF HINDU JURISPRUDENCE

Vol.1

(Vyavaharā Chapters of the Agnipurāṇa–
Text, Translation, Study)

SURES CHANDRA BANERJI

1996
Sharada Publishing House
DELHI-110052

First Published 1996

ISBN : 81-85616-41-8 (Set)

Published by :
B.L. Bansal for Sharada Publishing House,
40, Anand Nagar, Inderlok,
DELHI-110035. Ph. 5117390, 5116768.

Printed at :
Santosh Offset, DELHI-110035.

PRINCIPLES OF HINDU JURISPRUDENCE

Vol. 1

(Vyavaharā Chapters of the Agnipurāṇa–
Text, Translation, Study)

SURES CHANDRA BANERJI

1996
Sharada Publishing House
DELHI-110052

Contents

Preface

The *Agnipurāṇa* (Ag. p.). originally a work of the Pāñcarātras, is an encyclopaedic work. It is supposed to be a recast of an earlier Purāṇa of this name. The *Vahni-purāṇa*, which means the same as the *Agnipurāṇa*, is a different work.

The Ag. p. contains 383 chapters (Vaṅgavāsī ed.). The first chapter proposes to present the essence (*sāra*) of all knowledge which is divided into *Parā* and *Aparā*. The *Parā-vidyā* is stated to be that which leads to the attainment of the Supreme Being. The *Aparā-vidyā* consists of the four Vedas, the Vedāṅgas, Abhidhāna, Mīmāṃsā, Dharmaśāstra, Purāṇa, Nyāya, Vaidyaka, Gāndharva, Dhanurveda, Arthaśāstra, etc.

From various evidences this Purāṇa is supposed to have been compiled in the ninth century A.D.

It is difficult to say in which part of India it originated. The assumption of some scholars that Bengal or Bihar was its provenance is now proved to be based on such portions of the work as are spurious.

The Ag.p. has been studied from different angles. The Alaṃkāra chapters of it have been studied critically and shown to represent a tradition earlier than that of the Kashmirian school of Ānandavardhana. The polity in the work has been the subject of elaborate study. Its influence on the later works has been discussed by some scholars. The question of its chronology, the history of its compilation and evolution, its position among the Purāṇas, etc. have engaged the attention of others.

The Vyavahāra portion of the Ag. p. has not yet been studied as critically as it should be. But, this portion is indispensable for a study of the text-tradition of the Vyavahārādhyāya of the YS., and for that matter, of the evolution of secular Hindu Law. We propose, in this work, to present this portion of the work with *varia lectiones* noting the divergences from the text-traditions, as represented by the commentaries of Viśvarūpa, Vijñāneśvara and Aparārka. The text is followed by an English translation. After the translation we have given notes on some important words of the text, based on different commentaries. A Glossary of technical terms and difficult words, contained in the Vyavahāra portion of the work, has been added; in it the references to the places of the YS., containing the words, have also been noted. In a concordance, the Vyavahāra chapters of the Purāṇa, along with the corresponding sections of the YS., have been indicated. We have given a verse-concordance of the Purāṇic text and the YS. A similar concordance of the Purāṇic text and the *Nārada-smṛti* has also been added. Finally, we have noted the verses of the YS. missing in the Ag. p. and *vice versa.*

At the end, a verse-index of the Vyavahāra portion of the Ag. p. has been appended.

Calcutta, S.C. BANERJI

New Year's Day,

1991.

Works utilised in reconstructing the text

Ap.—*Yajñavalkya-smṛti* with the comm. *Aparārka* of Aparāditya

BK.—*Yājñavalkya-smṛti* with the comm. *Bālakrīḍā* of Viśvarūpa

Mit.—*Yājñavalkya-smṛti* with the comm. *Mitākṣarā* of Vijñāneśvara

—*Agnipurāṇa*, ed. Damale, Poona, Śaka 1716

—*Agnipurāṇa*, ed. M. Pandit, Śaka 1737

—*Agnipurāṇa*, ed. V.C. Śāstri, Śaka 1661

—*Agnipurāṇa*, *Bibliotheca Indica*, Calcutta

—*Agnipurāṇa*, ed. Khasniwale

—*Agnipurāṇa*, ed. Y.D. Badulikar

—*Agnipurāṇa*, Sarasvati Press ed., Calcutta

—*Agnipurāṇa*, Vaṅgavāsī ed., Calcutta, 1314 B.S.

—*Nārada-smṛti*, ed. K. Smṛititīrtha, Sanskrit College, Calcutta.

Introduction

Sources of the Vyavahāra portion of the Agnipurāṇa

The Vyavahāra portion of the Purāṇa leaves no doubt that it is borrowed partly from the *Nārada-smṛti* and largely from the *Yājñavalkya-smṛti.* It is quite in keeping with the eclectic manner in which the work was compiled. A glance at the verse-concordance, appended to this work, will show the proportion of its borrowings from these two works. Chronological considerations rule out the possibility of the above Smṛti works borrowing from the Purāṇa.

The text of the Ys., as commented upon by different commentators, shows considerable variations. The question arises—to which of the versions is the Purāṇic text most similar ? The question is difficult to answer. A comparison of the Purāṇa with the versions preserved in the commentaries reveals that the former differs both in the number and order of the stanzas besides their readings. Again, some verses and part-verses of the Purāṇa are missing in all the versions of the text. A few verses occur only in the BK., but not in the versions represented by other commentators. One verse occurs in the Mit. and Ap., but it is missing in the

BK. Quite a number of verses, found in all the versions of the Ys., does not occur in the Purāṇa.

In the circumstances, it is clear that the Purāṇic text does not agree fully with any one version of the Ys. The Ys., having been a popular work, must have constantly undergone changes in the hands of copyists. It is not unlikely that the compiler of the Purāṇa himself made some changes. Both the Mit. (c. 2nd half of the 11th. cent. A.D.) and Ap. (c. first quarter of the 12th cent. A.D.) are later than the *Agnipurāṇa* (c. 900 A.D.).[1] As Viśvarūpa is believed to have flourished about the first quarter of the ninth century, the Purāṇa should agree more closely with the *Bālakrīḍā.* This may explain the fact that, while a few lines of the Purāṇa occur in the BK., these are missing in the versions represented in the other two versions of the Ys. But, the divergences between the BK. and the Purāṇa are too many to warrant the assumption that the latter followed the former in toto. The conclusion is, therefore, irresistible that either the Purāṇa had an exemplar lost to us or that it introduced changes into the version current in its time.

Résumé of the contents of the Vyavahāra portion of the Agnipurāṇa[2]

The portion of the *Agnipurāṇa*, dealing with *Vyavahāra* or administration of justice, consists of six chapters (253-258). The contents of these chapters are summarised below.

1. The dates, as fixed by P.V. Kane, are given here.
2. For the meanings of the technical terms, used here, see Glossary.

CHAPTER 253

This chapter opens with the promise of narrating *Vyavahāra* which is stated to have four feet, four *sthānas* and four *sādhanas*. The four feet are *dharma* resting on truth, *Vyavahāra* on witnesses, *caritra* (document or customary law or conduct ?) on popular practice (?) and royal edict on the king's command. Of these, each succeeding is stronger than the preceding one. *Vyavahāra* benefits four, viz, the four stages of life. It affects four, viz. the perpetrator of an act, witnesses, the assessors as well as the king. It is stated to produce four, viz. *dharma*, *artha*, fame and popular esteem. It has eight limbs, viz. the king with his officers, the assessors, the law-book, the accountant, the scribe, gold, fire and water. It has three sources—passion, anger and greed. It consists of two modes of complaint—one based on suspicion and the other on facts. It is stated to have two openings, viz. the plaintiff and the defendant. It is said to have two courses, because it follows truth as well as false statements.

The following titles of dispute are then laid down :

(i) Ṛṇādāna—recovery of debt,

(ii) Nikṣepa—deposit of property with another,

(iii) Saṃbhūya-samutthāna—partnership business,

(iv) Dattāpradānika—resumption of gift,

(v) Abhyupetyāśuśrūṣā—non-service after undertaking it,

(vi) Vetanasyānapākarma—non-payment of wages,

(vii) Asvāmi-vikraya—sale by a non-owner,

(viii) Vikrīyāsaṃpradāna—non-delivery after sale,

(ix) Krītānuśaya[1]—rescission of sale,

(x) Samayasyānapākarma—breach of contract,

(xi) Sīmā-vivāda[2]—dispute relating to boundary,

(xii) Strīpuṃsaṃyoga—mutual relation between husband and wife,

(xiii) Dāyabhāga—partition of paternal property,

(xiv) Sāhasa—acts of violence,

(xv) Vāk-pāruṣya—abuse,

(xvi) Daṇḍa-pāruṣya—assault,

(xvii) Dyūta[3]—gambling,
Prāṇi-dyūta—animal-betting,

(xviii) Prakīrṇaka—miscellaneous.

---

1. The Purāṇa omits the line containing this term, but mentions the line referring to this title of law.

2. *Ibid.*

3. Both *dyūta* and *prāṇi-dyūta* appear to have been included under one title of law; otherwise the titles become nineteen instead of eighteen as stated in verse 2 of this chapter. The *Nārada-smṛti* (ed. N. Smṛtitīrtha, Calcutta, p. 60) includes these two under one title. Mit., Ap. and BK. mention *dyūta-samāhvaya* as one title of law in Ys.

Verse 31 of this chapter presents some difficulty. It says that Vyavahāra is *daśapada*; it is difficult to be reconciled with *aṣṭādaśapada* stated in verse 2, *Daśapada* Vyavahāra is said to be of a hundred kinds. Again, it is stated to have one hundred branches or ramifications owing to the diversity of human activities.

The king should look into judicial proceedings. In this matter, he is to be assisted by a council constituted by members who are learned, impartial and free from greed. If the king himself is unable to do so, he should appoint a Brāhmaṇa for the purpose. The members, who act under the influence of passion or greed, should be separately fined twice the value of the suit in question.

A complaint, lodged by a person wronged by others, is a subject of litigation.

A judicial proceeding consists of four parts, viz. (i) Writing the plaint, (ii) Writing the reply, iii) Writing the evidences furnished by the plaintiff, (iv) Judgment.

No counter-allegation can be made by the defendant against the plaintiff before the plaint, filed by the latter, is disposed of. One cannot lodge a complaint against a person against whom a plaint has already been filed by another. This rule is, however, relaxed in certain cases, e.g. violence. Sureties are allowed for both the plaintiff and the defendant. False complaints are liable to punishment.

Suits of certain types, e.g. those relating to violence, theft etc., should be tried immediately. Time may be allowed in other cases.

In a court of law, a person of the following descriptions may be taken as a liar both as a plaintiff and as a witness :—restlessness, unnatural facial expression, perspiration on forehead, etc.

If a man, who is summoned to the court, fails to say anything, he becomes liable to punishment. If witnesses are available for both the earlier and later transactions, those of the former should be interrogated; if the contention of the first party fails, then those of the second party should be asked to depose.

If of the many written charges, denied by the defendant, even one is proved he should be made liable for the rest.

Two cardinal principles are enunciated. One is that, in the event of conflict between two written texts of the law, usage should prevail. Another is that of Smṛti texts, those relating to *dharma* will outweigh those relating to *artha*.

Evidences are of two kinds—human and divine; the latter should be resorted to in the absence of the former which includes documents, possession and witnesses.

In all disputes, the latter transaction is stronger than the former. In cases of mortgage, acceptance of gift and purchase, however, the earlier transaction is stronger.

Possession by one person of the immovable property of another, without any objection by the owner, for twenty years leads to adverse possession on the part of the possessor. Such adverse possession for ten years gives right to the possessor in the case of movables. The following are excluded from the purview of the following properties—mortgage, boundary, deposit, property of an idiot, a minor or a female, or Brāhmaṇa versed in the Veda and royal property.

One, misappropriating a mortgaged property, has to restore it to the owner besides paying fine to the king.

Between a valid mode of acquisition and possession, the former is generally a stronger evidence; but possession for generations is stronger than acquisition. Valid acquisition without even slight possession is of no avail. Again possession without valid acquisition does not *ipso facto* become evidence.

If acquisition is challenged, the acquirer should prove it; in such a case, his heirs have no responsibility, because, in their case, possession is enough. If a man, the validity of whose acquisition is challenged, dies his heir should prove it; in such a case, possession without acquisition is of no use.

A trial under the influence of force and coercion is set aside. So also trials by certain persons, e.g. enemies, intoxicated persons, lunatics, women, etc., in certain places, e.g. inside one's house, outside the village, and at certain times, e.g. night.

A lost thing, if recovered, should be restored by the king to the owner on proper identification of it; a claimant failing to identify it properly is liable to fine. The king should restore to the owner his article that is stolen.

The rate of interest is 1/80 per *mensem* in a loan with security; in an unsecured loan, the rate is two, three, four and five per cent for the four castes in order. For all castes, however, the interest may be as agreed upon by one's ownself.

In a suit relating to debt, the creditor lawfully realising his legitimate dues, should not approach the king. If the debtor in such a case goes to the king, he becomes liable to punishment and to pay the just dues to the creditor.

CHAPTER 254

This chapter opens with matters relating to the creditor and the debtor. The general rule is that the debtor should be made to repay money to the different creditors in the order in which he borrowed from them; the topmost priority, however, is enjoyed by the Brāhmaṇa creditor followed by the king. In a suit relating to realisation of debt, the debtor should pay ten per cent of the proved amount to the king and the creditor, who has received the money, should pay five per cent. A debtor of low caste, who is in straitened circumstances, should be made to do the work of the creditor instead of repaying the money. A Brāhmaṇa debtor, however, who is destitute, should be made to repay the money gradually as and when he may have income.

One, inheriting the property of another, should pay off the latter's debt also. But, the son is not responsible for the father's debt incurred for drinking, gambling, satisfying his passion; the remainder of the fine or tax payable by the father as well as for making useless gifts. The husband is not responsible for the debt incurred by his wife. But, among cowherds, distillers of wine, actors, washermen and hunters, the husband should pay off the debt of the wife, because his livelihood depends on her.

A surety is allowed for producing the debtor, creating confidence in the creditor as well as paying the money on his behalf. In the event of the debtor's failure, the first two kinds of surety themselves should pay off the debt; in the case of the last kind of surety, his heirs are also bound.

A mortgaged property is lost to the mortgagor if it is not released even after the amount borrowed is doubled, i.e., the interest becomes equal to the principal. A mortgage for a specific period is lost if it is not redeemed after that time-limit. A usufructuary mortgage is never forfeited.

One should return, exactly in the same condition, an article deposited by another. The custodian, however, is not reponsible if the deposited article is stolen or lost due to the action of the king or God. The custodian is liable to punishment if he uses the thing for his own benefit or if it is lost after his refusal to return it when demanded by the owner.

---

1. For the meaning of the technical terms, used here, see Golssary.

CHAPTER 255

The number of witnesses in a case should be three or five. Even one person can be a witness if he is approved by both the parties to a suit. People of the following descriptions can be witnesses :—

(i) Ascetics, (ii) Charitably disposed, (iii) Born of a high family, (iv) Truthful, (v) Looking upon *dharma* as the most important pursuit in life, (vi) Upright, (vii) Possessed of son, (viii) Rich, (ix) Engaged in the performance of *pañcayajña*.

The general rule is that witnesses should be of the same caste as that of the litigant. As an alternative however, this restriction is waived, and any one is allowed to stand witness for any other person. Persons of the following description are disqualified as witnesses :—

(i) Woman, (ii) Old man, (iii) Boy, (iv) Gambler, (v) Intoxicated person, (vi) Lunatic, (vii) *Abhiśastaka*,[1] (viii) Bard, (ix) Heretic, (x) A perjurer, (xi) Deformed, (xii) Degraded, (xiii) Friend of the litigant, (xiv) Interested in the subject of dispute, (xv) Accomplice of the litigant, (xvi) Hostile to the litigant, (xvii) Thief.

No disqualification, however, stands in the way of one's standing witness in a suit in respect of theft, abuse, assault and *sāhasa*.[2]

It is a penal offence to suppress evidence if one is in the know of the matter.

---

1. See Glossary.
2. *Ibid.*

If there is divergence in the evidence, that given by the majority should be accepted. If the number of witnesses, giving divergent evidence, is equally divided, the evidence of those who are more qualified is acceptable. If the qualified persons, giving divergent evidence, are equally divided the evidence of the more qualified ones should be accepted.

Both the person who gives false evidence and the one who instigates him are liable to punishment. Though false evidence is usually condemned and is punishable, yet a witness is allowed to resort to it if a true statement is likely to lead to the death-penalty of a member of any of the four castes.

A document, relating to debt, should contain the following particulars besides the signatures with the father's name, caste and *gotra* of the parties concerned :—

Signature of witness, the year, month, fortnight, day of the transaction.

If the debtor or witness is illiterate, he should get his name written for him by another person. The scribe also should write his father's name, and put in his signature.

A document is valid even without witnesses, provided it is written by a person in his own hand, it is not fraudulent or not written under duress.

When a payment is made by the debtor, the creditor should give him a receipt, and record the payment on the back of the document.

Three generations remain bound for a debt incurred with a document.

Divine proofs (*divya*) are ordained in certain cases in the absence of human proofs. The following divine proofs are mentioned :—

> Balance, fire, water, poison and *Kośa.* The ordeal of ploughshare (*Phāla*)[1] is also ordained in certain cases.

The following are the various kinds of *Strīdhana* (woman's exclusive property) :—

> Given by father, mother, husband or brother, received before the nuptial fire, *Ādhivedanika*, presented by a *bandhu*, *śulka*, *anvādheyaka*,

The *strīdhana* of a childless woman, who is married according to any one of the four forms, viz. *Brāhma*, *Daiva*, *Ārṣa* and *Prājāpatya*, devolves on her husband after her death. If she leaves behind issues, her property is inherited by her daughters. In the other forms of marriage, viz. *Āsura*, *Rākṣasa*, *Paiśāca* and *Gāndharva*; the property of such a woman goes to her father. Ordinarily the husband has no right over the *strīdhana* of his wife as long as she is alive. But, he can use it in the following circumstances without being required to restore it to her:

> famine, religious rite of an unavoidable nature, disease, *Saṃpratirodhaka*.

To a wife, who has been superseded, and to whom no *strīdhana* has been given, the husband should give *strīdhana* equal to what has been spent on the subsequent marriage. If

1. see P.V. Kane, *History of Dharmaśāstra*, III, pp. 373-4.

strīdhana has already been given to her, she should be given half of what is prescribed above.

In the event of the denial of partition, it should be proved by agnates, *bandhus*, witnesses, documents as well as by means of the house and fields which are partitioned.

The son, begotten on another man's wife through levirate by a sonless person, becomes the heir of both the persons.

The sons are of the following kinds :

Aurasa, Putrikā-putra, Kṣetraja, Gūḍhaja, Kānīna, Paunarbhava, Dattaka, Krīta, Kṛtrima, Dattātmā, Sahoḍhaja, Apaviddha. Of them, in the absence of the preceding one, the succeeding one becomes heir. This is the law with respect to sons of the same caste as that of the father. A son, born to a female slave by a Śūdra, gets a share of the property according to the father's will. If partition is effected after the father's death, then the legitimate sons of the deceased should give him half the share (due to a son). The son of a female slave will take the entire property if the deceased has no legitimate son, married daughter or daughter's son.

In respect of the property of a deceased sonless person, the following is the order of succession :

> Wife, daughter (her son in her absence), parents, brothers, brother's son, *sagotra*, *bandhu*, pupil, fellow-student.

As regards re-united coparceners, the general rule is that the property of such a person is inherited by a re-united coparcener. But, a uterine brother, though not re-united, gets preference over a half-brother who is re-united.

Excluded from inheritance are the following :—

> An apostate, son of an apostate, an impotent person, a lame man, a lunatic, an idiot, a blind man, one affected with an incurable disease, and the like.

They are, however, entitled to maintenance. Their *aurasa*, and *kṣetraja* sons, if free from defects, will take their shares. Their daughters should be maintained so long as they are not married. The wives of the above disqualified persons, who are sonless, should also be maintained provided they are of good conduct. If they go astray or are not submissive should be banished.

CHAPTER 256

If the father makes a partition of the property, he may distribute shares among the sons at his will. He may give equal shares to them or give the greatest share to the eldest son. In the former alternative, he should give his wife, to whom no *Strīdhana* has been given by her husband or father-in-law, a share equal to that of a son.

After the death of the father the sons should divide the property as well as the debt equally among themselves. Whatever is acquired by a brother, without using the paternal property, need not be shared with other brothers. Sons of many brothers will inherit through their respective fathers i.e. the share of one brother will be equally divided among his sons. One who recovers a lost ancestral property, need not share it with his brothers. Similar is the case with what is acquired by means of one's own learning.

The mother's property will be inherited by her daughters.

Over the ancestral property, i.e., a property belonging to a forefather earlier than the father, the father and the son have equal right.

In the case where partition is made by brothers, it is the duty of those who have undergone sacraments (*Saṃskāras*) to perform the sacraments on those whose sacraments have not been performed. It is also the responsibility of the brothers to defray the expenses of the marriage of the unmarried sisters.

The quantum of the share of a son will depend on the caste of his mother. Thus, the sons of a Brāhmaṇa by his wives of the Brāhmaṇa, Kṣatriya, Vaiśya and Śūdra castes will get four, three, two, and one shares respectively. The sons of a Kṣatriya by wives of the three castes in order, will get three, two and one shares respectively. Those of a Vaiśya by wives of the two castes in order will get two and one shares respectively.

CHAPTER 257

In disputes relating to boundary, residents of neighbouring villages, elderly people, cowherds, tillers of the boundary etc. should fix the boundary which will be marked by charcoals, husk, tree, dam etc. In the absence of knowledgeable persons and marks, the king should fix the boundary. In the cases of breaking the boundary, misappropriation of a field and encroachment of a boundary, the punishments are respectively first, highest and lowest amercements.

A dam or well, encroaching on another man's land and causing slight loss, is permissible provided it is conducive to the welfare of many.

Liable to fines are those whose cow, buffalo, sheep or goat destroy the standing crops of another man.

The keeper of cattle must return to the owner, in the evening, the animals entrusted to him exactly in the condition in which these were given. He is to make good the loss for which he is responsible.

The buyer of an article is guilty if he makes a clandestine purchase, purchases it at an abnormalle low price or at an unusual hour. The owner, having come across his article lost or stolen, should cause the buyer to be apprehended, or if the time and place be unfavourable, himself catch him to by handed over to police. The buyer, however, becomes free from guilt by showing the seller to the owner. From the seller the buyer gets the price paid by him, the owner his article and the king realises fine. The owner has to prove his ownership; otherwise, he becomes liable to fine.

Manumission is obtained by slaves under the following circumstances :

(i) if enslaved forcibly,

(ii) if sold by thieves,

(iii) if a slave saves his master's life,

(iv) if a slave gives back to the master what has been enjoyed by him ever since his enslavement,

(v) if a slave repays the money borrowed from his master.

A man, misappropriating the property of a Gaṇa or violating a contract, becomes liable to punishment. One should give what one obtains being deputed by an association. If he does not voluntarily give it, he should be made to give it elevenfold. The same rule applies to *Śreṇis*, *Naigamas*, *Pākhaṇḍins*, besides *Gaṇas*.

By leaving a job after receiving wages for it, one should pay to the master twice the amount received. If wages are not accepted, but merely agreed to, an amount equal to what is agreed should be paid to the master. A person, who makes a servant work without settling wages, should be caused by the king to give the servant one-tenth of the merchandise, animals and corns as the case may be. The master has to pay at his will wages to a servant who does not keep to the proper time and place or does the work in an improper way.

In a *Glaha*, the keeper of the gaming house should take as his fee five per cent from a gambler who gains a hundred or more; from any other gambler he should take ten per cent. Those who play with false dice and by fraudulent means should be branded and punished by the king.

CHAPTER 258

Different kinds of penalty are prescribed for different kinds of abuse, e.g., abusing a man by stating his physical deformity, calling a man thief when he is not so, verbally breaking the head, etc. Punishment for abuse depends on the caste and lineage of the abuser and the abused. Abuse of people of a superior caste or status constitutes a more serious offence than that of those of an inferior caste or position.

In cases of assault, trial should be conducted, in the absence of witnesses, by taking into account marks, probability and public report. As in the case of abuse, punishment for assault also varies in accordance with the degree of the offence, the caste, lineage and status of the offender and the offended. The limb of a non-Brāhmaṇa, causing injury to a Brāhmaṇa, has to be cut off. Within the meaning of assault are included also obstruction to one's movement, eating and speech.

The fines, prescribed for striking, become twofold if many persons strike one.

Different kinds of injury to animals also are punishable. The cutting of branches and trunks of certain kinds of trees also makes the offender liable to punishment.

For aiding and abetting *Sāhasa* in various ways, one becomes liable to punishment.

Sexual union with a widow at will, not rushing to help when there are shouts for help, swearing improperly, emasculation of bulls and other animals, destruction of the foetus of a female slave; of father and son, sister and brother, husband and wife, preceptor and pupil one deserting the other without sufficient reason—these are penal offences.

Realisation of land-custom by a ferry-man, the washerman wearing other men's clothes, use of false weight, deceitful alteration of the balance, royal grant, passing counterfeit coins as genuine, posing as a physician not being actually so, improper confinement of a person, mixing of inferior substances with articles like medicine, oil etc., changing the value of a commodity, fixed by the king, in such a manner as to cause suffering to traders or loss or increase in value, non-delivery by a seller of a commodity at the agreed price, sale of an article to one person after selling it to another, sale of a defective article, rescission in respect of a commodity by one ignorant of the appreciation or depreciation, false statement about the quantity of a commodity, slipping away from the place of tax-collection—these are all offences which are punishable.

The profit and loss in a co-operative business are determined in proportion to the amounts invested by the members.

A thief is sentenced to death (if the theft is of a very serious nature). A Brāhmaṇa thief is branded and banished from the kingdom.

A stealer of cloth etc. and a knot-cutter should be deprived of their hand and tongs[1] respectively.

1. See footnote on the translations of 258,62b-63a.

In the second offence of similar kinds, they should be deprived of one hand and one foot.

Different kinds of penalty are prescribed for aiding and abetting murderers and thieves in various ways.

Incendiaries burning a house, a village, a pasture land etc. as also one who has sexual intercourse with the queen should be burnt in straw-fire.

Punishment for adultery varies with the caste and status of the offender and the woman involved.

Association of women with men, prohibited by her superiors, and of men with women, prohibited by their guardians, is punishable.

Sexual intercourse with cows and other beasts, prohibited female slaves, female slaves of others as also with female mendicants makes the offender liable to punishment. Defilement of a Brāhmaṇa with prohibited food is a penal offence.

For making a false statement in a court of law, stealing gold and selling bad meat (e.g. that of a dog) one should have one's limb[1] cut off besides paying the highest amercement. Those, who speak ill of the king, abuse him, beats the preceptor and leaks out royal counsel, should have their tongues cut off besides being banished.

Fines, unjustly realised by the king, should be given to Brāhmaṇas thirtyfold.

---

1. See footnote on the translation of 258.76a.

Main points of difference between the *Vyavahāra* Chapters of the *Agnipurāṇa* and the Vyavahārādhyāya of the *Yājñavalkya-smṛti*

A glance at the verse-concordance will reveal how the Purāṇa differs from the Smṛti both in the number and order of verses. Some verses of the former are missing in the latter and *vice versa.* The text of the Purāṇa, presented by us, will also show that it differs considerably from the Smṛti in the readings of the verses.

The Purāṇa omits the Smṛti provision regarding the qualifications of the members of the Court trying a suit. Probably these were too well-known to be mentioned.

As regards the sign of one who makes a false statement, the Purāṇa leaves out faltering speech, contradictory statements, failure to give a reply or to look up to another saying something, and the twisting of the lips. The Purāṇa does not mention the Smṛti provision regarding legal transactions relating to Pūgas, Śreṇis and Kulas. The Smṛti lays down a rule regarding the disposal of a treasure-trove discovered by the king or by any one else. The Purāṇa, perhaps, did not think it necessary to give the rule provided for exceptional circumstances and chose to give only general rules. The Purāṇa does not state the sin accruing to the king for not making over to the owner his stolen property which is recovered.

The Purāṇic stanza 255.35 is missing in the Smṛti. This stanza, in a different metre, appears to be an interpolation; it may have been introduced with the motive of instilling a sense of fear in the mind of the culprit by telling him that the natural objects like sun, moon etc. know the doings of a person, however secretly done. Stanza 258.83,[1] which is missing in the Smṛti, is an obvious attempt of the Purāṇa to hold out great reward for a king who metes out justice to his people.

In the section on witnesses, the Purāṇa makes a departure from the Smṛti by omitting the rule that anyone and every one can be a witness to certain offences; e.g. adultery, theft, abuse, assault and violence. It may reflect the change of outlook of a later society. While the Ys. lays down (II.68) that the number of witnesses should be at least three, the Purāṇa provides for five or three. In the same section, the Purāṇa omits the provision for expiation on the part of a witness who is allowed by law to make false statements under certain circumstances. The Purāṇa adds that, in cases of a little doubt swearing may be done with truthful speech, conveyance, weapons, cow, seeds of grain, gold, images of gods, feet of the preceptor. It is also possible by pious and charitable deeds.

In the section on Saṃvid-vyatikrama, the Purāṇa leaves out the injunction that the king should bid farewell to those who come in connexion with the work of a *Gaṇa* after duly honouring them.

---

1. The first two lines occur in the *Nārada-smriti,* p. 3, verse 33 (Calcutta Sanskrit College ed.)

Under Daṇḍapāruṣya, the Purāṇa omits the penal measure for causing damage to trees grown on certain spots.

Under Sāhasa, the Purāṇa does not mention that the word means forcibly taking away a common property; it also omits the penalty for it. In the same section, the Purāṇa omits the penalty for those who undertake to give evidence about a quarrel between the father and the son instead of putting a stop to it, as well as the fine for one who aids and abets such a feud. The Purāṇa also omits the penal measures provided for those who practise deceit in the sale of earth, skin, jewels etc., and indulge in several other kinds of fraud in connexion with the sale and mortgage of various articles. It also omits the penalty for causing obstruction to the sale of foreign goods at the legitimate price.

Under theft the Purāṇa omits the rule that the owner of a *vivīta* is responsible for theft committed there. If theft is perpetrated on the way, at a place other than a *vivīta*, the responsibility will attach to the *mārgapāla* (the protector of ways). In the same section, the Purāṇa omits the rule that penalty for theft will depend on the value of the article stolen; as it also leaves out the provision that, in awarding punishment, the place and time of occurrence, the age and capacity of the offender are to be considered. In the same section, the Purāṇa omits the death-penalty of a woman who is very bad or commits the offences of killing a man, destroying a foetus, breaking a *setu*.

Under Strī-saṃgraha, the Purāṇa does not mention the rule that a man, who committed adultery, should be apprehended by seeing fresh signs of enjoyment. In the same section, the Purāṇa omits the penalty for carrying away a girl decked for marriage as well as for the rape of a girl by one person and by many. The Purāṇa also leaves out the penal provision for a prostitute violating her contract with a man and *vice versa.* It omits the penalty for a person who indulges in sexual gratification with his woman in the places of her body excepting the female organ. It does not mention the penalty for a person having sexual union with a female mendicant and a Caṇḍāla woman.

In the miscellaneous section, the Purāṇa omits the penal provision for defiling, with prohibited food, the members of castes other than the Brāhmaṇa. It also leaves out the provision for exemption of penalty, under certain extenuating circumstances, for the owner whose four-footed animals cause injury or death to people. The work does not mention the penalty for one who fails to rescue a man from the attack of his animals having horns and teeth. The provision of penalty for one, who characterises a paramour as a thief or releases him after taking bribe, is omitted in it. Also omitted is the penalty for one who leaks out royal counsel. The Purāṇa leaves out the rule that the king should review a case that has been unfairly tried, and should punish those who tried the case as well as the persons who won it. Two explanations of this omission are possible. Either the Purāṇa does not recognize any appeal against the decision of a court or it does not contemplate trial in any court other than the council presided over by the king himself. The latter alternative lacks plausibility in view of the fact that it is not convenient for people, in the remote corner of a kingdom, to appear before the king in a litigation in which witnesses of the litigants' locality have to be present; in certain cases, the king's men have to inspect the place where the cause of action arises. The former alternative appears to deprive the litigant public of their fundamental right of appeal against a judgment which is vitiated or bad in law.

TEXT

अग्निपुराणे

त्रिपञ्चाशदधिकद्विशततमोऽध्यायः

व्यवहारप्रकरणम्

अग्निरुवाच–

व्यवहारं प्रवक्ष्यामि नयानयविवेकदम् ।
स चतुष्पाच्चतुः स्थानश्चतुः साधन उच्यते ॥१॥

चतुर्हितश्चतुर्व्यापी चतुष्कारी च कीर्त्यते ।
अष्टांगोऽष्टादशपदः शतशाखस्तथैव च ॥२॥

त्रियोनिर्द्व्यभियोगश्च द्विद्वारोद्विगतिस्तथा ।
धर्मश्च व्यवहारश्च चरित्रं राजशासनम् ॥३॥

चतुष्पाद्व्यवहाराणामुत्तरः पूर्वसाधकः ।
तत्र सत्ये स्थितो धर्मो व्यवहारस्तु साक्षिषु ॥४॥

चरित्रं संग्रहे पुंसां राजाज्ञायां तु साधनम् ।
सामा (द्युपायसाध्यत्वाच्चतुः साधन उच्यते ॥५॥

चतुर्णामाश्रमाणां च रक्षणात्स चतुर्हितः ।
कर्त्तारं साक्षिणश्चैव सत्या (भ्याः) न्राजानमेव च ॥६॥

व्याप्नोति पादशो यस्माच्चतुर्व्यापी ततः स्मृतः ।
धर्मस्यार्थस्य यशसो लोकपंक्तेस्तथैव च ॥७॥

चतुर्णां करणादेष चतुष्कारी प्रकीर्त्तितः ।
राजा सपुरुषः सभ्याः शास्त्रं गणकलेखकौ ॥८॥

हिरण्यमग्निरुदकमष्टाङ्गः समुदाहृतः ।
कामात्क्रोधाच्च लोभाच्च त्रिभ्यो यस्मात्तप्रवर्तते ॥९॥

अष्टपञ्चाशदधिकद्विशततमोऽध्यायः

वाक् पारुष्यादि प्रकरणम्

अग्निरुवाच–

सत्यासत्यान्यथास्तोत्रैर्न्यूनाङ्गेन्द्रियरोगिणाम् ।
क्षेपं करोति चेद्दण्ड्यः पणानर्धत्रयोदश ।।१।।

अभिगन्तास्मि भागिनीं मातरं वा तवेति च ।
शपन्तं दापयेद्राजा पञ्चविंशतिकं दमम् ।।२।।

अर्धोऽधमेषु द्विगुणः परस्त्रीषूत्तमेषु च ।
दण्डप्रणयनं कार्यं वर्णजात्युत्तराधरैः ।।३।।

प्रातिलोम्यापवादेषु द्विगुणात्रिगुणा दमाः ।
वर्णानामानुलोम्येन तस्मदेवार्धहानितः ।।४।।

बाहुग्रीवानत्रसक्थिविनाशे वाचिके दमः ।
शत्यस्ततोऽर्धिकः पादनासाकर्णकरादिषु ।।५।।

अशक्तस्तु वदन्नेवं दण्डनीयः पणान्दश ।
तथाशक्तः प्रतिभुवं दद्यात्क्षेमाय तस्य तु ।।६।।

पाषण्डनैगमादीनां स्थितिः समय उच्यते।
समयस्यानपाकर्म तद्विवादपदं स्मृतम् ॥२२॥

सेतुकेदारमर्यादाविकृष्टाकृष्टनिश्चय :।
क्षेत्राधिकारे यत्र स्युर्विवादः क्षेत्रजस्तु सः॥२३॥

वैवाहिको विधिः स्त्रीणां यत्र पुंसां च कीर्त्यते।
स्त्रीपुंसयोगसंज्ञं तु तद्विवादपदं स्मृतम् ॥२४॥

विभागोऽर्थस्य पैत्रस्य पुत्रैर्यस्तु प्रकल्प्यते।
दायभागमिति प्रोक्तं तद्विवादपदं बुधैः॥२५॥

सहसा क्रियते कर्म यत् किंचिद्बलदर्पितैः।
तत्साहसमितिप्रोक्तं विवादपदमुच्यते ॥२६॥

देशजातिकुलादीनामाक्रोशव्यंग (ग्य?) संयुतम्
यद्वचः प्रतिकूलार्थं वाक्पारुष्यं तदुच्यते ॥२७॥

परगात्रेष्वभिद्रोहो हस्तपादायुधादिभिः।
अग्न्यादिभिश्चोपघातैर्दण्डपारुष्यमुच्यते ॥२८॥

अक्षवज्रशलाकाद्यैर्देवनं द्यूतमुच्यते।
पशुक्रीड़ा वयोभिश्च प्राणिद्यूतं समाह्वयः ॥२९॥

प्रकीर्णकः पुनर्ज्ञेयो व्यवहारो नृपाश्रयः।
राज्ञामाज्ञाप्रतीघातस्तत्कर्माकरणं तथा ॥३०॥

व्यवहारोऽष्टादशपदस्तेषां भेदोऽथ वै शतम्।
क्रियाभेदान्मनुष्याणां शतशाखो निगद्यते ॥३१॥

व्यवहारान्नृपः पश्येज्ज्ञानिविप्रैरकोपनः।
शत्रुमित्रसमाः सभ्या अलोभाः श्रुतिवेदिनः॥३२॥

अपश्यता कार्यवशात् सभ्यैर्विप्रं नियोजयेत्।
रागाल्लोभाद् भयाद्वाऽपि श्रुत्यपेतादिकारिणः॥३३॥

सभ्याः पृथक् पृथग्दण्ड्या विवादाद्द्विगुणं दमम् ।
स्मृत्याचारव्यपेतेन मार्गेण धर्षितः परैः ॥३४॥

आवेदयति यद्राज्ञे व्यवहारपदं हि तत् ।
प्रत्यर्थिनोऽग्रतो लेख्यं यथावेदितमर्थिना ॥३५॥

समामासतदर्धाहर्नामजात्यादिचिह्नितम् ।
श्रुतार्थस्योत्तरं लेख्यं पूर्वावेदकसंनिधौ ॥३६॥

ततोऽर्थी लेखयेत्सद्यः प्रतिज्ञातार्थसाधनम् ।
तत्सिद्धौ सिद्धिमाप्नोति विपरीतमतोऽन्यथा ॥३७॥

चतुष्पाद्व्यवहारोऽयं विवादेषूपदर्शितः ।
अभियोगमनिस्तीर्य नैनं प्रत्यभियोजयेत् ॥३८॥

अभियुक्तं च नान्येन नोक्तं विप्रकृतिं नयेत् ।
कुर्यात् प्रत्यभियोगं तु कलहे साहसेषु च ॥३९॥

उभयोः प्रतिभूर्ग्राह्यः समर्थः काम्यनिर्णये ।
निह्नवे भावितो दद्याद्धनं राज्ञे तु तत् समम् ॥४०॥

मिथ्याभियोगाद्द्विगुणमभियोगाद्धनं हरेत् ।
साहसस्तेयपारुष्येष्वभिशापात्यये स्त्रियाः ॥४१॥

विचारयेत् सद्य एव कालोऽन्यत्रेच्छया स्मृतः ।
देशाद्देशान्तरं याति सृक्किणी परिलेढि वा ॥४२॥

ललाटं स्विद्यते चास्य मुखवैवर्ण्यमेव च ।
स्वभावाद्विकृतं गच्छेन्मनोवाक्कायकर्मभिः ॥४३॥

अभियोगेऽथवा साक्ष्ये वाग्दुष्टः परिकीर्तितः ।
संदिग्धार्थं स्वतन्त्रो यः साधयेद्यश्च निष्पतेत् ॥४४॥

न चाऽऽहूतो वदेत् किंचिद्धीनो दण्ड्यश्च स स्मृतः ।
साक्षिषूभयतः सत्सु साक्षिणः पूर्ववादिनः ॥४५॥

पूर्वपक्षेऽधरीभूते भवन्त्युत्तरवादिनः।
सपणश्चेद्विवादः स्यात्तत्र हीनं तु दापयेत् ॥४६॥

दण्डं पणं वसुं चैव धनिनो धनमेव च ।
छलं निरस्य भूतेन व्यवहारान्नयेन्नृपः ॥४७॥

भूतमप्यनुपन्यस्तं हीयते व्यवहारतः।
निह्नुते लिखितानेकमेकदेशविभावितम् ॥४८॥

दाप्यः सर्वो नृपेणार्थो न ग्राह्यस्त्वनिवेदितः।
स्मृत्योर्विरोधे न्यायस्तु बलवान् व्यवहारतः॥४९॥

अर्थशास्त्राद्धि बलवद्धर्मशास्त्रमिति स्थितिः।
प्रमाणं लिखितं भुक्तिः साक्षिणश्चेति कीर्त्तितम् ॥५०॥

एषामन्यतमाभावे दिव्यान्यतममुच्यते ।
सर्वेष्वेव विवादेषु बलवत्युत्तरा क्रिया ॥५१॥

आधौ प्रतिग्रहे क्रीते पूर्वा तु बलवत्तरा ।
पश्यतो ब्रुवतो भूमेर्हानिर्विंशतिवार्षिकी ॥५२॥

परेण भुज्यमानाया धनस्य दशवार्षिकी ।
आधिसीमोपनिक्षेपजडबालधनैर्विना ॥५३॥

तथोपनिधिराजस्त्रीश्रोत्रियाणां धनैरपि ।
आध्यादीनां विहर्तारं धनिने दापयेद्धनम् ॥५४॥

दण्डं च तत्समं राज्ञे शक्त्यपेक्षमथापि वा ।
आगमोऽप्यधिकोभुक्तिं विना पूर्वक्रमागताम् ॥५५॥

आगमेऽपि बलं नैव भुक्तिःस्तोकाऽपि यत्र न ।
आगमेन विशुद्धेन भोगो याति प्रमाणताम् ॥५६॥

अविशुद्धागमो भोगः प्रामाण्यं नाधिगच्छति ।
(आगमस्तु कृतो येन सोऽभियुक्तस्तमुद्धरेत् ॥५७॥

न तत्सुतस्तत्सुतो वा भुक्तिस्तत्र गरीयसी ।
योऽभियुक्तः परेतः स्यात्तस्य ऋक्थात्तमुद्धरेत् ॥५८॥

न तत्र कारणं भुक्तिरागमेन विना कृता ।
बलोपधिर्विनिर्वृत्तान् व्यवहारान्निवर्तयेत् ॥५९॥

स्त्रीनक्तमन्तरागारवहिः शत्रुकृतस्तथा ।
मत्तोन्मत्तार्तव्यसनिबालभीतप्रयोजितः ॥६०॥

असंबद्धकृतश्चैव व्यवहारो न सिद्ध्यति ।
प्रनष्टाधिगतं देयं नृपेण धनिने धनम् ॥६१॥

विभावयेन्न चेल्लिङ्गैस्तत्समं दातुमर्हति ।
देयं चौरहृतं द्रव्यं राज्ञा जनपदाय तु ॥६२॥

अशीतिभागो वृद्धिः स्यान्मासि मासि सबन्धके ।
वर्णक्रमाच्छतं : द्वित्रिचतुष्पञ्चकमन्यथा ॥६३॥

सन्ततिस्तु पशुस्त्रीणां रसस्याष्टगुणा परा ।
वस्त्रधान्यहिरण्यानां चतुस्त्रिद्विगुणा तथा ॥६४॥

ग्रामान्तरात्तु दशकं सामुद्रादपि विंशतिम् ।
दद्युर्वा स्वकृतां वृद्धिं सर्वे सर्वासु जातिषु ॥६५॥

प्रपन्नं साधयन्नर्थं न वाच्यो नृपतिर्भवेत् ।
साध्यमानो नृपं गच्छेद्दण्ड्यो दाप्यश्च तद्धनम् ॥६६॥

इत्याग्नेये महापुराणे त्रिपञ्चाशदधिकद्विशततमोऽध्यायः ॥२५३॥

1. ज चतुष्पाच्च चतु for स.... चतुः.

2. क अष्टांशो for अष्टाङ्गो.

4. ना व्यवहारोऽयमुत्तरः पूर्वबाधकः for व्यवहाराणा.... साधकः. क संवेष्टितो (च सम्योत्थितो) for सत्ये स्थितो.

5. ज, ना शासनम् for साधनम्. ज सामाभ्युपाय (editor of ना notes the v.l.सामाध्युपाय) for सामाद्युपाय.

6. ना कर्तृनथो साक्षिणश्च for कर्तारं... चैव.

7. ना, ज, छ पादगो for पादशो.

8. ना एषां for एव, चतुष्कारीति चोच्यते for चतु....र्तितः. ना सत्पुरुषः for सपुरुषः.

The portion from 9b to 11b is missing in च.

11. ज षड्भिस्तु (ना सतां तु) for सद्भिस्तु. ज, क, ख, ग, घ, च, छ तत्त्वषोढादिदर्शनात् (ङ तत्त्वं for तत्त) for तत्त्वं...नात्.

12. ना तदुत्तरं for त्वनन्तरः. ना स उदाहृतः (ज समुदाहृता) for समुदाहृतः.

13. ना धर्माभ्याम् for धर्मश्च. Mit. before YS.II.37 also reads like ना.

14. ना स्वं for स्व; निक्षेपो for निक्षेपं.

15. ना स्मृतम् for विदुः.

16. ना असम्यग् for च सम्यग्. Mit. before YS.II.175 reads like ना.

17. ज, ना अशुश्रूषाभ्युपेत्येतद् for अशुश्रूषा...तद्. Mit. before YS.II.182 also reads like ना and ज.

18. क, घ, ङ वेतनस्योक्तं.....विधिश्च यः for वेतन....क्रिया. Mit. before YS.II.193 reads the first line as भृत्यानां वेतनस्योक्तो दानादानविधिक्रमः.

19. ज प्रहृत्य for (अ)पहृत्य. ना (अ)समक्षं for परोक्षं. Mit. before YS.II.168 समक्षं for परोक्षं.

20. ना, Mit. before YS.II.254 यत्र प्रदीयते for यच्च...ते.

21. ज यत् for first यः. क, ख, ग, घ, ङ, च कृत्वा for क्रीत्वा; मूल्यं for मूल्येन. ज, ना, (Mit. before YS.II.177) यत् for यः.

22. क, ङ परं for पदं. नामैतद्

23. ना निश्चये for निश्चयाः; यस्तु स्याद्.

24. ना विवाहादि for वैवाहिको; नामतैद् for संज्ञं तु; पदमुच्यते for पदं स्मृतम्.

25. क, ङ (अर्थ)स्य योगस्तु for (अ)र्थस्य पैत्रस्य. ना पित्र्यस्य for पैत्रस्य; यत्र for यस्तु; दायभागः for भागं, Mit. before YS.II.114 reads the stanza as follows: विभागोऽर्थस्य पित्र्यस्य तनयैर्यत्र कल्प्यते । दायभाग इति प्रोक्तं व्यवहारपदं बुधैः ।। Mit. before II.254 क्रेतुः for क्रेत्रे.

26. ना सहो बलमिहोच्यते for विवाद...ते. Mit. under YS.II.230a reads like ना.

27. क, ङ देशकालक्रमादीनां for देश....दीनाम्. क, घ, ङ आक्रोशद्यङ्ग (ज आक्रोशत्यङ्ग). Mit. before YS.II.204 आक्रोशं for आक्रोश.

28. क, ङ पादमुखादिभिः for पादा.....भिः. ना भस्मादीनामुपक्षेपै (Mit. before YS.II.212 भस्मादिभिश्चोपघाती) for अग्न्या...तै.

29. ना व्रध्न (Mit. before YS.II.199 for वज्र. ज दैवतं for देवनं. ना जिह्मकारितम् for द्यूतमुच्यते. क, घ, ङ द्यूतं समादिशत् for द्यूतसमाह्वयः. Mit., ना reads the second line as पणक्रीडा वयोभिश्च पदं द्यूतसमाह्वयम्.

30. ना प्रकीर्णकें for कः. All the texts of the Purāṇa, consulted by us, read

निराश्रयः for नृपाश्रयः. Mit. before YS.II.295 reads the first line thus प्रकीर्णकेषु विज्ञेया व्यवहारा नृपाश्रयाः।

31. ख, ग, छ व्यवहारोष्टादशपद for व्यव... दशपद.

32. Mit., BK., Ap. विद्वद्भि... सह for ज्ञानि... पनः. The second line is read by Mit., BK., Ap. as धर्मशास्त्रानुसारेण क्रोधलोभविवर्जितः.

33. Mit., BK., Ap. व्यवहारान् नृपेण तु for सभ्यै.... येत्.

Mit., BK., Ap., ख, ग, छ स्मृत्येपेतादि for श्रुत्य

34. घ, च, छ, ज द्विगुणोदमः for ° णं दमम्. Mit., Ap., BK. मार्गेणाधर्षितः for मार्गेण धर्षितः.

35. Mit., Ap., BK. चेत् for यत्.

36. ङ, च श्रुतार्थस्यान्तरं for °स्योत्तरं.

39. BK. न चाभियुक्तमन्येन for अभि... च. न, Mit., Ap., BK. नोक्तं for त्यक्तं; च for तु.

40. Mit., Ap., BK. कार्य for काम्य. क, ङ, च भार्गवे for निह्नवे. Mit., Ap., BK. च for तु.

41. Mit., Ap., BK. मिथ्याभियोगी for ° योगात्; वहेत् for हरेत्; पारुष्यगोभि (Mit., Ap., BK. also क, ख, ग, ङ, च) for पारु..... भि; स्त्रियाम् for स्त्रियाः.

42. Mit., BK., Ap. विवादयेत् for विचारयेत्.

43. Mit., BK., Ap. च for वा.

44. Mit., BK., Ap. मुखं वैवर्ण्यमेति च for मुख... च. Mit., BK. च साक्ष्ये वा (BK. च for for वा) for (अ) थवा साक्ष्ये. Mit., BK., Ap. दुष्टः स for वाग्दुष्टः.

45. Mit., BK., Ap. किंचिद्धीनो (छ, ज धनी for द्धीनो) for किंचिद्दीनो।

Note: 42-45 (up to सत्सु) omitted in च.

46. छ, ज सगण for सपण.

47. छ, ज दत्तं for दण्डः. Mit., Ap., BK. दण्डं च स्वपणं चैव धनिने for दण्डः.... धनिनो. क, ख, ग, ङ, च, ज दूतेन for भूतेन.

48. छ, ज भूतमप्यर्थमप्यस्तं for भूत... स्तं. क, ङ दीयते for हीयते. Mit. लिखितं नैकमेकदेशे विभावितः (BK. लिखितोऽनेकमेकदेश..., Ap. निह्नवे लिखितेऽनेकमेकदेश...., छ, ज निखिलानेकम्) for लिखिता... तम्.

49. Mit., Ap. सर्व॰, अर्थ॰ (BK. सर्वान्, अर्थान्) for सर्वो, अर्थो.

50. Mit., Ap., BK. तु for हि.

51. Mit. सर्वेष्वर्थ for सर्वेष्वेव.

54. Ap. निहन्तारं (BK. हि हर्तारं) for विहर्तारं.

55. Mit. आगमोऽभ्यधिको (Ap. आगमोऽत्यधिको) for आग.... को. Ap., Mit. भोगात् (BK. भुक्तेः) for भुक्ति. Mit., Ap., BK. ° गतात् for °गताम्.

56b-57a Missing in Mit., Ap.

58. Mit., Ap., BK. रिक्थी for ऋक्थात्.

59. BK. बलोपधि for ब...धि.

60. Mit., Ap., BK. कृतांस्तथा for कृतस्तथा. क, ङ बलमन्त्रप्रयोजितः (Mit., Ap. बालभीतादियोजितः) for बाल...तः.

61. Mit. प्रनष्टाधिगतं for° शंतं.

62. Mit., Ap., BK. दण्डम् for दण्डम्. क, ङ जनपदस्य (Mit. जानपदाय) for जनपदाय.

Note: 57b-62 Omitted in च.

63. च सर्वर्णके for सबन्धके.

64. Mit., Ap., BK. सन्तति for सम्रति. Mit., Ap. परा for तथा.

65. Mit., Ap., BK. कान्तारगास्तु दशकं सामुद्रा विंशकं शतम्.

66. Mit., Ap., BK. नृपते for नृपति.

चतुःपञ्चाशदधिक-द्विशततमोऽध्यायः

ऋणादानप्रकरणम्

अग्निरुवाच–

गृहीतार्थः क्रमाद्दाप्यो धनिनामधमर्णकः ।
दत्त्वा तु ब्राह्मणायादौ नृपतेस्तदनन्तरम् ॥१॥

राज्ञाधमर्णिको दाप्यः साधिताद्दशकं शतम् ।
पञ्चकं तु शतं दाप्यः प्राप्तार्थो ह्युत्तमर्णिकः ॥२॥

हीनजातिं परिक्षीणमृणार्थं कर्मकारयेत् ।
ब्राह्मणस्तु परिक्षीणः शनैर्दप्यो यथोदयम् ॥३॥

दीयमानं न गृह्णाति प्रयुक्तं यः स्वकं धनम् ।
मध्यस्थस्थापितं तत् स्याद्वर्धते न ततः परम् ॥४॥

ऋक्थग्राह ऋणं दाप्यो योषिद्ग्राहस्तथैवच ।
पुत्रोऽनन्याश्रितद्रव्यः पुत्रहीनस्य ऋक्थिनः ॥५॥

अविभक्तैः कुटुम्बार्थं यद्दणं तु कृतं भवेत् ।
दद्युस्तद्‌कथिनः प्रेते प्रोषिते वा कुटुम्बिनि ॥६॥

न योषित् पतिपुत्राभ्यां न पुत्रेण कृतं पिता ।
दद्यादृते कुटुम्बार्थान्न पतिः स्त्रीकृतं तथा ॥७॥

गोपशौण्डिकशैलूषरजकव्याधयोषिताम् ।
ऋणं दद्यात् पतिस्त्वासां यस्माद्वृत्तिस्तदाश्रया ॥८॥

प्रतिपन्नं स्त्रिया देयं पत्या वा सह यत् कृतम् ।
स्वयं कृतं वा यद्दणं नान्यत् स्त्री दातुमर्हति ॥९॥

पितरि प्रोषिते प्रेते व्यसनाभिप्लुतेऽथवा ।
पुत्रपौत्रैर्ऋणं देयं निह्नवे साक्षिभावितम् ॥१०॥

सुराकामद्यूतकृतं दण्डशुल्कावशिष्टकम् ।
वृथाऽदानं तथैवेह पुत्रो दद्यन्न पैतृकम् ॥११॥

भ्रातॄणामथ दम्पत्योः पितुः पुत्रस्य चैव हि ।
प्रातिभाव्यमृणं साक्ष्यमविभक्तेन च स्मृतम् ॥१२॥

दर्शने प्रत्यये दाने प्रातिभाव्यं विधीयते ।
आद्यौ तु वितथे दाप्याावितरस्य सुता अपि ॥१३॥

दर्शनप्रतिभूर्यत्र मृतः प्रात्ययिकोऽपि वा ।
न तत् पुत्रा धनं दद्युर्दद्युर्दानाय ये स्थिताः ॥१४॥

बहवः स्युर्यदि स्वांशैर्दद्युः प्रतिभुवो धनम् ।
एकच्छायाश्रितेष्वेषु धनिकस्य यथारुचि ॥१५॥

प्रतिभूर्दापितो यत्र प्रकाशं धनिनो धनम् ।
द्विगुणं प्रतिदातव्यमृणिकैस्तस्य तद् भवेत् ॥१६॥

ससंततिस्त्रीपशव्यं धान्यं द्विगुणमेव च ।
वस्त्रं चतुर्गुणं प्रोक्तं रसश्चाष्टगुणस्तथा ॥१७॥

आधिः प्रणश्येद् द्विगुणे धने यदि न मोक्ष्यते ॥
काले कालकृतो नश्येत्फलभोग्यो न नश्यति ॥१८॥

गोप्याधिभोगिनो वृद्धिः सोपकारेऽथ भाविते ।
नष्टो देयो विनष्टश्च दैवराजकृताद्दते ॥१९॥

आधेः स्वीकरणात् सिद्धीरक्ष्यमाणोऽप्यसारताम् ।
यातश्चेदन्य आधेयो धनभाग् वा धनी भवेत् ॥२०॥

चरित्रबन्धककृतं सवृद्धं दापयेद्धनम् ।
सत्यंकारकृतं द्रव्यं द्विगुणं प्रतिदापयेत् ॥२१॥

उपस्थितस्य मोक्तव्य आधिर्दण्डोऽन्यथा भवेत् ।
प्रयोजकेऽसति धनं कुलेऽन्यस्याऽऽधिमाप्नुयात् ॥२२॥

तत्कालकृतपूल्यो वा तत्र तिष्ठेदवृद्धिकः ।
विनाधारणकाद्वाऽपि विक्रीणीतेससाक्षिकम् ॥२३॥

यदातु द्विगुणीभूतभृणमाधौ तदा खलु ।
मोच्यश्चाऽऽधिस्तदुत्पन्ने प्रविष्टे द्विगुणे धने ॥२४॥

वासनस्थमनाख्याय हस्तेऽन्यस्य यदर्पयेत् ।
द्रव्यं तदौपनिधिकं प्रतिदेयं तथैव तत् ॥२५॥

न दाप्योऽपहृतं तत्तु राजदैवततस्करैः ।
भ्रेषश्चेन्मार्गितेऽदत्ते दाप्यो दण्डश्च तत्समः ॥२६॥

आजीवन्स्वच्छया दण्ड्यो दाप्यस्तच्चापि सोदयम् ।
याचितान्वाहितन्यासनिक्षेपेष्वप्ययं विधिः ॥२७॥

इत्याग्नेये महापुराणे चतुःपञ्चाशदधिक-द्विशततमोध्यायः ॥२५४॥

1. Mit., Ap., BK. गृहीतानुक्रमात् for गृही. . . क्रमात्. BK. दद्याद् for दाप्यो; BK. दद्यात्तु for दत्त्वा तु; ब्राह्मणायैक Mit. ब्राह्मणायाग्रे for ब्रा. . . दौ. BK. नृपाय for नृपेतस्.
2. Mit., Ap. च for तु. ग, घ, च, द स्मृतम् for शतम्.
4. BK. गृह्णीत for गृह्णाति. Mit. चेत् for तत्.
5. BK. दद्यात् for दाप्यो.
6. Mit., Ap. कुटुम्बार्थे for °र्थः.
8. Mit., Ap., BK. पतिस्तांसां for पतिस्त्वासां.
9. BK. स्वयं कृतमृणं वापि for स्वयं. . . ऋणं.
10. BK. अपि for अथ. क, ङ निह्नुते for निह्नवे.
12. छ, ज ग्राह्यम् for साक्ष्यम्.
14. Mit., Ap., BK. ऋणं for धनं. Mit., BK. यः स्थितः for ये स्थिताः.
15. BK. स्थितेष्वेषु for श्रितेष्वेषु.
16. ग, छ, ज धनिने for धनिनो. धनम् for भवेत्.
17. ज स्वसन्तति for स. . . ति. Mit., Ap. संततिः स्त्रीपशुष्वेव for स. . . . व्यं. Mit., Ap., BK. त्रिगुणं for द्विगुणम्. BK. देयं for प्रोक्तं.

18. छ कालकृतं for °कृतो.

19. ज भोग्यो ना वृद्धिः (Mit., Ap. भोगे नो वृद्धिः) for भोगिनो वृद्धिः. हापिते for भाविते. ङ विशिष्टश्च for विनष्टश्च. क देशकालो विभाव्यते for दैव..द्दते.

20. BK. धनं वा धनिने वहेत् for धन... भवेत्.

21. ज चरित्रं for चरित्र. Mit., Ap. सवृद्ध्या for सवृद्धं, प्रतिपादयेत् for °दांपयेत्.

22. Mit., Ap. स्तेनो for दण्ड्यो.

23. Mit., Ap., BK. विक्रीणीत for °तें.

24. Mit., Ap. मोच्य आधिः for मोच्यश्चाधिः. ख, ग, घ, ङ, च, छ, ज उत्पाद्य for उत्पन्ने.

25. BK. भाजन for नासन. Mit., Ap. BK. अर्प्यते for अर्पयेत्. ग, घ, न तदर्पयेत् for यद...

26. Mit. तं तु for तत्तु. Mit., Ap., BK. दैविकं (ज दैवक) ज प्रेषै (Ap. भ्रंश) for भ्रेष.

27. Mit., Ap. तं चापि for तच्चापि. ज न्यासे for न्यास. Mit., Ap. निक्षेपादिष्वयं for नि...यं.

पञ्चपञ्चाशदधिक-द्विशततमोऽध्यायः

दिव्यप्रमाणकथनम्

अग्निरुवाच–

तपस्विनो दानशीलाः कुलीनाः सत्यवादिनः।
धर्मप्रधाना ऋजवः पुत्रवन्तो धनान्विताः॥१॥

पञ्चयज्ञक्रियायुक्ताः साक्षिणः पञ्च वा त्रयः।
यथाजाति यथावर्णं सर्वे सर्वेषु वा स्मृताः॥२॥

स्त्रीवृद्धबालकितवमत्तोन्मत्ताभिशस्तकाः।
रङ्गावतारिपाषण्डि कूटकृद्विकलेन्द्रियाः ॥३॥

पतिताप्तार्थसम्बन्धिसहायरिपुतस्कराः:।
असाक्षिणः सर्वसाक्षी चौर्यपारुष्यसाहसे ॥४॥

उभयानुमतः साक्षी भवत्येकोऽपि धर्मवित् ।
अब्रुवन्हि नरः साक्ष्यमृणं सदशबन्धकम् ॥५॥

राज्ञा सर्वं प्रदाप्यः स्यात् षट्चत्वारिंशकेऽहनि ।
न ददाति हि यः साक्ष्यं जानन्नपि नराधमः॥६॥

सकूटसाक्षिणां पापैस्तुल्यो दण्डेन चैव हि ।
साक्षिणः श्रावयेद्वादिप्रतिवादिसमीपगान् ॥७॥

ये पातककृतां लोका महापातकिनां तथा ।
अग्निदानां च ये लोका ये च स्त्रीबालधातिनाम् ॥८॥

तान् सर्वान् समवाप्नोति यः साक्ष्यमनृतं वदेत् ।
सुकृतं यत्त्वया किञ्चिज्जन्मान्तरशतैः कृतम् ॥९॥

तत् सर्वं तस्य जानीहि यं पराजयसे मृषा ।
द्वैधे बहूनां वचनं समेषु गुणिनां तथा ॥१०॥

गुणिद्वैधे तु वचनं ग्राह्यं ये गुणवत्तराः ।
यस्योचुः सक्षिणः सत्यां प्रतिज्ञां स जयी भवेत् ॥११॥

अन्यथा वादिनो यस्य ध्रुवस्तस्य पराजयः ।
उक्तेऽपि साक्षिभिः साक्ष्ये यद्यन्ये गुणवन्नराः ॥१२॥

द्विगुणा वाऽन्यथा ब्रूयुः कूटाः स्युः पूर्वसाक्षिणः ।
पृथक् पृथग्दण्डनीयाः कूटकृत् साक्षिणस्तथा ॥१३॥

विवादाद्द्विगुणं दण्डं विवास्यो ब्राह्मणः स्मृतः ।
यः साक्ष्यं श्रावितोऽन्येभ्यो निह्नुते तत्तमोवृतः ॥१४॥

स दाप्योऽष्टगुणं दण्डं ब्राह्मणं तु विवासयेत् ।
वर्णिनां हि वधो यत्र तत्र साक्ष्येऽनृतं वदेत् ॥१५॥

यः कश्चिदर्थोऽभिमतः स्वरुच्या तु परस्परम् ।
लेख्यं तु साक्षिमत् कार्यं तस्मिन्धनिकपूर्वकम् ॥१६॥

समामासतदर्धाहर्नामजातिस्वगोत्रकैः ।
सब्रह्मचारिकात्मीय पितृनामादिचिह्नितम् ॥१७॥

समाप्तेऽर्थेऋणीनाम स्वहस्तेन निवेशयेत् ।
मतं मेऽमुकपुत्रस्य यदत्रोपरिलेखितम् ॥१८॥

साक्षिणश्च स्वहस्तेन पितृनामकपूर्वकम् ।
अत्राहममुकः साक्षी लिखेयुरिति ते समाः ॥१९॥
अलिपिज्ञ ऋणी यः स्याल्लेखयेत् स्वमतं तु सः ।
साक्षी वा साक्षिणाऽन्येन सर्वसाक्षिसमीपतः ॥२०॥

उभयाभ्यर्थिते नैतन्मया ह्यमुकसूनुना ।
लिखितं ह्यमुकेनेतिलेखकोऽन्ते ततो लिखेत् ॥२१॥

विनाऽपि साक्षिभिर्लेख्यं स्वहस्तलिखितं च यत् ।

तत् प्रमाणं स्मृतं सर्वं बलोऽधिकृताद्दते ।।२२।।

ऋणं लेख्यकृतं देयं पुरुषैस्त्रिभिरेव तु ।
आधिस्तु भुज्यते तावद्यावत्तन्न प्रदीयते ।।२३।।

देशान्तरस्थे दुर्लेख्ये नष्टोन्मृष्टे हृते तथा ।
भिन्ने छिन्ने तथा दग्धे लेख्यमन्यत्तु कारयेत् ।।२४।।

सन्दिग्धार्थविशुद्ध्यर्थं स्वहस्तलिखितं तु यत् ।
युक्तिप्राप्तिक्रियाचिह्नसंबन्धागमहेतुभिः ।।२५।।

लेखस्य पृष्ठेऽभिलिखेत् प्रविष्टमधमर्णिनः ।
धनी चोपगतं दद्यात् स्वहस्तपरिचिह्नितम् ।२६।।

दत्त्वर्णं पाठयेल्लेख्यं शुद्ध्यै चान्यत्तु कारयेत् ।
साक्षिमच्च भवेद्यत्तु तद्दातव्यं ससाक्षिकम् ।।२७।।

तुलाग्न्यापो विषं कोषो दिव्यानीह विशुद्धये ।
महाभियोगेष्वेतानि शीर्षकस्थेऽभियोक्तरि ।।२८।।

रुच्या वाऽन्यतरः कुर्यादपरो वर्तयेच्छिरः ।
विनापि शीर्षकात् कुर्यात् नृपद्रोहेऽथ पातके ।।२९।।

नाऽऽसहस्राद्धरेन्फालं न तुलां न विषं तथा ।
नृपार्थेष्वभियोगेषु वहेयुः शुचयः सदा ।।३०।।

सहस्रार्थे तुलादीनि कोषमल्पेऽपि दापयेत् ।
शतार्द्धं दापयेच्छुद्धमशुद्धो दण्डभाग्भवेत् ।।३१।।
सचेलं स्नातमहूय सूर्योदय उपोषितम् ।
कारयेत् सर्वदिव्यानि नृपब्राह्मणसंनिधौ ।।३२।।

तुलास्त्रीबालवृद्धान्धपंगुब्राह्मणरोगिणाम् ।
अग्निर्जलं वा शूद्रस्य यवाः सप्त विषस्य वा ।।३३।।

तुलाधारणविद्वद्भिरभियुक्तस्तुलाश्रितः ।
प्रतिमानसमीभूतो रेखां कृत्वाऽवतारितः ।।३४।।

आदित्यचन्द्रावनिलोऽनलश्च द्यौर्भूमिरापो हृदयं यमश्च ।
अहश्च रात्रिश्च उभे च सन्ध्ये धर्मश्च जानाति नरस्य वृत्तम् ॥३५॥

त्वं तुले सत्यधामासि पुरा दैवविर्निर्मता ।
सत्यं वदस्व कल्याणि संशयान्मां विमोचय ॥३६॥

यद्यस्मि पापकृन्मातस्ततोमां त्वमधो नय ।
शुद्धश्चेद्गमयोर्ध्वं मांतुलामित्यभिमन्त्रयेत् ॥३७॥
करौ विमृदितव्रीहेर्लक्षयित्वा ततो न्यसेत् ।
सप्ताश्वत्थस्य पत्राणि तावत् सूत्रेण वेष्टयेत् ॥३८॥

त्वमेव सर्वभूतानामन्तश्चरसि पावक ।
साक्षिवत् पुण्यपापेभ्यो ब्रूहि सत्यं करे मम ॥३९॥

तस्येत्युक्तवतो लौहं पञ्चाशत्पलिकं समम् ।
अग्निवर्णं न्यसेत् पिण्डं हस्तयोरुभयोरपि ॥४०॥

स तमादाय सप्तैव मण्डलानि शनैर्व्रजेत् ।
षोडशाङ्गुलकं ज्ञेयं मण्डलं तावदन्तरम् ॥४१॥

मुक्त्वाऽग्निं मृदितव्रीहिरदग्धः शुद्धिमाप्नुयात् ।
अन्तरापतिते पिण्डे संदेहे वा पुनर्हरेत् ॥४२॥

पवित्राणां पवित्रत्वं शोध्यं शोधय पावन ।
सत्येन मामभिरक्षस्व वरुणेत्यभिशस्तकम् ॥४३॥
नाभिदघ्नोदकस्थस्य गृहीत्वोरुजलं विशेत् ।
समकालमिषुं मुक्तमानीयाद्यो जवान्नरः ॥४४॥

यदि तस्मिन्निमग्नाङ्गं पश्येच्चेच्छुद्धिमाप्नुयात् ।
त्वंविष ब्रह्मणः पुत्रः सत्यधर्मे व्यवस्थितः ॥४५॥

त्रायस्वास्मादभीशापात्सत्येन भव मेऽमृतम् ।
एवमुक्त्वा विषं शार्ङ्गं भक्षयेद्धिमशैलजम् ॥४६॥

यस्य वेगैर्विना जीर्णं शुद्धिं तस्य विनिर्दिशेत् ।
देवानुग्रान् समभ्यर्च्य तत् स्नानोदकमाहरेत् ॥४७॥

संश्राव्य पाययेत्तस्माज्जलात्तु प्रसृतित्रयम् ।
आचतुर्दशमादह्नो यस्य नोराजदैविकम् ।।४८।।

व्यसनं जायते घोरं स शुद्धः स्यादसंशयम् ।
सत्यवाहनशस्त्राणि गोबीजकनकानि च ।।४९।।

देवता गुरुपादाश्च इष्टापूर्त्तकृतानि च ।
इत्येते सुकराः प्रोक्ताः शपथाः स्वल्पसंशये ।।५०।।

इत्याग्नेये महापुराणे पञ्चपञ्चाशदधिकद्विशततमोऽध्यायः ।।२५५।।

2. Mit., Ap., BK. त्र्यवराः साक्षिणो ज्ञेयाः श्रौतस्मार्तक्रियापराः (BK. पञ्चयज्ञक्रियारताः) for the first line BK. सर्वे सर्वासु वा पुनः for सर्वे... स्मृताः.

3. Mit., Ap. transpose वृद्ध and बाल.

4. ज पतितान्नार्थ for पतितात्तार्थ. Mit., Ap., BK. साहसी दृष्टदोषश्च निर्धूताद्या (BK. निर्धूतश्चेत्य) स्त्वसाक्षिणः for the second line.

6. Ap., BK. षट्चत्वारिंशत्तमेऽहनि for स्यात्..ऽहनि.

8. Ap. च पातकिनां for पातककृतां.

9. Mit. स तान् सर्वानवाप्नोति for तान्...ति. BK. यत्त्वाया सुकृतं for सुकृतं यत्वया.

10. BK. पराजयसि यं मृषा for यं... मृषा; साक्षिद्वैधे प्रभूतानां for द्वैधे... वचनं.

11. Mit., Ap. गुणवत्तमाः for तराः. BK. यद्गुणवत्तरम् for ये...राः; यस्यादुः for यस्योचुः.

12. Mit., Ap. गुणवत्तमाः for तराः

14. BK. विवादद्विगुणं for ति...णं; द्रव्यं for दण्डं; भवेत् for स्मृतः; अन्येन for अन्येभ्यो.

15. BK. द्रव्यं for दण्डं. Mit., Ap., BK. साक्षी for साक्ष्ये. After this line Mit., Ap., and BK. add तत्पावनाय निर्वाप्यश्चरुः सारस्वतो द्विजैः.

16. Mit., Ap., BK. निष्णातः for (अ)भिमतः BK. वा for तु.

17. BK. वास for नाम. ज स्वगोत्रजैः for °कैः. BK. नाम्ना च for नामादि. Ap., BK. स for स्व.

19. Ap., BK. असमाः for समाः.

20. Omitted by Mit. and Ap. This verse has been attributed to Kārale by Mit. under YS.II.87, BK. समीपगः for °तः.

21. क, ख, ङ, ज लेखकोऽर्थास्ततो लिखेत् for लेखको... लिखेत्. क नयेत् for लिखेत्.

22. Mit., BK. तु for च. Mit. लेख्य for सर्वः

23. ख ज्ञेयं for देयं.

24. Mit., Ap भिन्ने दग्धेऽथवा (Ap. तथा) छिन्ने for भिन्ने... दग्धे.

25. Mit., Ap. संदिग्धलेख्य (Ap. लेख्ये for लेख्य) शुद्धिः स्यात्स्वहस्तलिखितादिभिः for the first line.

26. Mit., Ap. दत्त्वा दत्त्वर्णिको धनम् for प्रविष्ट... नः. BK. अधमर्णिकात् for °र्नः Mit., Ap., BK. वोपगतं for चोपगतं.

27. Mit., Ap वा for च, वा for second तु.

28. Ap. महाभियोगेत्वेतानि for °स्तेतानि.

29. Mit., Ap., BK. इतरो for अपरो. BK. राज for नृप.

30. BK. नासहस्रपरं for ना... रेत्. Mit., Ap. न विषं न तुलां for न... विषं; अभिशापे च for अभियोगेषु.

31. BK. कारयेत् for दापयेत्; पञ्चाशत् for शतार्धः. The second line is attributed to Kātyāyana in Mit. under YS.II.113.

32. सचेलस्नानम् for सचेलं स्नातम्.

33. क च for वा.

34. च स्थितः for श्रितः. च विभावितः for (अ)वतारितः. Ap. रेखाः (BK. लेखाः क, ङ लीलां, ख, ग लेखं) for रेखां.

35. It is quoted in the Mit. comm. on YS.II.100-102. It occurs in the *Mahābhārata*, Ādi. 68.29 and Anuśāsana 18.4 (Critical edition, Poona).

36. Mit., Ap, देव (ज, BK. देवै) for दैव; तत्सत्यं वद for सत्यं वदस्व.

38. Ap.° व्रींही for ° व्रीहे.

39. Mit., Ap. त्वमग्ने for त्वमेव. Mit., Ap., BK. कते for कारे.

40. क तथा for समम्. BK. क्षिप्रं for पिण्डं.

42. BK. मुक्ताग्निः for °ग्निं.°

43. The first line does not occur in Mit., Ap., BK. Mit. अभिशाप्य (Ap. अभिशास्य, क, ख अभिजाप्य) for अभिशस्त.

44. Mit., ज आनीयान्यो (Ap., BK. आनयेद्यो for आनीयाद्यो). क, ङ, च, ज जवी for जवात्.

45. Mit., Ap. गते for यदि. BK. गतेऽन्यस्मिन् for यदि तस्मिन्. BK. सत्यधर्मव्यवस्थित for सत्य... तः.

46. BK. अस्मान्मामभिशापात् for अस्मा.... त्, ख, ग, च साङ्गं for शार्ङ्गं.

47. Mit. जीर्येत् for जीर्णं

48. Mit., Ap. संस्राव्य for संश्राव्य. Mit. जलं for जलात्. Mit., Ap. अर्वाक् चतुर्दशात् for आचतुर्दशमात्.

49. Mit., Ap., BK. स्यान्न संशयः for स्यादसंशयम्.

49b-50. Do not occur in Mit., Ap. and BK.

षट्पञ्चाशदधिक-द्विशततमोऽध्यायः

दायविभाग कथनम्

अग्निरुवाच–

विभागं चेत्पिता कुर्यादिच्छया विभजेत् सुतान् ।
ज्येष्ठं वा श्रेष्ठभागेन सर्वे वा स्युः समांशिनः ।।१।।

यदि दद्यात् समानंशान् कार्या. पत्न्यः समांशिकाः ।
न दत्तं स्त्रीधनं यासां भर्त्रा वा श्वशुरेण वा ।।२।।

शक्तस्यानीहमानस्य किंचिद्दत्त्वा पृथक् क्रिया ।
न्यूनाधिकविभक्तानां धर्म्यश्च पितृतः स्मृतः ।।३।।

विभजेयुः सुताः पित्रोरूर्ध्वमृकथमृणं समम् ।
मातुर्दुहितरः शेषमृणात्ताभ्यऋृतेऽर्पयेत् ।।४।।
पितृद्रव्याविनाशेन यदन्यस्त्वयमर्जयेत् ।
मैत्रमौद्वाहिकं चैव दायादानां न तद्भवेत् ।।५।।

सामान्यार्थसमुत्थाने विभागस्तु समः स्मृतः ।
अनेकपितृकाणां तु पितृतोभागकल्पना ।।६।।

भूर्या पितामहोपात्ता निबन्धो द्रव्यमेव वा ।
तत्र स्यात् सदृशं स्वाम्यं पितुः पुत्रस्य चोभयोः ।।७।।

विभक्तेषु सुतो जातः सवर्णायां विभागभाक् ।
दृश्याद्वा तद्विभागः स्यादायव्ययविशोधितात् ।।८।।

क्रमादभ्यागतं द्रव्यं हृतमभ्युद्धरेच्च यः ।
दायदिभ्यो न तद्दद्याद्विक्षयालब्धमेव च ।।९।।

पितृभ्यां यस्य यद्दत्तं तत्तस्यैव धनं भवेत् ।
पितुरूर्ध्वं विभजतां माताप्यंशं समं हरेत् ॥१०॥

असंस्कृतास्तु संस्कार्या भ्रातृभिः पूर्वसंस्कृतैः ।
भगिन्यश्च निजादंशाद्दत्वऽशं तु तुरीयकम् ॥११॥

चतुस्त्रिद्व्येकभागाः स्युर्वर्णशो ब्राह्मणात्मजाः ।
क्षत्रजास्त्रिद्व्येकभागा विड्जास्तुद्व्येकभागिनः ॥१२॥

अन्योन्यापहृतं द्रव्यं विभक्ते यत्तु दृश्यते ।
तत्पुनस्ते समैरंशैर्विभजेरन्निति स्थितिः ॥१३॥

अपुत्रेण परक्षेत्रे नियोगोत्पादितः सुतः ।
उभयोरप्यसावृक्थी पिण्डदाता च धर्मतः ॥१४॥

औरसो धर्म्मपत्नीजस्तत्समः पुत्रिकासुतः ।
क्षेत्रजः क्षेत्रजातस्तु सगोत्रेणेतरेण वा ॥१५॥

गृहे प्रच्छन्न उत्पन्नो गूढजस्तु सुतः स्मृतः ।
कानीनः कन्यकाजातो मातामहसुतो मतः ॥१६॥

अक्षतायां क्षतायां वा जातः पौनर्भवः सुतः ।
दद्यान्माता पिता वा यं स पुत्रो दत्तको भवेत् ॥१७॥

क्रीतश्च ताभ्यां विक्रीतः कृत्रिमः स्यात् स्वयंकृतः ।
दत्तात्मातु स्वयं दत्तो गर्भे विन्नः सहोढजः ॥१८॥

उत्सृष्टो गृह्यते यस्तु सोऽपविद्धो भवेत् सुतः ।
पिण्डदोऽशहरश्चैषां पूर्वाभावे परः परः ॥१९॥

सजातीयेष्वयं प्रोक्तस्तनयेषु मया विधिः ।
जातोऽपि दास्यां शूद्रस्य कामतोऽशहरो भवेत् ॥२०॥

मृते पितरि कुर्युस्तं भ्रातरस्त्वर्द्धभागिकम् ।
अभ्रातृको हरेत् सर्वं दुहितृणां सुताद्दते ॥२१॥

पत्नीदुहितरश्चैव पितरौ भ्रातरस्तथा ।

तत्सुतो गोत्रजो बन्धुः शिष्यः सब्रह्मचारिणः ॥२२॥

एषामभावे पूर्वस्य धनभागुत्तरोत्तरः।
स्वर्यातस्य ह्यपुत्रस्य सर्ववर्णेष्वयं विधिः ॥२३॥

वानप्रस्थयतिब्रह्मचारिणामृक्थभागिनः ।
क्रमेणाऽऽचार्यसच्छिष्यधर्मभ्रात्रेकतीर्थिनः ॥२४॥

संसृष्टिनस्तु संसृष्टी सोदरस्य तु सोदरः।
दद्याच्चापहरेच्चांशं जातस्य च मृतस्य च ॥२५॥

अन्योदर्यस्तु संसृष्टी नान्योदर्योधनं हरेत् ।
असंसृष्ट्यपि चाऽऽदद्यात् सोदर्योनान्यमातृजः ॥२६॥

पतितस्तत्सुतः क्लीबः पङ्गुरुन्मत्तको जडः।
अन्धोऽचिकित्स्यरोगाद्या भर्तव्यास्तुनिरंशकाः ॥२७॥

औरसाः क्षेत्रजास्त्वेषां निर्दोषाभागहारिणः।
सुताश्चैषां प्रभर्तव्या यावद्वै भर्तृसात् कृताः ॥२८॥

अपुत्रा योषितश्चैषां भर्तव्याः साधुवृत्तयः ।
निर्वास्या व्यभिचारिण्यः प्रतिकूलास्तथैव च ॥२९॥

पितृमातृपतिभ्रातृदत्तमध्यग्न्युपागतम् ।
आधिवेदनिकं चैव स्त्रीधनं परिकीर्त्तितम् ॥३०॥

बन्धुदत्तं तथा शुल्कमन्वाधेयकमेव च ।
अप्रजायामतीतायां बान्धवास्तदवाप्नुयुः ॥३१॥

अप्रजस्त्रीधनं भर्तुर्ब्राह्मादिषु चतुर्ष्वपि ।
दुहितॄणां प्रसूता चेच्छेषेषु पितृगामि तत् ॥३२॥

दत्त्वाकन्यां हरन् दण्ड्यो व्ययं दव्याच्च सोदयम् ।
मृतायां दत्तमादद्यात्परिशोध्योभयव्ययम् ॥३३॥

दुर्भिक्षे धर्मकार्ये च व्याधौ संप्रतिरोधके ।
गृहीतं स्त्रीधनं भर्ता न स्त्रियै दातुमर्हति ॥३४॥

अधिविन्नस्त्रियै दद्यादाधिवेदनिकं समम् ।
नदत्तं स्त्रीधनं यस्यै दत्ते त्वर्धं प्रकीर्तितम् ॥३५॥

विभागनिह्नवे ज्ञातिबन्धु साक्ष्यभिलेखितैः ।
विभागभावना ज्ञेया गृहक्षेत्रैश्च यौतकैः ॥३६॥

इत्याग्नेये महापुराणे षट्-पञ्चाशदधिकद्विशततमोऽध्यायः ॥२५६॥

2. Mit., Ap. कुर्यात् for दद्यात्. कार्याः and पत्न्यः transposed.
3. Mit., Ap. धर्म्यः (Ap., BK. धर्मः) पितृकृतः, स्मृतः for धर्म्य...स्मृतः. क, ख, ग, घ, छ, ज कृतः for स्मृतः.
4. Mit., Ap. विभजेरन् for °जेयुः; अन्वयः (also BK. and ज) for अर्पयेत्.
5. Mit., Ap. पितृद्रव्याविरोधेन for पितृ...शेन; अर्जितं (also BK.) for अर्जयेत्.
6. क, घ, ङ, च अनेकपितृकार्याणां for °पितृकाणां.
7. Mit. चैवहि for चोभयोः.
8. BK. विभक्तेऽपि सवर्णायाः पुत्रो जातो for विभक्तेषु...सवर्णायां.
9. BK. अभ्युद्धरेत (क, ङ अभ्युद्धरेत्तु) for अभ्युद्धरेच्च.
10. BK. समाप्नुयात् for समं हरेत्.
12. BK. एकभागीना for °भागा. Ap. विड्जौ तु चेकभागिनौ for विड्जा..नः.
13. ख, ग अन्योन्यापकृतं for °हृतं. BK. विभक्तैर्यत्र for विभक्ते यत्तु. Ap. यदि for यत्तु.
14. Mit., Ap. असौ रिक्थी for असावृक्थी.
16. ख यतः for मतः.
17. Ap. स्मृतः for सुतः; क, ङ वापि for वा यं; Ap. दत्तकः स्मृतः for दत्तको भवेत्.
18. Ap. कृत्रिमश्च for कृत्रिमः स्यात्.
19. Ap. भवेत् and सुतः transposed.
20. Mit., Ap., BK. शूद्रेण for शूद्रस्य.
21. BK. भागिनम् for भागिकम्.
22. Mit., Ap. read the second line as तत्सुता गोत्रजा (Ap. गौत्रजो) बन्धुशिष्यसब्रह्मचारिणः.
23. ख, ग, घ, च पूर्वः स्यात् for पूर्वस्य.
26. Ap नान्योदर्यधनं for ना...धनं. BK. सोदरो for सोदर्यो.
27. Mit., Ap. क्लीबोऽथ पतितस्तज्जः for पतित...क्लीबः. BK. रोगी च for रोगाद्या. Mit. स्युः for स्तुं.
30. BK. सुत for पति. Mit. आधिवेदनिकाद्यं च for आधि...चैव.
31. Mit. अतीतायामप्रजसि for अप्रजा...यां.
33. Ap. सहोदयम् for च सोदयम्; सर्वम् for दत्तम्
35. Ap. देयम् for दद्यात्. BK. यस्या for यस्यै.
36. BK. देय for ज्ञेया; क्षेत्रक for क्षेत्रैश्च.

सप्तपञ्चाशदधिक-द्विशततमोऽध्यायः

सोमाविवादादिनिर्णय

अग्निरुवाच–

सीम्नो विवादे क्षेत्रस्य सामन्ताः स्थविरादयः।
गोपाः सीमाकर्षिणो ये सर्वे च वनगोचराः॥१॥

प्रणेयुरेते सीमानं स्थूलाङ्गारतुषद्रुमैः।
सेतुवल्मीकनिम्नास्थिचैत्याद्यैरुपलक्षिताम् ॥२॥

सामन्ता ना समग्रामाश्चत्वारोऽष्टदशापि वा।
रक्तस्रग्वसनाः सीमां नयेयुः क्षितिचारिणः॥३॥

अनृते तु पृथग्दण्ड्या राज्ञा मध्यमसाहसम्।
अभावे ज्ञांतृचिंह्नानां राजा सीम्नः प्रवर्त्तकः ॥४॥

आरामायतनग्रामनिपानोद्यानवेश्मसु।
एष एव विधिर्ज्ञेयो वर्षाम्बुप्रवहेषु च ॥५॥
मर्यादायाः प्रभेदेषु क्षेत्रस्य हरणे तथा।
मर्यादायाश्च दण्ड्याः स्युरधमोत्तममध्यमाः ॥६॥

ननिषेध्योऽल्पबाधस्तु सेतुः कल्याणकारकः।
परभूमिं हरन्कूपः स्वल्पक्षेत्रो बहूदकः॥७॥

स्वामिने योऽनिवेद्यैव क्षेत्रे सेतुं प्रकल्पयेत्।
उत्पन्ने स्वामिनो भोगस्तदभावे महीपतेः॥८॥

फालाहतमपि क्षेत्रं यो न कुर्यान्न कारयेत्।
स प्रदाप्योऽकृष्टफलं क्षेत्रमन्येन कारयेत् ॥९॥

माषानष्टौ तु महिषी सस्यघातस्य कारिणी।

दण्डनीया तदर्थं तु गौस्तदर्धमजाविकम् ॥१०॥

भक्षयित्वोपविष्टानां द्विगुणो वसतां दमः।
सममेषां विधीयते खरोष्ट्रं महिषी समम् ॥११॥

यावत् सस्यं विनष्टं तु तावत् क्षेत्री फलं लभेत् ।
पालस्ताड्योऽथ गोस्वामी पूर्वोक्तं दण्डमर्हति ॥१२।

पथिग्रामविवीतान्ते क्षेत्रे दोषो न विद्यते ।
अकामतः कामचारे चौरवद्दण्डमर्हति ॥१३॥

महोक्षोत्सृष्टपशवः सूतिकाऽऽगन्तुका च गौः।
पालो येषां तु ते मोच्या दैवराजपरिल्पुताः ॥१४॥

यथार्पितान्पशून गोपः सायं प्रत्यर्पयेत्तथा ।
प्रमादमृतनष्टांश्च प्रदाप्यः कृतवेतनः॥१५॥

पालदोषविनाशे तु पाले दण्डो विधीयते ।
अर्धत्रयोदशपणः स्वामिनो द्रव्यमेव च ॥१६॥

ग्रामेच्छया गोप्रचारोभूमिराजवशेन वा ।
द्विजस्तृणैधः पुष्पाणि सर्वतः सर्वदाऽऽहरेत् ॥१७॥

धनुःशतं परीणाहो ग्रामक्षेत्रान्तरं भवेत् ।
द्वे शते खर्वटस्य स्यान्नगरस्य चतुःशतम् ॥१८॥

स्वं लभेतान्यविक्रीतं क्रेतुर्दोषोऽप्रकाशिते ।
हीनाद्रहो हीनमूल्ये वेलाहीने च तस्करः॥१९॥

नष्टापहृतमासाद्ये हर्तारं ग्राहयेन्नरम् ।
देशकालातिपत्तौ वा गृहीत्वा स्वयमर्पयेत् ॥२०॥

विक्रेतुर्दर्शनाच्छुद्धिः स्वामी द्रव्यं नृपो दमम् ।
क्रेता मूल्यं समाप्नोति तस्माद्यस्तत्र विक्रयी ॥२१॥

आगमेनोपभोगेन नष्टं भाव्यमतोऽन्यथा ।
पञ्चबन्धो दमस्तस्य राज्ञस्तेनाथ भाविते ॥२२॥

हृतं प्रनष्टं यो द्रव्यं परहस्तादवाप्नुयात् ।
अनिवेद्य नृपे दण्ड्यः स तु षण्णवतिं पणान् ॥२३॥

शैल्किकैः स्थानपालैर्वा नष्टापहृतमाहृतम् ।
अर्वाक् संवत्सरात् स्वामी लभते परतो नृपः ॥२४॥

पणानेकशफे दद्याच्चतुरः पञ्च मानुषे ।
महिषोष्ट्रगवां द्वौ द्वौ पादं पादमजाविके ॥२५॥
स्वकुटुम्बाविरोधेन देयं दारसुतादृते ।
नान्वये सति सर्वस्वं देयं यच्चान्यसंश्रुतम् ॥२६॥

प्रतिग्रहः प्रकाशः स्यात् स्थावरस्य विशेषतः ।
देयं प्रतिश्रुतं चैव दत्त्वा नापहरेत्पुनः ॥२७॥

दशैकपञ्चसप्ताहमासत्र्यहार्धमासिकम्[।
वीजायोवाह्यरत्नस्त्रीदोह्यपुंसां प्रतीक्षणम् ॥२८॥

अग्नौ सुवर्णमक्षीणं द्विपलं रजते शते ।
अष्टौ त्रपुणि सीसे च ताम्रे पञ्चदशायसि ॥२९॥

शते दशपला वृद्धिरौर्णे कार्पासिके तथा ।
मध्ये पञ्चपला ज्ञेया सूक्ष्मे तु त्रिपला मता ॥३०॥

कार्मिके रोमवद्धे च त्रिंशद्भागः क्षयो मतः ।
न क्षयो न च वृद्धिस्तु कौशेये वल्कलेषु च ॥३१॥

देशं कालं च भोगं च ज्ञात्वा नष्टे बलाबलम् ।
द्रव्याणां कुशला ब्रुयुर्यत्तद्दाप्यमसंशयम् ॥३२॥

बलाद्दासीकृतश्चौरैर्विक्रीतश्चापि मुच्यते ।
स्वामिप्राणप्रदो भक्तत्यागात्तन्निष्क्रयादपि ॥

प्रव्रज्यावसितो राज्ञो दास आमरणान्तिकः ।
वर्णानामानुलोम्येन दास्यं न प्रतिलोमतः ॥३४॥

कृतशिल्पोऽपि निवसेत् कृतकालं गुरोर्गृहे ।

अन्तेवासी गुरुप्राप्तभोजनस्तत्तफलप्रदः ॥३५॥

राजा कृत्वा पुरे स्थानं ब्राह्मणान्न्यस्य तत्र तु ।
त्रैविद्यं वृत्तिमद्ब्रूयात्स्वधर्मः पाल्यतामिति ॥३६॥

निजधर्माविरोधेन यस्तु सामयिको भवेत् ।
सोऽपि यत्नेन संरक्ष्यो धर्मो राजकृतश्च यः ॥३७॥

गणद्रव्यं हरेद् यस्तु संविदं लङ्घयेच्च यः ।
सर्वस्वहरणं कृत्वा तं राष्ट्राद्विप्रवासयेत् ॥३८॥

कर्त्तव्यं वचनं सर्वैः समूहहितवादिनाम् ।
यस्तत्र विपरीतः स्यात्स दाप्यः प्रथमं दमम् ॥३९॥

समूहकार्यप्रहितो यल्लभेत तदर्पयेत् ।
एकादशगुणं दाप्यो यद्यसौ नार्पयेत् स्वयम् ॥४०॥

वेदज्ञाः शुचयोऽलुब्धा भवेयुः कार्यचिन्तकाः ।
कर्त्तव्यं वचनं तेषां समूहहितवादिनाम् ॥४१॥

श्रेणिनैगमपाषण्डिगणानामप्ययं विधिः ।
भेदं चैषां नृपोरक्षेत्पूर्ववृत्तिं च पालयेत् ॥४२॥

गृहीतवेतनः कर्म त्यजन् द्विगुणमावहेत् ।
अगृहीते समं दाप्यो भृत्यै रक्ष्य उपस्करः ॥४३॥

दाप्यस्तु दशमं भागं वाणिज्यपशुसस्यतः ।
अनिश्चित्यभृतिं यस्तु कारयेत् स महीक्षिता ॥४४॥
यो यावत्कुरुते कर्म तावत्तस्य तु वेतनम् ।
उभयोरप्यसाध्यं चेत् साध्ये कुर्याद् यथाश्रुतम् ॥४६॥

अराजदैविकं नष्टं भाण्डं दाप्यस्तु वाहकः ।
प्रस्थानविघ्नकृच्चैव प्रदाप्यो द्विगुणां भृतिम् ॥४७॥

प्रक्रान्ते सप्तमं भागं चतुर्थं पथि संत्यजन् ।
भृतिमर्धपथे सर्वां प्रदाप्यस्त्याजकोऽपि च ॥४८॥

गृहेशतिकवृद्धेस्तु सभिकः पञ्चकं शतम् ।
गृह्णीयाद्धूर्तकितवादितराद्दशकं शतम् ॥४९॥

स सम्यक् पालितो दद्याद्राज्ञे भागं यथा कृतम् ।
जितमुद्ग्राहयेज्जेत्रे दद्यात् सत्यं वचः क्षमी ॥५०॥

प्राप्ते नृपतिना भागे प्रसिद्धे धूर्तमण्डले ।
जितससमिके स्थाने दापयेदन्यथा न तु ॥५१॥

द्रष्टारो व्यवहाराणां साक्षिणश्च त एव हि ।
राज्ञा सचिह्ना निर्वास्याः कूटाक्षोपधिदेविनः ॥५२॥

द्यूतमेकमुखं कार्यं तस्करज्ञानकारणात् ।
एष एव विधिर्ज्ञेयः प्राणिद्यूते समाह्वये ॥५३॥

इत्याग्नेये महापुराणे सप्तपञ्चाशदधिक-द्विशततमोऽध्यायः

1. ख, ग, छ, ज स्थविरा गणाः for °रादयः. Mit., BK. कृषाणोऽन्ये (Ap. कृषाणाश्च), ज कृषाणा for कर्षिणो ये, Ap. ये चान्ये for सर्वे च.
2. Mit., Ap., BK. जनयेयु for प्रणेयु. BK. सीमान्तं for सीमानं. Ap., Mit., क, ङ, छ, ज स्थल for स्थूले.
3. Ap. समा for सम, BK. दशथि वा for दशापि वा. Mit., Ap., BK., ज धारिणः for चारिणः.
4. Mit., BK. प्रवर्तिता for प्रवर्तकः. BK. ज्ञान for ज्ञातृ.
5. Mit., Ap. प्रवहादिषु for प्रवहेषु च.
6. BK., Mit. प्रभेदे च (Ap. प्रभेदे तु) for प्रभेदेषु. Mit., Ap. सीमातिक्रमणे for क्षेत्रस्य हरणे. Mit., Ap. क्षेत्रस्य हरणे (BK. सीमातिक्रमणे) दण्डा for मर्यादापाश्च.... स्युः.
7. BK. हरेत् for हरन.
8. Ap. अविनिवेद्यैव (hypermetric). Mit., Ap. प्रतर्तयेत् for प्रकल्पयेत्.
9. Mit. न कुर्याद्यो न for यो न कुर्यान्निः स प्रदाप्यः कृष्टफलं (Ap., BK. तं प्रदाप्य कृष्टशदं) for स फलं.

Note: verses 8, 9 not found in च.

11. छ, ज, Mit., Ap. यथोक्ताद् द्विगुणो for द्विगुणो वसतां, Mit., Ap., BK. ऽवसतां)
12. क, ङ यावत्संख्यं for °संस्यं.
14. Mit., Ap. सुतिकागन्तुकादयः for सूतिका...गौः; न (Ap. च) for तु, Ap. राजदेव for दैवराज.

16. BK., Ap. स्वामिने for स्वामिनो. BK. धन for द्रव्य.

17. Mit. ग्राम्येच्छया for ग्रामेच्छया. BK. गोप्रचारभूमी for गो... भूमि Ap. समुपाहरेत् (BK., ज स्ववदाहरेत्) for सर्वदाहरेत्.

18. Ap. परीहारो for परीणाहो.

20. क, ङ कर्तारं for हर्तारं.

21. BK., Mit., Ap. अवाप्नोति for समाप्नोति. Mit., Ap तस्य for तत्र.

22. BK., Mit., Ap. तत्र for तस्य. Mit., Ap., ज राज्ञे तेनाविभाविते for राज्ञ... विते.

24. Mit., Ap. हरेत (BK. लभेत) for लभते.

26. Mit., Ap. यच्चान्यस्मै प्रतिश्रुतम् for यच्चा... तम्. BK. संश्रितम् for संश्रुतम्.

28. Mit., Ap., BK. परीक्षणम् for प्रतीक्षणम्.

29. Mit., Ap. transpose द्विपलं and रजते. BK. शतं for शते. BK. अष्टा तु त्रपुसीसे.

30. Mit. कार्पाससौत्रिके for कार्पा... तथा. Mit., Ap. वृद्धिः (BK. हानिः) for ज्ञेया. ख सौम्ये for सूक्ष्मे.

31. Mit., Ap. भागाः for भागः च (Ap., BK. स्यात्) for तु. BK. तथा for षुं च.

33. छ, ज, Mit., Ap. तन्निष्क्रयात् for निष्क्रयणात्. BK. भक्तस्तत् त्यागन्निष्क्रयादपि for भक्त... पि.

34. BK., Mit. आमरणान्तिकम् for कंः.

35. क, घ, ङ, च शिष्यो for शिल्पो. BK. कृतं for कृत.

36. Ap. त्रैविद्यान् for द्यं.

39. ख तेषां for सर्वैः. BK. वादिनः (ज वादिभिः) for वादिनाम्.

43. BK. कार्यं for दाप्यो; पाल्य for रक्ष्य.

44. Ap. तद्दशमं for तु दशमं. BK. महीभृता for °क्षिंता.

45. Mit., Ap. लाभं for कर्म.

46. Ap शाठ्यं for साध्यं, शाठ्ये (Also BK.) for साध्ये. BK. कृतम् for श्रुतम्.

47. Ap., BK. अराजदेविकात् for °दैविकं. BK. कर्ता च for कृच्चैव

48. BK. संत्यजेत् for संत्यजन्.

49. BK. गलत्सभिक for ग्लहे शतिक.

50. Ap. भागं राज्ञे दद्यात् यथाश्रुतम् for दद्यात्... कृतम्. BK. सत्यवचाः for सत्यं वचः.

51. Ap. भागे च नृपतिः (BK. नृपतिभागे तु) for नृपतिना भागे; transposes न and तु.

52. Mit., Ap. सचिह्नं for सचिह्ना.

त्रियोनिः कीर्त्यते तेन त्रयमेतद्विवादकृत् ।
द्व्यभियोगस्तु विज्ञेयः शङ्कातत्त्वाभियोगतः ॥१०॥

शङ्का सद्भिस्तु संसर्गात्तत्वं होढादिदर्शनात् ।
पक्षद्वयाभिसंबन्धाद्द्विद्वारः समुदाहृतः ॥११॥

पूर्ववादस्तयोः पक्षः प्रतिपक्षस्त्वन्तरः।
भूतच्छलानुसारित्वाद्द्विगतिः समुदाहृताः ॥१२॥

ऋणं देयमदेयं च येन यत्र यथा च यत् ।
दानग्रहणधर्मश्च ऋणादानमिति स्मृतम् ॥१३॥

स्वद्रव्यं यत्र विश्रम्भान्निक्षिपत्यविशङ्कितः।
निक्षेपं नाम तत्प्रोक्तं व्यवहारपदं बुधैः॥१४॥

वणिक्प्रभृतयो यत्र कर्म संभूय कुर्वते ।
तत्संभूयसमुत्थानं व्यवहारपदं विदुः॥१५॥

दत्त्वा द्रव्यं च सम्यग् यः पुनरादातुमिच्छति।
दत्ताप्रदानिकं नाम तद्विवादपदं स्मृतम् ॥१६॥

अभ्युपेत्य च शुश्रूषां यस्तां न प्रतिपद्यते ।
अशुश्रूषामुपेत्यैतद्विवादपदमुच्यतेते ॥१७॥

भृत्यानां वेतनस्योक्तादानादानविधिक्रिया ।
वेतनस्यानपाकर्म तद्विवादपदं स्मृतम् ॥१८॥

निक्षिप्तं वा परद्रव्यं नष्टं लब्ध्वाऽपहृत्य वा ।
विक्रीयते परोक्षं यत्स ज्ञेयोऽस्वामिविक्रियः ॥१९॥

विक्रीय पण्यं मूल्येन क्रेत्रे यच्च न दीयते ।
विक्रीयासंप्रदानं तद्विवादपदमुच्यते ॥२०॥

क्रीत्वा मूल्येन यः पण्यं क्रेता न बहुमन्यते ।
क्रीत्वा मूल्येन तु यः पण्यं दुष्क्रीतं मन्यते क्रयी ॥२१॥

पतनीयकृते क्षेपे दण्डो मध्यमसाहसः।
उपपातकयुक्ते तु दाप्यः प्रथमसाहसम् ॥७॥

त्रैविद्यनृपदेवानां क्षेप उत्तमसाहसः।
मध्यमो जातिपूगानां प्रथमो ग्रामदेशयोः॥८॥

असाक्षिकहते चिह्नैर्युक्तिभिश्चाऽऽगमेन च।
द्रष्टव्यो व्यवहारस्तु कूटचिह्नकृताद्भयत् ॥९॥

भस्मपङ्करजः स्पर्शे दण्डो दशपणः स्मृतः।
अमेध्यपार्ष्णिनिष्ठ्यूतस्पर्शने द्विगुणः स्मृतः॥१०॥

समेष्वेवं परस्त्रीषु द्विगुणस्तूत्तमेषु च।
हीनेष्वर्धं दमो मोहमदादिभिरदण्डनम् ॥११॥

विप्रपीड़ाकरं छेद्यमङ्गमब्राह्मणस्य तु।
उद्गूर्णे प्रथमो दण्डः संस्पर्शे तु तदर्धकः॥१२॥

उद्गूर्णे हस्तपादे तु दशविंशतिकौ दमौ।
परस्परं तु सर्वेषां शस्त्रे मध्यमसाहसः॥१३॥

पादकेशांशुककरोल्लुञ्चनेषु पणान्दश।
पीडाकर्षांशुकावेष्टपादाध्यासे शतं दमः॥१४॥

शोणितेन विना दुःखं कुर्वन्काष्ठादिभिर्नरः।
द्वात्रिंशतं पणान्दाप्यो द्विगुणं दर्शनेऽसृजः॥१५॥

करपाददतो भङ्गे छेदने कर्णनासयोः।
मध्यो दण्डो व्रणोद्भेदे मृतकल्पहते तथा ॥१६॥

चेष्टाभोजनवाग्रोधे नेत्रादिप्रतिभेदने।
कंधराबाहुसक्थ्नांच भङ्गे मध्यमसाहसः॥१७॥

एकं घ्नतां बहूनां च यथोक्ताद्द्विगुणा दमाः।
कलहापहृतं देयं दण्डस्तु द्विगुणः स्मृतः॥१८॥

दुःखमुत्पादयेद्यस्तु स समुत्थानजं व्ययम् ।
दाप्यो दण्डं च यो यस्मिन्कलहे समुदाहृतः ॥१९॥

तरिकः स्थलजं शुल्कं गृह्णन्दण्ड्यः पणान्दश ।
ब्राह्मणप्रातिवेश्यानामेतदेवानिमन्त्रणो ॥२०॥

अभिघाते तथा भेदे छेदे कुड्यावपातने ।
पणान्दाप्यः पञ्चदश विंशतिं तद्व्ययं तथा ॥२१॥

दुःखोत्पादि गृहे द्रव्यं क्षिपन्प्राणहरं तथा ।
षोडशाऽऽद्यः पणान्दाप्यो द्वितीयो मध्यमं दमम् ॥२२॥

दुःखे च शोणित्पादे शाखाङ्गच्छेदने तथा ।
दण्डः क्षुद्रपशूनांस्याद्द्विपणप्रभृतिक्रमात् ॥२३॥

लिङ्गस्यच्छेदने मृत्यौ मध्यमो मूल्यमेव वा ।
महापशूनामेतेषु स्थानेषु द्विगुणा दमाः ॥२४॥

प्ररोहिशाखिनां शाखास्कन्धसर्वविदारणे ।
उपजीव्यद्रुमाणां तु विंशते द्विगुणा दमाः ॥२५॥

यः साहसं कारयति स दाप्यो द्विगुणं दमम् ।
यस्त्वेवमुक्त्वाऽहं दाता कारयेत्स चतुर्गुणम् ॥२६॥

आर्याक्रोशातिक्रमकृद्भ्रातृभार्याप्रहारकः ।
संदिष्टस्याप्रदाता च समुद्रगृहभेदकः ॥२७॥

सामन्तकुलिकादीनामपकारस्य कारकः ।
पञ्चाशत्पणिको दण्ड एषामिति विनिश्चयः ॥२८॥

स्वच्छन्दविधवागामी विक्रुष्टेनाभिधावकः ।
अकार च विक्रोष्टा चण्डालश्चोत्तमान् स्पृशन् ॥२९॥

शूद्रः प्रव्रजितानां च दैवे पै(पि)त्रे च भोजकः ।
अयुक्तं शपथं कुर्वन्नयोग्यो योग्यकर्मकृत् ॥३०॥

वृषक्षुद्रपशूनां च पुंस्त्वस्य प्रतिघातकृत् ।
साधारणस्यापलापी दासीगर्भविनाशकृत् ॥३१॥

पितापुत्रस्वसृभ्रातृदंपत्याचार्यशिष्यकाः ।
एषामपतितान्योन्यत्यागी च शतदण्डभाक् ॥३२॥

वसानस्त्रीन्पणान्दण्ड्यो नेजकस्तु परांशुकम् ।
विक्रयापक्रियादानयाचितेषु पणान्दश ॥३३॥

तुलाशासनमानानां कूटकृन्नाणकस्य च ।
एभिश्च व्यवहर्ता यः स दाप्यो दण्डमुत्तमम् ॥३४॥

अकूटं कूटकं ब्रूते कूटं यश्चाप्यकूटकम् ।
स नाणकपरीक्षायां दाप्यः प्रथमसाहसम् ॥३५॥

भिषङ्मिथ्याऽऽचरन्दाप्यस्तिर्यक्षु प्रथमं दमम् ।
मानुषे मध्यमं राजमानुषेषूत्तमं तथा ॥३६॥

अवध्यं यश्च वध्नाति वध्यं यश्च प्रमुञ्चति ।
अप्राप्तव्यवहारं च स दाप्यो दममुत्तमम् ॥३७॥

मानेन तुलया वापि याऽशमष्टमकं हरेत् ।
द्वाविंशतिपणान्दाप्यो वृद्धौ हानौ च कल्पितम् ॥३८॥

भेषजस्नेहलवणगन्धधान्यगुडादिषु ।
पण्येषु प्रक्षिपन् हीनं पणान्दाप्यस्तु षोडश ॥३९॥

संभूय कुर्वतामर्घं सवाधं कारुशिल्पिनाम् ।
अर्थस्य ह्रासं वृद्धिं वा सहस्रो दण्ड उच्यते ॥४०॥

राजनि स्थाप्यते योऽर्थः प्रत्यहं तेन विक्रयः ।
क्रयो वा निःस्रवस्तस्माद्वणिजां लाभकृत्स्मृतः ॥४१॥

स्वदेशपण्ये तु शतं वणिग्गृह्णीत पञ्चकम् ।
दशकं पारदेश्ये तु यः सद्यः क्रयविक्रयी ॥४२॥

पण्यस्योपरि संस्थाप्य व्ययं पण्यसमुद्भवम् ।
अर्घोऽनुग्रहकृत्कार्यः क्रेतुर्विक्रेतुरेव च ॥४३॥

गृहीतमूल्यं यः पण्यं क्रेतुर्नैव प्रयच्छति ।
सोदयं तस्य दाप्योऽसौ दिग्लाभं वा दिगागते ॥४४॥

विक्रीतमपि विक्रेयं पूर्वे क्रेतर्यगृह्णति ।
हानिश्चेत् क्रेतृदोषेण क्रेतुरेव हि सा भवेत् ॥४५॥

राजदैवोपघातेन पण्ये दोषमुपागते ।
हानिर्विक्रेतुरेवासौ याचितस्याप्रयच्छतः ॥४६॥

अन्यहस्ते च विक्रीतं दुष्टं वा दुष्टवद्यदि ।
विक्रीणीते दमस्तत्र तन्मूल्याद्द्विगुणो भवेत् ॥४७॥

क्षयं वृद्धिं च वणिजा पण्यानामविजानता ।
क्रीत्वा नानुशयः कार्यः कुर्वन् षड्भागदण्डभाक् ॥४८॥

समवायेन वणिजां लाभार्थं कर्म कुर्वताम् ।
लाभालाभौ यथाद्रव्यं यथा वा संविदा कृतौ ॥४९॥

प्रतिषिद्धमनादिष्टं प्रमादाद् यच्च नाशितम् ।
स तद्दद्याद्विप्लवाच्च रक्षिताद्दशमांशभाक् ॥५०॥

अर्घप्रक्षेपणाद्विंशं भागं शुल्कं नृपो हरेत् ।
व्यासिद्धं राजयोग्यं च विक्रीतं राजगामितत् ॥५१॥

मिथ्या वदन् परिमाणं शुल्कस्थानादपक्रमन् ।
दाप्यस्त्वष्टगुणं यश्च स व्याजक्रयविक्रयो ॥५२॥

देशान्तरगते प्रेते द्रव्यं दायादबान्धवाः ।
ज्ञातयो वा हरेयुस्तदागतास्तैर्विना नृपः ॥५३॥

जिह्मं त्यजेयुर्निर्लाभमशक्तोऽन्येन कारयेत् ।
अनेन विधिराख्यात ऋत्विकर्षककर्मिणाम् ॥५४॥

ग्राहकैर्गृह्यते चौरो लोप्त्रेणाथ पदेन वा ।
पूर्वकर्मापराधी वा तथैवाशुद्धवासकः ॥५५॥

अन्येऽपि शङ्कया ग्राह्या जातिनामादिनिह्नवैः ।
द्यूतस्त्रीपानसक्ताश्च शुष्कभिन्नमुखस्वराः ॥५६॥

परद्रव्यगृहाणां च प्रच्छकागूढचारिणः ।
निराया व्ययवन्तश्च विनष्टद्रव्यविक्रयाः ॥५७॥

गृहीतः शङ्कया चौर्ये नाऽऽत्मानं चेद्विशोधयेत् ।
दाययित्वा हृतं द्रव्यं चौरदण्डेन दण्डयेत् ॥५८॥

चौरं प्रदाप्यापहृतं घातयेद्विविधैर्वधैः ।
सचिह्नं ब्राह्मणं कृत्वा स्वराष्ट्राद्विप्रवासयेत् ॥५९॥

घातितेऽपहृते दोषो ग्रामभर्त्तुरनिर्गते ।
स्वसीम्निदद्यात् ग्रामस्तु पदं वा यत्र गच्छति ॥६०॥

पञ्चग्रामी बहिः क्रोशाद्दशग्राम्योऽथवा पुनः ।
वन्दिग्राहांस्तथा वाजिकुञ्जराणां च हारिणः ॥६१॥

प्रसह्यघातिनश्चैव शूलमारोपयेन्नरान् ।
उत्क्षेपकग्रन्थिभेदौ करसंदंशहीनकौ ॥६२॥

कार्यौ द्वितीयापराधे करपादैकहीनकौ ।
भक्तावकाशाग्न्युदकमन्त्रोपकरणव्ययान् ॥६३॥

दत्वा चौरस्य हन्तुर्वा ज्ञानतो दम उत्तमः ।
शस्त्रावपाते गर्भस्य पातने चोत्तमो दमः ॥६४॥

उत्तमो वाऽधमो वापि पुरुषस्त्रीप्रमापणे ।
शिलां बद्ध्वा क्षिपेदप्सु नरघ्नीं विषदां स्त्रियम् ॥६५॥

विषाग्निदां निजगुरुनिजापत्यप्रमापणीम् ।
विकर्णकरनासौष्ठीं कृत्वा गोभिः प्रमापयेत् ॥६६॥

क्षेत्रवेश्मवनग्रामविवीतखलदाहकाः।
राजपत्न्यभिगामी च दग्धव्यास्तु कटाग्निना ॥६७॥

पुमान् संग्रहणे ग्राह्यः केशाकेशि परस्त्रियाः।
स्वजातादुत्तमो दण्ड आनुलोम्ये तु मध्यमः॥६८॥

प्रातिलोम्ये वधः पुंसां नार्याः कर्णावकर्तनम् ।
नीवीस्तनप्रावरणनाभिकेशावमर्दनम् ॥६९॥

अदेशकालसंभाषं सहावस्थानमेवच ।
स्त्री निषेधे शतं दद्याद् द्विशतं तु दमं पुमान् ॥७०॥

प्रतिषेधे तयोर्दण्डो यथा संग्रहणे तथा ।
पशून्न गच्छन्नशतं दाप्यो हीनां स्त्रीं गाश्च मध्यमम् ॥७१॥

अवरुद्धासु दासीषु भुजिष्यासु तथैव च ।
गम्यास्वपि पुमान्दाप्यः पञ्चाशत्पणिकं दमम् ॥७२॥

प्रसह्य दास्यभिगमे दण्डो दश पणः स्मृतः।
कुबन्धेनाऽऽङ्क्य गमयेदन्त्याः प्रव्रजितागमे ॥७३॥

न्यूनं वाप्यधिकं वाऽपि लिखेद् यो राजशासनम् ।
पारदारिकचौरं वा मुञ्चतो दण्ड उत्तमः॥७४॥

अभक्ष्यैर्दूषयन्विप्रं दण्डं उत्तमसाहसम् ।
कूटवादी स्वर्णहारी विमांसस्य च विक्रयी ॥७५॥

अङ्गहीनश्च कर्तव्यो दाप्यश्चोत्तमसाहसम् ।
शक्तो ह्यमोक्षयन् स्वामी दंष्ट्रिणः शृङ्गिणस्तथा ॥७६॥

प्रथमं साहसं दद्याद्विक्रुष्टे द्विगुणं तथा ।
अचौरं चौरोऽभिवदन्दाप्यः पञ्चशतं दमम् ॥७७॥

राज्ञोऽनिष्टप्रवक्तारं तस्यैवाऽऽक्रोशकं तथा ।
मृताङ्गलग्नविक्रेतुर्गुरोस्ताडयितुस्तथा ॥७८॥

तन्मन्त्रस्य च भेत्तारं छित्वा जिह्वां प्रवासयेत् ।
राजयानासनारोढुर्दण्डो मध्यमसाहसः ॥७९॥

द्विनेत्रभेदिनो राजद्विष्टादेशकृतस्तथा ।
विप्रत्वेन च शूद्रस्य जीवतोऽष्टशतो दमः ॥८०॥

यो मन्येताजितोऽस्मीति न्यायेनाभिपराजितः ।
तमायान्तं पुनर्जित्वा दण्डयेद्द्विगुणं दमम् ॥८१॥

राज्ञा न्यायेन यो दण्डो गृहीतो वरुणाय तम् ।
निवेद्य दद्याद्विप्रेभ्यः स्वयं त्रिंशद्गुणीकृतम् ॥८२॥

धर्मश्चार्थश्च कीर्त्तिश्च लोकपंक्तिरुपग्रहः ।

प्रजाभ्यो बहुमानं च स्वर्गस्थानं च शाश्वतम् ।
पश्यतो व्यवहारांश्च गुणाः स्युः सप्तभूपतेः ॥८३॥

इत्याग्नेये महापुराणे पञ्चाशदधिकद्विशततमोऽध्यायः ॥ २५८ ॥

1. Mit., Ap. त्रयोदशान् for ?दश.

2. Mit., Ap. ह for च. BK. हि.

3. BK. वर्णजातुत्तराधरम् for वर्ण.... रैः.

4. BK. प्रतिलोम for प्रातिलोम्य; चतुस्त्रिद्विगुणा for द्वि... गुणा; वर्णान्त्येष्वानुलोम्येन for वर्णा... न. Mit., Ap. तस्मादर्धार्ध for तस्मादेवार्ध. BK. हानतः for हानितः.

5. Mit., BK. शत्यस्तदर्धिकः for शत्य... ऽर्धिकः. ज शक्त for शत्य.

6. Mit., Ap., BK. दाप्यः for दद्यात्.

7. BK. दण्ड्यो for दण्डो; साहसम् for साहसः.

9. Mit. कूटचिह्नकृतो भयात् (Ap. कूटचिह्नकृताद्दते) for कूट... भयात्.

10. Mit., Ap. ततः for second स्मृतः.

11. Mit. समेष्वेव for वं. Mit., Ap., BK. अर्ध for अर्धः. Ap. प्रोक्तो for मोह.

12. BK. स्पर्शने for संस्पर्शे. Mit., BK. तदर्धिकः for तदर्धकः.

14. Ap., BK. करालुश्चतेषु for करोल्लुश्चनेषु. BK. पीडाकर्षाञ्जनावेष्ट्य for पीडा.... वेष्ट.

15. Ap. पीडां for दुःखं. BK. transposes दुःखं and कुर्वन्. Mit., BK. दण्ड्यो for दार्प्य.

16. Ap., BK. दन्त for दतो.

17. Ap. सक्थ्यंघ्रि for सक्थ्नां व. BK. उत्तम for मध्यम.

18. Mit., Ap. द्विगुणो दमः for °णा दमाः. Mit., BK. ततः (Ap. तथा) for स्मृतः.

19. Ap. समुत्थानधनव्ययम् for स...व्ययम्.

20. Mit., BK., Ap. दाप्यः for दण्ड्यः. BK. ब्राह्मणः for ब्राह्मण.

21. Mit., Ap. transpose भेदे and छेदे.

22. क, ङ क्षिप्रप्राण for छि...ण. BK. षोडभाद्ये for द्यंः ; द्वितीये (क, घ, ङ द्विगुणो) for यो.

23. Ap., BK. दुःखोऽथ for दुःखे च. Mit., Ap. तु for स्यात्.

24. Mit., Ap, ज, चं for वा; द्विगुणो दमः for णां दमाः.

25. BK. प्ररोहशाखिका for ˚शाखिनां; विंशति for विंशते.

26. Mit., Ap. यश्चैवं for यस्त्वेवम्. The second line is missing in च.

27. Mit. अर्घ्याधेप (Ap., BK. अर्घ्याक्रोश) for आर्याक्रोश. छ, ज प्रहारदः for कंः. BK. भेदकृत् for भेदकः. The second line is missing in क, ङ.

28. Second line missing in च.

29. The first line is missing in च. Mit. स्वच्छन्द for न्दे. BK. विक्रुष्टेनभिधावकः for वि...कः. Mit., Ap., BK. अकारणे for णं. Mit. स्पृशेत् for स्पृशन्.

30. Ap., BK., घ, ङ, च शूद्रप्रव्रजितानां for शूद्रः...नां.

31. BK. प्रतिघातकः for प्रंति...कृत्.

32. Mit. पितृ for पित्ता.

33. छ, Mit., Ap. विक्रयावक्रयाधात (BK. विक्रयापक्रयाधान) for विक्रय...दान.

34. Mit., Ap., BK. दमम् for दण्डम्.

35. Mit., Ap., BK., ज नाणकपरीक्षीतु for परीक्षायां; उत्तम for प्रथम.

36. Mit. दण्ड्य for दाप्य; पुरुषेषूत्तमं दमं (Ap. मानुषे तूत्तमं दमं) for मानुषे...तथा. BK. दाप्य उत्तमं राजमानुषे for राज...तथा.

37. BK. बन्ध्यं for वध्यं.

38. Mit., Ap., BK. दण्डं स दाप्यो द्विशतं for द्वा...दाप्यो. The portion from दाप्यो to कल्पितम् is missing in क.

39. The portion भेषज...पणान् is missing in क. BK. हीनं क्षिपतः for प्रक्षिपन् हीनं.

40. BK. साबाधं for सबाधं. Ap. ह्रासे वृद्धौ for ह्रासं वृद्धिं. Mit. जानतो दम उत्तमः for सहस्रो दण्ड उच्यते. BK. अर्थस्य हानौ वृद्धौ वा साहस्रो for अर्थस्य...सहस्रो.

41. Ap. राजभिः स्थापितो for राजनि स्थाप्यते. ख, ग, घ विक्रय for निःस्रव. Ap. लाभकः (BK. लाभतः) for लाभकृत्.

43. क, ङ, च, छ अथो for अर्घो. Ap. अनुग्राहकः for अनुग्रहकृत्.

44. BK. दिशां गते for दिगागते.

47. Mit. विक्रीय for विक्रीतं.

48. BK. पण्यानां तु विजानता for पण्या...ता.

49. BK. कृता for कृतौ.

50. Ap., BK. रक्षिता for रक्षिताद्.

51. BK. अर्घप्रक्षेपणाच्छुल्कं विंशद्भागं for अर्घ...शुल्कं. ख ससिद्धं for व्यासिद्धं.

52. Mit., Ap. अपासरन् for अपक्रमन्.

53. Ap. धनं for द्रव्यं.

54. BK. विधिनाख्यातम् for विधि...त.

55. BK. पूर्वकर्मापराधाद् for° धी.

56. Ap. नामजात्यादि for जातिनामादि.

58. Ap. आत्मानं चेन्न शोधयेत् for नात्मानं...येत्. Mit. गतं for हृतं.

59-60. Between these lines, Mit., Ap. read विवीतभर्तुस्तु पथि चौरोद्धर्तुरवीतके. In verse 60 BK. घातितापहृते for घातितेऽपहृते; ख reads यदि for यत्र.

61. BK. कृष्टाद् for क्रोशाद्; ग्राम्यपि वा तथा for °ग्राम्योऽथवा पुनः.

63. BK. द्वितीये for द्वितीय. क, ङ, च रक्षावहासाग्न्युदक for भक्ता...क. Ap. व्ययम् for व्ययान्.

64. Mit. transposes हन्तुः and वा. Mit., Ap., BK., ज जानतो for ज्ञानतो. ङ दण्ड for दम. ङ चोत्तमः सदा for चोत्तमो दमः.

65. Second line missing in Mit., Ap., BK. ज क्षिपेदप्सु for क्षिपेद्यस्तु.

66. Mit., Ap., BK. पति for first निज.

67. BK. transposes वन and ग्राम; विवीतादेश्च for विवीतखल.

68. Ap. परस्त्रिया for °स्त्रियाः. Mit., Ap., BK. सजाता for स्वजाता.

69. Mit., Ap. पुंसः for पुंसां. BK. स्त्रीणां नासादिकृन्तनम् for नार्याः...कर्तनं. Mit., Ap. कर्णादि for कर्णाव; सक्थिक्रेशावमर्थनम् for नाभि...नम्. BK. मर्शनम् for मर्दनम्.

70. Mit. सहैकासनमेव (Ap. सहैकस्थानमेव) for सहावस्थानमेव. BK. निषिद्धा for निषेध.

71. BK. अनिषेधे for प्रति°, हीनस्त्रीं°गां च (also Ap.) for हीनां...गाश्च.

73. The second line does not occur in the *Yājñavalkya-smṛti*.

74. Mit., Ap. ऊनं for न्यूनं; वाभ्यधिकं (also BK.) for वाप्यधिकं. Ap. पारदारिकचौरौ (BK. चौरो) for° चोर.

75. Mit. अभक्ष्येण द्विजं दूष्यो (Ap. द्विजं प्रदूष्याभक्ष्येण) for अभक्ष्यै...विप्रं. Ap., BK. दण्ड्य for दण्ड. Mit., Ap., BK., ज कूटस्वर्णव्यवहारी for कूट...हारी.

76. Mit., Ap., BK. त्र्यङ्ग for अङ्ग. BK. हीनास्तु कर्तव्या for हीन...व्यो. BK. दाप्या for दाप्य. Mit., Ap., BK. शक्तोऽप्यमोक्षयन् for शक्त...न्; दंष्ट्रिणां शृंगिणां for दंष्ट्रिणः शृंगिणः. BK. transposes दंष्ट्रिणः and शृंगिणः.

77. BK. दाप्यो for दद्याद्. Mit., Ap. जारं चौरेत्यभिवदन (BK. चौरं चोरेत्यतिवदन्) for अचौर्य...ऽभिवदन्.

78. Mit., Ap. तस्यैवा क्रोश कारिणम् for तस्यैवा...तथा. क, ङ तथैव for तस्यैव.

79. BK. राजशय्या for °याना. Mit. उत्तम for मध्यम.

81. BK. अपि for अभि. BK. तमागतं for तमायान्तं. Mit., Ap. न्यायेनापि for °नाभि; दापयेद् (also BK.) for दण्डयेद्.

82. BK. दण्डोऽगृहीतो for दण्डो गृहीतो.

83. The first two lines occur in the *Nārada-smṛti* (Calcutta Sanskrit College ed.), p.3, verse 33, with स्वर्गे for स्वर्ग.

ENGLISH TRANSLATION

CHAPTER 253

AGNI SAID

1. I shall narrate *Vyavahāra* which helps discrimination between justice and injustice. It consists of four parts, four stays and four means.

2. It benefits four, affects four and is said to do four things. It has eight constituents, eighteen titles and hundred branches.

3-4a. It has three sources, two modes of complaint, two openings and two courses. *Dharma*, the issue of the suit, customary law,[1] a royal edict—these are the four parts of judicial proceedings; each succeeding is superior to the preceding one.

---

1. This meaning is appropriate if we take the reading as in our text, Monier-Williams also gives this as a meaning of the word "Caritra". Some translate the word as "Conduct" (of the parties). Others take it to mean document evidently from the reading *Vaitram Pustakarna* instead of the reading in our text.

4b-5a. Among them, *dharma* rests on truth, the issue of the suit depends upon the witnesses, customary law on popular practice and success on the royal order.

5b. It is said to consist of four means as it has to be accomplished by the (four) expedients called conciliation, etc.

6a. It benefits four as it protects the four stages of life.

6b-7a. It is known to affect four as it concerns the perpetrator of the deed, the witnesses, the judges as well as the king, each by one quarter.

7b-8a. It is said to perform four acts as it produces the four, viz. *dharma*, *artha*, fame and regard among men.

8b-9a. The king with his officers, the assessors, the law-book, the accountant, the scribe, gold, fire, water—these are stated to be the eight constituents.

9b-10a. It proceeds from the three, viz. passion, anger and greed; so it is said to have three sources—these three cause disputes.

10b. It is known to have two modes of complaint, one based on suspicion, another on fact.

11a. Suspicion arises from (the defendant's) association with evil company. The factual complaint arises from the sight of stolen goods,[1] etc.

11b. It is said to have two openings as it relates to two parties.

12a. Of these two, the one who speaks first (i.e. lodges the complaint) is called *pakṣa* (plaintiff) and one who appears later is called *pratipakṣa* (defendant).

12b. It is said to have two courses as it follows true and false statements.

13. Debts worthy of being paid, not worthy of being paid, by whom, where and in what manner, the rules of gift and acceptance–(all this) is known (i.e. comprised in the title of law called) recovery of debt.

14. That is called by the wise deposit, which is a title of law, in which one, without any suspicion and in confidence, keeps one's own article in the custody (of another).

15. Where traders and others carry on a business jointly, it is called Partnership which is a title of law.

16. That is known as resumption of gift, which is a title of law, where a person having duly given a thing (to another) wishes to take it back.

---

1. It is obviously an instance of factual complaint; because there may be complaints about various offences besides theft. For the meaning of *ṣodhā*, see Glossary.

17. When a man, having undertaken service, does not render it, it is called Breach of Contract of service which is a title of law.

18. That is known as the title of law called non-payment of wages in which the rules regarding payment and non-payment of wages to servants are laid down.

19. That is known as (the title of law called) Sale by a non-owner in which a person sells, in the absence (of the owner), another man's property which is deposited, lost and found or after stealing it.

20. That title of law is called Non-delivery after sale in which a person, having sold an article for a price, does not deliver it to the purchaser.

21a. (That is called Rescission of purchase when) a purchaser, having purchased an article for a price. is dissatisfied with it.

21b. If a purchaser, having bought an article for a price, thinks it to be a bad purchase (he may return it to the vendor on the same day intact).[1]

22. The established convention among heretics, followers of the Nigama (i.e. Veda) and the like is called *Samaya* (compact). That (i.e. the breach of such a compact)

1. Verse 21 obviously drops two lines without which the sense is incomplete.

is known as the title of law called Breach of a Compact.

23. That dispute is one arising from a field where, in regard to a landed property, there are decisions about a bridge, field, boundary, cultivated and uncultivated pieces (of land).

24. That title of law is known to have the designation of Relation between husband and wife, where the rules of marriage and mutual duties of husband and wife are laid down.

25. That title of law is called Dāyabhāga by the learned in which partition of paternal effects is made by the sons.

26. That title of law is called *Sāhasa* in which an act is committed by force by people proud of strength.

27. That is called harshness of speech, of adverse import, which, mixed with abuse and insinuation, relates to (another person's) country, caste, family, etc.

28. Hurting another person's limbs with the hand, foot, weapons etc. and injury by fire and the like are called assault.

29. Playing with dice, small slices of leather,[1] little staves of ivory and the like is called gambling. Betting on animals and birds is called animal-betting.

1. According to Jolly.

30. Miscellaneous (disputes) comprise law-suits which relate to the king, (such as) violation of the king's order and not doing his work.

31. Judicial proceeding has ten titles; their varieties are one hundred. Owing to the differences of human activities, it is said to have one hundred branches.

32. The king, free from anger, should supervise judicial proceedings, accompanied by Brāhmaṇas. The members (of the council trying a suit) are of equal disposition towards enemies and friends, free from greed and versed in the Vedas.

33a. (The king), not supervising (a judicial proceeding) due to (other) work, should get a Brāhmaṇa appointed by the members.

33b-34a. The members, acting contrary to the Vedas and indulging in other malpractices owing to attachment, greed or fear, should be punished separately; (their) fine should be twice the value of the suit.

34b-35a. A subject of dispute is that which a person, being oppressed by others in a manner opposed to Smṛti and custom, reports to the king.

35b-36a. What is stated by the plaintiff should be written in presence of the defendant marked with the year, month, fortnight day, name, caste etc.

36b. The reply, given (by the defendant) who has heard the plaint, should be written in presence of the plaintiff.

37. Then the plaintiff should immediately get the evidence in support of his contention recorded. If it is established, he wins. The reverse is the case if it is otherwise.

38a. In disputes, this judicial procedure is shown to have four stages.

38b. One should not bring a counter-charge against him (who has lodged a complaint), without being acquitted of the charge.

39. One should not complain against a person accused by another, nor should one change what has been stated.[1] But in a feud (relating to abuse or assault) as also in acts of violence one can bring a counter-charge.

40a. The representatives of both parties, capable of the desired settlement, are acceptable.

40b. In the event of denial if the contention be proved (the defendant) should pay the money (to the plaintiff) and (a fine of) equal amount to the king.

41a. In a false complaint, (the plaintiff) should pay double the value of the suit.

---

1. The portion *tyaktam...nayet* is not clear. We have translated it taking *noktam*, as found in Ys., for *tyaktam*.

41b-42a. In *sāhasa*, theft, abuse, assault, *abhiśāpa*,[1] *atyaya*,[2] defamation of a woman, the court should try the suit immediately; in other cases, the time (of trial) can be according to will.

42b-44a. Moving to and fro, licking of lips, perspiring forehead, fading of complexion, unnaturalness in mental disposition, speech, body and act—a man having these (signs) is declared to be a liar in a complaint or oral evidence.

44b-45a. One who independently (of evidence) realises a doubtful amount, one who, while being asked for money (admitted by him or proved by evidence to have been borrowed by him), runs away, one who, being summoned, keeps silent—these are vile and punishable.

45b-46a. When there are witnesses on both sides, those of one who claims earlier transaction (are to be examined). The person, claiming earlier transaction, being defeated, (the witnesses) of the person claiming the latter transaction (should be examined).

46b-47a. If there is a dispute with wager, (the king) should make the defeated party pay the amount of wager and fine (to the

1. Complaint about a degrading act.
2. Mit.—*prāṇudhanātipntaḥ* i.e. taking away one's life and misappropriation of one's money.

king) and the claimed amount to the plaintiff).

47b-48a. The king should conduct judicial proceedings after setting aside a wrong statement[1] by means of the actual fact. In a judicial proceeding, even a fact, not properly presented, suffers.

48b-49a. If out of many charges, denied by a person, one is proved, he should be made by the king to give to the claimant all (i.e the things involved in other charges too). What is not stated (in the plaint) is not acceptable.

49b-50a. In a conflict between two Smṛti texts, equity, derived from usage, is strong. Dharmaśāstra is stronger than Arthaśāstra—this is the established rule.

50b-51a. Evidence is said to consist of documents, possession and witnesses. In the absence of even one of these, ordeal is said (to be evidence).

51b-52a. In all disputes whatsoever, the latter transaction is valid. In a mortgage and acceptance of gift, however, the earlier transaction is stronger.

52b-54a. A land (of one enjoyed by another in the presence of the owner) without protest (by the owner) for twenty years is lost (to the owner). A movable property (is lost to the owner) by ten-year (adverse

1. *Chalaṃ pramādābhihitam* (Mit)-stated inadvertently.

possession in the above manner). Mortgage, boundary, open deposit, property of an idiot or a minor, sealed deposit, property of the king, women and Brāhmaṇas versed in the Vedas—these are excepted (for the purpose of the operation of the law of adverse possession).

54b-55a. (The king) should make one, who misappropriates mortgages etc., pay the value to the owner and a fine equal to that, or according to capacity, to the king.

55b-56a. Valid acquisition is stronger than (possession) excepting hereditary possession. Even in valid acquisition, in which there is not the slightest possession, there is no strength.

56b-57a. Possession, with pure acquisition, becomes valid. Possession, with faulty acquisition, does not get validity.

57b-58a. The person, who acquires a property, if accused, should prove (the rightful acquisition); not his son or grandson—in their cases possession is stronger.

58b-59a. If a person, being accused (of illegal ownership), dies, his heir should prove it; in his case possession without valid acquisition is no excuse.

59b-61a. (The king) should set aside a judicial proceeding conducted under force and coercion. A trial, conducted by the following, is not valid—women, done at night, inside a house, outside a village, conducted by an enemy, intoxicated person, lunatic, a passionate fellow, a minor, one stricken with fear, one having no connexion with the matter (or, one not appointed as an agent by the parties concerned).

61b-62a. An article, lost and recovered, should be given by the king to the owner; one, failing to identify it by marks, should pay (as fine) an equal amount.

62b. The king should restore a stolen article to the citizen (concerned).

63. In a loan with pledge, the interest should be the eightieth part per month. Otherwise, the rates are two, three, four and five per cent for the castes in order.

64. The progeny (is the interest) in the case of animals and women. Eightfold, fourfold, threefold and double are the maximum interests for liquid substances, clothes, paddy and gold respectively.

65a. Ten per cent (per mensem) should be realised (as interest) from a person of a different village and twenty per cent from one who undertakes a sea-voyage.

65b. Or, among all castes everybody should pay the interest agreed to by himself.

66. One, realising money that is proved, need not report the matter to the king. The accused (from whom the creditor is justly

trying to realise his legitimate dues), approaching the king, becomes liable to punishment, and should be made to pay the (proved) amount (to the owner).

CHAPTER 254

1. A debtor, who has borrowed money, should be made to pay to creditors in the order (in which he borrowed), having first paid to a Brāhmaṇa and then to the king.

2. The debtor should be made by the king to pay ten per cent of the proved amount. The creditor, however, who has got the money, should be made to pay five per cent.

3. (A debtor) of a low caste, who is impoverished, should be made (by a creditor of the higher caste) to do work (for the latter) as discharge of debt. A Brāhmaṇa, however, who is impecunious, should be made to pay gradually according to his income.

4. If one does not accept one's own invested money which is offered, it should be kept with an arbitrator; after that it does not increase (i.e. bear interest).

5. One, who takes the heritage, should be made to pay the debt (of the person whose property one inherits), so also one who takes the wife (of the debtor); the son whose property is not

shared by others (should pay the debt of his father). Of a sonless person the heirs (should pay off his debt).

6. When the head of the family is dead or has gone abroad, the heirs should pay off the debt incurred by those, who are not divided, for the sake of the family.
7. A woman should not pay off the debt incurred by her husband and son, nor the father should repay the debt incurred by the son unless it is for the sake of the family; the husband should not pay the debt of the wife.
8. In the case of the wives of cowherds, distillers, actors (or dancers), washermen and hunters, the husband should pay off their debt as the occupation (of the husband) depends upon them.
9. A woman should pay the debt proved to have been incurred along with the husband or by herself; a woman is not required to pay off any other (debt).
10. The father having gone abroad, died or met with a calamity, the son and grandson should pay off his debt; in the case of denial, as much as is proved by witnesses (should be paid).
11. The son should not repay the debt of the father if it was for wine, (satisfaction of) passion, gambling, or if it is the balance of a fine or custom duty or incurred for useless charity.
12. In an undivided family, suretyship, debt and evidence are not known (to be allowed) as

between brothers, husband and wife, father and son.

13. Suretyship is ordained in regard to sight (i.e. production in court), confidence and payment; the first two should be fulfilled (by the surety himself) if there is breach (of the condition); of the surety of the other kind, sons too (are bound).

14. Where a surety for sight or for confidence is dead, his sons should not pay the money; the (sons of) those who stand guarantee for payment should pay (in the event of) their father's death.

15. If there are many sureties, they should pay money according to their own shares. If they are jointly responsible, (the money may be realised according to the will of the creditor).

16. Where a surety is openly made to pay the money to the creditor, the debtor should pay twice the amount; it will be the property of him (i.e. the surety).

17. In case of female beasts with their progeny, and paddy double (will be given to the surety). Cloth is said to be fourfold and a liquid substance eightfold.

18. A mortgage is lost if it is not released after the money is doubled. A (mortgage) for a fixed time is lost after the expiry of the period; a usufructuary mortgage is not lost.

19. No interest accrues if a mortgage for custody is enjoyed (by the mortgagee) and if a usufruc-

tuary mortgage is proved to be so. If a pledge is spoilt or destroyed by means other than acts of God or king, the loss should be made good.

20. A mortgage becomes valid by enjoyment (by the mortgagee). If it becomes useless even though protected, another thing should be mortgaged or the creditor should get the money.

21. One should be made to pay with interest the money which is lent on the guarantee of character. One should be made to repay what is borrowed with a promise.

22. A mortgage should be released to one who has come; otherwise, (the mortgagee) becomes punishable. In case the investor is absent, the money should be paid to a member of the (mortgagee's) family and the mortgaged property got back.

23. Or, with the value assessed at that time, the property should remain there without (further) interest. Or, if the debtor is not available, the property should be sold in presence of witnesses.

24. When a mortgaged debt is doubled, the mortgage should be released if twice the amount, produced from it, is credited.

25. That is called a sealed deposit which, kept in a vessel, is handed over to another person without declaring (the contents); it should be returned intact.

26. If it is stolen or lost by act of king or god, one should not be made to give it (i.e. its value). If it be lost after it is wanted (by the depositor), but not given (to him), (the custodian) should be made to pay a fine equal to it.

27. (The custodian), using at will (the article deposited without the consent of the depositor), should be punished and made to give the article with interest. This is the rule also with respect to what is obtained by request, what is deposited (by the custodian) with another person, a *nyāsa*[1] and a *nikṣepa*.[2]

Here ends the two hundred and fifty-fourth chapter, entitled *Vyavahāra* in the Mahāpurāṇa called Agni.

CHAPTER 255

1-2. Sages, people who are charitably disposed, of high lineage, truthful, regard *dharma* as the principal (end of life), straightforward, possessed of son, rich, engaged in the performance of five sacrifices—these persons, numbering five or three should be witnesses; witnesses should be of the same race and family or all may be (witnesses) for all.

3-4. A woman, an old man, a minor, a gambler, an intoxicated person, a lunatic,

1. See Glossary.
2. *Ibid.*

an *abhiśastaka*,[1] an actor, a heretic, a perjurer, one with deformed senses, an apostate, a friend, one connected with the subject (of trial), an associate, a thief—these are unfit to be witnesses. All are witnesses in theft, harshness (of speech and punishment) and *sāhasa*.[2]

5a. Even one pious man, approved by both (the parties to a suit) can be a witness.

5b-6a. A man, not giving evidence, should be made by the king to pay, on the forty-sixth day (of the suit) the entire debt with ten per cent.[3]

6b-7a. The vilest among men, who though aware, does not give evidence, is similar in sin to perjurers, and deserves equal punishment.

7b-10a. Cause the witnesses, in the presence of the plaintiff and the defendant, to hear thus —one who gives false evidence gets to all the regions of sinners, of those who commit grave sins, of the incendiaries as well as of the slayers of women and minors.

Know that all the merit, acquired by you through hundreds of other births, belong to the person whom you falsely defeat.

---

1. See Glossary.
2. *Ibid.*
3. According to the *Mitākṣarā* the ten per cent goes to the king.

10b-11a. In the event of difference (among witnesses), the evidence of the majority (should be accepted, and if the witnesses are equally divided, the word of the qualified (is acceptable). If there is division among qualified (witnesses), the evidence of those who are more qualified is acceptable.

11b-12a. He becomes the winner whose witnesses say that his statement is true. Defeat is certain for him whose (witnesses) speak otherwise.

12b-13a. Even when the evidence having been given by witnesses, other more qualified persons or double the number state otherwise, the former witnesses will be perjurers.

13b-14a. One who causes perjury and the perjured witnesses should be punished separately; they should pay a fine twice the value of the subject of dispute,[1] a Brāhmaṇa should be exiled.

14b-15a. One who, after being made to hear the evidence (along with other witnesses), conceals it from others under the influence of *tamas*[2] should be made to pay eight times as fine; a Brāhmaṇa, however, should be banished.

---

1. According to *Mitākṣarā*, twice the fine payable by the defeated party.
2. i.e. passion etc.

15b. One should give false evidence where a member of a caste will be sentenced to death (if the truth is spoken).

16. Whatever matter is mutually agreed to should be written in a document which is witnessed and in which the creditor's name is written first.

17. (The document) should mention the year, month, fortnight, the name, race, *gotra* fellow student, the names of own father, (i.e. the father of the creditor and of the debtor) and the like.

18. The matter being written out, the creditos should write in his own hand as follows : what is written herein above is approved by me, the son of so and so.

19. Witnesses of even number should write, after their fathers' names, thus—in this matter, I so and so am a witness.

20. A creditor, who is illiterate, should get his own opinion written by others. Or, (an illiterate) witness should cause his statement to be written by another witness in presence of all witnesses.

21. Then, at the end, the scribe should write thus–it is written by me, so and so, son of so and so, being requested by both (the parties).

22. All documents, written in one's own hand, though without witnesses, are known to be a proof provided these are

not written under duress or are not fraudulent.

23. The debt, incurred by a document, should be repaid by three generations. A mortgage is enjoyed so long as it is not given (back).

24. When a document exists in another land, when it is illegibly written, lost, effaced, stolen, rent, torn or burnt, another document should be caused to be written.

25. The removal of doubt about the purport of a document written in one's own hand may be done by means of the relation of time, place and men with the thing concerned through inference, evidence, marks, the relation between the disputants and probability.

26. On the back of the document, one should write what is paid by the debtor. The creditor should give an acknowledgment with his own signature.

27. Having repaid the debt, one should tear off the document or cause another to be written for the sake of discharge. What is done in presence of witnesses should be given in presence of witnesses.

28. Balance, fire, water, poison, *kośa*[1]—these are the ordeals for proving the innocence (of an accused); these are the ordeals in

---

1. For description see P.V. Kane, *History of Dharmaśāstra*, III, pp. 373-74.

grave complaints when the plaintiff is agreeable to accept the result of the ordeal (i.e. the punishment).

29. Or, at the option (of the plaintiff and defendant) one of the two may undergo (the ordeal) and the other may abide by the result (of the suit).

30. Do not allow the ordeal of plough, poison or balance below a thousand (i.e. when the value of the subject of dispute is below one thousand). In complaints affecting the king and relating to grave sins, the parties being pure should always undergo ordeals.

31. One should allow the ordeals of balance and the like in a dispute concerning a thousand. Allow the *kośa* even when the value is small. The innocent one should be made to pay half of a hundred, and the guilty person should be liable to punishment.

32. All ordeals should be caused to be undergone in presence of king and Brāhmaṇas after calling at sunrise (the accused) who has bathed with cloth on and has observed fast.

33. Balance is for women, minors, old people, the blind, the lame, the Brāhmaṇas and

the sick. Fire or water or seven *yavas* of poison for a Sūdra.[1]

34. The accused (or the plaintiff) being seapte in a balance, weighed against a weight equal to himself, is made to descend after marking a line by those who are versed in holding the balance.

35. Sun, moon, wind, fire, heaven, earth, water, heart, Yama, day, night, both junctures of day and *dharma* know the conduct of man.

36-37. O balance, you are the abode of truth formerly created by God. O auspicious one, tell the truth, absolve me of suspicion. O Mother, if I am a sinner, take me downward. If I am innocent, take me upward—utter this to the balance.

38. After marking the hands of one who has rubbed paddy, place on them seven leaves of *Ficus religiosa* and put as many pieces of thread around.

39. O fire, it is you who move about inside all creatures. Like a witness, having considered merit and sin, speak the truth (i.e. show it) in my hand.

40. Place in both the hands of him, who has said thus, a round red-hot iron ball weighing fifty *palas*.

---

1. This is the apparent meaning. But, according to the *Mitākṣarā* fire is for Kṣātriyās, water only for Vaiśyas and poison for Śūdras. *Yava*—a weight—6 or 12 mustard seeds—½ Guñjā.

41. Having taken it, he should slowly walk over all the seven circles; a circle should measure sixteen fingers and have as much interval between them.

42. He, having taken it, should slowly walk through seven circles and not less. A circle is known to be sixteen fingers (in diameter) and have as much intervening space (between one another).

43. One should be declared innocent if he remains unburnt after throwing away the fire (i.e. a hot iron-ball) and rubbing paddy (with his hands).

44-45a. (The accused) should dip into the water holding the thighs of one who stands in navel-deep water. If another man, speedily taking an arrow thrown at the very time (of the accused's dipping), finds him still submerged, the (accused) shall obtain acquittal.

45b-47a. "O poison, you are son of Brahman and established in truth; save me from this curse, by truth, be nectar to me." Saying this take *Śārṅga*[1] poison grown on the Himalayas. One should declare innocent the person who can digest it without having any effect.

47b-48a. Having worshipped the fierce deities, collect the water of their bath. Having

1. Extracted from *Śṛṅga*, a poisonous plant.

caused the accused to hear (about the result of drinking the water) make the (accused) drink three handfuls of it.

49b-50. Mounts, weapons, cows, seeds, gold, god, preceptor, sacrifices, works of public utility—swearing by these is easy in matters of small doubt.

CHAPTER 256

1. If the partition is done by the father, he may distribute shares among the sons as he wishes. Or, he may either give the greatest share to the eldest son or make all the sons share equally.

2. If he gives equal shares (to them) he should make (his) wives, to whom *strīdhana* has not been given by the husband or the father-in-law, share equally (with the sons).

3. One, who is fit (for earning) but unwilling (to accept any share of the paternal property), should be separated after giving him something (slight); partition (of sons) with a smaller or greater share is lawful if done by the father.

4. The sons should equally divide the heritage as well as the debt after (the death of) the parents. The daughters (should divide equally) the balance of the mother's money after repayment of debts;

in their absence, one should give this money (to the sons).

5. One's brothers have no right to what one earns without loss to the paternal property, what is got as a friendly gift and a nuptial present.

6. Division is known to be equal in the case of income from a joint undertaking. Those, who are sons of many fathers, receive shares through their (respective) fathers.

7. Both the father and the son have equal right to the land, *nibandha* or any (other) thing obtained from the grandfather.

8. A son, born to (the father's) wife of the same caste after the sons are divided, is entitled to a share. His share will be what remains out of the (brothers') shares after considering the income and expenditure.

9. One, who recovers a stolen hereditary property, should not share it with brothers nor what is acquired by learning.

10. What is given to one by the parents becomes his exclusive property. The mother, too, shares equally with those who divide (the paternal property) after the father's death.

11. The brothers, whose sacraments have not been performed, should be made by the brothers, whose sacraments have been

performed before, to undergo sacraments. The sisters also (should be given away by brothers in marriage) after giving a fourth part out of their (respective) shares.

12. The sons of a Brāhmaṇa, in accordance with their castes, should get four parts, three, two and one (respectively); the sons of a Kṣatriya get three, two and one part (respectively) and those of a Vaiśya two and one (respectively).

13. (The sons) should equally divide the property, stolen out of the entire property, which is found after partition—this is the rule.

14. The son, begotten by a sonless person through levirate on the wife of another, is lawfully the heir of both and the offerer of *piṇḍa* (to both).

15. *Aurasa* (son) is one who is born to the lawfully wedded wife; *putrikāputra* is like him. *Kṣetraja* is one who is raised on one's wife by a person of the same *gotra* or by any other person.

16. A son, born in the house in a clandestine manner, is known, as *Gūḍhaja*. *Kānīna* is one born to a maiden, and is known to be the son of (his) maternal grandfather.

17. *Paunarbhava* son is one born to a widow who has or has not been enjoyed (by her husband). That son, whom the mother

or the father gives, becomes *dattaka* (adopted).

18. *Krīta* is one who is sold by them (i.e. parents). *Kṛtrima* is one who is made a son by a person himself. *Dattātmā* is one who offers oneself. *Sahoḍhaja* is one who remains in the womb (of a woman when she is married).

19a. One, who is forsaken (by a person) and taken (by another) becomes a son called *Apaviddha*.

19b. Of these, in the absence of the preceding one, each succeeding is the offerer of *piṇḍa* and heir.

20. This rule is told by me with regard to the sons of the same caste. A son, born to a female slave by a Śūdra, takes a share according to the will (of the father).

21. If the father is dead, the brothers should make him a half sharer. If he is brotherless, he should take the entire property provided there are no sons of the daughters (of the deceased).

22-23. Wife, daughters, parents, brothers, brother's son, a person of the same *gotra*, a *bandhu*, a disciple, a fellow student—of these, in the absence of each preceding one the succeeding person takes the property of one dying childless. This rule holds good in all castes.

24. Of a *Vānaprastha*, a *Yati* and a Brahmacārin the heirs are respectively a spiritual brother living in the same hermitage, a good disciple and the preceptor.

25. A re-united coparcener (should give a share to the son) born to a re-united coparcener (after reunion) and take the property of a reunited coparcener who is dead. A uterine brother respectively gives and takes the share of a full brother when born and when dead.

26. A re-united half brother takes the property (of a brother), but not a half brother (who is not re-united). Even a brother, who is not re-united, should take the property of a brother (but) not a step-brother.

27. An apostate, his son, an impotent person, a lame man, lunatic, an idiot, a blind man, one afflicted with an incurable disease and the like do not have any share (of the paternal property); they are to be maintained.

28. Their *aurasa* and *kṣetraja* sons, who are free from defects, are entitled to shares. Their daughters, too, should be well-maintained till they are married (lit. made over to their husband).

29. Their sonless wives, too, who are of good conduct, should be maintained. Such as are unchaste and disobedient should be banished.

30. That which is given (to a woman) by (her) father, mother, husband and brother, what is obtained (by her) before the (nuptial) fire as well as the supersession fee are called *strīdhana*.

31. (So also are) what is given by *bandhus*, the bride's price and *anvādheyaka*. (Her) *bāndhavas* should get that (i.e. *strīdhana*) when she dies childless.

32. In all the four (forms of marriage) beginning with *brāhma*, the *strīdhana* of a childless woman belongs to (her) husband; if she has children, it belongs to her daughters. In the remaining (forms of marriage), that goes to (her) father.

33. One, not giving a girl after betrothing her, is punishable and should pay the expenses along with interest (to the bridegroom's party). If she dies, (the bridegroom's party) should take what has been given (to the bride's party) after calculating the expenses on both sides.

34. The husband should not give (his) wife the *strīdhana* taken at the time of famine, on the occasion of a religious ceremony, at the time of disease and siege.

35. One should give the superseded wife a solatium equal (to what has been spent on the subsequent marriage or to what has been given to the other wife), if no *strīdhana* has been given to her. If (*strīdhana*) has been given, half is declared.

36. In case partition is concealed, is to be ascertained by agnates, *bandhus*, witnesses, documents as well as by the house and fields which have been separated.

Thus ends the 256th chapter, called *Dāyavibhāga*, of the Mahāpurāṇa entitled Agni.

CHAPTER 257

1-2. In a dispute relating to the boundary of a field, residents of neighbouring villages, the elderly people and the like, cowherds, the tillers of the boundary; all the people living in the forest—these should fix the boundary marked by big charcoals, husk, tree, dam, ant-hill, *nimnāsthi*[1] and *caitya*[2] etc.

3. Residents of neighbouring villages, numbering four, eight or ten, putting on red garlands and clothes and moving on the ground, should fix the boundary.

4. In the case of falsehood (on the part of those who mark the boundary) they are to be punished by the king with the middle amercement. In the absence of knowledgeable persons and marks, the king is the settler of the boundary.

---

1. The meaning is not clear. Some take it as two words—*nimna* moat and *asthi* bone.

2. See Glossary.

5. This very rule is to be known with respect to groves, *āyatanas*,[1] villages, tanks, pleasure-gardens, houses and aqueducts of rain-water.

6. In the cases of breaking the boundary, misappropriation of a field and the encroachment on boundary, people are to be punished with the lowest, highest and middle amercements.

7. (The construction of a dam), conducive to welfare, encroaching on another man's land, should not be prohibited if it causes slight loss (or obstruction); so also a well on a small land containing plenty of water.

8. If one constructs a dam in a field without telling the owner, the owner will enjoy the produce, in his absence the king.

9. One, who (having promised before the owner) does not till a land, though ploughed (to some extent), nor gets it tilled by another person, should be made to give (to the owner) the estimated produce of the uncultivated land; the land will be caused to be cultivated by another person.

10. A she-buffalo, destroying the corns, should be fined eight *māṣas*, a cow half of that,

1. *niveśanaṃ palālakūṭādyarthaṃ vibhakto bhū-pradeśāḥ* (Mitākṣarā). A place separated for heaps of husk and straw.

a goat and a sheep half of that (i.e. of what is ordained for a cow).

11. Double is the punishment for those which sit (on the land) after eating corns. (The punishment of these animals) is ordained to be equal (in such a case). The (punishment for the) ass and the camel is equal to that for a she-buffalo.

12. The owner of the land should get as much corns as are destroyed. The keeper should be beaten, and the owner of the cow deserves the fine stated earlier.

13. There is no fault if (animals eat corns) without any intention (on the part of their owner) in a field near a village and on the outskirts of a protected land near a village. If they are grazed intentionally, one deserves punishment like a thief.

14. A big stud-bull, animals which are consecrated, a cow that has calved (not earlier than ten days) and a cow that has strayed away should be set free. Those, however, which have keepers, should be set free, if afflicted by an action of god or king.

15. The keeper of cows should return the animals in the evening in the same condition in which these were given (to him). One who is paid should be caused to make good those which are dead or lost through negligence.

16. In the event of loss (or death of cattle), due to the fault of the keeper, he is to be fined thirteen *paṇas* and a half, and the owner should be paid the price of the lost animals.

17. The pasture will be in accordance with the wish of the villagers, the size of the land or the will of the king. A twice-born person should always collect, from all places, grass, fuel and flowers.

18. The space, intervening between a village and a field, should spread over a land measuring a hundred *dhanus*; a *kharvaṭa* should measure two hundred (*dhanus*) and a city should have an intervening space of four hundred (*dhanus*).

19. One should recover one's own property sold by another. The blame will be of the buyer if he makes a clandestine purchase. If he (i.e. the buyer) purchases it from a vile person secretly at an (abnormally) low price and at unusual time he is (regarded as) a thief.

20. Having come across one's article, lost or stolen, one should cause the buyer to be apprehended. The place and time being unfavourable, a person should catch hold of (the buyer) and himself hand him over (to the policeman, etc.).

21. (The buyer of a lost or stolen article) becomes, free from fault by the sight of

the seller (i.e. by showing the seller to the owner). From the seller the owner gets his article—the king (realises) fine and the buyer the price (paid by him).

22. The lost thing should be proved (by the owner to be his own) by means of a valid mode of acquisition and (evidence of) enjoyment. Otherwise, if he fails to prove it, the king has to be paid a fine of one-fifth of the article.

23. He who recovers an article, stolen or lost, from the hand of another person not reporting the matter to the king, should pay a fine of ninety-six *paṇas* to the king.

24. If a thing, lost or stolen, is recovered by customs officers or policemen, the owner may get it within a year; after the lapse of this period the king (gets it).

25. For an one-hoofed animal (the owner recovering his lost property) should (pay to the king), as fee for maintenance, four *paṇas*, five for a human being, two *paṇas* each for a buffalo, camel and cow, a quarter each for a goat and a sheep.

26. One should give things, excepting one's wife and sons, without detriment to the interest of one's dependants; there being descendants, the entire belongings should not be given or what has been promised to others.

27. The acceptance of a gift, particularly of an immovable property, should be open. What is promised should be given; one should not take back a thing after giving it.

28. A wait of ten, one, five and seven days, a month, three days and a fortnight respectively (are ordained for examining) seeds, iron, draught - animals, jewels, female slaves, milch animals and male slaves.

29. Gold is not reduced in fire, in the case of silver two *palas* in a hundred (are lost), eight in the case of tin and lead, five in that of copper and ten in case of iron.

30. In the case of woollen and cotton goods, there is an increase of ten *palas* in a hundred, in the case of middle quality (an increase of) five *palas* should be known; in the case of fine goods (the increase) is known to be three *palas*.

31. In the case of embroidered things as well as those made of fur, a deficiency of a thirtieth part is known. In the case of silk goods and barks, there is neither deficiency nor increase.

32. (A craftsman) should doubtlessly be made to give what the experts in the things (concerned) say after ascertaining the place, time, enjoyment, the durability or otherwise of the thing that has suffered reduction.

33. One, who is enslaved forcibly as also one who is sold by thieves are released. So also (is a slave) who saves the life of his master. Slaves are also set free if they give back (to the masters) what has been enjoyed by them (ever since their enslavement) and also by the re-payment of the money (borrowed by the slaves).

34. A man, fallen from mendicancy, becomes the king's slave till death. Slavery takes place among the members of castes in the regular order and not in the reverse order.

35. A pupil, even after mastering a craft, should live in the preceptor's house for the stipulated period getting food from the preceptor and giving him the proceeds (from the craft in question).

36. The king, having made a place in the city and put there Brāhmaṇas devoted to the Vedic triad and engaged in occupations (fixed by the king), should tell them, "Let your own *dharma* be observed."

37. The customary law, not conflicting with one's own *dharma*, as well as the law formulated by the king are to be carefully preserved (i.e. honoured).

38. (The king) should banish from the state one who misappropriates a property belonging to a *Gaṇa* and violates a contract.

39. All should act up to the advice of the well-wishers of an association. There one

who acts in a contrary manner should be made to pay the first amercement.

40. One should make over what one, being deputed for the work of an association, obtains. If he does not voluntarily give it, he should be made to give it elevenfold.

41. Men, thinking of the affairs, should be versed in the Vedas, pure and free from greed. The word of those well-wishers of the association should be acted upon.

42. This is the rule for *Śreṇis Naigamas*, *Pākhaṇḍins* and *Gaṇas* too. The king should maintain their distinction, and protect their hereditary calling.

43. One, who has accepted wages, should pay (the master) twice (the amount) if he leaves the job. If wages are not accepted (but agreed to), he should pay an amount equal (to what has been agreed to). The appurtenances should be preserved by the servants.

44. The person, who makes (a servant) work without settling the wages, should be caused by the king to give (the servant) one-tenth of the merchandise, animals and corns.

45. The master has his will (in the payment of wages) to (a servant) who does not keep to the (proper) place and time, and does the work in an improper way; if excess (of profit) is made (by the servant), an extra (amount) should be paid (to him).

46. If a work cannot be done even by both, one should get wages in proportion to the work done by him; if it is accomplished (by both), (the master) should pay as stipulated.

47. A bearer should be made to give a vessel destroyed by a cause other than an act of the king or god. One who impedes a procession should be made to pay double the wages (taken by him).

48. (A servant), leaving his job after a procession, is started (should be made to pay) one-seventh (of his wages to the master); leaving the work on the way he should pay one-fourth and the entire wages on the midway. (The master, too), who makes a servant leave his job (at these places) should be made to pay (the servant in the above manner).

49. In a *Glaha*, the keeper of the gaming house should take (as his fee) five per cent from a cunning gambler who gains a hundred (or more); from any other gambler he should take ten per cent.

50. He (i.e. the master of the gaming house), being duly protected, should pay to the king the share as stipulated. He should recover (from the defeated party) what is won (by the other party), and make it over to the winner; being forgiving he should tell the truth (to the gamblers for their confidence).

51. The king, having obtained his share, should cause to be given (to the winner) the amount won (by him) in the open assembly of gamblers in the presence of the master of the gaming house, but not otherwise.

52. The gamblers themselves are the observers of the judicial proceedings (in respect of gambling); they alone are the witnesses. Those who play with false dice and by fraudulent means should be branded and banished by the king.

53. Gambling should be made to have one supervising officer for the detection of thieves. This very rule applies to animal-betting (known as) *Samāhvaya* or *Āhvaya*.

CHAPTER 258

Fire said

1. If one abuses a man who is deformed, lacking in some organ or diseased, by speaking the truth, by falsehood and sham eulogy, he should be fined thirteen *paṇas* and a half.

2. The king should make one, who abuses another by saying 'I shall have sexual union with our sister or mother', pay a fine of twenty-five *paṇas*.

3. Half (the usual fine) should be imposed (for abusing) inferiors and double for

abusing other men's wives and the superiors. Penalty should be inflicted in accordance with the superiority and inferiority of castes and lineages.

4. In the slander of castes in the reverse order, fines are twofold and threefold; in the regular order, that is halved.

5. In the verbal destruction of the hand, neck, eye and thigh the fine is one hundred. Half of that is prescribed for (similar abuse) with respect to the foot, nose, ear, palm and the like.

6. One, who is incapable (of doing mischief), is to be fined ten *paṇas* by saying so. On the other hand, he, who is capable, should give a surety for his release.

7. Middle amercement is the fine for abuse mentioning a degrading act (i.e. associating the person abused with acts like *brahma-hatyā* which causes degradation to a man). The (abuser) should be made to pay the first amercement if he utters an abuse associating a man with an *upapātaka*.

8. The highest amercement is the fine for the abuse of those who are versed in the Vedic triad, kings and gods. The middle (amercement) is (the punishment for the abuse) of the race and *Pūga*, the first for (the abuse) of the village and the country.

9. In the case of assault, in the absence of witnesses, trial should be conducted by taking into account marks, *yukti* and public report due to the apprehension of the marks being false.

10. If ashes, mud or dust (thrown by a person) touches another, then (the accused) is to be fined ten *paṇas*. (The fine is) known to be double for touching another with impure things, heel or water spat out.

11. Such is the fine (for the offence against) a person equal in status as well as (against) another man's wife. Double the fine is ordained for the offence against superiors. Half (of it) is prescribed as fine for (similar offence against) an inferior person. There is exemption of fine (for the offence) committed under delusion or intoxication.

12. The limb of a non-Brāhmaṇa, causing injury to a Brāhmaṇa, is to be cut off. The first amercement is the fine for raising a weapon (for striking). Half of that is prescribed for touching (another with the weapon).

13. Ten and twenty (*paṇas*) are the fine (respectively,) for raising the hand and the foot (with the object of striking). Middle amercement (is the fine) for all (castes) for raising weapons for striking at each other.

14. Ten *paṇas* are the fine for dragging one by the foot, hair, cloth or hand. One hundred *paṇas* are the fine for causing injury, dragging, tying with a piece of cloth, striking with the foot (all committed one after the other).

15. A person, causing injury to another with wood and the like, should be made to pay a fine of thirty-two *paṇas* if there is no blood-shed; in case blood is seen, double (the fine) is known.

16. Middle amercement is the fine for breaking a person's hand, foot, tooth, cutting off the ear or nose, bursting a boil as well as for striking one almost to death.

17. Middle amercement is the fine for causing obstruction to one's movement, eating and speech, for injury to the eye and the like as well as for breaking one's neck, arm or thigh.

18. The prescribed fines are twofold for many striking one person. The article, taken away during a quarrel, should be given (back to the owner); the fine, however, is twofold.

19. One, who causes injury to another, should bear the expenses incurred (by the aggrieved person) in getting the wound healed up and pay the fine prescribed for a particular dispute.

20. A ferry-man, realising land-custom, should be fined ten *paṇas*. This indeed is (the fine) for not inviting a neighbouring Brāhmaṇa (to *Śrāddha* etc. when one has the capacity to do so).

21. One should be caused to pay five *paṇas*, ten and twenty respectively for striking at a wall, breaking and felling it, as well as the expenses for reconstructing it.

22. One, throwing into (another man's) house, a thing that causes injury as also that may cause loss of life, should be made to pay a fine of sixteen *paṇas* (for the first offence); for the second offence the fine is the middle amercement.

23. The fine, for causing bleeding injury to small beasts as well as for cutting off their accessory limbs, should be two *paṇas* etc. is order (e.g. two *paṇas*, four *paṇas*, six *paṇas*, eight *paṇas* etc. in accordance with the gravity of the offence).

24. For cutting off the genital organ and causing death (to the above animals), (the fine is) middle amercement or the price (of the animal). Twice the fines (is ordained) for these offences towards big animals.

25. For cutting off the branches and the entire trunks of the trees having branches that sprout up as well as of those on which people subsist, the fines are twenty *paṇas*

and twice that amount and so on (i.e. 20, 40, 80 etc.).

26. One, who makes another commit *sāhasa*, should be caused to pay double the fine. He, who causes another person (to commit *sāhasa*) by saying this, 'I shall give (you money)' (should be made to pay) fourfold.

27-28. One, who abuses a respectable person, transgresses his order, beats the wife of the brother, does not pay the promised money, breaks a sealed house, commits mischief to owners of neighbouring lands and houses and to persons of one's own family—the fine of these people is fifty *paṇas*; this is the decision.

29-32. One who has sexual relation with a widow at will, one who does not rush to help when there are shouts for help (by people in distress), one who abuses without any reason, a Caṇḍāla touching a person of of superior caste, a Śūdra who feeds the mendicants (like Digambaras) in rites in honour of deities or of the manes, one who swears improperly, an unfit person doing the work of one who is fit, one who emasculates bulls and small animals, deceives others in ordinary things, one who destroys the foetus of a female slave; of father and son, sister and brother, husband and wife, preceptor and pupil the one deserting the other who is not degraded—these have to undergo a fine of one hundred *paṇas*.

33. A washerman, wearing the cloth of another person, should be fined three *paṇas*. In case of his sale (of the cloth) mortgage, gift or loan at request (he is to be fined) ten *paṇas*.

34. One who deceitfully alters the balance, a royal grant, a standard of weight or a coin and one who carries on transactions with these should be made to pay the highest amercement.

35. In the examination of coins, one, who says that a counterfeit coin is not so and that a genuine coin is counterfeit, is to be made to pay the first amercement.

36. A physician, acting falsely (i.e. posing as a physician not being actually so) towards lower animals, human beings and king's men should be made to pay (respectively) first, middle and highest amercement.

37. One, who confines a person not deserving confinement, sets free one who should be confined or one who (is confined but) has not yet undergone trial should be made to pay the highest amercement.

38. One, who misappropriates one-eighth (of an article) with (a false) standard of weight or balance should be made to pay twenty-two *paṇas*. In the case of greater or less quantity misappropriated, the fine will be

fixed (in accordance with the increase or decrease).

39. One, mixing inferior substances with commodities like medicine, oil, salt, fragrant substances, paddy, molasses etc., should be made to pay sixteen *paṇas.*

40. A fine of one thousand *paṇas* is ordained for those who make the value (fixed by the king) such as causes suffering to craftsman and artisans doing co-operative business or cause diminution or increase in the value.

41. The king being near, day-to-day sale or purchase should be in accordance with the value fixed (by him). For the merchants, the difference from that (i.e. what is fixed by the king) is known to be the profit-earner.

42. One who immediately purchases or sells (articles) should take (a profit of) five per cent on commodities of one's own country and ten per cent on those obtained from a foreign land.

43. The price, equitable to (both) the purchaser and the seller, should be fixed on a commodity after considering the cost of the article.

44. One, who does not deliver to the buyer a commodity the price of which has been accepted (by him), should be made to give it along with interest or with the profit

obtained in another region if the buyer comes from that place.

45. The original buyer not having taken delivery of an article sold, the loss, if any, due to his fault, will be his (i.e. buyer's) alone.

46. If in a commodity which, though asked for by the buyer, has not been given to him, there is any defect due to a disturbance caused by the king or God, the loss will be of the seller alone.

47. A fine of twice the value (of the commodity concerned) will be imposed on a person who, after selling it to one party, (again) sells it to another, or sells a defective article as one free from defect.

48. By a trader, ignorant of the depreciation and appreciation of commodities, rescission should not be made; if he does so, he becomes liable to a penalty (equivalent to) one-sixth of the commodity.

49. Among merchants, working for profit in a co-operative business, the profit and loss are determined in proportion to the amount (invested by them) or in accordance with the contract.

50. (Among the partners of a co-operative concern), a person should restore the thing which has been lost due to his working in a manner prohibited (by others), acting contrary to (others') order

or through inadvertence. One saving a thing from a calamity gets a tenth part of it.

51. The king should take as tax one-twentieth of the price fixed (by him for a commodity). If an article, which is prohibited to be sold or which is the king's due, is sold, it goes to the king.

52. One making a false statement about the quantity (of a commodity) or slipping away from the place of tax-collection or who buys or sells a disputed article should be made to pay (as fine) eight times the value of the commodity (concerned).

53. If (of those who run a co-operative business) dies abroad, his share should be taken by (the deceased person's) heirs (like son etc.), the *bāndhavas* (i.e. close relatives on the maternal side, like maternal uncle etc.) or the agnates (i.e. *Sapiṇḍas* excepting son etc.); in their absence, the king should take it.

54. The (partners) should remove the deceitful (partner) without (giving him) a share of the profit. One, who is incapable, should get (his work) done by another person. By this is stated the rule in respect of (sacrificial priests called) Ṛtviks, cultivators and craftsmen (like dancer, actor, carpenter, etc.).

55. A thief is apprehended by policemen, etc. either by (seeing in his possession) the stolen article or by tracking him down. An old offender as well as one, whose whereabouts are unknown, should also be apprehended.

56. Others, too, who conceal their caste, name etc., are addicted to gambling, women and drinking, and have their faces shrunk up and voice broken.

57. Those who enquire about others' things and house, move about in disguise, have no income but expenditure as well as those who sell lost articles (should also be apprehended).

58. He who, apprehended on the suspicion of theft, does not prove his innocence, should be made to give the stolen article and given the punishment due to a thief.

59. (The king) should make a thief give the stolen article and get him slain[1] by striking him in various ways. (He) should brand a Brāhmaṇa (thief), and banish him from his own kingdom.

60. If a murder or theft has occurred (in a village), the fault is of the head of the village if the thief has not gone out (of the village). The (people of the) village, within the boundary of which the sign of

---

1. This punishment, according to the Mitākṣarā is awarded when the theft is of a very serious nature.

the thief is seen, or the (inhabitants of a) place where such signs are found, should give it (i.e. restore the stolen article).

61a. (If a murder or theft takes place) beyond one *Krośa*, five or ten villages (should restore the stolen article).

61b-62a. Those, who snatch away prisoners, steal horses or elephants as well as those who forcibly kill others—(the king) should get them placed on the stake.

62b-63a. A stealer of cloth etc. and a knot-cutter should be deprived of their hand and tongs[1] (respectively). In the second offence they should be deprived of one hand and one foot.

63b-64. The first amercement is the fine for consciously providing a thief or murderer with food, a stimulant substance, fire, water, advice, materials and expenses. The first amercement is the fine for striking others with a weapon as well as for causing abortion.

65-66. (The penalty) is highest or lowest amercement for murdering the wives of particular persons (e.g. Brāhmaṇas, etc.).

67. Those, who burn a field, house, a forest, a village, a pasture ground or a threshing floor, and one, who has sexual intercourse with the queen, should be burnt in the strawfire.

---

1. The thumb and forefinger, together, used like tongs, in seizing another person's article.

68. A man, about to have sexual intercourse with another man's wife, should be apprehended knowing it by (signs like) snatching each other by the hair. If this takes place with respect to a woman of the same caste, the fine is the first amercement. The middle amercement is the fine if it occurs with respect to a woman in the regular order (i.e. if the woman is of inferior caste).

69a. If this occurs with respect to a woman in the reverse order (i.e. if the woman is of a higher caste), then the men (concerned) will have death (as penalty) and the ears of the woman will be cut off.

69b-70a. The pressing of the waist-knot, the breasts, the wrapper, the navel and the hair (of a woman), talking to a woman at an improper place or time, staying with her (on the same seat)—(these are the signs by which a man is known to be about to enjoy a woman).

70b-71a. A woman (talking to or associating with a) man (with whom) association is prohibited (by her husband or father) should pay one hundred (*paṇas*) as fine; a man, (violating the prohibition of his superiors with respect to a woman), should give two hundred (*paṇas*).

71b. A man, having intercourse with beasts, a woman of low class as well as cows should be made to pay a hundred (*paṇas*).

72. A man should be made to pay fifty *paṇas* as fine for having intercourse with female slaves who are restrained (from having sexual enjoyment with other men) and with a female slave dependent on others though they are approachable (from the point of view of caste).

73. Ten *paṇas* are known to be the fine for forcible sexual intercourse with a female slave. For intercourse with a Caṇḍāla woman or a female mendicant, one should be made to move about (after being branded with ugly signs).

74. The highest amercement is the fine for one who makes a lesser or greater entry in a royal grant or releases one who has abducted another man's wife.

75-76a. The highest amercement is the fine for one who defiles a Brāhmaṇa with prohibited food. One, who makes a false statement (in a court of law), steals gold as well as one who sells bad meat (e.g. that of a dog), should be deprived of their limb,[1] and should be made to pay the highest amercement.

76b-77a. A man, though capable, not saving a person (who has been attacked) from animals having teeth or horns should pay the first amercement and twice as much if the victim shouts for help.

---

1. The Mitākṣarā reads *tryaṅga* for *aṅga*, and explains it as nose, ear and hand.

77b. One calling as thief one who is not a thief should be made to pay a fine of five hundred (*paṇas*).

78-79a. One, who speaks ill of a king, one who abuses him, sells things attached to a dead body, beats the preceptor, one who leaks out the counsel of the king—(the king) should banish them after cutting off their tongues.

79b. The middle amercement is the fine for one who gets upon the royal vehicle or seat.

80. Eight hundred (*paṇas*) are the fine for one who pierces both the eyes (of a person), one who (being an astrologer other than the king's preceptor or well-wisher) forecasts the king's harm and a Śūdra living as a Brāhmaṇa.

81. (The king) should impose double the fine on one who, though justly vanquished, thinks, 'I am unconquered' after defeating him again while he approaches.

82. The king, who has unjustly realised fine, should himself give it, increased thirty-fold, to Brāhmaṇas after consecrating it to Varuṇa.

83. *Dharma*, material prosperity, fame, popularity, *upagraha*,[1] great honour from the

> subjects and eternal residence in heaven—these seven merits accrue to a king who (justly) supervises judicial proceedings.

Here ends the 258th chapter entitled abuse etc., in the Mahāpurāṇa called Agni.

---

1. The meaning of this word is not clear, their to jouy, at means addition of wealth. In view of *artha* (material prosperity), stated already, this meaning seems to be redundant. The editor of the *Nārada-smṛti* (Calcutta Skt. College) explains it as regard by the subjects. But, as the word is preceded by *loka-paṅkti* (popularity) and *prajābhyo bahumānam*, this meaning also seems to be tautologus.

EXPLANATORY NOTES

CHAPTER 253

1. व्यवहार

Kātyāyana defines it as follows :
वि नानार्थेऽव संदेहे हरणं हार उच्यते ।
नाना संदेहहरणाद् व्यवहार इति स्मृतः ।।

33. श्रुत्यपेतादि

'Ādi' perhaps refers to prescriptions of Smṛti and customary law.

34. विवादाद् द्विगुणम्

Mit., Dīp.—twice the amount of fine to be imposed on the defeated party in a suit.
Ap.—money involved in the suit. Mit—rejects the suggestion that *vivāda* means reject of dispute; because it is meaningless in abduction of women, etc.

CHAPTER 254

5. पुत्रोऽनन्याश्रितद्रव्य:

According to Ap., it means a son who is independent of others in respect of property. In other words, it means a son whose property is not under the control of any other brother.

17. स्त्रीपशव्यम्

Women slaves and beasts.

27. न्यास

According to Bāl., a thing deposited after declaring its nature.

निक्षेप

According to Bāl., a thing kept with one for being handed over to another.

CHAPTER 255

3. उन्मत्त

According to Vīr., violent as by madness etc.

रंगावतारिन्

According to Bāl., *malla* i.e. athlete, wrestler, boxer, etc.

According to Ap., *naṭādi*, i.e. actor and the like.

पाखण्डिन्

One who does not recognize Vedic authority (Vīr. and Āp.).

4. आप्त

Relative (Vīr).
Related by birth or learning (Ap.).

निर्धूत

Banished from village (Dīp.).

5b-6a. According to Bāl., it applies to disputes of all kinds though only *ṛṇa* is mentioned. According to Ap., it relates to disputes about debt alone.

11. प्रतिज्ञा

According to Ap., it means what is to be established, and, therefore, includes the kinds of reply called प्रत्यवस्कन्दन (confession with a plea) and प्राङ्न्याय. Bāl. points out that the rule holds good where a witness testifies to the truth of the entire प्रतिज्ञा, and not of a part thereof.

13. कूटकृत्

According to Ap., it may also mean one who forges a document.

14. विवादाद् द्विगुणम्

Double the amount involved in the suit.
(Ap., Dīp., Vīr.).

25. प्राप्ति

Residence of the plaintiff and the defendant at the same place (Bāl.).
Residence of the above persons at the same place and same time. (Ap.).

हेतु

Impossibility of perjury etc. (Bāl).
Inference (Ap.)

CHAPTER 256

7. निबन्ध

Something settled by the king, e.g. cess from a ferryman (Vīr.).

Fixed grant of gold etc. made by the king (Dīp).

11. असंस्कृताः

संस्कार means marriage (Bāl)., *jātakarma* etc. (Ap., Dīp)., initiation, marriage, etc. (Vīr.).

तुरीयकम

According to Jīmūtavāhana, in his *Dāyabhāga* (J. Vidyasagara's ed., 1893, p. 70), followed by Raghunandana, this word means 'vivāhocita-dravya' and not a fourth part. Jīmūtavāhana points out that, if it means 'one-fourth, then in the case of one brother and four sisters the brother will have nothing—this is absurd.

22. दुहितरः

It means पुत्रिकापुत्र (Dīp.).

25. संसृष्ठी

Such a reunion is possible between father and son, between brorhers, between a person and his paternal uncle. Bāl. does not recognize the last kind. Ap. recognises the second kind only.

27. अन्धः

Congenitally blind (Dīp.).

31. शुल्कम्

It means *ādhivedanika* (Bāl.)
Uterine brother, according to Bāl.

33. दण्डचः

According to Ap., it will apply to one who withholds a girl after betrothal to a groom free from the defects of impotency, etc.

दत्तम्

According to Vīr., it applies only to the *Āsura* form of marriage.

34. सप्रंतिरोधक

The carrying away of one's things after forcibly obstructing him (Bāl., Dīp.). Such distress in which no loan is obtained (Ap.). According to some, it means the siege of a city.

35. समम्

Equal to what has been given to the other wife.

(Ap., Dīp., Vīr).

CHAPTER 257

18. खर्वट

A place other than a village, but inferior to a town (Ap.).
Bāl. reads *Karpaṭa*, and explains it as a place having the characteristics of both a village and a town.

31. कार्मिक

According to Ap., a piece of cloth with the figure of a man or woman woven in it.

36. स्वधर्म

It includes, according to Bāl, dissuasion of the king if he strays away from the right path.

38. चतुष्पाद् व्यवहार:

A judicial proceeding consists of the following four stages :—

(i) Filing of the plaint,

(ii) Reply of the defendant,

(iii) Recording of evidence by plaintiff,

(iv) Judgement.

35. पूर्ववादिन:

Mit—the word *pūrvavādiān* means the party claiming priority; not the party which lodges the complaint first.

50. अर्थशास्त्रात्

Here *arthaśāstra* means the portion of *dharmaśāstra* dealing with *artha* (i.e. temporal matters) and not works like the *Arthaśāstra* of Kauṭilya. On this, see R.C. Hazra in *Our Heritage* (*Calcutta Sanskrit College Journal*), XII, 1964.

CHAPTER 258

A man of inferior caste and qualification (Bāl.). According to Bāl, it means age and indirectly qualification.

4. A Kṣatriya or Vaiśya, abusing a Brāhmaṇa, shall pay 100 (double of 50) and 150 (50×3) *paṇas* respectively. According to Mit., a Śūdra, abusing a Brāhmaṇa, shall have his tongue cut off or undergo other corporal punishment. According to Dīp. and Vīr., however, in such a case, a Śūdra shall pay 200 *paṇas*. For abusing a Kṣatriya or Vaiśya, he shall pay 150 and 100 *paṇas* respectively.

GLOSSARY

(*in English alphabetical order*)

The technical terms and difficult words in the Vyavahāra Chapters (253-58) of the *Agnipurāṇa*[1] have been explained. All the various meanings of a word, and not necessarily the one intended in the context, have been noted. The places of the Ys., containing these terms, have also been indicated.

Abhiśastaka 255.3

Used in the following senses :—

(i) Murderer of a Brāhmaṇa.

(ii) Murderer of a Brāhmaṇa woman who has bathed after her monthly impurity.

(iii) Guilty of a mortal sin.

(iv) Murderer of a Brāhmaṇa or Kṣatriya who has studied the Veda or had been initiated to some sacrifice.

Ādhi 254.18.

"Pledge or mortgage of a chattel or immovable property to the creditor himself with or without possession. "HDH, III, p. 419. f.n. 681.

YS. II. 2.23, 25 etc., II.6.90.

1. The following abbreviations have been used :

HDH—*History of Dharmaśāstra* by P.V. Kane.

M. Wms.—Sanskrit-Engilsh Dictionary by Monier-Williams.

Mit.—*Mitākṣarā* commentary of Vijñāneśvara on Ys.

MS.—*Manu-smṛti.*

YS=*Yājñavalkya-smṛti.*

Ādhivedanika 256.30.

A kind of *Strīdhana* (q.v.) presented to a woman by her husband on his marrying another woman.

YS. II. 8.143, 148.

Āgama 253, 55,56

valid mode of acquisition.

YS. II. 2.27

Anvādheyaka 256.31.

A kind of *Strīdhana* (q.v.) obtained by a woman, after her marriage, from her husband or parents.

YS. II. 8.144.

Anvāhita 254.27.

(From Anvādhi)

Sub-mortgage, i.e. mortgage of a property by the mortgagee.

YS. II. 4.67.

Apaviddha 256.16.

One cast off by one's parents and accepted by another person as his son.

YS. II. 8.132.

Aupanidhika 254.25.

Derived from *Upanidhi* which means a sealed deposit, i.e. an article deposited with a person in a sealed container without disclosing the contents.

For *Upanidhi*, see YS. II. 2.25.

Caitya 257.2.

Used in the following senses :—

(i) A pile of stones forming a landmark.

(ii) A monument.

(iii) A place of worship.

(iv) A temple.

(v) A tree grown by the side of a street.

(vi) A village-tree on which deities are worshipped.

Dattaka 256.17.

A boy who, being given by his parents, in adopted by a person as his son.

YS. II. 8.130.

Dattātmā 256.18.

A boy who, either bereft of parents or forsaken by them, offers himself to a person as his son.

YS. II. 8.131.

Ḍāyāda 259.5.

A person entitled to inheritance.

YS. II. 8.118, 119.

Dhanus 257.18.

A measure of length equal to four *hastas*.

Divya 255.28.

Divine proof; e.g. ordeal of fire, water etc.

YS. II. 2.22.; 7.95,97.

Gaṇa 257.42.

(i) An association of merchants etc.

(ii) A guild of horse-dealers.

(iii) An association of men living in a village and such other places.

(iv) An association of warriors etc. who pursue the same vocation.

YS. I. 13.361; II. 15.157, 192.

Gūḍhaja 256.16.

A son born to a woman during the absence of her husband, the real father being unknown.

YS. II. 8.129.

Glaha 257.46.

Wager mutually agreed upon by gamblers.

YS. II. 17.199.

Hoḍha 253.11

Stolen article. Some analyse the word as *ha* (healy)+ *Ūḍha* (carried away. (Under *Manu-smṛti* ix. 260, Kullūka explains it as *hṛta-dravya*. Under Yr. ii. 5 Mit. says *hoḍhā loptram*.

Iṣṭāpūrta 255.50

The components are *Iṣṭa* and *Pūrta*. *Iṣṭa* means

(i) Whatever is offered in the *Gṛhya* fire and the three *Śrauta* fires and gifts made in side the *Vedī* in the *Śrauta* sacrifices.

(ii) Honouring a guest and performance of *Vaiśvadeva*.

(iii) Oblation to fire, penance, truthfulness, Vedic study hospitality, performance of *Vaiśvadeva*.

Pūrta has been defined as

(i) Dedication of deep wells, oblong large wells tanks, temples, distribution of food and maintenance of public gardens.

(ii) To the above are added, by some, gifts made at the time of the eclipse or on the sun's passage into a Zodiacal sign or on the twelfth day of a month.

(iii) Nursing of those who are ill.

Kānīna 256.16.

Son of an unmarried woman.

YS. II. 1.129.

Kharvaṭa 256.18.

(i) "Mountain-village" (M. Wms).

(ii) *Kharvaṭasya pracurakaṇṭaka-santānasya grāmasya.* (Mit. on YS. II. 10.167).

YS. II. 10.167.

Kṛtrima 256.18.

A parentless boy adopted by a person as his son after alluring him with money, land, etc.

YS. II. 8.131.

Kṣetraja 256.15.

A kind of son, begotten by a person by means of *Niyoga* levirate on the wife of a sonless person.

YS. I.3.69; II. 8.128, 141.

Mahāpātakin 255.8.

One who has committed a *Mahāpātaka* (grave sin). The *Mahāpātakas* are as follows :

(i) Murder of a Brāhmaṇa.

(ii) Drinking of wine called *surā*.

(iii) Theft of gold belonging to a Brāhmaṇa.

(iv) Incestuous connexion with one's mother.

(v) Association with one who has committed anyone of the above sins.

For *Mahāpātaka*, see YS. I.3.77; II.5.73 etc.

Naigama 257.42.

The Pāśupatas etc. who accept Vedic authority.

YS. II. 15.192.

Nikṣepa 254.27.

(i) "A deposit entrusted to a man after counting the article in his presence". (HDH, III, p. 454).

(ii) "Deposit of one's articles with another through confidence" (*Ibid.*)

(iii) "Delivery of one's articles to another for handing over to a third". (*Ibid.*).

YS. II.4.67. III. 5.230.

Nyāsa 254.27.

(i) An open deposit for safe custody.

(ii) "Handing over to some member in the house an article in the absence of the head of the house for delivery to the head of the house". (HDH, III, p. 455).

(iii) Mental appropriation or assignment of various parts of the body to tutelary deities.

YS. II. 4.67.

Pāṣaṇḍin 257.42.

Heretic like a Buddhist.

YS. I.6.130; II. 5.70 etc.

Paunarbhava 256.17.

Son of a woman called *Punarbhū*. *Punarbhū* generally means a remarried widow. Seven kinds of *Punarbhū* were usually known. See HDH, II (Pt. 1), pp. 608-9.

YS. I. 10.222, II. 8.130.

Pratibhū 254.14.

Surety; one standing guarantee for another.

YS. II. 3.54, 55 etc.

Pūga 258.8.

Any combination or body of an association, corporation, union,

YS. II. 2.30; II. 18.8 211.

Putrikā 256.15.

(i) One's daughter's son appointed to be one's own son.

(ii) One's daughter appointed as one's son.

YS. II. 8.128.

Ṛkthin 254.5

Literally meaning 'one who possesses ṛktha' (inheritance); heir.

For *Ṛktha*, see YS. II. 3.51; II. 8.117 etc.

Sāhasa 255.4; 258.26.

(i) "Punishment, fine (regarded as of three kinds, the highest being called *Uttama*, half of that *Madhyama* and half of that *Adhama*" (M. Wms.). The lowest one is also called *Prathama.*

(ii) Violence, rape, felony.

YS. II. 20.230.

Sahoḍhaja 256.18.

A kind of son; he is brought with a woman pregnant at the time of her marriage.

YS. II. 8.131.

Samāhvaya 257.53.

Betting, especially on animals.

YS. II. 18.203.

Saṃsṛṣṭin 256.25.

One re-united with coparceners after partition of the property.

YS. II. 8.138, 139.

Śreṇī 257.42.

A guild or association of traders dealing in the same

articles.

YS. I.13.361; II. 2.30, II. 15.192.

Strīdhana 256.2.

A woman's exclusive property given to her by her parents, brother or husband and by others on certain occasions. A property over which she has absolute right. For various kinds of *Strīdhana*,

See MS. IX.194.

YS. III. 8.143, 145 etc.

Upanīdhi 253.54 Sealed deposit.

YS. II.2.

Śulka 256.31.

(i) Bride's price; i.e. money paid by the bridegroom's party to the bride's guardians.

(ii) Toll, tax, especialiy money levied at ferries, passes and roads.

YS. II. 3.47; II. 8.144 etc.

Tarika 258.20

Officer in charge of tolls payable by boats.

YS. II. 22.263.

Upapātaka 258.7.

A class of sins lighter than *mahāpātaka* (q.v.); i.e. incest, giving up of Vedic study, fornication, etc.

YS. II. 18.210; III. 5.2 etc.

Vivīta 257.13.

An enclosed or preserved spot of land, such as pasture-ground.

Vyavahāra 258.

(i) Legal istration.

(ii) Administration of Justice.

(iii) Contract.

(iv) Competency to manage one's own affairs; majority.

YS. I. 13.360; II. 1.1 etc.

Vṛddhi 253. 63,65

Interest.

The following kinds of Interest appear to have been in vogue in ancient India :

(i) Kālikā—payable monthly.
(ii) Kāritā—fixed by mutual agreement.
(iii) Kāyikā—in the form of daily phyical labour.
(iv) Cakravṛddhi—compound interest.
(v) Śikhā—realised daily.
(vi) Bhoga—interest in the form of enjoyment (eg. rent of a house, fruits of crops, etc.).
YS. II. 3.37,38 etc.

Concordance of Vyavahāra Chapters of the *Agnipurāṇa* and the Vyavahāra sections of the *Yājñavalkya-sṃrti*

Topic	*Chapter of Agnipurāṇa*	*No. of section in the Vyavahārādhyāya of the Yājñavalkya-smṛti*
Sādhāraṇa Vyavahāramātṛkā, Asādhāraṇa-Vyavahāramātṛkā	253	1-3 (part)
Ṛṇādāna (part)	254	3,4
Sākṣī	255	5,6,7
Dāyavibhāga	256	8
Sīmāvivāda	257	9, 10, 11, 12, 13, 14, 15, 16, 17.
Vāk-pāruṣya		
Daṇḍa-Pāruṣya		
Sāhasa	258	18-25
Vikrīyāsaṃpradāna		
Sambhūya-samutthāna		
Steya		
Strī-saṃgrahaṇa		
Prakīrṇaka		

Verse—concordance of the Vyavāhara Chapters of the *Agnipurāṇa* and the Vyahahārādhyāya of the *Yājñavalkya-smṛti*

Agni-purāṇa	*Text as in the Mitākṣarā*	*Yājñavalkya-smṛti Text as in Aparārka*	*Text as in Bālakrīḍā*
Chap. 253			
32	1 (part)	1 (part)	1 (part)
33	3 a, 4 a	3 a; 4 a	3 a, 4 a
34	4 b, 5 a	4 b, 5 a	4 b, 5 a
35	5 b, 6 a	5 b, 6 a	5 b, 6 a
36	6 b, 7 a	6 b, 7 a	6 b, 7 a
37	7 b, 8 a	7 b, 8 a	7 b, 8 a
38	8 b, 9 a	8 b, 9 a	8 b, 9 a
39	9 b, 10 a	9 b, 10 a	9 b, 10 a
40	10 b, 11 a	10 b, 11 a	10 b, 11 a
41	11 b, 12 a	11 b, 12 a	11 b, 12 a
42	12 b, 13 a	12 b, 13 a	12 b, 13 a
43	13 b, 15 a	13 b, 15 a	13 b, 15 a
44	15 b, 16 a	15 b, 16 a	15 b, 16 a
45	16 b, 17 a	16 b, 17 a	16 b, 17 a
46	17 b, 18 a	17 b, 18 a	17 b, 18 a
47	18 b, 19 a	18 b, 19 a	18 b, 19 a
48	19 b, 20 a	19 b, 20 a	19 b, 20 a
49	20 b, 21 a	20 b, 21 a	20 b, 21 a
50	21 b, 22 a	21 b, 22 a	21 b, 22 a
51	22 b, 23 a	22 b, 23 a	22 b, 23 a
52	23 b, 24 a	23 b, 24 a	23 b, 24 a
53	24 b, 25 a	24 b, 25 a	24 b, 25 a
54	52 b, 26 a	25 b, 26 a	25 b, 26 a
55	26 b, 27 a	26 b, 27 a	26 b, 27 a

Agni-purāṇa	*Text as in Mitākṣarā*	*Text as in Aparārka*	*Text as in Bālakrīḍā*
56a	27 b,	27 b,	27 b,
56b-57a	X	X	229
57b	28 a	28 a	28 a
58	28 b, 29 a	28 b, 29 a	28 b, 30 a
59	29 b, 31 a	29 b, 31 a	30 a, 32 a
60	31 b, 32 a	31 b, 32 a	32 a, 33 a
61	32 b, 33 a	32 b, 33 a	33 a, 35 a
62	33 b, 36 a	33 b, 36 a	35 b, 38 a
63	37	37	39
64	39	39	40
65	38	38	41
66	40	40	42
Chap. 254			
1	41	41	43
2	42	42	44
3	43	43	45
4	44	44	46
5	51	51	47
6	45	45	48
7	46	46	49
8	48	48	50
9	49	49	51
10	50	50	52
11	47	47	53
12	52	52	54
13	53	53	55
14	54	54	56
15	55	55	57
16	56	56	58
17	57	57	59

Agni-purāṇa	*Text as in Mitākṣarā*	*Text as in Aparārka*	*Text as in Bālakrīḍā*
18	58	58	60
19	59	59	61
20	60	60	62
21	61	61	63
22	62	62	64
23	63	63	65
24	64	64	66
25	65	65	67
26	66	66	68
27	67	67	69
Chap. 255			
1	68	68	70
2	69	69	71
3	70	70	72
4	71	71	73
5	72 a, 76 a	72 a, 76 a	74 a, 75 a
6	76 b, 77 a	76 b, 77 a	75 b, 76 a
7	77 b, 73 a	77 b, 73 a	76 b, 77 a
8	73 b, 74 a	73 b, 74 a	77 b, 78 a
9	74 b, 75 a	74 b, 75 a	78 b, 79 a
10	75 b, 78 a	75 b, 78 a	79 b, 80 a
11	78 b, 79 a	78 b, 79 a	80 b, 81 a
12	79 a, 80 a	79 b, 80 a	81 b, 82 a
13	80 b, 81 a	80 b, 81 a	82 b, 83 a
14	81 b, 82 a	81 b, 82 a	83 b, 84 a
15	82 b, 83 a	82 b, 83 a	84 b, 85 a
16	84	84	86
17	85	85	87
18	86	86	88
19	87	87	89
20	X	X	90

Agni-purāṇa	*Text as in Mitākṣāra*	*Text as in Aparārka*	*Text as in Bālakriḍā*
21	88	88	91
22	89	89	92
23	90	90	93
24	91	91	94
25	92	92	95
26	93	93	96
27	94	94	97
Chap. 255			
28	95	95	99
29	96	96	99
30	99	99	100
31	X	X	101
32	97	97	102
33	98	98	103
34	100	100	104
35	X	X	X
36	101	101	105
37	102	102	106
38	103	103	107
39	104	104	108
40	105	105	109
41	106	106	110
42	107	107	111
43	108 a	108 a	112 a
44	108 b, 109 a	108 b, 109 a	112 b, 113 a
45	109 b-110 a	109 b-110 a	113 b-114 a
46	110 b-111 a	110 b-111 a	114 b-115 a
47	111 b-112 a	111 b-112 a	115 b-116 a
48	112 b-113 a	112 b-113 a	
49	113 b	113 b	117 b

Agni-purāṇa	*Text as in Mitākṣāra*	*Text as in Aparārka*	*Text as in Bālakriḍā*
Chap. 256			
1	114	114	118
2	115	115	119
3	116	117	120
4	117	117	121
5	118	118	122
6	120	120	123
7	121	121	124
8	122	122	125
9	119	119	126
10	123	123	127
11	124	124	128
12	125	125	129
13	126	126	130
14	127	127	131
15	128	128	132
16	129	129	133
17	130	130	134
18	131	131	135
19	132	132	136
20	133	133	137
21	134	134	138
22	135	135	139
23	136	136	140
24	137	137	141
25	138	138	142
26	139	139	143
27	140	140	144
28	141	141	145
29	142	142	146
30	143	143	147

Agni-purāṇa	*Text as in Mitākṣāra*	*Text as in Aparārka*	*Text as in Bālakriḍā*
31	144	144	148
32	145	145	149
33	146	146	150
34	147	147	151
35	148	148	152
36	149	149	153
Chap. 257			
1	150	150	154
2	151	151	155
3	152	152	156
4	153	153	157
5	154	154	158
6	155	155	159
7	156	156	160
8	157	157	161
9	158	158	162
10	159	159	163
11	160	160	164
12	161	161	165
13	162	162	166
14	163	163	167
15	164	164	168
16	165	165	169
17	166	166	170
18	167	167	171
19	168	168	172
20	169	169	173
21	170	170	174
22	171	171	175
23	172	172	176

Agni-puraṇa	*Text as in Mitākṣāra*	*Text as in Aparārka*	*Text as in Bālakriḍā*
24	173	173	177
25	174	174	178
26	175	175	179
27	176	176	180
28	177	177	181
29	178	178	182
30	179	179	183
31	180	180	184
32	181	181	185
33	182	182	186
34	183	183	187
35	184	184	188
36	185	185	189
37	186	186	190
38	187	187	191
39	188	188	192
40	190	190	194
41	191	191	195
42	192	192	196
43	193	193	197
44	194	194	198
45	195	195	199
46	196	196	200
47	197	197	201
48	198	198	202
49	199	199	203
50	200	200	204
51	201	201	205
52	202	202	206
53	203	203	207

Agni-purāṇa	*Text as in Mitākṣāra*	*Text as in Aparārka*	*Text as in Bālakriḍā*
Chap. 258			
1	204	204	208
2	205	205	209
3	206	206	210
4	207	207	211
5	208	208	212
6	209	209	213
7	210	210	214
8	211	211	215
9	212	212	216
10	213	213	218
11	214	214	219
12	215	215	220
13	216	216	221
14	217	217	222
15	218	218	223
16	219	219	224
17	220	220	225
18	221	221	226
19	222	222	227
20	263	263	228
21	223	223	229
22	224	224	230
23	225	225	231
24	226	226	232
25	227	227	233
26	231	231	237
27	232	232	238
28	233	233	239
29	234	234	249
30	235	235	241
31	236	236	242

Agni-purāṇa	*Text as in Mitākṣāra*	*Text as in Aparārka*	*Text as in Bālakriḍā*
32	237	237	243
33	238	238	244
34	240	240	246
35	241	241	247
36	242	242	248
37	243	243	249
38	244	244	250
39	245	245	251
40	249	249	255
41	251	251	257
42	252	252	258
43	253	253	259
44	254	254	260
45	255	255	X
46	256	256	261
47	257	257	262
48	258	258	263
49	259	259	264
50	260	260	265
51	261	261	266
52	262	262	267
53	264	264	268
54	265	265	269
55	266	266	270
56	267	267	271
57	268	268	272
58	269	269	273
59	270	270	274
60	271 a, 272 a	271 a, 272 a	275 a, 276 a,
61	272 b, 273 a	272 b, 273 a	276 b, 277 a

Agni-purāṇa	*Text as in Mitākṣāra*	*Text as in Aparārka*	*Text as in Bālakriḍā*
62	273 b,	273 b,	277 b,
	274 a	274 a	278 a
63	274 b,	274 b,	278 a,
	276 a	276 a	280 a
64	276 b,	276 b,	280 b,
	277 a	277 a	281 a
65	277 b	277 b	282 b
66	279	279	283
67	282	282	286
68	283 a	283 a	287 a
	286 a	286 a	288 a
69	286 b	286 b	288 b
	284 a	284 a	289 a
70	284 b	284 b	289 b
	285 a	285 a	290 a
71	285 b	285 b	290 a
	289 b	289 b	293 b
72	290	290	294
73	291 a	291 a	295 a
74	295	296	298
75	296 a,	295 a,	299 a
	297 a	296 a	300 a
76	297 b	296 b	300 b
	300 a	299 a	303 a
78	302 a	301 a,	305 a
	303 a	392 a	306 a
79	302 b	301 b,	305 b
	303 b	302 b	306 b
80	304	303	307
81	306	305	309
82	307	306	310
83	X	X	X

Concordance of the Vyavahāra Verses of the *Agnipurāṇa* (Chapter 253) and the stanzas of the *Nārada-smṛti*.

Chapter 253 of the Agnipuraṇa contains 66 verses. Of these, the first thirty stanzas, excepting the first line of the first stanza, are found in the *Nārada-smṛti*. We give below a concordance of the stanzas in these two works.

Agnipurāṇa (Chap. 253)	Nārada-smṛti
1 a	X
1 b	I. 8 a
2	I. 8 b, 9 a
3 a	I. 9 b
3 b, 4 a	I. 10
4 b, 5 a	I. 11
5 b, 6 a	I. 12
6 b, 7 a	I. 13
7 b, 8 a	I. 14
8 b, 9 a	I. 15
9 b, 10 a	I. 26
10 b, 11 a	I. 27
11 b, 12 a	I. 28
12 b	I. 29 a
13	Vyavahārapadas I. 1 (P. 10)
14	II. 1 (P. 31)
15	III. 1 (P. 32)
16	IV. 1

1. The text, edited by N. Smrtitirtha, Sanskrit College, Calcutta, has been used here.

17	V. 1
18	VI. 1
19	VII. 1
20	VIII. 1
21	IX. 1 a, 2 a
22	X. 1
23	XI. 1
24	XII. 1
25	XIII. 1
26	XIV. 1
27	XV. 1
28	XV. 4
29	XVI. 1
30	XVII. 1

Note : The first two lines of 258.83 of the *Agnipurāṇa* are identical with I. 33 of the *Nāradasmṛti.*

Verses of the *Yājñavalkya-smṛti* (Vyavahārādhyāya) missing in the *Agnipurāṇa* (Vyavahāra Chapters)

Several verses or parts of some verses of the YS. are not found in the *Agnipurāṇa.* We state below the passages of the YS., according to the three well-known commentators, which do not occur in the Purāṇa.

Mitākṣarā	*Aparārka*	*Bālakrīḍā*
2	2	2
14	14	14
30	30	31
34	34	36
35	35	37
36 b	36 b	38 b
72 b	72 b	74 b
83 b	83 b	85 b
189	189	193
228	228	234
229	229	235
230	230	236
239	239	245
246-48	246-48	252-54
250	250	256
271 b	271 b	275 b
275	275	279
278	278	284
283 b	283 b	287 b
287	287	291
288	288	292
289 a	289 a	293 a
291 b	291 b	295 b
292	X	X
293-94	292-93	296-97
296 b	295 b	299 b

Mitākṣarā	*Aparārka*	*Bālakrīḍā*
298	297	301
299	298	302
300 b	299 b	303 b
301	300	304
302 b	301 b	305 b
305	304	308

Verses of the Agnipurāṇa (Vyavahāra Chapters) not occurring in the *Yājñavalkya-smṛti* (Vyavahārādhyāya)

Agnipurāṇa

Chapter	Verse	
253	56 b-57 a	
255	20	Occurs only in B.K.
	31	-Do-
	35	
	43 a	
258	45	Occurs in Mit. but, not in Ap. and B.K.
	83	

REFERENCES

We note below the important books and papers on the *Agnipurāṇa* Editions published by Vaṅgavāsī with Bengali translation, and by Ānandāsrama, Poona, 1900, Bibliotheca Indica, Calcutta, 1873-79, and by Veṅkaṭeśvara Press, V.E. 1977 (=1921 A.D.).

English translation by M.N. Dutt, Vols. I-II, Calcutta.

BOOKS ON AGNIPURĀṆA

De, S.K., *History of Sanskrit Poetics*, Calcutta, 1960, pp. 97-100.

Gyani, S.D., *Studies in the Agnipurāṇa*, Banaras, 1964.

Hazra, R.C., *Studies in the Puranic Records*, etc., Dacca, 1940, pp. 134 ff, *passim.*

Kane, P.V., *Hiṣtory of Dharmaśāstra*, I, pp. 160 ff.

Mishra, B.B., *Polity in the Agnipurāṇa*, Calcutta, 1965.

Sastri, H.P., *Cat. of Skt. Mss in Asiatic Society*, Calcutta, V., Preface, pp. cxlvii-cxlviii.

Wilson, H.H., *Essays*, Vol. I, pp. 89-90.

Verma, R., *Agnipurāṇa kā kāvyaśāstrīya bhāg* (in Hindī), Delhi, 1959.

PAPERS

De, S.K., *Poona Orientalist*, II, pp. 15-17.

Farquhar, J.N., *Outline* etc., p. 179.

Hazra, R.C., Our Present Agnipurāṇa, *Indian Historical Quarterly*, XII, 1936.

———The Genuine Āgneya-purāṇa alias Vahni, *Our Heritage*, I, 1958 (Part II), II, 1954.

———Discovery of the Genuine Āgneya-purāṇa, *Journal of the Oriental Institute*, Baroda, V, 1955-56.

Raghavan, V., *Indian Historical Quarterly*, X, 1934, p. 767 ff.

INDEX TO VERSES

of the Vyavahāra chapters (253-258)
of the *Agnipurāṇa*
(Pratikas of the first Lines are given)

Engendering the Divine Image

Engendering the Divine Image

Conversations with Dalit Women's Experience

Nelavala Gnana Prasuna

Christian World Imprints

First Published in 2020 by

Christian World Imprints
Christian Publishing & Books from India
C-3, Wazirpur Industrial Area
Delhi-110052
cwidelhi2017@gmail.com
www.ChristianWorldImprints.com
Phone: +91 11 41526079

ISBN: 978-93-5148-421-9

Printed in India.

Dedicated to my father-in-law

Dedicated to

Rev. J. John Sundaram

1940 - 2009

Dedicated to my beloved Dad Mr Nelavala Devasahayam

Contents

Foreword

This publication is a welcome resource in the theological genre of Dalit Theology and Feminism. Several Dalit theologians, scholars and activists have made their contributions to the body of Dalit Theology in the past four decades or so. All these works have their own independent value and distinction due to the fact that every single work and contribution analyses, reflects and articulates the special context, its challenges and hopes of the Dalit communities both inside and outside the Churches. Over the past few decades, I have had the opportunity to meet with some very interesting contemporaries, friends, scholars, other Dalits, about who we write about, and read some of these works. One such author is the Rev. Dr. Gnana Prasuna Nelavala, an ordained pastor of the South Andhra Lutheran Church and a Theologian currently teaches at the Gurukul Lutheran Theological College and Research Institute, the surrogate mother that gave birth to Dalit Theology both as an academic discipline and one for theological praxis. She is a first-generation ordained minister and academician in her family.

Prasuna Nelavala in this work deals with one of the most critical and controversial disciplines within Dalit Theology and Dalit Feminist Hermeneutics. Dalit women in the church, it is said, are 'thrice discriminated' by 'patriarchy, caste and religion'! Not only does she walk the path of understanding the language of Dalit Feminism, she also deals with the ambiguity of 'thinking and concepts' of Hermeneutics to help its readers to understand the ways of interpretation within the social, gender and complex ecclesiological facets. In this publication, she argues that both 'Dalit Theology and Feminist theology' have inaugurated a fresh impetus in transformative and liberative interpretations on Biblical texts and understanding, not only limited to academics but also opening the scope for social transformation of Dalit communities, more specially women. The author, through her argumentation passionately demands the need to provide intentional, positive and creative spaces for Dalit women to articulate and affirm their identities, and claim their visibility within the contexts of the 'missionary interventions and the conversion from Hinduism to Christianity.' Through the conversion process, she argues that 'Dalit women's identity has lost or broken, and that there is an urgent need to recover the lost identity'.

The author further analyses the processes of identity formation of Dalit women through the cascade of the caste system, patriarchy and social exclusion and juxtaposes this on the 'identity and the Imago Die in Dalit women.' She then attempts to 'depatriarchalize theology and liberate the Image of God from patriarchy and the prejudiced systems that keep women oppressed and discriminated. Drawing from several feminist thinkers, she further attempts to articulate tools of analysis to understand 'traditional theology and interpretations', read hermeneutical principles, based on scriptures proposing the 'Images of God' that reflects liberative and transformative Dalit Feminist Hermeneutics.

This publication approaches the challenges and controversies in Dalit Feminist Hermeneutics in an attractive and contemporary method and deals with the main issues in a fresh style and methodology. The author explores the potential of Dalit Women to become agents of change and hope. Her study provides concrete examples of the challenges, struggles, and hopes of Dalit Women in the SALC.

In many ways, this is a path breaking research that contributes to a gender, caste and social transformation of and within the church through a liberative, inclusive and a just Dalit Feminist Hermeneutics. This publication is her original Doctoral dissertation (adapted for publication), relevant to students of theology and teachers of Dalit Theology and Dalit Feminism.

Rev. Dr. Chandran Paul Martin, ELCA

Preface

The experience of the struggles, sufferings, aspirations and victories of Dalit women is the starting point in theologizing and constructing Dalit Feminist Hermeneutics in India. This work explores how the resources that are available among Dalit women in the South Andhra Lutheran Church contribute to the construction of a distinct Dalit Feminist Hermeneutics drawing strength from both the feminist and Dalit hermeneutics as engendered by the experiences of Dalit women.

This work traces the tremendous transformation that took place in the lives of Dalit women in South Andhra Lutheran Church. The reasons for this transformation are: Missionary intervention and their strategies in uplifting the Dalit community and the conversion of Dalits from Hinduism to Christianity. Certainly Dalit women have acquired new identities. However, the identity the out caste women received as "Christian" and "Dalit" is not a complete one. Although there is a transformation, they bear a false image for themselves as secondary citizens and as out castes. The research probed into this status of the Dalit women in South Andhra Lutheran Church.

The identity formation begins at home. The historical, socio-cultural and religious rules and norms play a significant role in the identity formation. In the life of Dalit women, the real identity as a human being created in the image of God and as a Christian resurrected to new life is lost in the Dalit women. The focus of the work is one way to recover Dalit women's identities and to formulate new images for them to live a life in fullness by using their experience as a primary resource.

The Work concludes with a reflection on the implications of this research both to those who are in the academy and those who are outside it. The research restates that those who are privileged in claiming new identities need to use their articulations and academic language to bring transformation and complete conversion among the faith community.

Acknowledgements

A large community contributed towards publication of my research work. Though it is not possible to thank each one, I can at least start.

My research was made possible by the Lutheran world Federation that funded my studies and United Evangelical Lutheran Churches in India (UELCI) for providing me number of opportunities to do a contextual research. I owe my special thanks to the Senate of Serampore College for granting me approval to publish my doctoral thesis. My student life in Gurukul Lutheran Theological College & Research Institute was deeply formative period. I owe particular thanks to my teachers, who taught me. My engagement with international, national and ecumenical conversation has also been massively influential in my theological research I must thank all those who I have had a privilege of conversing with. I thank my church the South Andhra Lutheran Church for endorsing me for theological education. I owe gratitude to the Rt. Rev. K. Chandra Sekhar who gave me permission to conduct survey for my thesis. I am thankful to the folk I did interviews with. I am obliged to Bishop Rt. Rev. O. Michael Benhur for his confidence in me and for his constant support and encouragement.

Another learning community for me was my students. The students, I have been privileged to teach and journey with at Indian Theological Seminary, Mennonite Brethren Centenary Bible College and Gurukul Lutheran Theological College & Research Institute have been the source of great theological stimulation. I am grateful for the support of wonderful colleagues in all these institutions who have supported my theological journey, especially Dr Gladson Jathanna for his contributions in bringing out this work.

There have been many other people who played significant role through the years that have led to this publication. I am grateful to my beloved guru and guide Sis. Dr. Pushpa Joseph for making it possible by offering valuable suggestions and insights. Particular thanks must go to Mr. Arun Kumar Wesley for his careful reading of the original dissertation and his penetrating questions and insights and his precious editorial comments which enhanced the quality of this work. I also thank Rev. Renee Coulson for her contributions in bringing out this work. I have great pleasure in acknowledging many other friends such as Mrs Vijaya Frederick who have been the source of inspiration and support over the years. Friends and mentors are special gifts, and I am blessed with plenty of them. Various friends have also served as precious conversation partners in making this work possible. Thanks for their love and friendship.

I am most grateful to another important and personal set of communities whose love has been incredible. Friends of Bethlehem Lutheran Church (IELC), Avadi, St Peter's Lutheran Church (IELC), Vellanoore, and St. Peters Lutheran Church (SALC), Satyavedu for their prayers and emotional support.

I am grateful to my sister Surekha, and brother-in-law John Vararpasad Rao who have been an immense support all through this work. I also thank my brothers Samuel Kumar and John Sukumar and sisters-in-law Rita and Daisy Baby for their support.

A very special note of thanks to Rev. Dr. John Samuel, Principal, Gurukul for his extreme encouragement, inspiration and support in making this possible. A special gratitude to the publishers Christian World Imprints for publishing this book. I greatly acknowledge Rev. Dr. Chandran Paul Martin, my mentor whom I always admire, for writing foreword to this book.

This would not be possible without the immense support of my husband and my dear friend Rev. J. Meega Maraivanan for standing beside me throughout my career. He has been my continuing inspiration and motivation to move forward in my theological career. I always acknowledge and value greatly the unfailing support, love, encouragement, and understanding of my beloved husband. I also thank my sweet children: Anurag and Dravid who have endured assertions very often of 'Amma is busy with her thesis!' with an understanding that goes beyond their age. I acknowledge greatly their sacrifice, understanding, assistance and all their emotional support in completing my doctoral studies and in publishing this work.

Most of all, I want to thank my parents, Ms. Bodipedda Devadanamma and Mr. Nelavala Devasahayam whose love and support have been incredible over the years, and who taught me most of all what it means to be a person. I dedicate this book to the memory of my father Nelavala Devasahayam. I remain deeply grateful to him for his boundless love and support to me. My father passed away a few months before as I was finishing this book. I also dedicate this book to my father-in-law, Rev. J. Johnsundaram who passed away 10 years ago. He is a man of vision, compassion and mission who made a great impact on 1000s of people.

1

Introduction
Journey Towards Dalit Feminist Hermeneutics

1.1. Introduction

This research is a study on the status and identity of Dalit women in South Andhra Lutheran Church (SALC) with the purpose of using their experiences as resources in developing Dalit feminist hermeneutics. The term status denotes the place that a person occupies and the dignity as well as the privileges that a person enjoys in society.[1] Status is a relative rank that an individual holds with rights, duties, and lifestyle, in a social hierarchy based upon honour or prestige. A status also can be assigned to individuals at birth without reference to any innate abilities as an ascribed status. Ascribed status is typically based on sex, age, race, family relationships, or birth. A status can also be achieved, requiring special qualities and gained through competition and individual effort. An achieved status is based on education, occupation, marital status, accomplishments, and other factors.[2] Thus status is one's own condition which consists of certain rights and duties and involves the role of a person as an important aspect in different areas of life and conditioned by one's own caste, birth, age, gender, class, colour, education, and occupation.[3]

Status is a relative concept that refers to a person's position or standing in society. In general, status has an evaluative element such as high status or low status.[4] People have more than one status in society and play multiple roles. Status of a person leads to a formation of one's identity. Identity in fact refers to who or what one is as a person. Status and identity are inseparable. In Indian culture, a name is more than a label that assists the other to refer to a person. It carries with it the identity of one's family and place of birth; in some parts of south India it also indicates one's community or caste. It indicates birthright, association, location, and caste of a person. In the Indian social hierarchy, caste identity leads either to power and privilege or to powerlessness and an unprivileged life. One's status determines one's identity.

In India, the status of a Dalit woman can be better understood in the words of Gail Omvedt, a feminist sociologist. Indian society is hierarchical social unit categorized by caste and patriarchy which have religious sanction, wherein one's status in life is marked by birth. She describes the Hindu caste system as a pyramid of earthenware pots set one top of another: Brahmins at the top, Kshatriyas, Vaisyas, Sudras and the untouchables at the bottom respectively. But, within each earthenware pots men are at the top and women of that caste are at the bottom. At the very bottom are Dalits and below are the Dalit women like crushed and wasted powder.[5] Dalit women's identity in India is prescribed and ascribed by the dominant traditions and cultures. In general, Dalit women's status is located in the context of a predetermined condition of caste in Indian society. Dalit feminists affirm that Dalit women are 'thrice oppressed,' and so they are 'Dalit of the Dalits, Oppressed of the Oppressed, Downtrodden among the Downtrodden, and backward among the backwards.'[6] They are oppressed due to their caste, gender and class. Untouchability, subordination, marginalization, disparities, exploitation, deprivation and discrimination are the common features of Dalit women.[7] However, educational policies and reservations have helped Dalit women to a certain extent to attain literacy and employment increasing thereby their status and identity in society.

Identity involves psychological, spiritual and material influences. The understanding of identity involves both identity at an individual level and identity at a group level. Identity on individual level involves distinctive characteristics such as personality, physical and intellectual trait; and identity on a group level involves social categories such as group-belonging, class, nationality and sex.[8]

Christian mission has brought about a change in the Indian social living by providing men and women of out castes and lower classes dignity, integrity and recognition. The basic affirmation of God's love which brought this change continues to work in India in various ways as theology – God-talk to work and seek opportunities for social welfare. Dalit theology and feminist theology in India have brought about tremendous transformation in Indian society by their contextual interpretations of the Bible. Dalit interpretation is not only limited to academics but also to social liberation of Dalits. However, both Dalit and feminist interpretations have remained largely as academic exercise to the majority in India. Most of the debates still take place at the theoretical level. This study seriously challenges the distance that exists between the academic world and the world of Dalit women, and attempts to bridge the gap.

For a Dalit feminist theologian, the contexts of academics and Dalit women are central in theologizing. The Dalit feminist theologian takes into account the Dalit communities of faith and their connection with the interpretation of the

Bible in theological articulations. In this case, V. Devasahayam, a Dalit theologian provides a theoretical framework. Like other liberationists, Devasahayam says:

> Theology is a reflection on human experience from the perspective of one's faith. Human life is the focus of theology. Theology is concerned not primarily with either the religious metaphysic or rituals, not even with soul after death but with human person as he/she lives in this world of theology, forgets human concerns and human experiences that theology stands discredited as irrelevant.[9]

As Devasahayam points out, theology is a dynamic and an ongoing business involving the lives of people. Thus, this study raises questions about the ways in which the biblical text is read, understood, and taught and interpreted in the dominant theologies as they are not involved much with human life situations. It confronts assumptions, belief systems and the doctrines of faith and the whole of Christian life from the perspective of a Dalit woman as bearing the image of God and as a human being. This study by taking both academics and the day-to-day lives of Dalit women as the basis for Dalit feminist hermeneutics, reconsiders the traditions, practices, scriptures and theologies within the framework of Dalit and feminist hermeneutics.

Dalit feminist scholarship in India is now making room to deal with the issues of gender, caste and class, as Dalit women suffer triple disadvantages of being women as belonging to lower caste and lower class. Monica Melanchthon, while discussing Dalit woman in her work 'Indian Dalit Women and the Bible: Hermeneutical and Methodological Reflections,' declares:

> As Dalit women emerge as an identifiable category, they are playing a very significant role within the Dalit movement, addressing issues of untouchability, identity, justice, etc. Despite this, people have tried to define the Dalit woman as the 'divisive force,' a tool being used to divide the Dalit movement and the women's movement, an 'imaginary category' with no real identity of her own. But, she is actually an 'emerging category' that needs to be recognized and given space, for the caste-class-gender combination affects her in ways very different from other women within the structures of Indian society.[10]

Melanchthon considers Dalit women as belonging to an 'imaginary category' and 'emerging category' in Indian society. She also mentions that people have tried to say that a Dalit woman has 'no real identity of her own.' The real identity of Dalit women as created in the 'Image of God' has been obscured by the oppressive sinful structures of caste system and patriarchy. The identity they have now and that which is imposed upon them is evolved out of purity-pollution syndrome as untouchable, polluted, dirty, etc. I argue along with Melanchthon that the real identity of the Dalit woman is lost in this network. It is broken into various pieces under the umbrella of caste, class and gender.

This research therefore asserts that the 'obscured identity' of Dalit women has to be given a face-lift and restored in the theological articulations not only at the academic level but also in the daily lives of Dalit women. Melanchthon further says that the Dalit readings are committed to the cause of justice, and the ultimate goal of Dalit readings is to instill in the community a stand to strive for liberation and new identity.[11] Repaired and restored identity is a liberated new identity. This research uses identity as a tool in analysing the status of Dalit women and strives for new identities for them.

1.2. Statement of the Problem

This is a work on the status and identity of Dalit women in the South Andhra Lutheran Church with the intention to develop Dalit feminist hermeneutics for the liberation of Dalit women, using their experiences as resources to bring out its implication for those who are in the academy and to those outside.

1.3. Elaboration of the Problem

Dalit and Feminist movements in India share a common concern and discuss the issues common to them, of oppression and liberation. But, both have failed in giving space to the experience of Dalit women which is different and distinct from their male and other female Indian counterparts.[12] Their oppression is complex due to their caste, class and gender. However, Dalit feminists share an explicit sense of identity with the essential articulations raised by both these movements. For the Dalit feminist movement, the self-definition and the location of Dalit women in society are of serious concern.[13] It is essential therefore for Dalit women to define their identity in the given context of their day-to-day experiences.

Dominant Dalit ideologies seem to be less perceptive of the cause of Dalit women. They seem to be comfortable with the existing social structure within the Dalit families. For example, M.C. Raj and others are pleased in projecting the equality of women and men in the Dalit communities while acknowledging the fact that even the patriarchal features have entered into Dalit families.[14] Raj says elsewhere that Dalit women are the home managers and they manage the finances at home. But, the question here is what finances? Dalit women are the managers of their survival. The management for survival multiplies their burden. For example, Kumari, one of the respondents shared that she has freedom to work outside the home and she has freedom to manage money but that is very meager she receives for her labor. She questions back, "how can I manage the family with this meager amount?" And she says, "there were times when we suffered even to provide milk for her infant." Therefore, the argument that women are the managers ignores the fact that 'family management' in the Dalit families is not an opportunity to exercise freedom, but an obligation which is sometimes forced upon them for their survival and that of their family members including the husband. Ideologically speaking, Dalit women suffer more disadvantages in the families, as Dalit family is patriarchal in nature as do their families.

Sangeetha (name is changed); a respondent tells her plight in the family. Sangeetha is an orphan woman brought up by her relatives. While she was doing her nursing she fell in love with a Lutheran Dalit Christian man. In the process, she became pregnant before marriage. The boy's parents who are illiterates but very sensitive to this issue organized the marriage. Now they are living in a joint family. Her husband could not find any job as he failed in his B.A. (Bachelor of Arts). She could not find job either since the village in which they are living has no hospital. So Sangeetha's husband began to work in his agricultural field as a laborer for others, against his parents' and his wife's wish. But, with his hard earned money he drinks arrack every day. He never gives money for the family expenses. Meanwhile they gave birth to three girl children. When the researcher asked her, "Why they did not go for family planning?" she answered, "My husband wanted a boy child to continue his family name." She added, "Even his parents are not able to control him. I can't leave him either, I have to suffer forever. I believed him and I came after him, I should live with him." And she said, "His cousins found job for me and my husband in a nearby shoe-making factory. After working for a few months with a new found occupation and salary he bought a bike on loan. One day, as he was riding the bike drunk heavily he met with an accident. Still there is no change in him." Sangeetha's story represents millions of Dalit women in India. A number of similar stories are found in the field research to authenticate the Dalit woman's plight.

While such pathetic Dalit women's living stories give us a clue to their status in their families, Kancha Ilaiah in his article 'Why I am Not a Hindu,' declares that Dalit family is more democratic![15] How is it possible to have democracy in the patriarchal structure? Can democracy and patriarchy go together as they are two different entities? If the purpose of democracy is to provide freedom and the purpose of patriarchy is bondage, how is it possible to call patriarchy democratic? Ilaiah, of course, notices the fact that there are oppressive practices like wife-battering in the Dalit families. However, he says 'the beaten up wife has a right to make the attack publicly by shouting, abusing the husband, and if possible by beating the husband in return.'[16] In reality, may be a few women might be beating their husbands back. However, it is observed that the Dalit woman yells back not because of 'democratic patriarchy' but because of the socio-economic situation she is in. However, the theological, ministerial, and pastoral concern is not to encourage beating each other but treating each other with dignity.

Feminists like Kalpana Kannabhiran assert that all communities' women are badly discriminated and so all women are Dalits. The struggles however of Dalit women are unique. For example, the low status based on caste impurity is not experienced by caste women. The impure caste identity destroys the image of Dalit women. Thus, the caste-gender dynamics is not correctly understood by both the Dalit movement and the Feminist movement in India.

At this stage, it is also equally important to recognize and acknowledge Dalit male theologians' attempt in re-articulating theology from the perspective of Dalit women. For example, Devasahayam is keen on developing a partnership of men and women in the Christian community, within the Dalit movement and in the theological task.[17] Maria Arul Raja's articulations are one of solidarity with Dalit women and their struggles.[18] However, the 'otherness' is obvious in their articulations.

Very few have recognized and appropriated into their articulations on the issues of gender, caste and class as they touch the lives of Dalit women in India who live outside the academy, living under triple disadvantages. Given the fact that the majority of Indian Dalits (particularly women), who listen to the Bible view it as a source of inspiration in their daily lives and not a document under scientific scrutiny. Therefore, a Dalit feminist theologian needs to be more responsible while reading and interpreting the biblical text. One needs to be vigilant, for as Melanchthon says:

> The Bible was shaped in a male-dominated world, councils of men determined the canon itself, and over the centuries, male theologians and scholars interpreted texts that were considered to subordinate women. It is therefore a difficult and complex task to reconsider those texts from the perspective of women and bring to the fore an interpretation that reveals God's concern for the whole humanity. Besides, it has been proven that the oppressed often internalize the ideals and values of the oppressor, and women are much more apt to do this because of their belief in scripture as the divine word. Hence, sometimes women are highly resistant to feminist interpretations.[19]

Melanchthon further states that creative imagination retells biblical stories in a new dimension from a feminist perspective. It reformulates biblical vision from the perspective of the discipleship of equals. Only then the Bible can become Holy Scripture for women.[20] The contexts that shape one's interpretation of the Bible are limitless and each offers a unique meaning for theological reflection. The Black women's community has discovered the body and bodily experiences as a means of worship. In creative imagination, when women share their experience, they come across similarities and differences which strengthen them to break their oppression. For Evangeline Anderson-Rajkumar for example, Dalit body is a subversive tool for theologizing. Anderson-Rajkumar says:

> Dalit theologizing therefore has to take the body of a Dalit seriously as the primary criteria for theologizing in the Indian context. The body of a Dalit has to be affirmed in to. When we turn a body inside out,

> we can realize the utter commonness of all human beings on earth, at par with each other – the organs functioning in the same way as it should – in all males and all females – regardless of whether it is a white or black body, or a Christian, or rich, or a tribal body. A Dalit body indeed functions as the hermeneutical principle to de-robe our theologies and ideologies of the layers of masks and markers that we don in order to sustain the difference.[21]

Dalit women's bodies need to be resurrected from their imposed identity as impure and polluted bodies. Rosangela Soares De Oliveira emphasizes the need for a hermeneutical approach when she says: "Telling story makes one aware of being a subject in history. From word to word, from tear to tear, from smile to smile, women are discovering themselves as resurrected bodies present in history."[22] This hermeneutical step helps us to fill in gaps, imagine new beginnings and new endings to biblical stories, and expand the personalities of women in the texts who often do not even have names.[23]

1.4. The Need for Dalit Feminist Hermeneutics

Feminist perspective has not been central to Dalit hermeneutics, even though it was sensitive to the issues of women. Similarly caste perspective has not been central to feminist hermeneutics and so was not sensitive to the issues of Dalit women. In such a scenario, where the sufferings and experience of Dalit women are not taken into consideration, an urgent need is felt in this study to develop Dalit feminist hermeneutics.

The experience of Dalit women is different and distinct from their male and other female Indian counter parts. The multifaceted oppression of Dalit women due to their caste, gender, class, and of being women from the third world need to be tested out. Hence, Christian Dalit women ought to seek justice from the scriptures placing their struggles at the center of biblical interpretation.

Contextual theology in the context of Dalit women is to converse with the realities of their own context in the light of their own faith-experience. Thus, hermeneutics becomes necessarily a discourse between the biblical text and the text of the day-to-day socio-political reality within the particular context of Dalit women. Therefore, the need is to formulate Dalit feminist hermeneutics to widen theological articulations from the perspective of the Dalit women in India.

1.5. Significance of the Research

This work is unique because this is the first study which is done concerning the status and identity of SALC women in order to understand them less superficially and so minister to their deepest needs more adequately. This study contributes towards the theology in action method of understanding, reflection, interpretation and articulation of Indian Christian Theology at large. It contributes methodologically to the wider feminist movement in India. The theological enterprise in this study takes both the academic circles and the grassroots in to serious consideration where the Bible becomes a major socio-religious context.

In this study, I presuppose two phases in the lives of Dalit women in SALC. The first one is that Dalit women are transformed at various levels and enjoy better status due to the entrance of missionaries and their reformative activities; the second is that violence against Dalit women continues to exist at various levels in spite of the transition and transformation.

As the Bible remains a significant social space of common ground between the biblical world and Dalit world (particularly the world of SALC Dalit women), the correlation between these two worlds is given paramount importance in this study.

The text, as well as the context, Devasahayam precisely states, is the site where the battle between the oppressed and the oppressor is played out. He says that theologizing within the framework of the Bible will facilitate understanding and acceptance of new ideas. Devasahayam further acknowledges the fact that the Indian Dalit families cherish and value the Bible very much.[24] For Dalit theologians (women and men), the context is the starting point for reading the Bible and doing theology. For doing theology and reading the Bible, hermeneutics is imperative.

People take part in the process of hermeneutics in their day-to-day lives. People read, listen and see various things in their daily lives and they do not leave them as they are. But they try to understand the meaning of those things, explain and discuss their understanding with others. Hermeneutics plays a significant role from the moment learning begins. Felix Wilfred goes further and states, "There is no area of human life and expression where hermeneutics is absent or does not play a significant role, whether people are aware of it or not. The interpretation is part and parcel of the society and it affects the society."[25]

Hence, the common aspect of Christian theological hermeneutics has to do not only with the doctrines and the Bible but also with the community we belong to and the communion we feel in and through the horizons of understanding. As the Bible is given the highest place in the life of Christians, it is highly essential to interpret it in a meaningful way according to the context. In the past in the Indian Church history, the Bible was misused and abused in various ways to justify exclusion, gender exploitation and other forms of oppression. Hence, inventing new ways of interpreting the scriptures is an urgent need in order to project the Bible as upholding the liberative spirit. Much work has been done in that vein but much more remains to be done on the part of Dalit theology. A sense of urgency is expressed in this dissertation in creating awareness among women to define their identity and to instill self-acceptance, as the image of God, and as equal with men, which eventually leads to developing Dalit feminist hermeneutics which is in spirit liberative and thus transformative.

Proceeding with the assumption that the role of the reader is of central importance in the process of interpretation, it is necessary at this point to state my own location and identity as the status of Dalit women is taken as text. I am a third generation Christian woman born into a middle class home which was rooted in Lutheran Christian faith, reared in a middle class socio-economic set up as my parents are teachers. Currently, I am married and I have two sons. Both my spouse's secular as well as theological education and my own allow us to lead a fairly middle-class lifestyle. My experience as a Dalit Christian Lutheran woman becomes imperative for doing theology. My experience as an insider of SALC becomes a tool and the norm for my research.

Conversion from Hinduism to Christianity is a key element in shifting women from lower class to middle class. My great grandparents were 'no people.' But a drastic shift from 'no people' to Christian Community took place with the conversion of my grandparents. Scholars give various reasons for the mass conversions from Hinduism to Christianity among the Dalit communities. Reasons may differ from person to person. It is important to acknowledge John C.B. Webster's observation; the dynamics of the mass conversions was the quest for dignity, and respect that Christianity offered to them. My grandmother (father's mother) did not give birth even after ten years of her marriage. While she was in crisis, some unknown evangelists visited their village and proclaimed the Gospel to her and affirmatively told her that if she believes in Christ, she will be blessed with a child. They prayed together and she believed in Christ. Later after a few months, she was surprised to know that she had conceived. She delivered her first born boy baby and she named him Devasahayam which means God's help, as she believed that Christ helped her. She then took baptism and became a Christian. Along with my grandmother, her entire family took baptism. My mother's parents were also converted to Christianity, seeing the miracle as my grandmother (mother's mother) is a sister of my father's father. The transformation began with the conversion of my grandparents. Since then a great change was observed in their lives and in their villages as well, as their children were put up in mission schools and were educated and acquired dignified positions.

Most of my childhood was spent in rural villages where the caste system was predominant. As there were no churches in villages our home would be turned into a church where my parents used to conduct Sunday worship services. We as children were nurtured in Christian faith. We used to have regular family prayers both in the morning and evening. Our parents taught us to have regular personal devotions too.

As my parents were teachers they rented houses in the main villages and we lived along with the caste people. We escaped the stigma of untouchability to a great extent as it was the customary attitude towards Dalit Christians. Christmas and birthday celebrations were used by us as great occasions to invite our neighbours those belonging to other religions and castes as well to share the gospel and also to dine with each other. At the same time, we were also invited by them to participate in their special ceremonial celebrations.

As my parents were government employees, we enjoyed relatively improved economic status. To give an example, when I was in the 8th class, my parents were working in a village called Dhamanellore which had schooling only up to Upper Primary level (7th Grade). Therefore, my parents found admission for me in a girls' hostel. The hostel being petty in basic facilities, I did not like the hostel, particularly the food served in that place. My father arranged for me to eat food in a small hotel which was close to the hostel that was run by a Brahmin lady. The bills were paid during the first week of every month. I was the only person who had that facility and enjoyed better socio-economic status among 25 girls because my parents were financially stable.

The early childhood metaphors of the experiences of faith, confrontation with caste system and improved status in socio-economic field have been significant to me in my self-comprehension and in articulating theology. These experiences have been fixed in my mind and contributed significantly in my identity formation and later have taken an academic shape due to my university and theological education as well. This is the current context out of which I write. I confess that the interpretative choices I make in the hermeneutical process that follow in the work are influenced by my own personal identities, identity of my faith community particularly women and by my ideological position.

1.6. Limitations

As SALC is a vast area to cover, I have chosen to do a field study only in 20 villages and 10 towns from Nellore and Chittore districts. 300 women at random have been interviewed to collect data. The experience of the struggles and strengths of Dalit women is the backdrop in formulating Dalit Feminist Theological Hermeneutics in this research work.

1.7. Hypotheses

The work presumes that social factors like education, employment, economic status, community life and religious factors such as conversion and the church life significantly influence women's status in SALC. Based on this, I have formulated the following hypotheses for empirical testing and validation:

1. The intervention of Christian Missionaries' and conversion from Hinduism to Christianity are the two key elements that created a shift in the status of Dalit women. However, gender discrimination is not completely eliminated in the church.
2. Education and employment played a major role in recovering the positive identity of SALC women.

1.8. Objectives

1. The major intention of this study is to investigate the rationale behind the shifting status of women in SALC.
2. To examine the levels of caste oppression and gender discrimination both in the church and society.
3. To delve into 'the identity of SALC women and the self-image' that they carry for themselves.

1.9. Aims

In simple terms, this study aims at three things: To critically and analytically assess the status of Dalit women in South Andhra Lutheran Church; to explore new possibilities of re-covering the lost and broken identities and re-imaging God to uphold Dalit woman's dignity as the image of God and thus create space in the theological academia for the voices of Dalit Feminist theologians. As it is clear from the arguments made already (that the theological scholarship cannot take place only within the halls of academy, particularly in the context of Dalit women), this work aims at bridging the gap between academics and the daily lives of Dalit women.

1.10. Use of the Term Feminism/Feminist

Feminism as a term has many connotations and definitions. It is often criticized and regarded generally as anti-cultural and anti-religious. It has been often blamed as a product of western colonialism. For many of the Second and Third World women, the term 'feminist' is associated with White European/American women. African and Latino feminists have suggested that the term 'feminism' should be displaced or replaced with a propagation of names and self-identifications according to specific context.[26]

Madhu Kishwar, the editor of 'Manushi' refuses to call herself a 'feminist.' Kishwar argues that the dominant 'isms' including feminism are inadequate in their expressions. She asserts that she never felt at a loss to work for the liberation of women even without identifying herself with feminism.[27] In contrast, Aruna Gnanadason an Indian feminist theologian says it would be unfair to brand western feminist theological efforts as inappropriate and irrelevant to Indian pluralistic context as it is frequently done.[28] Nevertheless, feminism is an academic development for re-imagining the position of women in patriarchal societies and religions. The term 'feminism' has been defined by various scholars in various ways,[29] and the definition of feminism changes in relation to the context of the experiences, realities, consciousness, and actions of individual women as well as a group. It is also conditioned by the way a feminist perceives the reality around in the light of the prevalent cultural, religious and economic situation.

Womanist theology is a reaction to male chauvinism in Black theology and racial prejudice in feminist theology. The term 'Womanist' was coined by Alice

Walker, and she defined womanist as committed to survival and wholeness of entire people, male and female. Womanist theologians contributed using their methodologies towards the theology of women in various ways to raise a voice against the oppression of women in all forms. When Black theologians articulated theology in terms of 'the black experience,' men's experience alone was included and the struggles of women were systematically excluded. The racial oppression which is unique to Black women was not included in the feminist theological articulations as well.[30] Hence, womanist theology emerged to discover theology in new ways from the perspective of their gender, race and class, while sustaining its connections with the Black theology and also with feminist theology.[31]

It is apparent by the articulations of womanist theologians that womanist theology not only gives attention to the gender perspective but also to the racial and class perspective. As a Dalit feminist, I find additional significance in the term womanist.

However, this research employs the term feminism with its prophetic and critical edge, while not undermining the significance of womanist concerns because of the similar struggle that I experience as a Dalit Christian Lutheran woman in India. In fact as Alice Walker points out 'womanism is to feminism as purple is to lavender.'[32]

Since the term 'feminist' stirs up reactions, emotions, and prejudices, it is essential for me to define my own position. I have my own identities as a woman, as a Dalit, as a Christian, as a Lutheran and as a theologian. I find the term feminism potential in taking up all these identities seriously in advocating equal rights. Feminism has paved the way for women to raise their voices. Western feminist liberation theologies have helped Indian women in their understanding and analysis of their experience. Therefore, I prefer to use the term feminist. I am arguing in this dissertation that the experiences of women both in their oppressed and liberated status are imperative in Dalit feminist hermeneutics that relate women with the academia.

1.11. Research Methodology

Research methodology refers to the techniques that a particular discipline uses to analyse data to acquire knowledge. Research methods are indispensable in the development of a discipline and the expansion of a field and its application. Such research can become scientific investigation only when scientific methods are applied.[33]

Scientific research is 'a systematic, controlled, empirical, critical investigation of natural phenomena, guided by theory and hypotheses about the assumed relations among such phenomena.'[34] Sebastian Periannan says:

> As an applied science, social research plays a vital role in social sciences. The distinctive schedule followed in social research begins with theory,

> runs through the phases of data collection and analysis and returns to theory.[35]

This work is both analytical and descriptive and inter-disciplinary in nature. Hence, it is socio-theological and hermeneutical. The methodology used attempts to gather fresh information through questionnaires, group discussions, and case histories. The effort is to arrive at a Dalit feminist framework, as a transforming movement to change power relations between women and men.

It is also descriptive and empirical relying on quantitative methods such as questionnaire and qualitative methods such as group discussions and interviews. The term empirical means 'observable' and it involves gathering fresh data to test statements. Descriptive method is different from other types of research methods, because the aim of descriptive method is not to determine causal relationships between variables.[36] Its aim is to describe the nature of a situation, as it exists at the time of the study, to explore the causes of particular phenomena.[37] Descriptive research method involves collection of data in order to test the hypotheses or to answer questions concerning the current status of the subject of the study.[38] Descriptive study determines and presents the way things are. Descriptive method is concerned with the existing social problem, its basic nature, and cause. The main objective of this method is to acquire knowledge. It also helps the researcher to keep in touch personally with the respondents. V. M. James says:

> Descriptive approach brings the researcher and the respondents face to face, and their cooperative efforts help to build up a better research study. Personal contact with the respondents enables the researcher to draw precise information from them and analyze the data in the light of his / her experience.[39]

Accuracy is given much importance in this method. In descriptive studies, the researcher is expected to have prior knowledge of the research problem. These studies do not confine themselves to any particular method, but apply any or all methods depending on the necessity.

1.11.1. Tools of Data Collection

The accidental sampling and survey method is used for the objective investigation of given phenomenon that is to find out the transition levels of women in SALC. I personally visited villages and towns and collected the required data. The interviews were conducted in Telugu the local language. The interviews and group discussions were recorded by means of taking notes and recording on the tape. While care was taken to translate as accurately as possible, I then transcribed and translated their responses into English. The data were later analyzed and interpreted.

Since SALC is scattered around Nellore, and Chittore districts in Andhra Pradesh and Chennai in Tamil Nadu, 20 villages and 10 towns from Nellore and

Chittore were chosen for investigation. It is assumed that the living conditions of the urban Dalit women are different from those of their rural counterparts. Therefore, in the research work both urban and rural Dalit women were chosen to assess the status. 300 women were interviewed from the above said areas. Selected respondents represented three generations having different educational standards. Both working and non-working women were included in the sample.

1.11.1.1. Accidental Sampling Method

Most of the researchers use a number of non-probability (or non-random) sampling techniques such as accidental sampling, quota sampling, purposive or known group sampling and snowball sampling, because these techniques are less complicated, less expensive, and can be carried out on 'the spur-of-moment' to take advantage of available and perhaps unanticipated respondents, without the statistical complexity of probability sample.[40] As such, for the present research work, the accidental sampling method has been chosen.

In the accidental sampling method, generally the sample is selected without applying the criteria of the proportion of sex, age, caste and other social stratifications. In the accidental sampling method, sample selection is almost readily available. In fact groups that are readily available are sampled. There is no attempt at randomization.[41] The merits of accidental sampling are as follows:-

i. It tends to be economical to gather samples.
ii. It is an appropriate method in situations where the field work has to be done quickly, perhaps in order to reduce memory errors.
iii. It is independent of the existence of sampling frames and may be the only practical method of sampling a population for which no suitable frame is available.[42]

However, like other samplings, accidental sampling also has its own demerits:

i. In this method there is no way to compute sampling biases.
ii. In this type of sampling, it is not possible to generalize.
iii. In this type of sampling, the investigator very often develops a tendency to select those respondents whom he or she knows.[43]

1.11.1.1.1. Methods of Data Collection

The field research was rather easy as I moved within most of the selected areas. I experienced a closer rapport with women than ever before during the research. Although total coverage of SALC is a welcome effort, time factor and resources at my disposal made it difficult to go in for a study of the entire Dalit women's community in SALC.

1.11.1.1.1.1. Questionnaires

Appointments were made with women for interviewing. Help from three local people was sought in distributing questionnaires. Questionnaires were prepared in which individuals responded on written forms and for illiterate respondents and the ones who could not read in English, local friends and the researcher read out the questions and translated them and recorded their response. The thrust of the questionnaire was to measure the actual situation of Dalit women. Since participatory interaction with the villagers was a conscious choice, the questions were unlimited for the interview. The effort was to let their voices be heard. The researcher personally met the respondents. The interview schedule intended to focus on the perception that the Dalit women have of themselves as Dalit women. The responses of the respondents were classified into 5 variables such as, general, economic, social, political and theological. 300 women were interviewed. The survey took 'Dalit Women' as an entity of analysis.

1.11.1.1.1.2. Personal Interviews

It was informed over phone to a few of them and appointments were made depending on the time and need. In the first meeting, the reason and the nature of the research were stated and questionnaires were distributed. Duration of one or two days was given so that the participants had time to think through. During the second meeting the researcher interviewed them. The researcher also met women's fellowship groups in various congregations, particularly on Sundays.

The participants were informed of their right to refuse to answer if they did not want to answer any question. They were assured of confidentiality. It was made clear that names would not be mentioned in the book if the respondents were not willing. Periodical visits and prior acquaintance helped to establish a good rapport and trust.

1.11.1.1.1.3. Focus Groups

A focus group interview is a structured group process with 10 to 15 participants. Groups were informed to come together in order to collect comprehensive information about a particular topic. In the focus groups, the interaction between me and the group, as well as the interaction between group members, helped to draw out information and insights. The dynamic interchange between the group members resulted in the generation of unbiased information concerning women's issues. The researcher also faced a potential weakness in the focus groups, when a few members did not express their personal opinions, and were conformed to a popular opinion or to a particular group member's opinion.

The focus group discussions aroused self-awareness among women who participated in the discussions. Their self-esteem was boosted up. Sometimes the meeting ended with heated discussions on issues like 'covering head,' 'women's ordination,' 'impurity based on menstruation,' 'silence of women according to

Paul's admonitions' etc. Group discussions also helped the group to understand the intensity of caste in the villages and particularly in rural schools. The group discussions helped us to understand the important role played by the teachers in the eradication of the caste differences and untouchability at least in schools and hostels. Women's meeting in the group demonstrated the level of their democratic functions in the church and society. The information on the topic, 'the image of God,' was collected as God's identity is reflected in God's image. Collected information was used in formulating Dalit feminist hermeneutical study of the image of God.

1.11.1.1.4. Narrations of Personal Stories

Story telling is important for many reasons. It is not just a telling of stories for the sake of story. It is a way of acknowledging the truth of the past, giving voice to one's experience and legitimating one's experience for the purpose of being able to face the horror of the past and be healed. It is principally telling a form of one's own story as a narrative of what led up to the present. The stories shared are apt examples of continued suffering and also serious resistance against the suffering. The stories provided space for dialogue with each other and for questioning the doctrines of faith and culture. These stories convey the message of oppression and torture in Christian homes to the larger community. At the same time, they convey the message to the dominant and particularly to the church to revise and to re-articulate her theological language. They also communicate that women need someone to share their experiences. These stories also reveal the hidden strength of resistance of women towards oppression of various kinds. The stories bear witness to the respondents' pain and tears of continued oppression that are found inherent in Christianity and church as well. Despite the struggles, women are resisting the oppression and discrimination. Their present stories are tomorrow's history. These stories will remain as tools of transformation. Selected stories are used in this dissertation to support the statements.

1.11.2. Data Used

1.11.2.1. Primary Data

In most of the cases the researcher herself personally interviewed the respondents and collected the data. In a few cases three of her friends helped to collect the data. In addition, respondents were mostly interviewed one by one, separately. Each interview lasted nearly 45 minutes to one hour. A few of them shared their personal stories during the time of interview, which were a process of healing and ventilation of emotions. This has been one of the most ambitious and comprehensive work of the researcher. Most of the contacted respondents co-operated well with the researcher in conducting this study.

1.11.2.2. Secondary Data

The secondary data needed for the study were collected from web sites, books, dailies and periodicals.

1.11.3. Analysis of the Data

Analysis of the data is important as it enables the researcher to tell the story of the people as the focus of research. The purpose of analysis is to summarize the conceptual observation in such a manner that yields answers to the research questions. Usual statistical methods such as tabulation, numerical calculation and percentage analysis are used during the analysis. Age, education, marital status, occupation, income, caste, social evils, religion, politics, health, patriarchy and theology are employed in the analysis of the data. Interpretations were made on the basis of the data and important findings.

Data for the study were both quantitative and qualitative. The research helped to draw conclusions from observations made during the interviews.

1.11.4. Limitations of the Empirical Research

Even though enough care was taken to obtain accurate data, there is a possibility for some respondents to hide the facts and give false information, especially on economic status, and habits of drinking, wife battering, and caste due to their indifference, suspicion, inhibitions, and lack of awareness of civic and academic investigations. A few of them, in spite of violence and subordination faced by them, wanted to protect their husbands and so did not reveal the facts.

1.11.5. Difficulties Faced by the Researcher

Apart from the above limitation, during the data collection, the researcher faced a few difficulties as below:-

1. Some respondents answered a few simple questions, and refused to answer questions related to economic status, polygamy, prostitution, etc.
2. A few from lower income levels expected some material benefits from the researcher.
3. A few expected immediate intervention in solving the problems. For example, in the areas where prostitution is rampant, respondents expressed fear and insecurity, and they were expecting the researcher to take some steps to remove prostitution from their area.

1.12. Theoretical Tools Used in the Research Work

A tool here refers to a conceptual framework to analyze certain realities. Different theoretical tools have been used by feminist scholars to analyze women's experience in the society to understand the status of women in a given context. Some of them include education, occupation/employment, income, financial independence, labour, sex ratio, marriage laws, health care, reproductive rights, cultural mobility and many more. In using the above tools, statistics are considered important information for research scholars to find the status of women in a given context.[44]

Anderson-Rajkumar while discussing the tools of analysis in her doctoral dissertation, quotes an Indian feminist scholar Bina Agarwal who uses poverty, discriminatory wages for women and men, increasing alienation from resources, decreasing employment opportunities for women (replacement by machine or man), homogenization of cultural values and practices brought about by modern media, rising consumerism and so on to study the gender inequalities in a given society.[45] This thesis uses 'identity' as a theoretical tool to analyze the status of Dalit women within the framework of feminist and Dalit hermeneutics.

1.13. Plan of Research

To accomplish the aims stated above, the work is presented in six chapters including introduction and conclusion. The introductory first chapter situates the study, indicates its point of departure and gives an overview of its relevance, importance, aims, scope and limitations of the study. This chapter also gives details about the research method followed in collecting data and the tools used in analyzing the collected data. It also discusses the theoretical tools used in the dissertation.

The second chapter presents the readers with a brief assessment of Indian Theological enterprise from a Dalit feminist perspective. Different theologies such as Missionary theology, early Indian Christian Theology, Dalit Theology and Feminist Theology are assessed in this chapter in order to show the readers the importance and the need for developing Dalit feminist hermeneutics.

The third chapter presents the Data and findings. Preliminary findings from the collected data provide an understanding of the current experience of both rural and urban women in SALC. It is found that there is a good percentage of transition in the lives of Dalit women in SALC. Two reasons were traced out for this transition: Missionary intervention and conversion from Hinduism to Christianity. Yet at the pragmatic level Dalit women maintain inferior and subordinate status in the family, church and society. They affirm that the Bible approves such a status for women. A person's family, socio-cultural, and religious factors play a significant role in formulating 'an image' for oneself. The basic theological issue emerged out of this chapter is 'Dalit women as the Image of God.'

Chapter four provides a theoretical framework for the context of overall analysis. This chapter begins with definitions and the nature of identity. Six selected approaches to identity such as historical, socio-cultural, post-modern, post-colonial, narrative and feminist are presented, while offering a brief critique of each approach from a Dalit feminist perspective. The focus of the chapter is

'Dalit feminist identity.' The chapter poses a few questions like "Can Identity be lost? If so, is there a possibility to recover that lost identity? What are the alternatives which lead to the process of recovering the lost identity?" On the whole, this chapter emphasizes the fact that Dalit women's identity is lost, and that there is an urgent need to recover the lost identity.

'Image of God and image of Dalit women' is an important issue raised in this chapter. The image often generates identities. Hence, by drawing on the work of several feminist and Dalit scholars, the final chapter has made an attempt to 'depatriarchalize' the patriarchal ideology in imaging God and Dalit women. By using the work of various Dalit theologians and feminist theologians, the chapter shows how a Dalit feminist theologian can deconstruct those patriarchal interpretations. The chapter revisited the image of God while depending heavily on the scriptural resources and has attempted to show how God can be imaged in various metaphors that are enhancing and empowering the image of Dalit women in recovering their identity as the image of God. This chapter proposes to do a theological exercise in revisiting the Image of God from the perspective of Dalit women using biblical and theological resources. Three images such as God as Life, God as Swathantra (freedom) and God as Shakti (Power) have been reclaimed.

The concluding sixth chapter provides a brief summary and then moves on towards the implications of this study. This chapter journeys from a broken identity of Dalit women to an achieved identity. This study concludes that Dalit women have acquired new identities in society by conversion from Hinduism. Although SALC women have acquired new identities in the field of economics, education and employment, it is observed that conversion from Hinduism to Christianity did not transform their secondary status in the family, church and society. This is mainly because converted Christians brought their caste along with them to new religion. Therefore, outcaste identity among Dalit Christians and superior caste identity among caste Christians remained with them. As a result caste conflicts continue in the church and society. Secondly, both Hinduism and Christianity and scriptures of both religions are predominantly patriarchal. Hence, Christianity reinforces patriarchal ideology. Therefore, this chapter stresses the fact that conversion from Hinduism among South Andhra Lutheran Christians is not a complete conversion but a partial one. In other words, what I mean here is, the conversion is not holistic. Both caste and patriarchy which are oppressive ideologies in nature play a dominant role in church and society and reinforce exclusion and impurity of Dalit women. Therefore, Dalit Christian women even after acquiring better status and identities suffer broken identities as impure, inferior and secondary. The chapter, hence, proposes a theological journey from broken identities towards an achieved identity which is holistic.

1.14. Conclusion

Dalit women who are in the lowest rung of the Indian society in spite of the progress and education are in need of empowerment and enlistment. The dehumanizing bondages of caste, class and gender have to be eliminated and their right to live with human dignity has to be restored in order for them to have their own identity. In this struggle for justice and liberation, Dalit women have to be concretized through constant participatory efforts.

The need of the hour is to expand the theological understanding and the practices that creatively engage our specific contextual realities in more decisively constructive ways. Adequate attention needs to be paid and addressed by the church in her theological discourses to promote basic education, employment opportunity, better working atmosphere, equal wages, etc., in the rural areas. Violence against women in any form has to be addressed more seriously by the church. As women become more conscious that Dalit women's rights are human rights, the church can become a human rights promoting agency, hence fulfil the Kingdom values. Social stigma on Dalit women often remains untouched by the church directly. Efforts are needed to eradicate caste and patriarchal ideologies within the church.

It is usually said that there is a gap between the academic world and the day-to-day life situations of people.[46] But, even the academic world relies on the contextual realties of the people for the theories. However, theories tend to be divorced from real life.[47] Thus, attempts are made to bridge the gap and make the academic work relevant and meaningful. The attempts in this venture have been that of feminist and Dalit theologians as they rely on the contextual realities of the oppressed and women in particular in their struggle for equality, dignity and status.

End Notes

1. Ila Mukharjee, *Social Status of North Indian Women* (Agra: Shivalal Agarwala & Company, 1972), iii.
2. Merriam-Webster, Online Dictionary, *www.merriam-webster.com/dictionary/status* (accessed on 2.8.2008).
3. N. G. Prasuna, *A Study of Feminist Hermeneutics and its Impact for the Liberation of Dalit Women,* M. Th. Thesis (Gurukul Lutheran Theological College & Research Institute, 1997), 9.
4. John C. B. Webster, et.al. ed., *From Role to Identity: Dalit Christian Women in Transition* (Delhi: ISPCK, 1997), 2.
5. Aruna Gnanadason, "Dalit Women: The Dalit of the Dalit" in *A Reader in Dalit Theology,* edited by Arvind P. Nirmal, and V. Devasahayam (Madras: Gurukul Lutheran Theological College and Research Institute, 1985), See Gail Omvedt, *Dalits and the Democratic Revolution: Dr. Ambedkar and the Dalit Movement in Colonial India* (New Delhi: Sage Publications India Pvt. Limited, 2004).
6. Harshard R. Trivedi, *Scheduled Caste Women: Studies in Exploitation* (Delhi: Concept Publishing Company, 1977), 1-2.

7. Leo Sequeira, "Human Response to Dalit Women Today" in *Dalit Women in India: Issues and Perspectives,* edited by P. G. Jogdand (New Delhi: Gyan Publishing House, 1995), 121; Neelam Gorhe, "Social Development and Dalit Women" in *Dalit Women in India: Issues and Perspectives,* 147; Kumud Paawade, "The Life of a Dalit Woman" in *Dalit Women in India: Issues and Perspectives,* 157.
8. J. C. Turner and H. Giles, *Intergroup Behaviour.* (Oxford: Blackwell, 1981), 49.
9. V. Devasahayam, "Doing Dalit Theology: Basic Assumptions" in *Frontiers of Dalit Theology,* edited by V. Devasahayam (Madras: Gurukul Summer Institute, 1996), 273.
10. Monica Melanchthon, "Indian Dalit Women and the Bible: Hermeneutical and Methodological Reflections" in *Gender, Religion and Diversity,* edited by Ursula King and Tina Beattie (London: Continuum, 2005), 216.
11. Monica Melanchthon, "Indian Dalit Women and the Bible," 216.
12. Nivedita Menon, "Nation, Identity, Citizenship: Feminist Critique in Contemporary India" in *Political Ideas in Modern India: Thematic Explorations*, edited by Vrajendra Raja Mehta, Thomas Pantham (New Delhi: Sage Publications, 2006), 358; Mamata Rajawat, et.al. ed., *Encyclopedia of Dalits in India*, Vol.1 (New Delhi: Anmol Publications, 2004), 187.
13. Nivedita Menon, "Nation, Identity, Citizenship," 221.
14. See M. C. Raj, *Dalitology: The Book of the Dalits* (Tumkur: Ambedkar Resource Centre/Rural Education for Development Society, 2001).
15. All Dalit women do not yell at their husbands. Kancha Ilaiah, "Why I am not a Hindu" in *Gender & Caste: Issues in Contemporary Indian Feminism,* edited by Anupama Rao (New Delhi: Kali for Women & Women Unlimited, 2003), 88.
16. Kancha Ilaiah, substantiates his argument, that *padapuja* (worshiping the foot of husband) that is peculiar to Hindu caste women are not observed among Dalit women. Similarly caste women refer to their husbands with respect, that which is not present in the Dalit communities. It is true, Dalit women do not perform pada pujas to their husband, and do not address their husbands like the caste women, and they do yell at their husbands and sometimes beat them. But does this mean equality and democracy? See Swathi Margaret, *http://www.sannaduttgu.com/INSIGHT/editorial_swathi_margaret,* (Accessed on 3rd June, 2005).
17. V. Devasahayam, "Dimensions of Dalit Dilemma" in *Prejudice: Issues in Third World Theologies,* edited by Andreas Nehring (Madras: Gurukul Summer Institute, 1996), 273-301.
18. I had an opportunity to sit in his classes; his interpretations are sensitive towards the struggles of Dalit women.
19. Monica Melanchthon, "Indian Dalit Women," 221.
20. Monica Melanchthon, "Indian Dalit Women," 221.
21. Evangeline Anderson-Rajkumar, "Dalit Body: A Subversive Tool for Theologizing in Context" in *God's Image,* Vol. 26, No. 3, (September 2007), 42.
22. Rosangela Soares De Oliveira, "Feminist Theology in Brazil" in *Women's Visions,* edited by Ofelia Ortega (Geneva: WCC Publications, 1995), 74-75.
23. V. Devasahayam, Introduction, *Frontiers of Dalit Theology;* V. Devasahayam, *Doing Dalit Theology in Biblical Key* (Chennai: ISPCK/Gurukul, 1997), 4; See V. Devasahayam's brilliant work on Bible studies, *Outside the Camp: Bible Studies in Dalit Perspective* (Chennai, Gurukul: 1992); Arvind P. Nirmal, *Heuristic Explorations* (Madras: The Christian Literature Society, 1990), 145-146.
24. Felix Wilfred, *Asian Dreams and Christian Hope: At the Dawn of the Millennium* (Delhi: ISPCK, 2000), 248.
25. See. Delores S. Williams, "Womanist Theology" in *Women's Visions,* edited by Ofelia Ortega (Geneva: WCC Publications, 1995), 112-126; Madhu Kishwar, "A Horror of 'Isms': Why I do not Call Myself a Feminist" in *Feminism in India,* edited by Chaudhuri Maitrayee (New Delhi, Women Unlimited: 2004), 26-51; Nalini Arles, "Pandita Ramabai: An Appraisal from

Feminist Perspective, in *Bangalore Theological Forum*, Vol. XXXI, No.1 (July, 1999): 64-86; Prasanna Kumari, "Introduction" in *A Reader in Feminist Theology,* edited by Prasanna Kumari (Madras: Gurukul, 1993), v; Elisabeth Schussler Fiorenza, "Foreword" in Gabriele Dietrich, *A New Thing on Earth.* (Delhi: ISPCK, 2001), x.

27. Madhu Kishwar, "A Horror of 'Isms': Why I do not Call Myself a Feminist" in *Feminism in India.* 26-51.
28. See Aruna Gnanadasan, "Feminist Theology: An Indian Perspective" in *Readings In Indian Christian Theology*, edited by R. S. Sugeertharajah & Cecil Hargreaves (Delhi: ISPCK, 1993), 60-61; Kamala Bhasin and Nighat Said Khan, "Some Questions on Feminism and Its Relevance in South Asia" in *Feminism in India*, 6.
29. Huge work has been done on the definitions on feminism. I cite here a few important definitions. Elizabeth Schussler Fiorenza says feminism as "women's liberation movement for social and ecclesial change." Elizabeth Schussler Fiorenza, "Emerging Issues in Feminist Biblical Interpretation" in *Christian Faith,* edited by Judith Weidmann (New York: Harper and Row, 1984), 37; Letty M. Russel, feminism "represents a search for liberation from all forms of dehumanization on the part of those who advocate full human personhood for all of every race, class, sex, sexual orientation, ability and age."; Letty M Russell, *Church in the Round: Feminist Interpretation of the church* (Louisville: Westminster/John Knox Press, 1993), 22; According to Ann Tolbert, feminism attempts "a critique of the oppressive structure of society and it is primarily a movement towards equality in which oppressed and oppressor are finally reconciled in a renewed humanity." Mary Ann Tolbert "Defining the Problem: The Bible and Feminist Hermeneutics" in *Semeia: an Experimental Journal for Biblical Criticism* (Chicago: Scholars Press, 1983), 115; Katherine D Sakenfeld defines feminism as "contemporary prophetic movement that announces judgment on the patriarchy of contemporary culture and calls for repentance and change." Katherin Doob Sakenfeld, "Feminist Uses of Biblical Material" in Letty M Russel, *Feminist Interpretation of the Bible,* edited by (Philadelphia: The Westminster's Press, 1985), 55; Devise L. Carmody declares feminism as "an advocacy of women's equality with men, sensitivity to the injustices women have suffered and the resolution that women came into their own without delay." Devise L Carmody, *Feminism and Christianity* (Abingdon: Nashville, 1982), 21. Thus feminism as a movement emerged from the women's understanding of their power toward transformation for equality for women against the patriarchal social order. Serene Jones, *Feminist Theory and Christian Theology: Cartographies of Grace* (Minneapolis: Fortress Press, 2000), 52.
30. Delores Williams critiques feminism for it meets the needs of white women. She asserts that white women involved in oppressing black women on the basis of race and that racial oppression is not addressed in feminism. See S. Y. Mitchem, *Introducing Womanist Theology* (Mary knoll: Orbis Books, 2002), 4; see Jacquelyn Grant, *White Woman's Christ and Black Woman's Jesus* (Atlanta: Scholars Press, 1989); Delores Williams, *Sisters in the Wilderness: The Challenge of Womanist God-Talk* (Maryknoll: Orbis Books, 1993).
31. Womanist theology remains faithful to the church traditions which gave them opportunities in life. Linda Thomas defines Womanist theology as: "critical reflection upon black women's place in the world that God has created; it takes seriously black women's experience as human beings who are made in the image of God; it affirms and critiques the positive and negative attributes of the church, the African American community, and the larger society." Linda Thomas, "Womanist Theology, Epistemology, And a New Anthropological Paradigm", *www.crosscurrents.org/thomas.htm.* (accessed on 13th September 2008). Womanist theology is known for its analysis of religion and society in light of the triple oppression of racism, sexism and classism that portrays the experience of many black women. Alice Walker and other womanists pointed out that black women experience is different and more intense kind of oppression from that of white women.

32. Alice Walker, in *Search of our Mothers' Gardens: Womanist Prose* (London, The Women's Press: 1984), xii.
33. P. Saravanavel, *Research Methodology* (Allahabad: Kitab Mahal Agencies, 2005), 31.
34. Fred Kerlinger, *Foundations of Behavioral Research*, (3rd Edition) (New York, Holt, Rinehart and Winston: 1986); Cited by S. Sebastian Periannan, *Social Research Methodology: An Introduction* (Chennai: Department of Christian Studies, University of Madras: Reprint 2010), 19.
35. S. Sebastian Periannan. *Social Research Methodology*, 71.
36. S. Sebastian Periannan. *Social Research Methodology*, 81.
37. S. Sebastian Periannan. *Social Research Methodology*, 81.
38. S. Sebastian Periannan. *Social Research Methodology*, 81.
39. James. V. M. "An Analysis of the Impact of Socio-Cultural factors on the Health of the Respondents of North Chennai" *M. Phil Thesis* (Unpublished) (Chennai, Annamalai University Archives: 2008).
40. S. Sebastian Periannan, *Social Research Methodology*, 138.
41. John C. Reinard, *Introduction to Communication Research* (Madison: WCB Brown & Benchmark Publishers, 1994), 226.
42. P. Saravanavel, *Research Methodology*, 202.
43. P. Saravanavel, *Research Methodology*, 202. 203.
44. See Evangeline Rajkumar, "The Image of God: in the light of women's experiences in an Indian perspective" *D. Th. Thesis* (Unpublished) (Bangalore, UTC Archives: 1999).
45. Bina Agarwal, ed., *Structures of Patriarchy* (New Delhi: Kali for Women, 1988), 103.
46. *dalitstudies.org.in/.../Report_on_the_Dalit_Women_Conference_Mar_2010.pdf* (accessed on 20.9.2010).
47. Bruce Nicholls, "Is the Kingdom Coming?" in *Third Way*. Vol. 4, No. 7, July-August (1980), 17. 16-31.

2

Theological Enterprise In India
A Dalit Feminist Assessment

2.1. Introduction

Untouchability against Dalits is widely spread and practiced in India in spite of the Indian Constitutional dictum that untouchability is a crime. Dalits are generally banned and segregated from full participation in Indian social life. They continue to be the victims of a cruel and oppressive socio-religious order. They were made to believe, that they were born as polluted beings and so untouchables. Fear, insecurity, inferiority, servility, hopelessness, and despair have enslaved millions of Dalits in India. They have been targets of frequent attacks of retribution and violence in the hands of the so called upper castes. Most of the atrocities against Dalits are caste based and committed by the dominant castes. Dalits are isolated in the villages. They are restricted to have access to public services, to own properties, to have good employment opportunities. They are abused at the hands of the police and upper-caste community members on a regular basis.[1]

"A marked feature of Hindu society is its legal sanction for an extreme expression of social stratification in which women and the lower castes have been subjected to humiliating conditions of existence."[2] The caste system which is peculiar to India is a longest surviving hierarchical system.[3] Manu has described a way of life for Dalits[4] which denied their right to property, education and even to negotiate for equal wages. In brief, Manu says, Dalits are impure products, they are impure and an intermixture of four varnas. They have to be treated like dogs, they are untouchables, should live beyond the burial ground. There should not be any interaction between Chandalas (out caste) and Brahmins, and food should be thrown to them and they should eat with crows and dogs. On December 27, 2006, Dr. Manmohan Singh openly acknowledged the parallel between the practice of "untouchability" and the crime of apartheid. Singh described "untouchability" as a "blot on humanity." He challenged the nation that "even after 60 years of constitutional and legal protection and state support, there is still discrimination against Dalits in many parts of our country."[5] He is the first sitting Prime Minister to make an open acknowledgment of caste discrimination in India. Despite this, Dalits continue to live in segregated settlements.

However taking hold of the Indian Constitution, Dalits have enjoyed certain privileges and access to new avenues. A lot has been done for the emancipation and empowerment of Dalits since Independence. However, Dalits are lagging behind in all areas of their life which need a careful attention. The caste stigma is far so difficult to remove from the Indian mind. The questionable part of Indian Christianity is that, even after baptism in the name of Christ, Indian Christians obviously practice Hindu caste system which has divided the Indian society. Baptism into Christianity could not bring much transformation in Indian Christianity. The caste system has strong caste roots in Indian Christianity which further create distinctions, divisions and segregations. As early Indian Christian theological articulations were Brahminical in nature and, they have not been of help to a majority of Christians who are Dalits in India. The identity of Dalits that is prescribed by Manu continues to damage the psyche and the life of Dalit Christians in particular and Dalits in general in India. The identity that is dismantled and broken by the caste system needs a recovery. As early Indian Christian theology was inadequate to deal with Dalit issues theologically, Dalit theology has emerged to recover the lost and broken identity. And again the identity of Dalit women faces triple disadvantages by being a woman, by being a Dalit and by belonging to a lower class. Dalit theology deems to address the caste issues, and has thus attacked Manu and his dictum but could not give much attention to gender discrimination that was dictated by Manu. Dalit women live under broken identities. The concern that is dealt in this entire work is, recovering the identities of Dalit women where lives are broken by patriarchal structures both in the church and society in India. The hypothesis of this chapter is that the church and the early Indian Christian theologies did not deal with the caste system adequately that oppressed millions of people. And also contextual Indian theologies such as feminist theology and Dalit theology did not give enough attention to the struggles of Dalit women. Hence, this chapter is an assessment of Indian Christian theology from the Dalit Feminist perspectives. Indian Christian theologies such as Missionary theology, Early Indian Christian theology, and Feminist theology and Dalit theology are analyzed from the Dalit feminist perspective.

2.2. Missionary Theology

Missionary theology has often been criticized by Dalit theologians for its inadequate approach for various reasons. Missionary theology is not holistic because it did not take into the account of the struggles of Dalits in its articulations, although mass conversions are from Dalit communities. On the other hand missionaries were working out a theology to make it relevant in Indian context by sanskritizing it in various forms. For example, Robert D Nobili, called himself as a European Brahmin and changed his eating habits, dressing pattern according to Brahmin religion, learnt Sanskrit and wrote many works in Sanskrit.[6] However, the approach of foreign missionaries to castes was not uniform. On the one hand, for those who were poor and untouchable, missionaries broke the boundaries of caste and embraced them, and on the other, for those who belonged to the caste, missionaries altered themselves to suit the style of the castes: they wore saffron clothes, read Vedas (Hindu scriptures), drew parallels between the Bible and Hindu scriptures, composed Christian songs in Sanskrit with Brahminical tunes and invited Hindu priests and *pandits* for inter-religious dialogues. Most of the missionaries who were scattered all over India from the 15th to the 20th centuries, worked on two issues: to promote the social development and to promote the gospel. R. S. Sugirtharajah explains the discrepancies in the missionary theology: "On one level, the missionaries projected the Bible as the new Moses, leading an Exodus from Caste-ridden Hinduism. But on another level, the missionaries were reluctant to press home the egalitarian potency of the gospel."[7] These two different missionary approaches existed simultaneously in the Indian caste context. Moreover, missionaries differed in their services, responsibilities, theological positions, and their intellectual and educational status as they were from different backgrounds and different countries. Added to that, their objectives were different which reflected their interpretations of theology. While some missionaries with a strong personal commitment were dedicated to the social development of the Dalits, others were committed to bringing the gospel in India by using Indian philosophical systems.[8] On the other hand, Samuel Jayakumar who did an extensive study on the missionary contribution says:

> ...despite failures and mistakes committed by missionaries, the social transformation of the Dalits was due to changes intentionally brought about by Christianity in the converts' physical surroundings, material wellbeing, and emotional condition by bringing about a climate of affection and loyalty. This they did by replacing the negative aspects of Dalits' lives, such as shallowness, lack of purpose or zeal, with positive Christian attributes such as deeper meaning in life, spirit of adventure and ambition. The change of the mental and spiritual climate in the attitudes or consciousness of the poor and the oppressed was an important contribution to their social mobility.[9]

Affirming what Jayakumar says one can note that in spite of their different approaches to different castes, the transformation of Dalits took place with the entrance of missionaries. The formation of South Andhra Lutheran Church in India was a result of missionaries' intervention. The whole system of transformation of Dalits came about through missionary activity when the Hermannsburg Missionary, Rev. August Mylius arrived in Andhra Pradesh and baptized the first converts in Sulurpet and established the first Church at Naidupet on 27th September 1865.[10] It has to be appreciated and noted that Father Mylius questioned the caste system. For example, while he was serving as a pastor at Naidupet, Venkatagiri Raja (king) sent communication to him saying that he would like to be baptized on one condition that Holy Communion should be given separately to him. Father Mylius bluntly rejected his request and declined to baptize him if he was not going to take part in the Holy Communion along with others.[11] While admitting the fact that missionary theology was inadequate in dealing with all the social evils particularly caste system, it needs to be commended for its tremendous work that brought incredible transformation among Dalit communities and particularly among Dalit women all over India. To give an example for the appreciation for missionary praxis oriented theology, Danamma an elder from Naidupet tells her story. She shares her experience of transition. She began sharing an experience that left hurt and humiliated feelings in her:

> We migrated from a nearby village six decades ago to Naidupet, a small town in Nellore District. I went to fetch water from the well that was near the Hindu temple. They did not allow me to draw water from the well. Caste women drew water with their utensils and poured into my container. One day I touched one high caste woman accidentally; she right away went home and washed herself, changed her clothes and came back. To such an extent untouchability was practiced during those days. But, now God brought a great change in our lives and in their lives as well. I share this with great joy, I am in my sixties now, I affirm with full volume, "Our Great God blessed us abundantly. Now we can look down at caste people, because we have better education, better employment, we have acquired properties. God brought us to the top positions from the least positions. We have a special identity as Christians now. We are proud to be Christians. All this happened due to women Missionaries who sacrificed their life for our sake and provided us education and thereby we have acquired dignity in this society.

Dalit women were transformed due to the advent of missionaries. However, the church and theology did not deal with the issue of caste theologically and therefore caste divisions and oppressions are visible in the Indian church. Dalit women are the most oppressed in the church. Dalit women's identity is considered impure by the society. Though they are not considered impure in the church, they are considered inferior and less than caste Christians. In the construction of Dalit feminist hermeneutics, the experiences of Dalit women, their sufferings, struggles, strengths, aspirations and hopes have to be given primary importance. Dalit feminist hermeneutics finds the transforming connections between the living stories of Dalit women with the biblical text, its context and its stories.[12]

Although, there is considerable transformation among Dalits and especially Dalit women, Missionary theology did not deal with the caste politics adequately.

2.3. Early Indian Christian Theology

Another milestone in the theological development in India is the birth of Indian Christian Theology. Early Indian Christian Theology needs to be viewed as the fruit of reflection born out of a crucial contextual theological research.[13] It is a result of the experiences and efforts made by the caste converts to help Indian Christianity to come out of the monopoly of Hellenistic, Latin, German and Anglo-American influences. The immediate context in which Indian Christian theology emerged was religious pluralism. The second context was that of socio-political struggles. It has to be noted that Christian mission and foreign imperialism came together and appeared to support and benefit mutually, while they were often in sharp disagreement with each other. In such a context, to a normal educated Hindu, Christian faith became a foreign faith of the oppressors. Hence, the majority of Hindus looked down upon Christianity as the religion of the pagans as it is even today. Nationalism was the unavoidable fruit of imperialism and it helped Indians to desire for self-rule than foreign rule. Christian missions evoked Hindu religious self-consciousness while colonialism provoked Indian political self-consciousness.

Arvind P. Nirmal says that Indian Christian theology is a serious theological research into the total body of the existing Christian theology rather than a separate movement.[14] He further says that, the new insights offered by Indian Christian theology have their immediate relevance for the Indian context and the new insights have contributed to the growth of total theological knowledge. He says for example, the contributions of Indian theological thinking on the question of religious pluralism cannot be ignored. It has to be recognized that these contributions are significant for the nature of Christian theology as a whole.[15]

Predominantly, Indian Christian Theology in the past has been an attempt to work out its theological system in terms of either Advaita Vedanta or Vishista Advaita. This was probably inevitable as the majority of the early Indian theologians were enlightened Hindus and were influenced by Western thought. Thus, their philosophical understanding was Hindu/Brahminical and Western religio-philosophical system. Their initial theological attempt was to reform both Hinduism and Indian society. It was an attempt to bridge the gap and maintain their being as both Christian and Indian simultaneously. The main concern was to communicate the gospel in thought patterns common to the Indian mind, and to balance Christianity with Hinduism. For example, Brahmabandab Upadyaya followed Jnana Marga, and finds Sankara's Advaita Vedanta as the suitable foundation for natural theology in India. A. J. Appasamy followed Bhakti Marga and he articulated theology on the lines of Ramanuja's Vishishta Advaitha Vedantha and M. M. Thomas followed Karma Marga.[16] To a certain extent, early Indian Christian Theology made the gospel relevant in the context of Indian nationalism, religio-cultural pluralism, and socio-economic development. It marked thus the inauguration of Indian biblical scholarship and creative theological formulations.

It is equally important to observe the fact as it is noted in the previous section that the approach of Missionaries to different castes was not uniform. On the one hand for those who were poor and untouchables, Missionaries broke the boundaries of caste and embraced them and on the other, for those who belonged to high caste, Missionaries altered themselves according to the life belonging to the castes, wore saffron clothes, read Vedas (Hindu scriptures), drew the parallels between the Bible and Hindu scriptures, composed Christian songs in Sanskrit with Brahminical tunes and invited Hindu priests and Pandits for inter religious dialogues. Nirmal thus calls early Indian Christian theology as 'Brahminic tradition.'[17] The chief attempt of Indian Christian Theology was to re-interpret the Gospel message and Jesus Christ through different concepts and symbols drawn from Hindu religious and cultural traditions. Early Indian Christian theology was predominantly caste oriented. For example, Brahmabandhab Upadhyay; a Bengali Brahmin, Nehemiah Goreh; a Marathi Brahmin, Narayana Vaman Tilak; Brahmin, Sadhu Sundar Singh: the twice born caste called Sikh, H A. Krishna Pillai; Vaishnavite non-Brahmin, A J Appasamy; Saivite, P Chenchaiah; a non-brahmin twice born caste and V Chekkarai; a Chetty non-brahmin.[17] Early Indian Christian Theology is uncritically Brahminical philosophical in its own scope in working out the indigenous theology. It thus attempted to re-evaluate and re-imagine Christianity in the religiously pluralistic cultural context of India.

However, Indian Christian theology which developed basically out of the backdrop and experience of caste Christians inherited the caste system. Caste system was not questioned as discriminatory or oppressive in their articulations; consequently, the caste system became a delicate reality in the Indian church. Early Indian Christianity never deemed caste system as contrary to the values of the Gospel and justice and so did not take into account the experiences, needs and issues of Dalit community.

Indian Christian theology is inadequate because its formulations were Western, classical Indian Christian and class-based. It failed to address the gospel in a holistic way. It failed to liberate Indian society from the social evils such as the caste system and patriarchy, thus did not attempt to contextualize theology in the context of Dalit community. Devasahayam states that Indian Christian theology failed in several ways: firstly, it has failed to relate the idea of God to the all-pervasive caste reality; secondly to explicate God as the reality that rescues us from every form of enslavement of oppression; thirdly to analyze major structures of oppression in the Indian context; fourthly to recognize the world of the most oppressed people in India, the Dalits; fifthly to discern the signs of the times and recognize the present moment as that which mediated the reality of God.[18] Thus, the dichotomy of theory and practice in Christian churches and the subsequent discrimination of Dalits have kindled the quest for Dalit identity in the church. The failure of the caste Christians to recognize the identity of Dalits in their theological formulations has occasioned for the emergence of Dalit theology.

2.4. Dalit Theology

Dalit theology sprouted because early Indian Christian theology failed to address the issues of Dalits in its articulations. As a result of the dichotomy of theory and practice in Christian churches and the subsequent discrimination of Dalits and the failure of the caste Christians to recognize the identity of Dalits in their theological formulations, Dalit theology emerged. For the last three decades Dalit Theology has been involved in determining a new theory of Indian Christian Theology. In search of the articulations of the real life experiences of Dalit Christians who comprise 250 million, Dalit theology has become an innovative dimension of Indian Christian Theology.[19] M. E. Prabhakar identifies diverse factors that contributed to the emergence of Dalit theology: Caste discrimination; Issues of the masses not addressed; Re-conversions of Christian Dalits to Islam during the first half of the 1980s particularly in Tamil Nadu as a protest against inequality and injustice in church and society; re-conversions of Christian Dalits to Hinduism under socio-political influences; the dual identity of Christian Dalits as Harijans and Christians to meet the economic and religious needs; the rising consciousness and increasing struggles of all Dalits against dehumanization and deprivation; uncontrollable atrocities against Dalits; formation of commissions on caste-issues by Church Councils at the national and or synod levels; the study-action programmes; and the formation of the Christian Dalit Liberation Movement as an all-India forum for promoting Dalit struggles against the caste system both within and outside the churches.[20] For the last three decades, Dalit theology has been involved in determining a new direction and theory for Indian Christian Theology. In search of the articulations of the real life experiences of Dalit Christians, Dalit theology has become an innovative dimension of Indian Christian Theology.[22] As this study works within the framework of Dalit hermeneutics, Dalit theological articulations are discussed throughout this chapter very often as well in other chapters. Hence, I move to the development of Indian feminist theology.

2.5. Feminist Theology in India

Another important dimension of Indian Christian theology is the birth of feminist theology. Indian feminist theology which emerged in 1970s gained its inspiration from the secular women's movement in India. Feminist theologians in India initiated a space for themselves in the theological disciplines and began to work out a methodology to read and understand the scriptures, theology, traditions, and culture afresh.

However, Indian feminist theologians have once again not adequately reflected upon caste-gender dynamics in their feminist positions as early feminist ideologies are once again caste ideologies. There are many reasons one can trace for its failure. Firstly, Indian Feminist Christian Theology has followed the pattern of secular feminist movement in India and the model of early Indian Christian theology. Secondly, early models of Indian feminist theology once again were caste models. It was so because Indian feminist theology was predominantly caste based; Where the struggles of Dalit women were not given adequate attention. Thirdly, much work has not been done from Protestant perspective and most of the theologians are Catholics and much connection could not be drawn. Fourthly, the experience of Indian women in general is basic in formulating feminist theology in India. Then again, one cannot ignore the articulations of feminist theologians in India from the perspective of Dalit women. Aruna acknowledges that "every struggle of women," particularly of women in the periphery of society – Dalit women, tribal women is a struggle for life.[23] Stella Baltzar in her article, "Hermeneutics of Subaltern Praxis: With Special reference to Dalit Women," says, hermeneutics in the context of Dalit women should be contextual.[24] Gabriele Dietrich, in her recent article, "Emerging Dalit Feminism," expresses her solidarity with the Dalit women and at the same time confesses that because of her own position as a privileged person she cannot internalize nor have a complete understanding of Dalit pathos.[25]

2.6. Feminist Hermeneutical Search of Identity

As I endeavor into the theological enterprise of Dalit feminist identity, I find feminist/womanist theological voices around the world as potential and relevant in my endeavour. They stress the fact that women suffer false identity due to injustice caused by patriarchy and emphasize on recovering the true identity by liberating themselves from patriarchy.[26] Women's experience and praxis are the foundational resources upon which feminist theology endeavours to reconstruct and create new forms resulting in their enhancement of dignity and creativity. The use of women's experience and practice indicate a new departure in the feminist theological journey in searching for new identities.[27] Phillis Trible's hermeneutics encompasses explication, understanding and application from past to present, subject to the experience of the reader; this process is always compelling and never ending. As the total process of understanding hermeneutics employs many adequate methodologies. For her, hermeneutical clue is "an issue and that issue is feminism as a critique of culture."[28]

Gayathri Chakravorty Spivak says that language is one of the many elements that allow us to make sense of things, of ourselves and others. She says, "I am thinking of course, gestures, pauses, but also of chance, of the sub-individual force-fields of being which click into place in different situations, swerve from the straight or true line of language in thought. "Making sense of ourselves is what produces identity."[29]

This study takes the experience of 'Dalit women: Dalit among the Dalits or downtrodden among the downtrodden,[30] as a basic foundation in its articulations. In the construction of Dalit feminist hermeneutics, the experiences of the Dalit women, their sufferings, struggles, strengths, aspirations and hopes are given primary importance in searching for alternative identities. Secondly, liberation of Dalit women is of serious concern. On the practical level, this research argues for the liberation of Dalit women at personal, social, political, psychological and spiritual levels. The imposed identities such as untouchable, inferior, subordinate, unclean, and weak, have broken the image of Dalit women. They have lost their identity as bearers of the image of God. Hence, this work proposes liberation for Dalit women that provide them dignity so that their self-image can be boosted up.

The dichotomy of theory and practice in Christian churches and the subsequent discrimination of Dalits have kindled the quest for Dalit identity in the church. Mohan Larbeer says:

> Dalit identity, as such, means developing the Dalit perspective, which means searching for a new identity, self-awareness, self-esteem and rejection of the stereotyped morals and values of the caste system. It gives us the consciousness, which implies a vision of the heritage of our fore parents. It is the beginning of a new search for our roots, to anchor us firmly to ourselves.[31]

Larbeer rightly points out that Dalit theology is a search for a new identity. The identity that has been imposed on Dalit women is a false identity. Identity is not something that is separate from experience. Identity predetermines experience.[32] The purpose of applying this tool is to answer questions such as: What are the attitudes and values of the self of Dalit women? What is Dalit woman's identity? How do external forces such as caste, class and patriarchy shape the identity of Dalit women? Human beings construct an image of themselves to maintain their identities.

Dalits were open to Christianity and colonial power. Conversion was seen as a means to secure a new identity which was a 'powerful and effective system.' Those who converted saw the Bible as the symbol of their new status and the guarantor of the benefits of their new mode of identity. "Conversion to Christianity (and Buddhism) implied liberation from the rigid and oppressive caste and communal structure of Hindu society. Christianity offered and affirmed human dignity and worth in the sight of God for the Dalit converts."[33] The Bible came to be used by the Dalits to assert different identities, corresponding to two distinct social and political contexts. In the context of colonialism, in which the Dalits converted to Christianity, acquiring a new social identity in the process helped them to adapt to the changed circumstances that colonialism had brought. The Bible was one of the key 'gifts' which the missionaries gave to indigenous people around the world in exchange for their obedience to the church and, in many situations, to the colonial power. At this stage the Bible was used as a tool of homogenization by the missionaries who supposed it to be the text of 'civilization.'[34]

Experience plays a key role in formulating Dalit hermeneutics as in other contextual hermeneutics. Dalit theologians find the interconnectedness between the experiences of Dalits and the experiences of the marginalized of the Bible. Jesurathnam affirms that "there are certain points of convergence in the matrixes of both the biblical and Dalit world." He states that "the biblical dictum of a preferential option for the poor and the Dalit struggle for equality are points of convergence.[35] Jesuratnam claims that the Dalit hermeneutical process leads to retelling the biblical texts several times to address Dalits or other marginalized people. Not only is the context of the Dalits vital to Dalit hermeneutics but also the connections between Dalits and the Bible. Dalit hermeneutics is a discovery of the connections between the biblical world and the world of Dalits more accurately.[36] As said above, Dalits are often kept as illiterates and biblical teaching has been used to exploit them. It is important to understand how the Bible plays a significant role in the lives of people. Maria Arul Raja proposes the re-telling of the biblical stories from the perspective of the Dalit community", as it will be an appropriate method to bring about transformation in the hearers.[37]

As Dalit experiences play a key role in formulating Dalit hermeneutics, Leonardo Boff articulates that hermeneutics has two eyes, 'one before and one behind.' With the eye behind, Dalit hermeneutics looks at past history and the people as the creators of history. With the 'eye before,' hermeneutics looks at the present realities. The two eyes are 'two horizons; horizons of the past and horizons of the present.'[38] Hence, in Dalit hermeneutics, the context of the text and the context of the reader are important components.[39] Fusion between these two horizons is essential to arrive at a meaningful interpretation. For Anderson-Rajkumar, the first and foremost imperative is that the Dalit hermeneutical methodology should challenge to de-link the historical experience of suffering of Dalits under the structures of caste system on the one hand, and to challenge the uncritical acceptance of caste stratification as normal / universal and unbreakable on the other.[40]

Dalit hermeneutics works towards the liberation of Dalits from the psychological, cultural and social oppression. It empowers Dalits to get organized in their struggle for freedom. A. P. Nirmal compares the Dalit struggle for liberation with that of the slaves in Egypt by identifying five important features of their struggle as mentioned in the Deuteronomic creed; the affirmation of one's roots, collective struggle, the experience of suffering and of liberation, and the vision of liberation and of restoration (Deut 26:5-12).[41] For Nirmal, theology begins with human life in totality rather than with God. The primary datum for doing theology is human life. He points out that Dalit hermeneutics is a collective struggle for liberation and restoration. It is community oriented. God in Dalit hermeneutics is an inclusive God. Devasahayam sees God as one who always takes the side of the oppressed and works for their liberation. In the process of reading the text, the Dalit reader notes how God acts on behalf of the oppressed; therefore, the message of the text is that God continues to do the same today.[42] For Amaladoss, the God of the Bible is a God of all, who opts 'preferentially' but not 'exclusively' for the poor. Moreover, in his opinion, Dalits will not be liberated unless the whole caste system as a hierarchical ordering of society is changed. Challenges to the system must come thus not only from Dalits, but also from others who are in solidarity with them.[43]

Dalit theologians declare over and over again that God's realm includes those who have been left out. God's image has been viewed as inclusive in Dalit theology. One has to note that the Bible takes the central place in Dalit theological discourse. In simple terms, Dalit theology is biblical. The Bible is seen as a source of power and comfort in moments of crisis, both personal and communal. It is not only a source for Dalit theology, but biblical study is also recognized as an important method for theologizing and reflection. The Bible is the potential basis that provides an identity and stability with the Christian tradition to the Dalits and therefore holds center stage.[44] However, Dalit hermeneutics in the context of Dalit community which includes both women and men needs to be handled with care as the patriarchal and racial oppression is pervasive in the Bible too. Along with Rosemary Radford Ruether this work contends that whatever promotes the dignity of a human being has to be taken as liberative and whatever negates the dignity of human being has to be regarded as not liberative. What kind of image Dalit women have about themselves? What kind of identities they maintain for themselves?

2.7. Dalit Feminist Hermeneutics: An Added Dimension to Indian Christian Theology

Dalit feminist hermeneutics is a creative adventure in which the interpreter enters into a dialogue with the text until it is appropriated in one's own context as to make it intelligible for oneself. In this process, the interpreter reads the text, understands it in the context of the reader. This formulates the potential fusion of connecting the horizon of the interpreter's context and the context of the text which will result in transformation.

Listening to the stories of Dalit women as accurately as possible is necessary in formulating Dalit feminist hermeneutics. Hence this work takes the experience of 'Dalit woman: the oppressed of the oppressed' as a basic foundation in its articulations. While reading from Dalit context Raja says:

> Dalit reading of the Bible is a transformative / pragmatic approach which focuses – not on the author / redactor and his/her intention

> nor on the deep structures of the external architecture of the text, but, on the flesh-and-blood persons of the Dalit community hearing / reading the text. This reading-experience is defined by the intimate conversation between the totality of the history, context, social relationships, horizon and world-view of the Dalitness and that of the biblical text.[45]

For Raja, the cultural context of the Dalit community is the norm in forming Dalit hermeneutics. However, Dalits are often kept as illiterates, and biblical teaching has been used to exploit them. It is important to understand that the Bible plays a very significant role in the lives of people; it speaks to people and exists as a living entity in the lives of the people. Hence as Raja proposes, the re-telling of the biblical stories from the perspective of Dalit community has to be done with much care in theological engagement.[46]

As Melanchthon rightly points out, for a community that was denied access to the scriptures, the Bible becomes the good news. It is something unique to Dalits. Dalit Christians found dignity and decorum, equality and equal opportunity, and a sense of worth and confidence in the 'presence' of the Bible.[47] In other words, the Bible helped them to recover their identity as the children of God. They find connections with the identity of the community of Israel who were liberated from their bondage in Egypt. In due course of time, the Bible replaced the world-view of the Hindu Scriptures and displaced the Hindu Vedas. The Bible became the Christian "Veda," filling that emptiness and supplying the Dalits with a framework for knowledge that they did not have to begin with, and which they desired.[48] Thus the Bible has been regarded as *Satya Veda Grandham* in Telugu and *Parisudda Vedagamam* in Tamil by Christians in general.

The English translation of the term hermeneutics is from *hermeneuein* the Greek word which means to interpret, explanation, exposition, expression, intelligible reading or even translation. Hermes was the Greek god responsible for transmuting what is beyond human understanding into a form that human intelligence can grasp. The Greeks related Hermes with the discovery of language, writing, and eloquence among other things. The traditional meaning of hermeneutics is principles of interpretation.[49] In the hermeneutical dialogue process, the reader's presuppositions, awareness, beliefs, knowledge, experiences of failures, success, dilemmas, competence, hopes, community expectations, desires etc., influence either consciously or subconsciously the construction of meaning and relevance of the text. However, in the hermeneutical process, a gap continues to exist between context/understanding of the reader and that of the author of the text. A dialogue between the reader's context and the author's as well leads to fusion of horizons of understanding between the reader and the text which brings transformation on the part of the reader. For Phillis Trible, hermeneutics encompasses explanation, understanding and application from past to present, subject to the experience of the reader; this hermeneutical process is always compelling and never ending.[50] Thus, Dalit feminist hermeneutics is the need of the hour to bring connections between the experiences of Dalit women and the text.

The following chapter of this thesis is set to present data on the experiences and the analysis of Dalit women in the South Andhra Lutheran Church. The third chapter provides resources to this work to develop Dalit feminist hermeneutics. The experiences of Dalit Christian Lutheran women are of various kinds. The stories of those experiences are both success-oriented and failure as well. However, those experiences are the main sources in constructing feminist theological hermeneutics.

2.8 Conclusion

Missionary theology, early Indian Christian theology, Indian feminist theology and Dalit theology and Tribal theology and other similar theologies arose in the context. However, early Indian Christian theology has to be regarded as a result of the experiences and efforts made by the caste converts to help Indian Christianity to come out of the monopoly of Hellenistic, Latin, German and Anglo-American influences. The immediate context in which Indian Christian theology emerged is the religious pluralism. The second context is that of socio-political struggles. It has to be noted that Christian mission and foreign imperialism came together and appeared to support and benefit mutually, while they were often in sharp disagreement with each other. In such a context, to a normal educated Hindu, Christian faith became a foreign faith of the oppressors. Hence, the majority of Hindus looked down upon Christianity as the religion of the pagans as it is even today. Nationalism is the unavoidable fruit of imperialism and it helped Indians to desire for self-rule than foreign rule. Christian missions evoked the Hindu religious self-consciousness. Colonialism provoked Indian political self-consciousness.[51] It is in such a context Indian Christian theology sprouted.

However, from then Indian Christian Theology and Indian theological hermeneutics grew in various arias. Indian Christian Theology grew towards Indian Christian Theologies such as Dalit Theology, Feminist Theology, Tribal Theology, Adivasi Theology, and Eco Theology and so on in order to make theology relevant to Indian contexts and communities. It is observed in this chapter that the theologies such as the early Indian Christian theology, feminist theology, and Dalit theology did not give adequate attention to the struggles and experiences of Dalit women. Hence, Dalit feminist theological hermeneutics is essential in order to empower Dalit women.

End Notes

1. *Johnson Thomaskutty,* India: "Hidden Apartheid of Discrimination" in *www.mapint.org/dalits,* (accessed on 2.10.2008); Human Rights Watch reports that in India 165 millions of Dalits are condemned to a lifetime abuse simply because of their caste, *www.hrw.org/english/docs/2007/02/13/india15303.htm,* (accessed on 5.10.2008); Hillery Mayell "India's Untouchables face Violence and Discrimination" For National Geographic News, 2003, news.nationalgeographic.com/news/2003/06/0602_030602_untouchables.html, (accessed on 10.10.2008) Andhra Pradesh "Discrimination Against Dalits Decried," *The Hindu,* Online Edition of India's National News Paper, Thursday, April 12, 2007, Goranga P. Chatopadhyaa, "The Dalits: A Fresh approach towards Interpreting their Experience of Reality" in R.M. Sankar Ed. 3; Surepally Sujatha, "The Status of Dalits," *International Humanist News, www.iheu.org/node/1813,* (accessed on 8.10.2008).
2. M. E. Prabhakar, "Caste-Class, Patriarchy and Doing Dalit Theology" in *Frontiers of Dalit Theology*, 79.
3. It is known as Chaturvarna Vyavastha which includes the four castes into the caste system such as Brahmins, Kshatriayas, Vishyas and Sudras. In this caste hierarchy, the three top varnas are "twice born castes" and Sudras and Dalits are subject to exploitation, discrimination, humiliation, deprivation and untouchability.
4. G. S. Ghurye, *Caste and Race in India* (Bombay: Popular Prakasham, 2005), 80; Sabhyasachi Bhattacharya, *Development of Modern Indian Thought and the Social Sciences,* (Oxford: Oxford University Press, 2008), 231; Richard W. Taylor, *Religion and Society: The First Twenty - Five Years 1952-1978,* (Bangalore: Christian Institute for Religion and Society, 1962), 49; A. Ramaiah, "The Dalit Issue: A Hindu Perspective" in *Frontiers of Dalit Hermeneutics.* 85. Oliver Mendelsohn & Marika Vicziany, *The Untouchables: Subordination, Poverty and the State in Modern India.* (Cambridge: Cambridge University Press, 1998), 6-7.
5. See for more details "Indian Leader Likens Caste System to Apartheid Regime" in www.guardian.co.uk/worl/2006/dec/28/india.mainsection, (accessed on 5.10.2008).
6. R. S. Sugirtharajah, *The Bible and the Third World: Pre-colonial, Colonial and Post-colonial Encounter* (Cambridge: Cambridge University Press, 2001), 231.
7. Cited by N. Surekha, "Liberation Beyond Borders: Dalit Feminist Hermeneutics and Four Gospel Women" Doctoral Dissertation (New Jersey: Drew University, 2008), 10.
8. N. Surekha, "Liberation Beyond Borders," 10.
9. Samuel Jayakumar, *Dalit Consciousness and Christian Conversion: Historical Resources for a Contemporary Debate* (Chennai: Mission Educational Books, 1999), 285.
10. For more details see, *Souvenir of the Centennial (1865-1965): Celebrated by the South Andhra Lutheran Church and Her Founding Missions at Tirupati, Chittor District Andhra Pradesh,* (Madras: Diocesan Press, 1966); See also *50 Years History of Hermannsberg Evangelical Lutheran Church Mission of South Andhra Lutheran Church from 1865-1915.*
11. Hugald Grafe, *The History of the Work of Hermannsburg Mission & Evangelical Lutheran Mission (ELM) for the South Andhra Lutheran Church* (Chennai: ICSA Books, 2010), 19.
12. Evangeline Anderson-Rajakumar, "Dalit Body: A Subversive Tool for Theologizing in Context" in *God's Image* Vol. 26 No. 3, Sep (2007), 40-43; Surekha Nelavala, "Smart Syrophoenician Woman: A Dalit Feminist Reading of Mark 7: 24-31" in *Expository Times*, Vol. 118 No. 2 Nov (2006) 64-69; M Kamala Raja Selvi, "The Dalit Women: the fourth class citizen" in *Frontiers of Dalit Theology.* 119.
13. Sunand Sumitra, *Christian Theologies from an Indian Perspective* (Bangalore: Theological Book Trust, 1995), 7 & 28.
14. Sunand Sumita, *Christian Theologies from an Indian Perspective* (Bangalore: Theological Book Trust, 1995), 7 & 28.

15. Arvind P. Nirmal, "Theological Research: Its Implications for the Natuare and Scope of the Theological Task in India" in *For the Sake of the Gospel,* Gnana Robinson Ed. (Madhurai: T. T. Publications, 1980), 81.
16. See. William A Dyrness and Veli-Matti Karakainnen Eds. *A Global Dictionary of Theology: A Resource for Worldwide Church* (Downers Grove: InterVarsity Press, 2008), 419-421; See also Robin Boyd, *Introduction to Indian Christian Theology.*
17. Arvind P. Nirmal, "Theological Research: Its Implications for the Nature and Scope of the Theological Task in India," 81.
18. James Massey, "Need of Dalit Theology" in *CTC Bulletin, www.cca.org.hk/resources/ctc/ctc01-04i.htm.* (accessed on 2.11 2008). See Robin Boyd, *Introduction to Indian Christian Theology*
19. V. Devasahayam, "Introduction" in *Frontiers of Dalit Theology.*
20. For other details cf. A. Maria Arul Raja, "A Dialogue Between Dalits and Bible: Certain Indicators for Interpretation." *Journal of Dharma* XXIV:l (1999), 41; cf. Jose Kananaikel, *Christians of Scheduled Caste Origin* (Delhi: Indian Social Institute, 1986), 1, K. Jesuratnam, "Towards a Liberative Dalit Hermeneutics: Re-reading the Psalms of Lement" in *http://www.religion-online.org.* (accessed on 15th February 2008); Dalit theologians has extensively written on the "Dalit Theology" and I mention here few significant works James Massey "Scheduled Caste: A Special Reference to Scheduled Caste Origin,"*Religion and Society* Vol. XXXXVIII, No.3 , (March, 1991), 30-38, See Abraham A.M. Ayrookuzhiel Ed. *The Dalit Desiyata: The Kerala Experience in Development and Class Struggle*, (New Delhi: ISPCK, 1990). James Massey Ed. *Indigenous People: Dalits-Dalits Issues in Today's Theological Debate,* (New Delhi: ISPCK, 1994); *Roots: A Concise History of Dalits*, (New Delhi: ISPCK, 1994); *Dalits in India: Religion as a Source of Bondage or Liberation with Special Reference to Christians* (New Delhi: Manohar, 1995); Xavier S. J. Irudayaraj, *Emerging Dalit Theology*, (Madras: Jesuit Theological Secretariat, 1990). V. Devasahayam Ed. *Frontiers of Dalit Theology*, (Chennai: Gurukul/ ISPCK, 1997), *Dalits and Women: Quest for Humanity.* (Chennai: Gurukul Summer Institute, 1992), James Massey, M. E. Prabhakar Ed. Towards Dalit Theology, (Delhi: CISRS/ISPCK, 1988), George Soares-Prabhu, "The Table Fellowship of Jesus: Its Significance for Dalit Christians in India Today", *Jeevadhara* XXII: 128 (1992), 140-159, M. Gnanavaram, "Dalit Theology and the Parable of the Good Samaritan." *JSNT50* (1993), 59-83; Dhyanchand Carr, "A Biblical Basis for Dalit Theology", in *Indigenous People*. 231-249.
21. M. E. Prabhakar, "The Search for a Dalit Theology" in *Indigenous People: Dalits, Issues in Today's Theological Debate,* James Massey Ed. (New Delhi: ISPCK, 1994), 202.
22. Dalit theologians have extensively written on the "Dalit Theology" and I mention here a few significant works: A. Maria Arul Raja, "A Dialogue Between Dalits and Bible: Certain Indicators for Interpretation" *Journal of Dharma,* XXIV: l (1999), 41; James Massey "Scheduled Caste: A Special Reference to Scheduled Caste Origin", *Religion and Society* Vol. XXXXVIII, No. 3, (March, 1991), 30-38; Abraham A. M. Ayrookuzhiel, ed., *The Dalit Desiyata: The Kerala Experience in Development and Class Struggle* (New Delhi: ISPCK, 1990); James Massey Ed. *Indigenous People: Dalits - Issues in Today's Theological Debate* (New Delhi: ISPCK, 1994); *Roots: A Concise History of Dalits* (New Delhi: ISPCK. 1994); *Dalits in India: Religion as a Source of Bondage or Liberation with Special Reference to Christians* (New Delhi: Manohar, 1995); Xavier S. J. Irudayaraj, *Emerging Dalit Theology* (Madras: Jesuit Theological Secretariat, 1990); V. Devasahayam, Ed., *Frontiers of Dalit Theology* (Chennai: Gurukul/ISPCK, 1997); *Dalits and Women: Quest for Humanity* (Chennai: Gurukul Summer Institute, 1992); James Massey & M. E. Prabhakar, Eds., Towards Dalit Theology (Delhi: CISRS/ISPCK, 1988); George Soares-Prabhu, "The Table Fellowship of Jesus: Its Significance for Dalit Christians in India Today", *Jeevadhara,* XXII: 128 (1992), 140-159; M. Gnanavaram, "Dalit Theology and the Parable of the Good Samaritan", *JSNT50* (1993), 59-83; Dhyanchand Carr, "A Biblical Basis for Dalit Theology", in *Indigenous People*, 231-249.

23. Aruna Gnanadasan, "Towards a Feminist Eco-theology for India" in *A Reader in Feminist Theology*, 96; "Women's Oppression: A Sinful Situation" in *With Passion and Compassion: Third World Women Doing Theology,* Virginia Fabella & Mercy Amba Oduyoye Eds. (Mary Knoll: Orbis, 1988), 69-76.
24. Stella Baltazar, "Hermeneutics of Subaltern Praxis: With Special Reference to Dalit Women" in *Frontiers in Dalit Hermeneutics.* 29.
25. See Gabriele Dietrich, "Emerging Dalit Feminism" *in God's Image* Vol. 26, No. 3 (September 2007).
26. *Feminist / Womanist theology is an ocean. It is impractical to cite all those works in this dissertation. Hence I cite important works of them.* Letty M Russell, *Church in the Round: Feminist Interpretation of the church* (Louisville: Westminster/Johnknox Press, 1993), 22; Katherin Doob Sakenfeld, "Feminist Uses of Biblical Material" in *Feminist Interpretation of the Bible,* edited by Letty M Russel, (Philadelphia: The Westminster's Press, 1985), 55; Elizabeth Schusller Fiorenza, *In Memory of Her: A Feminist Theological Reconstruction of Christian origins* (New York: Cross Road, 1983), 90; Susan Rakoczy IHM, in *Her Name: Women Doing Theology,* (Pietermaritzburg: Cluster Publications, 2004), 4; See Delores S. Williams, "Womanist Theology" in *Women's Visions;* Delores S. Williams, "Womanist Theology: Black Women's Voice," in edited by James H. Cone and Gayraud S. Wilmore, *Black Theology: A Documentary History,* Vol. II, 265-272; Linda Thomas, "Womanist Theology, Epistemology, And a New Anthropological Paradigm", *www.crosscurrents.org/thomas.htm.* (accessed on 13th September 2008); Alice Walker, *In Search of our Mothers' Gardens: Womanist Prose* (London: The Women's Press, 1984).
27. Letty M. Russell, "Authority and the Challenge of Feminist Interpretation," *Feminist Interpretation of the Bible.* 138-139, 137-146; See Sarojini Nadar, "Subverting gender and ethnic assumptions in biblical narrative: Exploring the narrative voice of Ruth" in *Journal of Contextual Theology*, 6 (2), 69-81; Sarojini Nadar, "A South African Indian Womanist Reading of the Character of Ruth" in *Other Ways of Reading: African Women and Bible,* edited by Musa W. Dube (Atlanta: Society of Biblical Literature/WCC Publications, 2001), 159-175; Philis Trible, *God and the Rhetoric of Sexuality* (Philadelphia: Fortress Press, 1978), 7-8 & 23.
28. See for further details, Letty M Russell, "Authority and the Challenge of Feminist Interpretation.,"
29. Gayathri Chakravorty Spivak, *Outside in the Teaching Machine* (New York: Routledge, 1993), 179.
30. Dalit scholars are aware of the fact that Dalit women are Dalits among Dalits. Few selected works are cited here. Sanjay Paswan and Paramanshi Jaideva Eds., *Encyclopedia of Dalits in India: Human Rights: Dimension in Dalit Problems* (Delhi: Kalpaz Publications, 2003), 261; Barbara R. Joshi, *Untouchables: Voices of the Dalit Liberation* (London: Zed Books, 1986), 86; Hans Ucko, the *People and the People of God: Minjung and Dalit Theology in Interaction* (Munster: LIT, 2002), 103.
31. See for more details, Mohan Larbeer, "Dalit Identity: A Theological Reflection" in *Frontiers of Dalit Theology.* 378.
32. Anne Patel-Grey, "Aboriginal Spirituality and Theology" in *Prejudice: Issues in Third World Theologies Ed* Andreas Nehring (Madras: Gurukul Summer Institute, 1996), 261.
33. J. Paul Rajasekar, "Lutheranism in Asia and the Indian Sub-continent" in *The Future of Lutheranism in a Global Context,* Arland Dean Jacobson and James Aageson Eds. (Augsburg: Augsburg Fortress, 2007), 74.
34. Sathinathan Clark, "Transforming Identities, De-textualizing Interpretation, and Re-modalizing Representation: Scriptures and Subaltern Subjectivity in India" in *Theorizing Scriptures; New Critical Orientations, to a Cultural Phenomenon,* Vincent L Wimush Ed. (New Jersey: Rutgers University Press, 2008), 98-100.

35. K. Jesurathnam "Towards a Dalit Liberative Hermeneutic: Re-reading the Psalms of Lament," in *Bangalore Theological Forum*, 34.1 (June 2002), 2-3.
36. K. Jesuratnam, "Towards a Dalit Liberative Hermeneutics: Re-reading the Psalms of Lament". *http:///www.religion-online.org/* (accessed on 10th March 2008).
37. K. Jesurathnam "Towards a Dalit Liberative Hermeneutic: Re-reading the Psalms of Lament," in *Bangalore Theological Forum*, 34.1 (June 2002), 2-3.
38. Leonardo Boff, *Faith on the Edge* (San Francisco: Harper & Row, 1989), 19; Cited by M. Gnanavaram, *"Some Reflections on Dalit Hermeneutics,"* in *Frontiers of Dalit Theology.* 329.
39. M. Gnanavaram, "Some Reflections on Dalit Hermeneutics," 329.
40. Evangeline Anderson-Rajkumar. *Skin, Body, Blood: Explorations for Dalit Hermeneutics. www.womenutc.com/07womenrsrcsindia_art04evangeline.htm - 29k,* (accessed on 5th September 2008).
41. Arvind P. Nirmal, "Towards a Christian Dalit Theology," in *A Reader in Dalit Theology,* Ed A. P. Nirmal (Chennai: Gurukul,) 65-69; *Heuristic Explorations* (Madras: The Christian Literature Society, 1990), 145-146.
42. See V. Devasahayam, "Introduction," in *Frontiers of Dalit Theology*; V. Devasahayam, *Doing Dalit Theology in Biblical Key*, 4.
43. Prem Kumar Shinde Ed. *Dalits and Human Rights: Dalits: Security and Rights Implications* (New Delhi: Isha Books) 2005), 105.
44. See Dhyanchand Carr, "Dalit Theology is Biblical and it makes the Gospel Relevant," in *A Reader in Dalit Theology*, 71-84.
45. "Reflections on a Dalit Reading of the Bible" and "New Exorcism and Dalit Assertion" in *Frontiers in Dalit Theology*, 336- 355.
46. Monica Jyotsna Melanchthon, "Dalit Readers of the Word: The Quest for Hermeneutics and Method" in *Frontiers in Dalit Hermeneutics*, Ed James Massey (Bangalore: BTESSC/SHATRI, 2005), 51.
47. Monica Jyotsna Melanchthon, "Dalit Readers of the Word: The Quest for Hermeneutics and Method" in *Frontiers in Dalit Hermeneutics*, 51.
48. Thomas Thangaraj, "The Bible as Veda: Biblical Hermeneutics in Tamil Christianity," in *Vernacular Hermeneutic,* R. S. Sugirtharajah Ed. (Sheffield: Sheffield Academic Press, 1999), 138-139.
49. G. Isaiah, "Homiletics" in *UBS Journal*, Vol. 2 No.1 (March 2004), 58; R. J. Coggins & J. L. Houlden Eds. *A Dictionary of Biblical Interpretation* (London: SCM Press, 1990), 282.
50. Phillis Trible, *God and the Rhetoric of Sexuality* (Philadelphia: Fortress Press, 1978), 7-8.
51. Phillis Trible, *God and the Rhetoric of Sexuality,* 7-8.

3

Presentation of Data and Findings of the Status and Identity of South Andhra Lutheran Church Women

3.1. Introduction

The second chapter is a Dalit feminist theological assessment of Indian theologies. The chapter assessed various Indian theologies such as Missionary theology, early Indian Christian theology, feminist theology and Dalit theology. The chapter has concluded that every theology is a contextual theology which arose in its own context. However, both Feminist theology and Dalit theology did not take the experiences of Dalit women seriously hence the chapter proposed that it is essential to do Dalit feminist hermeneutics in order to empower Dalit women. Having said that Dalit feminist hermeneutics is necessary to empower Dalit women, the research undertaken is an empirical research in order to arrive at conclusions.

This chapter situates the universe of the research and presents the summary of the research findings of Dalit women in South Andhra Lutheran Church. In essence, the study does not aim at problem-solving explanations of factors of change in the status of women in SALC as much as a descriptive study bound by its research design. But, the findings of the study as summarized in this chapter provide the clues for further research. Research findings from the collected data provide an understanding of the current experience of both rural and urban women in SALC with regard to their status and identity. Before discussing the status and identity of Dalit women in SALC, a brief historical sketch of SALC is provided as background.

The transformation of Dalits came about through missionary activity in the 19th century. Missionary intervention brought a substantial change in the lives of Dalit men and women in the state. The Telugu Christian community in Andhra Pradesh is an ethno-religious community who form the second largest religious minority. According to the Census of India, there are over a million Christians in Andhra Pradesh, consisting of 1.5 % of the state's population.[1] Although Christianity was in existence in Andhra Pradesh since ancient times, it is only after 1759 A.D. with the entrance of East India Company that Andhra Pradesh opened up to a Christian influence. The Rev. George Crann and Rev. Augustus Des Granges were the first Protestant missionaries sent by the London Missionary Society (LMS) to Andhra Pradesh in 1804. They set up their station at Vishakapatnam in 1805.[2] As early as 1805, they mastered Telugu and began translating the New Testament into Telugu. Ananda Rayara, one of the early Brahmin converts in India (who is said to have been in the court of Tipu Sultan, but had his roots in Andhra) assisted the early missionaries in the translation of the scriptures, and by 1809 the Gospels of Matthew and Luke were completed and in the next three years, the four Gospels were published in Telugu. After the death of George Crann in 1809, a new batch of missionaries, Revs. Lee, Gordon and Pritchett took over the good work done by the founding fathers and the first completed New Testament in Telugu was printed in Madras.[3] The American Baptist Mission and Godavari Delta Mission established their stations in 1836. They were followed by Church Missionary Society in 1841 and then American Lutheran Mission in 1842.

In Andhra Pradesh most Telugu Christians are Protestants belonging to major Indian Protestant denominations such as the Church of South India, the Andhra Evangelical Lutheran Church, the South Andhra Lutheran Church, the Samavesam of Telugu Baptist Church and several others. The Christian organizations in Andhra Pradesh run thousands of educational institutions and hospitals contributing significantly to the development of the state. Telugu Christians are found in all walks of life and have contributed much to the development of the state.[4]

3.2. Beginnings of SALC

John Christian Frederick Heyer, the first Lutheran missionary arrived in India in the year 1842. Then he went back to Pennsylvania to continue his studies and travelled back to India a second time in 1847. He spent a decade, mainly in the Guntur district of Andhra Pradesh, in southern India, where he ministered. He established a number of hospitals and a network of schools throughout the Guntur region. The Andhra Evangelical Lutheran Church was constituted in 1927 as a result of the Guntur Mission by John Christian Frederick Heyer of Pennsylvania Synod Society on July 31, 1842.[5]

Like many other churches in India SALC also came into existence through missionary intervention. Many Missionaries (47 male and 28 female) have done tremendous work towards the transformation of the community of Dalits in South Andhra Lutheran Church. They have established schools, hostels, orphanages, old age homes, hospitals, industrial schools and Bible training schools for men and women. Thus Dalit Christian women in the southern parts of Andhra Pradesh had access to education that paved their way for employment. The transformation activities concentrated on the upward mobility of Dalit Christians from lower class to middle class. Their status in education, employment, economy, and religion has improved. They have had thus the benefit of a better status when compared to Dalit women of other religions.

The Lutheran Mission work started by Father C. F. Heyer was continued by Hermannsburg Evangelical Lutheran Mission (HELM). Rev. August Mylius arrived in Andhra Pradesh in 1867. He began his work in Sullurpet living in the Travellers Bungalow. A man by name Rangayya was the first person to be baptized along with his two children. The baptismal name given to Rangayya was Johannes, and children were named as Jesudasen and Gabriel. His wife Maria was a Roman Catholic even before her marriage with Rangayya. (He was in a love relationship with Maria, and their relationship was set right according to Christian principles with the marriage. After his marriage he was baptized). Rangayya became the first Indian mission catechist.[6] By buying a house for 100 rupees, Mylius established a permanent residence and founded the first Church at Sullurpet in 1866.[7] Thus the South Andhra Lutheran Church has a history of 145 years.[8] The South Andhra Lutheran Church was under the Hermannsburg Evangelical Lutheran Mission from 1865 to 1914, from 1920-1929 under the Ohio Evangelical Lutheran Mission and from 1930-1941 under the American Lutheran Church. Only after Indian Independence in 1947, the Church came to be known as the South Andhra Lutheran Church.[9] At present, the Church has 44 parishes, five secondary schools, five boarding homes and hostels, a couple of technical schools and institutes and a hospital. In 1909, the Church had 3200 baptized members, in 1965 its numbers increased to 16,000, and in 2009, its membership increased to 33,863.[10] Thus the Telugu-speaking South Andhra Lutheran Church came into existence. SALC is located in Nellore, Chittore and Cuddapah districts of Andhra Pradesh and Chennai in Tamil Nadu.

3.3. Findings from the Field Research

To find out the transition levels of women in SALC, the sampling and survey method was used to reach the objective investigation of the given phenomenon. I personally visited villages and towns and collected the required data. The interviews were conducted in Telugu the local language. The interviews and group discussions were recorded by means of taking notes and recording on tape. While care was taken to translate the notes as accurately as possible, the same was transcribed and translated into English. The data was later analyzed and interpreted.

The research was undertaken in three districts – Chittoore, Nellore and Cuddapah. The twenty villages and ten towns of the districts chosen were, Sullurpet, Naidupet, Rapur, Gudur, Puttur, Venkatagiri, Kota, Sri Kalahasthi, Tirupathi, Nellore, Renigunta, Doravarisatram, Tada, Thogaramudi, Mutchalgunta, Rosanoor, Krishna Samudram, Bucchinayudu Kandriga, Anepudi,

Poolathota, Nellore Palli, Kammarpalem, Kallur, Pellakuru, Pindipalem, Ojili, Yerpedu, Mannarpolur, Dakkili, Satyavedu and Thummur.

It was assumed in the study that the living conditions of the urban Dalit women were different from those of their rural counterparts. Therefore, in the study both urban and rural Dalit women were chosen to assess the status. The selected respondents represented three generations having different educational standards. Both working and non-working women were included in the sample.

As the status as a noun refers to the position of an individual in relation to another, especially with regard to social or professional standing.[11] In modern times, the concept of status has been broadened to encompass all culturally prescribed rights and duties inherent in social positions, whatever their origin. Some of the criteria by which status is judged are leadership, dominance, ability, accomplishment, occupation or other means of recognition[12] designated by title, degree, membership, dress, behaviour or other devices of securing attention. For David Popenoe, 'status is a position in the social structure of an organized group or society.'[13] Status of a person leads to the formation of one's identity and it refers to who or what one is as a person. Status and identity are inseparable; one's status determines one's identity. In general, status has an evaluative element such as high or low status. "Age, sex, birth, genealogy, and other biological and constitutional characteristics are the very common basis of status. Nevertheless status is a phenomenon, not of the intrinsic characteristics of man, but of social organization."[14] People who have a high status will have better identity and the ones with low status develop poor identity. As elaborately discussed in Chapter I, Dalit women in India generally assume and presume low status for themselves. In most cases, Dalit women in India with the internalized low status have a poor self-image and identity due to their caste and gender.

Identity in Indian circles has a peculiar connotation as name, place of birth etc., identifying one's caste. So, 'Who are you'? 'What is your full name?' are serious identity-related questions in the present day Indian scenario. Indians everywhere are generally curious to find out the caste of another person. As experience plays a key-role in this work, I bring out one of my experiences related to caste here.

The Gurukul Lutheran Theological College gave me an opportunity to have my internship in South Africa. I stayed from August to October, 2008 in South Africa. I met many South African Indians and spent most of the weekends with them. I had a very good time with many people there. But often, I was challenged by the identity question. Some of them asked me to display 'my full name.' It did not strike me for some time; since I was informed that a typical caste system is not practised among South African Indians. One person embarrassed me by asking and asked me, whether my name contains names like 'Naidoo' or 'Naidu' or any other family names. Although they do not practice a typical caste system, they were only curious to know who I was. However, it was only an innocent curious probe. Despite this, I was treated like one among their family members. The question here is, 'the question of identity' which carries humiliating emotional situations.

Both caste and gender identities play a key role in shaping the status of women in India. Although SALC women are not any different, it is assumed that a considerable transition took place among SALC women. This transition may be due to various factors such as missionaries' intervention in the 19th century and new developments such as urbanization, industrialization, modernization and globalization. These factors have added density to the values and norms relating to the status and identity among women and men of Dalit communities in SALC.

But, this study does not claim universality as it applies accidental sampling method for its analysis of the status and identity of Dalit women in SALC. The significant message of the survey is that Christianity has brought a new status and a new identity to SALC women. However, it is indispensable in this work to take into account of in-depth understanding of the facts which would enable us to understand the shift in the status dynamics of Dalit Christian women. The status and identity of Dalit women comprises the subject matter of the present study in this chapter. It is proposed to analyze the changes observed in the status of Dalit women in SALC with respect to educational, employment, social, and religio-cultural backgrounds. An attempt in this chapter is made toward identity of SALC women; and it is a 're-description' in nature; it becomes a process of de-constructing any given ideological framework in the hermeneutics of suspicion to the prevalent elements that deny, dehumanize and destroy the identity of women.

3.3.1. General Information

There is a wide range of difference in age spread in the total number of 300 sample respondents. They range in age from 21 to 70; most women are married and live with their husbands and have an average of 3.7 children. Only five women in our study did not live with their spouses, 3 of them are divorced, 2 of them are separated and 18 are widowed and 7 of them are unmarried. Regarding personal belongings, 70 percent of the respondents own vehicles, 36 percent have land ownership and 80 percent of them live in their own houses.

The analysis of the income level of the respondents shows that it ranges from a minimum Rs. 2000 to 27,000 (74/100). The average income level of the respondents is Rs. 13,555 per month.

3.3.2. Educational Status

Access to education brings changes in the cognitive ability of a person. Education is essential for women in creating a critical outlook to think, questions, to reflect on and to act on. It is education that gives access to knowledge and information and to new ideas to facilitate women to empower themselves. As per the educational survey by the Government of India in 2001, 52.9 per cent boys and 56.9 per cent girls dropout at Upper Primary Level.[15] Official figures report that approximately seven million children are out of school in India. In spite of the reservation policies and programmes of Government of India, Dalit women lag behind others. Compulsory elementary education still remains a distant dream for many Dalit girl children in India.[16]

But, in contrast to the above discussion, the survey in SALC reveals that there is a substantial transition in the educational status of women. It is found that the literacy level of the women is 97.40 percent. Christianity was introduced in Andhra Pradesh as the religion of liberation to Dalit women in many aspects. Christian missionaries established schools in Andhra Pradesh in general and provided education to Dalits in particular. Roman Catholic Church, Canadian Baptist Mission, American Lutheran Evangelical Mission, Church Missionary Society and the London Missionary Society were a few of these who started schools. The American Baptist Mission succeeded in establishing a boarding school for girls at Nellore in Andhra in 1841. Late in 1848, the Free Church of Scotland Mission established a school for Dalits. During 1860s, the Lutheran Mission opened a school at Gudur, particularly for girls particularly. Since then a great change took place in the educational status of women in SALC.

The educational data of the respondents reveal that except for 5 women who are above the age of 65 who are illiterate, and rest of them had access to education. 10 respondents are retired teachers, 10 women have an average education level of primary school and 25 women are above 10th class up to post graduation. The field research proves that 100 per cent literacy has been achieved among the third generation Christians as against the status of Dalit women in other parts of India. It is found in the field survey that the women above age 65 who belong to the first generation of Christians in the villages are illiterate and continue to live as labourers. But, they are conscious of their grand children's education and very determined to educate their children. The survey revealed that urban women who belong to the second generation are mostly teachers who were educated in the missionary schools.

As found in the field research, all the children go to school. The women who had primary education still work as agricultural labourers. They responded that their children should not suffer like them and they must live better. So they need to study. When respondents were asked how far they are prepared to educate their children, their instant response was, if assistance is given to them, all the respondents were prepared to educate their children and grandchildren to their desired level.

Considerable transformation is observed in the lives of the second generation urban women in SALC due to their education. The third generation women are entering university studies and getting into different fields of education. Respondents opted that education and standard employment is essential for girls to have a better status in society. Education is considered both an end and a means to the empowerment of women by the respondents.

All the teachers responded that the education is the only tool, which can uproot inequality in the villages due to caste system and patriarchy. Education is the foundation stone for all-round development of an individual. It is also the strongest means of strengthening the capabilities of women in particular. It is observed that education among SALC women has certainly brought a considerable change that has led them to acquire a middle class status which gave them the acquired identity.

3.3.3. Status in Employment

Education leads to employment, employment in turn helps a person to have a better status and identity. Employment certainly holds the key to improvement of status and it determines the levels of food availability, nutrition and the level of the other basic essential demands. It also determines the structure of the house-hold and the relationships within the family.[17] The privileges credited to employed life were not equitable to the Dalit women in Indian society. The untouchables being on the lowest rung of the social ladder were denied entry in secured occupations which yielded regular income.[18] That means the position which caste occupies in the hierarchy is largely governed by the nature of occupation which that caste follows in societ.[19] Scavenging, sweeping, cleaning etc., are considered as unclean occupations, because they are commonly associated with certain stigmas such as disagreeability, unseeability and untouchability.[20]

About 90% of the illiterate women in rural areas are cultivators or agricultural labourers. Dalit women work in agriculture as labourers, casuals and bonded labourers. Census 2001 reveals that 42.95 percent of the rural female population was working as agricultural labourers. National Commission for Enterprises in the Unorganized Sector (NCEUS, August 2007) report observes that 46.7% SCs and STs and 33.9% are from other castes. The NCEUS report also observes that "working as agricultural labourers seemed to be the last resort, given its low social status, low earnings, irregular employment often reinforced by social oppression in the event of assertion of rights or dignity." The National Sample Survey (NSS) 2004-05 and 1999-2000, the percentage of rural women (regular) workers in the total workforce was 3.7, while that of SCs / STs was 3.1 percent.[21] Around 13 million children under the age of 14 work as child labourers.[22]

On the contrary, the observation in SALC reveals a significant breakthrough in the employment panorama of Dalit women due to the intervention of missionaries. Modern influences like industrialization created new opportunities for occupations especially for third generation Christian women, by opening up new job channels. For instance, international companies like APACHI Foot-ware Company provides better employment and better remuneration for Dalit women. 5 respondents reported that they are working in APACHI Foot-ware, and that has changed their dress code too as women have to wear uniform with pants and T-shirts and earn Rs. 5000 a month with 10th class qualification.

Field research reveals that 97 percent women are employed at different levels and enjoy better status. Most of them have come up to the middle class from the lower class by owning economic assets. Employment in different sectors has paved way to a middle class status and new identity of SALC women. Thus, tremendous change can be observed in the lives of SALC women due to their employment.

3.3.4. Status in the Family

The status of Indian Dalit women in the family depends upon the religious, traditional and cultural taboos related with their roles and duties. In general, their position in the family is secondary and subordinate. Dalit women are the main bread-winners in the family, yet they are considered as low, subordinate and inferior. Their day begins at 5 a.m. and ends late in the night both in the rural and urban families. The Dalit woman is expected to do twofold duties, which are both productive and unproductive. The jobs women do at home such as cooking, washing, laundering, cleaning, sweeping, mopping, fetching water, fetching firewood and fodder from long distance, shopping, tending the cattle and so on are considered unproductive jobs by the economists.

The respondents were asked about the involvement of male children in cooking; 79 percent of them said, men do not involve and only 21 percent said, they involve in cooking. Stereotyped duties of men and women at home such as cooking etc., are associated with less importance and low status. In simple terms, the status of Dalit women in the family is low, inferior and subordinate in spite of their education and employment.

To the question on their status and how they are treated in the family, 50 percent of the respondents disagreed that they are treated as subordinates and 5 percent strongly disagreed, while 41 percent of them strongly agreed and 2 percent agreed. The educational and economic status reveals that SALC women acquired better status and identities of their own. However, 50% of women are treated as subordinates in their families. Domestic violence is found in most of the families. Women also involve in productive jobs such as agricultural labourers, industrial workers and support the family income and national income. Unemployment is not found among the Dalit women. All illiterate women work as labourers in different economic sectors and educated women are employed in one way or the other.

Access to education brings changes in the cognitive ability of a person. Education is essential to women's capacity to question, to reflect on and to act on. It is education that gives access to knowledge and information and to new ideas to facilitate women to empower themselves. Employment certainly holds the key to improvement in the status and it determines the levels of food availability, nutrition and the level of the other basic essential demands. It also determines the structure of the house-hold and the relationships within the family.[23]

With regard to economic freedom in the family, 75 percent of the respondents said they have the economic freedom and only 25 percent of the women said, they do not have the freedom in economic matters. 40 percent of the respondents said that their husbands hold the decision-making authority, 36 percent said that both consult and take decisions, 17 percent of the women said, they decide on their own and the ones who answered that they decide on their own are mostly widows and separated women. A few of them are the wives of drunkards and so they decide by themselves as their drunkard husbands are not really responsible. 4 percent said, 'father will decide,' and only 1 percent said, others will take decision in the family.

The traditional family structure in SALC is a joint family. In this system, when a son marries, he along with his wife and their children continue to reside with his parents. The daughter on the other hand goes to her husband's home and lives with his parents, unmarried siblings, and the families of his married brothers. Boys stand as the carriers of the family name. Hence it is assumed that there is a preference for a boy child. With regard to the preference of a boy child, 68 percent said, 'no preference for a boy child' and 31 percent said, 'yes.' One respondent shared her story of her husband's preference for a boy child to carry his family name. To cite an example, Sangeetha shard her story during the field research:

Sangeetha is an orphan brought up by her relatives. While she was undertaking training to become a nurse, she fell in love with a Lutheran Christian man who is a Dalit. In the process, she became pregnant before marriage. The boy's parents were illiterates but very sensitive to this issue organized their marriage. Now they are living in a joint family. Her husband failed in graduation. So he could not find any job and she could not find job either because they are living in his village. He began his work as an agricultural worker as he has a small portion of agricultural field, as labourer for others, against his parents' and his wife's wish. But, with his hard earned money he began to drink arrack every day. He never gave money for the household expenses. Meanwhile they gave birth to three girl children. When I asked her why you gave birth to three girl children, she answered, "My husband wanted a boy child to continue his family name, he makes my in-laws cry every day. He beats me every day. Even his parents are not able to control him. I can't leave him either, as I have to suffer forever. I believed him and I came after him, I should live with him whatever he does."

The Dalit woman as a daughter-in-law and wife experiences relatively powerlessness and suffering. Until she bears a son she faces hardship especially in the hands of the mother-in-law. Bearing a son is the first definite rise in her status in the family. In turn when the daughter-in-law becomes the mother-in-law, she exercises her power over her daughter-in-law.[24]

The stories shared during the field research reveals that most of the women are not enjoying the equal status but live in a depressed mood. One respondent shared, "God wanted me to have peace in my life, so God allowed my husband to consume poison and commit suicide. I am relieved from torture." Another respondent shared, "Separation from my husband helps me to live in joy. While my husband was with me, I was in tears every day. Now I am in peace." These statements prove two facts: that the volume of violence is too high in the Christian Dalit families; and the women in SALC are resistant towards violence in the families to the extent of praising God for the death of and separation from their husbands. However, our concern here is not separation or death on the part of perpetrators but transformation and liberation from sexist violence for both the oppressed and the oppressor in the families.

3.3.5. Status in the Church

The survey on the opinion of how women are treated in the church reveals that, 79 percent of the respondents strongly disagreed that they are treated equally and 4 percent disagreed while 16 percent strongly agreed in this regard. With regard to women's involvement in the Church's ministry, 100 percent of the respondents are involved in praying and singing, 61 percent are involved in women's ministry, 41 percent are involved in cleaning the church, 35 percent are involved in Sunday school ministry, 31 percent are involved in fund raising, and 20 percent respondents are involved in youth fellowship.

However, most of the respondents do not treat themselves as equal to men. The notion of woman's ontological inferiority is related to the idea of woman's impurity or ritual pollution in several traditions. This is particularly true in Hinduism, where the hierarchy of castes is linked to purity and pollution. Women, through their bodily activities of menstruation and childbirth and their work in food preparation and cleanup, are linked to ritual impurity and thus equated to the Sudras, the ritually impure caste.

Judaism also has a strong tradition of woman's ritual impurity through her bodily functions of menstruation and childbirth. This deeply affects daily life. A woman must segregate herself from her husband and male relatives for part of each month. The dichotomy of purity and impurity is correlated with the sacred and the profane. In temple Judaism, this meant that women were forbidden to approach the Holy of Holies and confined to the outer court. Women's impurity is compared to the impurity of the profane Gentile world. In the separations of the pure and the impure, the woman falls on the impure side of the separation by which men keep themselves pure and holy to come into the presence of God.[25]

The Leviticus passage asserts, "When a woman has a discharge of blood that is her regular discharge from her body, she shall be in her impurity for seven days, and whoever touches her shall be unclean until the evening. Everything upon which she lies during her impurity shall be unclean; everything also upon which she sits shall be unclean. Whoever touches her bed shall wash his clothes, and bathe in water, and be unclean until the evening (Lev 15:19-23 (NRSV)). This has a strong impact on SALC women. The text clearly indicates that to menstruate is to remain in a state of ritual impurity. The Indian Church in the context of Hindu teachings has adopted the system that women are impure during menstruation. Hence, they are prohibited from touching the Bible, reading the Bible, and participating in the Holy Communion. The concept of treating women as impure is reinforced in the religious realms which also prohibited women to the ordained ministry until recently. Hence, it is essential to understand the opinion of SALC women on the issue of menstruation as this becomes an instrument for many women in disconnecting themselves from the religious activities during menstruation.

Regarding their opinion on menstruation and their participation in the Church activities during menstruation, the survey reveals that 91 percent of the respondents agreed that women are treated as impure, 3 percent 'strongly agreed,' and 5 percent 'disagreed' that women are treated as impure. The opinion on menstruation reveals that 77 percent of the respondents said that it is an aspect of divine creation and 22 percent of them replied, 'they do not know.' The survey on the opinion on women participating in communion during menstruation shows that 68 percent of the respondents revealed that they can take part, 18 percent said, 'do not know' and 13 percent stated, 'after bath they can take part.'

Although, women through Women's Maha Samaj make an incredible contribution not only towards the emancipation of women but also towards the growth of the Church, however, women are not involved in church administration at the higher level, but at the local congregational level. The survey revealed that 64 percent of the respondents stated that women should involve in church politics and administration, 23 percent replied, 'should not' and 13 percent said, 'do not know.' The question related to personal approach in political involvement in the Church has revealed that 63 percent respondents said, 'like to be involved in the church politics,' 23 percent replied, 'do not like to be involved' and 13 percent said, 'other reasons.'

3.3.5.1. Women and the Bible

Dalits were open to Christianity and colonial power. Conversion was seen as a means to secure a new identity which was a 'powerful and effective system.' Those who converted saw the Bible as the symbol of their new status and the guarantor of the benefits of their new mode of identity. 'Conversion to Christianity (and Buddhism) implied liberation from the rigid and oppressive caste and communal structure of Hindu society. Christianity offered and affirmed the human dignity and worth in the sight of God for the Dalit converts.'[26] The Bible came to be used by the Dalits to assert different identities. In the context of colonialism, in which the Dalits converted to Christianity, acquiring a new social identity in the process, which helped them to adapt to the changed circumstances that colonialism had brought.

Experience plays a key role in formulating Dalit hermeneutics as in other contextual hermeneutics. Dalit theologians find the interconnectedness between the experiences of Dalits and the experiences of the marginalized of the Bible.[27] As said above, Dalits are often kept as illiterates, and biblical teaching has been used to exploit them. It is important to understand how the Bible plays a significant role in the lives of the people.

As the study revealed, 72 percent of respondents read Bible twice a day, 20 percent read whenever they have time, and 7 percent replied, "They can't read the Bible." To the question on understanding the Bible at the time of reading, the analysis indicates that 89 percent of the respondents said, 'yes' and 11 percent stated that they do not understand.

When the respondents were asked to explain their intimacy with the Bible, they shared that the Bible is given the highest place in their life. 85 respondents said that they keep the Bible on their bed while sleeping, believing that it will protect them from danger. They regard the Bible as the highest one and so 20 of them said that they will not touch the Bible during menstruation as they assume that they will make the Bible unholy during that time, if they touch it. To cite an example, one respondent shared that she gives importance to the Leviticus text (Lev 15: 19-23) and says women are impure during menstruation. In their church she said, "Women before attaining age and women after menopause clean even the altar." Surprisingly, it is not the pastor of the congregation reinforcing this oppressive system. It is the women themselves apply their reading of the text to their life situations and disregard themselves as inferior and impure.

3.3.5.2. Women's Ordination

Looking at the subject from a global perspective, women's ordination has been both a topic of heated debate and a topic of no significance depending on the inroads the subject has made into the minds of Christians around the globe. However, it has become today a burning issue for a vast number of Christians. Several scholarly books and articles have discussed the topic, and the theological arguments for and against the ordination of women. Women's ordained ministry is one of the most remarkable and significant developments in the recent history of Christianity.

Due to the missionary movements, women were empowered in the 70s in a remarkable way. During the 70s, the women's movement in India was revived and the observance of the International Women's Year and Decade took place. Women's issues began to be identified and addressed by the church women leaders too during this period. The question of ordination of women, and equal participation in the church activities were also addressed simultaneously. Nevertheless, in the mid 70s the growing consciousness and constant efforts of church women leaders and as well as open-minded men, the ordination of women was accepted by the Church of South India. The first woman ordained in India is Rev Elizabeth Paul.[28] Since then Church of North India and Lutheran Churches have begun the ordination of women. SALC ordained women and the first Women's Ordination took place on 12 January 2011 at Tirupathi, and four women were ordained. The researcher is one among them.[29] SALC women were overwhelmed by the Women's Ordination. The data on women's ordination divulges that 60 percent of the respondents stated that ordained women should be allowed for church ministry, 21 percent stated, 'do not know' and 18 percent said, 'should not be allowed.' However, a majority of women accepted women's ordination and it is a welcome move.

3.3.5.3. Image of God

We live out the images that inform us. The images of the divine, other people, one's self are profoundly interrelated within each person's imagination. They affect every relationship, including with the divine. The divine is described as a mystery greater than any image or name can contain. However, human minds used images to relate to the divine being. Therefore, it is essential and crucial that the study examines the images that shape and shaped the lives of SALC women.

People's understandings and experiences of God, of self, and of others are fixed in their memories and emotions through the images. These can be accessed and changed primarily through the use of images any time. Hence, along with the conceptual level of understanding God, self and the other, it is crucial to combine the experiences of the alternative images of God, self and others in order to represent a holistic transformation. Each one's imagination draws from the raw materials of external sights, sounds and smells, as well as from the experiences of self, others, and divine. The process by which images of God are created and revisited throughout life is unique for each person, depending on the socio-religious and cultural context. Each person is continually forming and re-forming her/his internal imagery as he/she interacts with the representations of self, with God and the other. Therefore, while a shared cultural and religious background can cause significant similarities to the imaginations of self, God and others, a particular person's internal configuration of significant representations and relationships is unique at any particular time. [30] Hence, in this chapter, I explore this uniqueness through life history interviews with women. In my research with these women, we found out that each woman's images and experiences are unique. We also examined their stories together as a group and found common themes in the dynamic of their imaging God. As chapter IV is fully devoted to discuss the image of God, now I will move on to the analysis of data collected on 'the image of God'.

Some of the responses drawn from both the personal interviews and group discussions are very revealingly biblical, literal and patriarchal: 'God is the Father,' 'Jesus has called God the Father,' 'God is he,' 'Jesus is he,' and 'Holy Spirit is he,' 'therefore we can address God only in male terms,' 'man is created in the image of God,' 'woman is the rib of man,' 'woman is a helper to a man,' 'woman is the cause of sin therefore weak,' 'Paul commanded women to be silent,' 'Jesus' disciples are male therefore women need not be ordained,' and 'Jesus said to Mary at the tomb not to touch him, but he asked Thomas to touch him, so woman is a sinner,' 'women have to cover their heads because the Bible teaches so,' 'women should not take communion and step into the altar during menstruation, because the Bible says they are unclean during that time' and 'women have to obey their husbands.' These responses are the result of their reading of the Bible according to the traditional interpretations. Women are thus the silent spectators of their own oppression, violence and secondary position. They plainly admit that they are impure beings. They have internalized the aspect that they cannot be equal to men because 'man is created in the image of God and woman is created from his rib,' so a woman can never claim equality.

To the question whether they are created in the image of God, 98 percent said, 'yes' and the remaining 2 percent stated, 'no.' To the question whether they bear God's image, 76 percent of the respondents stated, 'yes' and 24 percent stated, 'no.' As data reveals, 75% percent of the respondents said, 'yes' and 25 % said, 'no' to the question whether God is in their image? To the question how they 'image God,' 95 percent of the respondents stated that they view God as the Father, three percent said both (the Father & the Mother), 1 percent stated 'do not know,' and 0 percent stated 'mother.' As many as 80 percent of the respondents expressed that God is viewed as their friend, healer, and the life giving spirit during the group discussions.

3.6. Caste System and Women in SALC

The villages in Andhra Pradesh are divided into *Harijanawada* (Dalit colony)[31] and *Ooru* (the place where caste people live, the village). Dalits are barred from entering the village because of the fear of spreading an atmosphere of pollution. They need to keep a distance of seventy-four feet from the caste people. It is believed that their shadow is capable of polluting the well; hence, they are not allowed to come close to the public wells used by Hindus. When caste Hindus carry water to their homes, the very sight of Dalits is considered to pollute the water. Hence, they throw out the water they are carrying and fetch fresh water.[32] Even the sound waves from the mouth of the Dalits are considered defiling and so they had to cover their mouth with a little pot when they speak with a Hindu. In some places, Dalits had to tie a long broom at the back, when they walk the streets of the village so that they sweep off their own foot prints. Dalits in the villages are thus pushed to the margins.[33] The researcher observed during the field research that most Dalit families in the villages live in mud-walled, mud-floored, one-roomed, thatched huts. A good percentage lives in the colony houses constructed by the government with one hall and kitchen.

Discrimination on the basis of caste continues more obviously in the villages. All respondents agreed that caste is observed very strictly during the time of marriages. Most of them are of the opinion that inter-caste marriages can solve caste problems to a great extent. A few respondents are involved in inter-caste marriages. Inter-caste marriages are found among a few families. A few Dalit men married caste women and a few Dalit women have married caste men. They gave a very positive response and advocated inter-caste marriages to eradicate the caste system. One among them is Daizy (Name changed on request by the respondent); a Dalit Christian married a Kamma (one of the forward castes) man. However she says it took a long time for boy's parents to accept them. All of them agreed that all marriages occur within each Dalit sub-caste and inter-caste marriages among Dalit sub-groups are not much encouraged.

Dalits continue to live in segregated settlements in the rural areas. The caste stigma is not removed from the Indian mind. While much has been done in India to transform Indian society, the reforms have not brought much change in Indian caste orthodoxy as the caste system has strong roots in Indian Christianity which has further created distinctions, divisions and segregations. Even early Indian Christian theological articulations were Brahminical in nature and scope, and thus were not of help to the majority of Christians who are Dalits in India. Nevertheless, taking hold of the Indian Constitution, Dalits have enjoyed certain privileges and access to the new avenues.

However with reference to caste 100 percent of the respondents categorize themselves as Adi Andhra Christians and to the question about the understanding of the term Dalit, 66 percent of them said that the term Dalit means low caste, 26 percent said 'outcastes,' and 8 percent stated 'do not know.' One respondent said, "Caste system itself is humiliating and I experienced in the Degree College when I freshly joined for my B.Sc. We have a women's waiting room in our college where all female students use that room when there are no classes. I experienced a pain as a Dalit Christian, as the caste girls and Dalit Christian girls sit in separate groups. They used to talk to each other but caste division was clearly visible." One respondent said, "It was humiliating to see the children separately sitting in the hostel, and outcaste girls addressing high caste girls of the same class as Reddemma and Naidamma (these names give status), whereas high caste girls address low caste girls in a humiliating way and particularly affixing their caste name just to humiliate them. It was so humiliating."

Caste discrimination and humiliation is very much prevalent in all areas of life of women: 50 percent of women faced discrimination in the village, 25 percent in town, 21 percent at the educational place and 4 percent of them at work. In the group discussion, respondents were asked to share their caste related experiences. 78 percent of them responded that they felt uncomfortable while mentioning their caste name and only 22 percent of them said that they felt comfortable. Untouchability as a social institution was and is kept alive by the use of brute force. The caste Hindus insist on enforcing the inferiority of the Dalits in many ways, and if they tried to improve their standards of living they were cruelly persecuted. Perhaps the most effective weapon which helped in the perpetuation of untouchability was the institutionalized bias and denial of access to educational resources. Untouchability is very much related to the patriarchal/ Brahmanic control over high caste women's sexuality which was essential for maintenance of caste privilege. Dalits all over India have tried to change their lifestyles, marriage practices and caste names but to no effect. Schools are of no exception. Untouchability is very much practiced in schools in Andhra Pradesh.[34] It is untouchability more than anything else that is responsible for the denial of human rights to the Dalit women. Commenting on untouchability, Maria Arul Raja states in his article 'Perspectives of Dalit Hermeneutics':

> Dalit communities are kept in close proximity of the caste communities for exploitative purposes. Besides at the same time, they are kept apart as untouchables from the so-called mainstream at the periphery of the Indian society in each village as *colony or cheri.* This dichotomy of being wanted as well as being rejected by the power-wielding caste communities creates a situation of ambiguity of incorporating the sensibilities at once of tenets of major religions and elements of subaltern religious praxis.[35]

A careful analysis of individual violence as well as nationwide reveals that they are caste based most of the time. A large number of Dalit women live in an atmosphere of constant violence and violated situations. Dalit women are those whose labor, laughter and life are spent for the sake of upper caste men, women and their own men physically. Dalit women are the people who are emotionally humiliated in every walk of life. They are socially neglected, ignored, dismantled, diminished and distorted human beings. Dalit women are oppressed psychologically and made to feel shame on account of their caste. A report by the Bureau Police Research and Development in Crimes in India 1997, in a comparative analysis of crimes against women in the various states, ranks Andhra Pradesh as the second highest state in dowry deaths, fourth for rape of girls below the age of sixteen, and seventh for molestation.[36] The above section on educational and economic transformation has brought new identities to SALC women. However, caste plays a dominant role in the formation of identity of a person in India. Hence, it is essential to study the impact of caste on SALC women both in the church and outside.

To the question of respondents' participation in the caste people's family functions, 61 percent stated that they sometimes participated, 34 percent said that they never turned up, 5 percent said, they always attended the family functions of the caste people.

Regarding caste discrimination in the church, the data reveals that 58 percent experienced caste discrimination some times, 31 percent responded that they 'never' experienced and 11 percent stated 'it is always practised.'

On the question regarding inter-caste marriages, 77 percent of women were positive towards inter-caste marriage and only 22 percent of the respondents were against inter caste marriage. During my field study, I came across three women among whom one married a Dalit Christian man and two Dalit Christian women married the caste men. All three of them are very strong in stating, "Caste system will be broken only through inter-caste marriages." It is a good move for inter-caste marriage as observed during the field research. Padma, a caste convert from Hinduism shares her success story of her marriage to a Dalit Christian man:

> I am basically a Hindu and from a forward caste background. My father died when I was young. I had a heart problem when I was a child. During that time I was admitted to the general hospital at Chennai. There the Christian evangelists visited hospital often and shared about God and God's loving care. In my difficult times as I was young I accepted Jesus as my saviour and became a Christian. After a few years, my entire family converted to Christianity. They found more peace in Jesus when they attended Christian meetings and prayers. At one time I had an opportunity to undergo a theological training so that I can serve the Lord. I was delighted to join the studies. As I was 37 year old and due to my health conditions I lost interest in getting married. But, during my theological training I came across a divorced man who was 45 years old. My family did not accept to arrange this marriage because the boy comes from out caste although he is a Christian. Although we all go to the same church, my mother and brothers are not happy. My Christian friends organized the wedding for us. I am happy with my husband. He is very good. He loves me so much. He has no bad habits. God has given me a blessed life. My mother-in-law and other family members love me. We have no caste barriers. The God who loves me and my husband had taken out the caste barriers in us. At first my family members were not happy and did not accept us. But, now they accepted us. Inter-caste marriages will transform our Christian community.

Although, caste discrimination is on a high level, it was found in the field research that resistance to caste also is on the rise. For example, one of the respondents by name Nagaratnamma who is a 55-year-old illiterate woman constructed a house on her own. There was some problem during the construction. At that time the Panchayat President who belongs to Reddy caste used abusive words and spoke against Dalits using the term 'mala.' She felt very much insulted. As part of her resistance, she filed a case against him and the case was in the court for six years and finally she won the case. However, the above description is very clear to state that caste-based violence either emotionally or physically is very much visible and prevalent at different levels in the church and society.

Identity of SALC women remains the most urgent topic to be researched in this work as the data explores, caste serves as the essential and determining quality of identity. Identity as an outcaste carries a burden of low self image that leads to serious identity crisis among SALC women. The living experience of SALC women has become a strong foundation for them to tell stories of recovering lost identities. In the process of recovering lost identities as human beings created in the image of God, teachers play a significant role in eradicating caste system in the schools and from the minds of children in SALC. In the South Andhra Lutheran Church, a majority of women are in the teaching profession. Respondents expressed that the caste system and gender inequalities exist in the schools among children, especially in the villages. But, most of them shared their experiences as they have been used as tools in the hands of God to bring transformation among the children of various castes in schools. One retired teacher reported that she stood firm in eradicating the caste system in the school. Rajamma, a teacher from Naidupet shares her experience of the caste system:

> At first I was posted in Rajupalem village. There Reddys, Pantakapulu, Girijan, and Harijan children were there in the school. The high caste children sit on the bench and Girijans (ST) and Dalit children were not allowed to sit on the benches. Once, I made Dalit and Girijan children sit on the benches, the women of Reddy caste came to school and fought with me very badly. They even commanded me not to allow "their children to come and sit with our children." I used to tell them, I cannot show caste favoritism here, if some officials come for inspection I will get into problems. We will not allow such practices in the school. I used to go to each house especially Girijan children, I used to bring them to my house and teach them how to be clean. During Christmas I used to buy dresses for them, there was some change and then I brought them together.

Vimala Vijayasree another teacher who is in service shares that she is used by the Hand of God to transform school children. Vimala Vijayasree says:

> In villages there is still a caste feeling. People call caste names like washer men, potters, mala, madiga, yandulu; likewise people are recognized by caste names only. "In 1983," she recalls her experience, "I worked in Chillakuru. That was the time, when women were not allowed to work. In such a village I was posted as a teacher. I observed during midday meals time that children used to sit in different rows. Then I understood that each row belongs to a particular caste. I was

> so upset and felt so bad because I was not able to do anything in the beginning because it is such a problematic place. When I asked the children why they are sitting in separate rows, the caste children said that 'they are *mala vallu*' (one of the derogatory name of outcastes), so they don't want to sit with them. Then I asked 'who are you?' They said 'we are *reddys*' (one of the high caste names in Andhra Pradesh). I put this problem in the prayer for one month. Especially during school assembly I used to share about this caste problem. After a month a miracle took place, to my surprise they came together, sat together and it was wonderful. As a teacher I was able to clear the untouchability in the school among children.

Education and employment certainly played a key role in helping Dalit Christian women to achieve an identity in society. According to the field research, rural women still maintain themselves as untouchables and they are not in a position to fight untouchability. They simply admit it as sanctioned by the society. The educated urban Dalit Christian women claim an achieved identity as professionals, educators, and as transformers. Rt. Rev. Chandra Sekhar, the then Bishop of SALC said, in our discussions, that women in his church have become a stronger wing of the church in praying, house visiting, and counselling. Women have become a strong force in taking the gospel to the villages. They claim their identity as women of God.

However, the research advocates that women have become strong in asserting that they are 'people with courage and dignity.' This becomes a feminist hermeneutical clue in formulating Dalit feminist theological hermeneutics.

3.7. Violence Against Women

In spite of the attention paid to the issue of violence against women in recent years, the research endeavour worldwide reveals that it is on the rise. Violence against women is certainly a cross-cultural phenomenon all over the world. Violence against women is partly as result of gender relations that assumes men to be superior to women. Given the subordinate status of women, much of gender violence is considered normal and enjoys sanction. Manifestations of violence include physical aggressions such as beating, buring, murder, physical assault, rape and sexual assault, physical assault, emotional abuse through insults, humiliation, coercion, blackmail, control over speech and actions, prostitution, genital mutilation, sexual harassment and pornography etc. The term violence has many synonyms such as mistreatment, cruelty, ill-treatment, maltreatment, neglect, exploitation, sadism, aggression, hostility, brutality, blood-shed, abuse, misuse and overuse. Violence may be physical, emotional, verbal, theological, cognitive, sexual, visual, institutional, structural, economical, political, social and ecological, eve-teasing, ragging etc. These expressions of violence take place in a man-woman relationship within the family, state and society.

Women are subject to violence even before birth in many societies in India. In many cultures, girl children are seen as less valuable than boy children, in part because when they grow up, girls are expected to marry and live with husband's families, whereas a boy and his future bride will take care of boy's parents. Additionally in India, inheritance and the family name are typically transmitted though male children. Therefore, there is a preference for a boy child and the birth of a second daughter is not welcomed. There is a saying that is attached to the birth of a girl child which is degrading: "If you tell lies, you will give birth to girl children." It means, if you want a boy child, then tell the truth always. The selective abortion of girl fetuses, infanticide of girl-newborns, and the underfeeding and death by malnutrition of girl children have resulted in the widespread reduction in female children worldwide each year (a phenomenon known as missing girls).[37] The family socializes its members to accept hierarchical relations expressed in unequal division of labour between the sexes and power over the allocations of resources.

Violence against women has been clearly defined as a form of discrimination in numerous documents. The World Human Rights Conference in Vienna, first recognized gender-based violence as human rights violation in 1993. In the same year, United Nations declaration, in 1993, defined violence against women as "any act of gender-based violence that results in, or is likely to result in, physical, sexual or psychological harm or suffering to a woman, including threats, coercion or arbitrary deprivations of liberty, whether occurring in public or private life."

Violence is abusive action resulting in reaction and silencing of human beings or cultures including customs, institutions, agencies and structures that are insensitive to God's creation and the people who have been created in God's image. However, the study does not include violence that occurs in combination with crimes, such as robbery, murder, etc. Nor does it include prostitution, sexual harassment, or trafficking in women that are more relevant to other societies. The study includes violence against women and most commonly related issues such as dowry, forced widowhood and discrimination. These the researcher feels are common issues that distort the identity of women in South Andhra Lutheran Church.

3.7.1. Dowry-related Violence Against Women

Dowry system is a universal phenomenon among all castes in India. It is associated with social status and family prestige. It affects Dalit families too. Although, giving dowry is an offence but an ideological part of the well to do, upper class and upper caste sections. This practice is fast spreading firmly among the Dalit families too. The South Andhra Lutheran Church is no exception to this among her members. The respondents stated that dowry practice is widespread in the community. The overall survey of the data reveals that 68 percent of them agreed that they have either given or taken dowry, only 32 percent stated 'no,' to dowry practice. Kalpana Sharma while discussing on issue of dowry says:

> Dowry is a symptom of a deeper disease that relates to how our society values women. The original concept of streedhan (gift to a girl during wedding) was based on providing a newlywed girl with some things that she could cherish and call her own. Today this concept has been vulgarized to symbolize all the things that not even the bridegroom, but his family wants to have as their own. Customs like dowry can end only when the people involved, the young men and women, decide to go against the tide, demand simpler weddings and say a firm "no" to the vulgar demands that constitute a dowry. Marriages may not be made in heaven, but they should not end up sending people into the hellhole of lifelong debt and misery.[38]

The dowry system causes damage to the identity and status of women in Indian society. Dowry is an issue that systematically gives rise to the preference of boy child, with less education for the girl child. A few responses were: "If we educate a girl child to higher level, at the time of marriage we have to find a boy with higher qualification than our daughter; the more the boy is qualified, the more dowry is demanded." So parents limit the education for girl children to certain level such as teachers training, nursing etc.,

The dowry system often leads to violence against women in one way or the other. To cite an example, Ruth Mary from Tada says that she had a painful experience. Her marriage broke up due to the dowry problem. Ruth Mary is engaged to a teacher who belongs to a Lutheran Christian family before the wedding. It was expected that the dowry demanded must be handed over by the bride's family to the bridegroom's family. After the engagement, her marriage was dropped, due to the dowry problem. After the engagement, the bridegroom's family demanded more dowry assuming that the bride's family can offer to give more. As the bride's family could not give more, the wedding was cancelled. Ruth says, "My parents have spent a lot of money by borrowing on high interest to celebrate my engagement. Who should be blamed for this? It is a mental shock for my parents. Now to find another bridegroom for me is a complicated matter."

The above instance clearly shows that dowry system is a practice in SALC. Although respondents are of the opinion that the dowry system is evil, most of them involve in either taking or giving dowry. Dowry is very much linked to the status and identity of women. Dowry damages the identity of women as it makes them vulnerable before marriage and after.

3.7.2. Violence Related to Alcoholism

Domestic violence against women is a culturally accepted standard of behaviour. Dalit community which is an endemic part of the Indian society is highly patriarchal and hierarchical in nature. The family is the strong protective agent of patriarchy in the Dalit community. Dalit men are highly expressive of their detestation against Manu's dictums with regard to caste. Yet they observe Manu's dictums sincerely in case of women's status. Quarrels after drinking liquor are quite common in the Dalit families. 37-year-old Kumari, the victim of the alcoholic husband comes from Puttur shares her memories of hunger and want. While sharing her story, her voice faltered and her eyes were crammed up with tears. She tells her story:

> I was born in a Christian family. I lost my mother when I was a child. My father is a drunkard. I was put up in the Mission school in Naidupet; I studied up to 10th class. I also learnt tailoring. I could not excel in studies due to domestic problems. After the completion of my 10th class, my school authorities gave me a sewing machine, so that I can earn my livelihood. But, my father sold it and spent that money on drinking alcohol. I worked as an agricultural labourer. After a few months, my father arranged my marriage with another aged drunkard, who was already married. Unfortunately, we came to know this after marriage. Meanwhile, I gave birth to two children. My husband was unemployed; I used to go and work as an agricultural labourer and earn a few rupees. But, many times even that hard earned money used to be snatched away by my husband. Even I could not give milk to my child. Some times when my child cried I gave warm water mixed with sugar to the child. I was living in utter poverty. After giving birth to my second child, my husband left me and joined his first wife. But, I never regretted for that. Then my aunty put me as a caretaker in an orphanage, where my children's studies and other needs are taken care of and I am given Rs.1000/- as pocket money. I am happy now. It is good he left me. I am at peace.

Examination of the data on addiction to alcohol consumption in South Andhra Lutheran Church reveals that alcoholism is rampant. The research highlights that women had experienced problems related to the alcohol consumption by 55 percent of the husbands, 41 percent of fathers and 4 percent of sons. The evil/good effects that the respondents have endured due to alcoholism are given in quotations. The following statements were made by the respondents. They expressed insecurity, shame, hurt, sufferings, poverty, wife-battering, bitter and sad experiences, sleepless nights and so on. Especially during summer season men have more access to local arrack, and almost every day they drink. Alcoholic husbands beat their wives on a regular basis. Alcoholism and wife battering is found even among the educated urban families. Some young girls reported that their fathers drink and create confusion in the homes. Alcoholism has a bad effect on the psyche of women too, particularly girl children. Although, education and employment have transformed Dalit Christian families to a greater extent, violence against women due to alcoholism remains a serious issue in most of the SALC families as the research indicates. This gives rise to an identity crisis. Even teachers, who claim a good and respectable status in the society and church experience shame due to their alcoholic husbands, fathers, brothers and sons.

3.7.3. Violence Related to Widowhood

Widows in India form a social sub-group whose status draws particular attention in research. Widows in India are deprived of their basic right to live as they are not allowed to wear colourful clothes or flowers. They are not allowed to participate in any auspicious occasions of the family and in the community. Widow re-marriage is restricted. Widows among Dalit communities reported loneliness, fear of the future, worry about money, and emotional imbalance. Depression is common among them. Many find it difficult not to have a male member beside them, citing issues of security, economic depravity, lack of identity and the like.[39]

To the question on 'forced widowhood,' 82 percent of the respondents said, 'it is an inhuman act against women who have lost their husbands,' while 18 percent of the respondents stated, 'it is good.' In answer to the question on the opinion on widow remarriage, the data analysis reveals that 80 percent answered it can be allowed; only 20 percent of the women respondents said it cannot be allowed.

On the survey of widow remarriage, the data analysis shows that 51 percent of the respondents said that it is sometimes allowed. 48 percent of the respondents answered that it is restricted and only 1 percent said that it is freely allowed. When asked about the widows and how they are treated in their place,. 72 percent of the respondents replied that widows are treated as inauspicious. 17 percent of the respondents said that widows are treated with respect and the rest of the 11 percent replied that widows are even excluded from auspicious celebrations.

It is surprising to note that there are many young widows in the South Andhra Lutheran Church. They are deprived of their basic needs and rights to live. They are considered to be inauspicious. Their presence makes people uncomfortable. They are not invited for auspicious programmes. To be a widow is a kind of excommunication from the family and society. Forced widowhood is very much practised. The researcher witnessed the ritual of widowhood in a Christian home. A certain Dalit Christian man passed away and the corpse was kept in front of the house. The wife was brought to the corpse of her husband and she was made to bend on her husband's corpse and she was bathed by the older women before the whole community that was gathered there. After the bath, the corpse was taken out for burial. Immediately she was forced to dress up like a bride, to wear a costly silk sari, to apply turmeric on her face, put on flowers and many bangles. She was supposed to dress up as a bride. I was also invited for the thanksgiving prayer day. On that day once again the older women removed her flowers and broke the bangles, removed her *Thali* (The wedding symbol tied around her neck by the husband at the time of wedding) and wrapped her a white sari. Then she was made to cover her face completely and brought before the pastor. Then the prayers began and she was in that position until the prayer meeting was over. It is really heart-aching to see such inhuman activities even among the educated Dalit Christians. One respondent stated about the experience of enforced widowhood: "People remind me every day that I am inauspicious." Another respondent shares her sad and painful experience which she is continuously experiencing due to her widowhood. 25-year-old Deva Krupa from Thummur says, "I became a widow after two years of my marriage. I am considered *asubham* (inauspicious); I am not invited to participate in any *shuba karyams* (auspicious functions). Early in the morning, if someone sees my face on the street, they show an irritable expression on their face and sometimes they even scold me."

Widowhood is both a crisis and a problem. Soon after widowhood, the widow is excluded from caste rituals and ceremonies. She is subjected to total segregation. The reason behind this segregation and putting restrictions is to prevent any kind of intimacy with men. A study conducted by the Govt. of India in 1994 revealed that 88% widows remained in their dead husbands' village. Only 3% shared the same hearth with their in-laws. Less than 9% lived with their parents. This is an important indicator of the economic status of the widows in the country and speaks volumes of their position. The problem of widowhood in India is critical both in terms of its emotional depth as well as the sheer number of persons caught in the cruel practice. The figures narrate the touching tale. The institution of widowhood with all its hardships and disadvantages is a result of discrimination between the sexes, which characterizes the prevailing archaic system. According to the 1991 Census, there are 33 million widows all over India constituting 8% of the total female population. In terms of prevalence of widowhood, India ranks amongst the highest in the world. The story of the daily deprivations of these 33 million widows is never told in public. Widowhood compels them to be away from the mainstream. Thus they are forced into a life of colorlessness, hopelessness and loneliness.

Widows in India no doubt are marginalized experiencing powerlessness, physical abuse, and social segregation and in some parts of India being abandoned by their families, in addition to economic hardships.[40]

3.7.4. Wife Battering

Battering of wife is the most pervasive age-old method of subjugating a woman to male domination in marital life. In the Dalit families it is very common because most of them are addicted to alcohol, and women become the victims of serious mental and physical violence. However, the field research revealed that 77 percent of women said, they don't have experience of wife battering. And 23 percent of the respondents stated that they have experienced wife battering in one way or the other. Wife-battering often is related to alcoholic addiction. Victoria Devi, a retired teacher in Sullurpet, a victim of alcoholic husband shares her story:

> I was born in a good Christian family. I was brought up in good discipline. I am married to my cousin who was a bus conductor. I have two children and three grand children. My husband comes home drunk every day. It used to be a painful experience to me every day. I am a retired teacher. I had a dignified profession; I am very much respected in society for my discipline and lifestyle. But, at home I was tortured by my husband. He used to beat me every day. He used to scold our neighbors. He forgets relationships when he is drunk. Once my husband came home drunk heavily, he hit me on my face with the swing (which is made up of iron and used to draw water from the well) of the well. The swing fell on my mouth and I lost my tooth completely. She added, "What else can I say about my experience with my alcoholic husband?" But, now I am glad that my husband committed suicide. My husband's death made me free. God wanted me to have peace in my life and took him off.

3.8. Intervention of Missionaries

As mentioned in the introductory chapter, transformation of women started in Andhra Pradesh in 1860s, with the opening of the Lutheran Mission School in Gudur, Nellore district. The extraordinary industrious and sacrifices with focused goal on educating women have brought considerable transformation as the research revealed. Although, Indian society treats Dalit Christians as lower castes or outcastes, SALC women's inner psyche tells them that they are chosen by God and cleansed by God and so have an identity as Christians, which claims a special dignity. SALC women have a number of successful stories. The respondents while sharing their stories mentioned that their success was due to missionaries' intervention and conversion to Christianity. Due to this, South Andhra Lutheran women are entering into better positions and raising their voices and sharing their stories of resistance. The above discussion reveals that the status and identity of women in SALC has been transformed to a great extent.

Mrs. Woerrlen established a boarding school for women and girls in 1901 at Gudur and later it was moved to Nayudupet.[41] Miss Gertruth Kettne was very much interested in Bible women's work and she also established a boarding school for widows, and embroidery schools, and elementary schools for girls in Nayudupet.[42] Miss Margaret Stahl was involved very much in building a missionary hospital at Renigunta. In 1922, the Women's Missionary Conference (WMC) took the initiative of raising funds for the construction of a hospital in Renigunta, in Andhra Pradesh. The women also supported the work of the India mission by marketing and selling their craft, lace and embroidery work created by young women attending the Lace School at Gudur through the India Lace Department.[43] Miss Stahl established a nursery school for girls in 1940, and it was upgraded to a middle school and finally it became a high school for girls.[44] Since the missionary period a great transition took place in the life of women in SALC in uplifting them.

When the respondents were asked to mention the name of the missionaries, 22 percent mentioned the name of Mrs. Margaret Elizabeth Stahl, 28 percent mentioned Miss. Dorathi Mayer's name, 5 percent mentioned Miss. Gertrud Kettner's name, and 5 per cent mentioned the name of Miss Lilyan Mayer and 2 per cent mentioned Miss Helen Agnes Schaefer. One percent mentioned the names of Ms. Swan, Ms. Brousius, Miss. Wize, Ms. Cornelius and Miss. Boehr. Three per cent mentioned Ms. Murray's name. 50 percent acknowledged Indian women's name such as Ms. Katakshamma Paul Raj and one percent mentioned Ms. K. Suseelamma, Mrs. Premalatha Benjamin. Although, Katakshmma, Suseelamma and Premalatha are Indians, the impression the researcher gets is that their impact on SALC is tremendous.

Christianity in India would not have spread as it did without the partnership of native Bible women with the western missionaries. The interactions of the Bible women with Western missionaries certainly influenced the way the native women identified their 'self.' Leena Manorama who is in her 70s, a daughter of Upadeshi (Pastor) shares that the Bible women played multiple roles: Being very strong in the faith, they played a very significant role in spreading the gospel to their community members; they maintained different identities by being one with the natives and with the missionaries. They were also home makers, convincing family members to roam around with the missionaries to spread the gospel. They had thus a role to play at home and a role to play outside the home. Most of the Bible women who worked with the Hermannsburg Mission had the approval of their families. This certainly transformed their status and professional identities. "Their tremendous commitment had contributed to the growth of SALC," says Devadanamma, a respondent. Since then women are part of the church ministry in one way or the other.

To the question, what do you know about the missionaries, 50 percent mentioned that the 'missionaries stood for discipline, sacrifice, love and zeal to transform people.' To the question what is the contribution of women missionaries, the respondents opined that, their extraordinary industrious work and sacrifice with the particular purpose of educating women have brought considerable change and transition in the lives of Dalit women. Eighty seven percent answered that missionaries gave the Gospel, education, food, employment, dignity and discipline to them. A few of them responded that the missionaries gave status and dignity particularly to Dalits and Dalit women. Some of the names of women missionaries repeatedly heard during the field work are Mrs. Margaret Elizabeth Stahl and Miss. Dorathi Mayer. The respondents who studied in missionary schools are eyewitnesses to the work done by women missionaries. They acknowledge that the discipline and the devotion to God that they have learnt from the missionaries are instrumental in the transition in their lives and in their communities as well. The sacrifices that the missionaries have made towards the establishment of SALC and the development activities that they had taken up are fresh in the memories of the respondents. 70 percent of the respondents mentioned that 'they were actively involved in awakening their minds, as they thought this was essential for their converts to live a fuller life with dignity and identity.' Mr. Devasahayam, a retired teacher who was participating in one of the group discussions shared his empowered and more self-confident experience. He said, "The education that he had in the mission school taught him to be dignified, sincere and disciplined in their duties." As he was appointed for a teaching position, he went for the first time to the caste people's area (as the schools were situated in the village), Anepudi, wearing white dress and putting on shoes. The village people got annoyed, as he hailed from the nearest Harijana Wada where his relatives still live. The villagers blocked the way and they warned him not to wear shoes when he enters the village next day.

Devasahayam did not oblige them and the following day he went in the same manner and the villagers did not allow him to enter the village. When he responded by saying, "I am posted by the Government, if you have any disagreements you can go and report to the government," the villagers remained silent. He said with an overwhelming joy, that after a few months, they had no word against him, and some of the caste women took his children to their house, bathed them and served food to them. He says, "It is because of the discipline, dignity and the knowledge of Christ that I acquired from the missionaries, I was able to resist the caste oppression." Another respondent shared her story and narrated how the dreams of her unschooled parents have come true in her life which empowers other Dalit women who struggle to survive and come up in life. Devadanamma tells her story:

> I was born in a Dalit family. My parents belonged to a lower class and outcaste community. They were illiterates, living in Harijanawada (Dalit colony) of Rosanoor. They were converted to Christianity seven decades ago. They were living in poverty, as labourers. My grandmother used to go and work in the stone work in the hills. They faced all kinds of humiliation as the caste people oppressed them. My parents had a dream. One fine day my father announced that 'my daughter and sons will study.' Some of the villagers from his community asked him about the dream as there was no school in the village. My father sharply replied that I will put them in Naidupet Mission School. The next morning he set off with his daughter and sons to Naidupet Mission School. Missionaries gave me admission in girl's hostel and my brothers were put up in the boy's hostel. I am

> proud to say that I am the first woman to study SSLC from my village, and I am the first teacher posted in my own village. 'How wonderful it is to teach to Kshatriya caste children,' who treated us untouchables? Even those small children call my parents by name adding a derogative terminology and we have to address small children respectfully. As days passed by, even some of the caste people fell in love with me and I earned a good name in teaching. I even had training in tailoring and did embroidery on saris and sold them to the caste women. I am very much industrious. I married my cousin who is also a teacher. My husband and I as teachers made a tremendous impact on the villagers wherever we taught. Our house used to be a 'house church' as there were no churches in the villages. We used to invite caste people to our homes for Christmas celebrations and we used that occasion to proclaim the gospel. We are blessed with four children and I am proud that my two daughters became theologians. Both my sons are in the teaching line like us and are making an impact on the people. My parents were bold enough to execute their dream for their children that they should be like one among the caste people. Their dream came true. All this transformation took place in our family because of the missionaries and our conversion to Christianity.

Devadanamma is so strong that one should have a dream, hope, boldness, education and the fear of God. All these things will transform life. It is challenging to listen to such success stories of Dalit women in SALC. 50 percent of the respondents belonged to the second generation, 45 percent belonged to third generation and 5 percent belonged to the first generation.

3.9. Conclusion

Caste and gender are endowed with the essential and determining quality of identity and status in the Indian context. The experience of living as a minority (outcaste and woman) within a dominant patriarchal caste culture is a hard-hitting experience in India. The woman, the black, an outcaste etc., are categorically fixed with certain identities that tie them to a set of prejudiced stereotypes, determining their status. For a Dalit woman, identity as an outcaste and as a woman, carry a double burden and lead to identity crisis. However, the responses also reveal that women have assumed a secondary and an inferior status by themselves. They consider themselves inferior to men and not equals. The hypothesis anticipated in this thesis is that attributing masculine images to God played a major role in confirming the secondary and inferior status to women.

In this chapter I have tried to analyse and discover the status of Dalit women in South Andhra Lutheran Church: what is the status of SALC women in the family, church and society, what improvements have emerged in the status of women in SALC, who were instrumental in bringing a change and what were the constraints which create blockages in the way of their progress. Taking hold of the Indian Constitution, Dalits have enjoyed certain privileges, and have accessed new avenues. A lot has been done for the emancipation and empowerment of Dalits since Independence. Dalit Christian men and women have been transformed have become middle class. Their status in education, employment, economy, and religion has improved. They have had thus the benefit of a better status when compared to Dalit women of other religions. In spite of the transformation, Dalits however continue to live in segregated settlements in Andhra Pradesh. This is so since the Indian social order is so strong that down through the centuries it has denied human rights to Dalits. In turn, their physical, psychological, emotional, economic and social growth standards hampered.[45] Caste stigma is yet to be removed from the Indian mind. While much has been done in India to transform the Indian society, the reforms could not bring much change in Indian Christian caste orthodoxy. The caste system has taken strong roots in Indian Christianity which further creates distinctions, divisions and segregations.

However, given the fact that SALC women are acquiring new identities, the need of the hour is to expand the theological understanding and the practices that creatively engage our specific contextual realities in more decisively constructive ways. Adequate attention needs to be paid and addressed by the church in her theological discourses to promote basic education, employment opportunity, better working atmosphere, equal wages, etc., in the rural areas. As women become more conscious that Dalit' women's rights are human rights, the church has to become a human rights promoting agency, hence fulfil the Kingdom values as social stigma on Dalit women often remains untouched by the church directly. Efforts are needed to eradicate the caste system from within the church. Additional efforts have to be made to eliminate social evils such as dowry, alcoholism, forced widowhood, polygamy and wife-battering which had been harming the life of SALC families and the future generation.

Dalit feminist theologians can grapple with the transformative theological articulations only by rooting themselves in the contextual experiences of Dalit women. Our theologies need to find a profound connection between academic theologies and the day-to-day lives of the people. There should be a link between theologies and faith, passion and justice. The experiences of Dalit Christian women serve as a critical paradigm for the interpretation of the Bible in developing a Dalit feminist hermeneutics. The field research brings out the present status of Dalit women in SALC. It has revealed: A tremendous change in the status in the various fields is observed in the lives of SALC women. However, in spite of the transformation, subordinate, inferior and secondary position is maintained at various levels. The study understands that educational, economic and political status alone cannot recover the lost identity of Dalit women as the image of God. Theological interpretation is essential in order for them to understand that they are created in the image of God.

Hence, the study comprehends that re-imaging a theology from the perspective of Dalit women is the need of the hour. Gustavo Gutierrez provides us with a representative methodology. Like other liberationists. In this view, Gutierrez rejects the idea that theology is a systematic collection of timeless and culture-transcending truths that remain static for all generations. Rather, theology is in a flux; it is a dynamic and ongoing exercise involving contemporary insights into knowledge, humanity, and history. Gutierrez emphasizes that theology is not just to be learned, it is to be done. In his thinking, 'praxis' is the starting point for theology that involves revolutionary action on behalf of the poor and the oppressed. These theological perceptions will continually emerge. He writes that the theology of liberation is a theological reflection born of the experience of shared efforts to abolish the current unjust situation to build a different society, freer and more human.[46] Therefore, liberation and transformation is of paramount importance for Dalit feminist hermeneutics. Dalit feminist theology thus raises new questions about ways in which the biblical text is understood and taught and interpreted in the dominant theologies. It challenges the creating of a poor self-image in the Christian Dalit women. Dalit feminist theology critiques the past and the present which has a profound influence on the identity of Dalit women. It confronts assumptions, belief systems and the doctrines of faith and the whole of Christian life from the perspective of woman's identity both as the image of God and a human being. Dalit feminist theology both as an academic discipline and as an activist liberation movement reconsiders the traditions, practices, scriptures and theologies using hermeneutics of suspicion. A perspective from this angle holds hope everywhere for women, and especially to SALC women who have begun the process of change in a small way.

This chapter although does not claim universality, it gives us the facts of the life of Dalit women in India in general and Dalit Christian women in particular. The study clearly states that SALC Dalit Christian Lutheran women in Andhra Pradesh have been transformed to a great extent. Their status and identity has been changed. However, the study also tells that most of the respondents are of the opinion that they are subordinate as they believed that God created them as helpers to male counterparts although they are also created in the image of God. Although, it is important to note that the identities of Dalits have been recovered to a great extent due to the conversion to Christianity and a Christian influence, it is equally important to note the fact that the identity of women remained lost in various aspects as it is revealed in this chapter.

One can imagine in India, how in the Indian social hierarchy, caste identity leads either to power and privilege or to powerlessness and an unprivileged life. Hence, it is essential in this study to look for theoretical perspectives in search of an identity of Dalit women. Hence, next chapter is set to study different identity theories.

End Notes

1. Telugu Christian, Wikipedia, *the Free Encyclopedia* (accessed on 9.9.2010).
2. Telugu Christian, Wikipedia, *the Free Encyclopedia* (accessed on 9.9.2010).
3. Telugu Christian, Wikipedia, *the Free Encyclopedia* (accessed on 9.9.2010).
4. Telugu Christian, Wikipedia, *the Free Encyclopedia* (accessed on 9.9.2010).
5. Telugu Christian, Wikipedia, *the Free Encyclopedia* (accessed on 9.9.2010).
6. http://www.uecf.net/articles/a16.htm (accessed on 10.9.2010).
7. "The Lutheran Enterprise in India: Hermannsburg and Ohio in India, Rev. C. W. Oberdorfer, Gudur" in *Gospel Witness*. Vol. XXXIV, No. 3 (November 1938), 96. See Centennial, Souvenir, South Andhra Lutheran Church, 1865-1965, 3.
8. "The Lutheran Enterprise in India," 97.
9. "Editorial" in Souvenir, SALC 125th Anniversary, (1991), 7-8 *www.gracelutheranchurch.ca/MMS_LuthHist.html* (accessed on 24.6.2009), *Andrew S. Burgess, Ed., Lutheran World Missions (Minneapolis: Augsburg Publishing House, 1954)*, 20-34.
10. *Andrew S. Burgess, Ed., Lutheran World Missions*, 20-34.
11. Bishop Rev. Chandra Sekhar gave these details in a personal interview. Also see http://www.uelci.org/member-churches.asp (accessed on 10.11.2009).
12. dictionary.reference.com/browse/status (accessed on 23.9.2010).
13. P. Nirmala Bhai, *Harijan Women in Independent India*, 12.
14. P. Nirmala Bhai, *Harijan Women in Independent India*, 12.
15. *International Encyclopedia of Social Sciences* (The Macmillan Co. and the Free Press, Vol. 15 (1968), 250. Cited by P. Nirmala Bhai, Harijan *Women in Independent India* (New Delhi: B. R. Publishing Corporation, 1986), 9.
16. Source from Selected Educational Statistics, 2001-02 quoted by Janaki Rajan "Dropout or Pushed out?" In *Combat Law*, February-March (2006), 37.
17. 90 % of Dalit women are still illiterates. J. Muthumari who is a professor in the University of Madras brings out various reasons for more dropouts among Dalit girls, there are various reasons for this: Resistance from the family to send girls to schools, fear of insecurity in villages, lack of physical facilities like accommodation, school, transport and medical facilities. The girls were forced to take care of the siblings when the parents are away at work, and to do domestic chores which prevent them from attending school. Many were forced to get married at young age, which stop them from schooling. J. Muthumari, "Dalit Women in India," *www.asiasource.org/asip/dalits.cfm - 62k* (accessed on 10.4.2009).
18. Y. B. Abbasayulu, *Scheduled Caste Elite: A Study of Scheduled Caste Elite in Andhra Pradesh* (Osmania University: Hyderabad, 1978), 24.
19. Suneila Malik, *Social Integration of Scheduled Castes* (New Delhi: Anubhav Publications, 1979), 18.
20. N. Patnaik, *Caste and Social Change: An Anthropological Study of Three Villages* (Hyderabad: National Institute of Community Development, 1969), 11.
21. S. N. Dubey, *Administration of Social Welfare Programmes* (Bombay: India Somaiya Publication Pvt. Ltd. 1970), 10.
22. The Hindu 'higher' castes, it said, were least likely to be agricultural labourers. The report, "Conditions of Work and Promotion of Livelihoods in the Unorganized Sector", said the work participation rates for women belonging to the S.C.s and the S.T.s was significantly higher than those for women in general. *www.aicuf.net/studentnews.pdf* (accessed on 14.4.2009).
23. Thomas Chandy, "Where are the children in the elections? All Political parties must make investing in children a national priority." In *The Hindu*, Wednesday, April 15, (2009), 11.
24. Y. B. Abbasayulu, *Scheduled Caste Elite: A Study of Scheduled Caste Elite in Andhra Pradesh* (Hyderabad, Osmania University, 1978), 24.

25. Sumitra Bhave, *Pan on Fire: Eight Women Tell Their Story* (Indian Social Institute, Delhi: 1988), xii, N. G. Prasuna, "The Dalit Woman" in *Frontiers of Dalit Theology,* edited by V. Devasahayam (Madras: Gurukul Summer Institute, 1996), 102-103.
26. Judith Plaskow, *Standing Again at Sinai* (San Francisco: Harper and Row, 1990), 94.
27. J. Paul Rajasekar, "Lutheranism in Asia and the Indian Sub-continent" in *The Future of Lutheranism in a Global Context,* edited by Arland Dean Jacobson and James Aageson (Augsburg: Augsburg Fortress, 2007), 74.
28. Jesurathnam affirms that "there are certain points of convergence in the matrixes of both the biblical and Dalit world." He states that "the biblical dictum of a preferential option for the poor and the Dalit struggle for equality are points of convergence... K. Jesurathnam "Towards a Dalit Liberative Hermeneutic: Re-reading the Psalms of Lament," in *Bangalore Theological Forum,* 34.1 (June 2002) 2-3; He claims that the Dalit hermeneutical process leads to retelling the biblical texts several times to address Dalits or other marginalized people. Not only is the context of the Dalits vital to Dalit hermeneutics but also the connections between Dalits and the Bible. Dalit hermeneutics is a discovery of the connections between the biblical world and the world of Dalits more accurately. Jesuratnam, Towards a Dalit Liberative Hermeneutics: Re-reading the Psalms of Lament. *http:///www.religion-online.org/* (accessed on 10th March 2008).
29. R. Annie Watson, "Visibility of the Invisible" in *Construction of the Other, Identification of the Self: German Mission in India,* Edited by Martin Tamcke and Gladson Jathana, (Zurich: LIT Verlag Munster, 2012), 368.
30. The then bishop Rev. Chandra Sekhar ordained four women, namely, Rev. Vijaya Victor, Rev. Nelavala Gnana Prasuna, Rev Smitha Das and Rev. Sirisha Kasamala.
31. Jennie S Knight, *Feminist Mysticism and Images of God: A Practical Theology,* (St Louis, Missouri: Chalice Press, 2011), 2.
32. *Harijana Wada* is place where Dalits live, a Dalit colony and it has different names in different areas like *Mala Wada, Madiga Wada, Harijana Wada* etc.
33. I referred to one my childhood stories wherein I mentioned that I had a similar experience in the 1st chapter of this work. However, field research did not reveal that it is in practice now.
34. One of the respondents who are above 75 years old shared that their foreparents used to tie the long broom at their back so that they will not leave their foot prints.
35. To prove these statements, illustration is presented from the field study in the next chapter.
36. A. Maria Arulraja, SJ "Perspectives of Dalit Hermeneutics" in *Gurukul Journal of Theological Studies: Issue on Dalit Theology,* Vol. XVI, No. 1&2, January & July (2005), 24.
37. See for an elaborated discussion on anti-arrack movement raised in Andhra Pradesh. Rekha Pande, "Solidarity, Patriarchy and Empowerment: Women's Struggles against Arrack in India" in *Feminist Politics, Activism and Vision: Local and Global Challenges,* edited by Luciana Ricciutelli, Angela Miles and Margaret H. Mcfadden (ZED Books Ltd., 2004), 212-226.
38. Lisa Aronson Fontes and Kathy A. McCloskey, "Cultural Issues in Violence Against Women" in Claire M. Renzetti, Jeffrey L. Edleson and Raquel Kennedy Bergen Eds. *Violence Against Women,* (Second Edition), (New Delhi: Sage Publications, 2011), 153.
39. Kalpana Sharma is a Chief of the Mumbai Bureau and the Deputy editor with the Hindu, said on 19 March, 2006 and is published in India Together, *www.indiatogether.org/2006/mar/ksh-marriage.htm.*
40. Anjali Raj, "Lifted from the Funeral Pure but Left in the Cremation Ground: Aruttu-Kattatha Widows of Kulthalai Taluk" in *God's Image,* Vol. 26, No. 3, September (2007), 13-2. Anjali Raj reports her findings in her field research.
41. M Sivagami and M Thamilrasan, "Empowering Widows for Development," in *Problems of Widows in India* edited by P. Adinarayana Reddy, (New Delhi: Sarup & Sons, 2004), 92-95.
42. *See Ambassadors for Christ in India, Helen Agnes* (Archives: Gurukul Lutheran Theological College & Research Institute, 1980).

43. "The Autobiography and Family History of Gertruth Kettener," *Women's Missionary Outlook* (Archives, Gurukul Lutheran Theological College & Research Institute, 1980).
44. "The Autobiography and Family History of Gertruth Kettener," Mrs. Wilhemina Young Kuhlman was inspired to form a women's missionary organization when she attended along with her husband, the 1913 convention of the Evangelical Lutheran Joint Synod of Ohio and Other States (JSO) Men's Missionary Conference held in Sandusky. As a result, the first meeting of the Women's Missionary Conference (WMC) took place at St. Paul's Lutheran Church, Toledo, Ohio, on September 24-26, 1913. From 1919 to 1928 the WMC established various departments of work: Junior, Life Membership and Memorial, Statistical, Thank offering, India Lace, Literature, Extension, and Special Needs. Each department concentrated on a specific aspect of WMC work to support mission endeavours of the church-at-large.
45. *Ambassadors for Christ in India, Helen Agnes* (Archives: Gurukul, 1980), 19.
46. See Buta Singh, *The Dalits and Dalit Awakening in India* (New Delhi, Gyan Publishing House: 2004), 45.
47. See Gustavo Gutierrez, *A Theology of Liberation,* (Maryknoll, N.Y.,: Orbis Books, 1973).

4

The Concept of Identity Theoretical Perspectives in Search of a Dalit Feminist Identity

4.1. Introduction

Identity remains one of the most urgent as well as a passionately discussed topic in the Indian theological scene and world-wide. What is identity? When does identity emerge? What are the characteristics of identity? Can identity change over time? Or is it fixed? Can identity be lost? If so, can it be recovered? How can it be recovered? Can one's past experiences affect one's present or future identity? What roles one's family, school, church, religion, society and cultural values play in the formation of one's identity? These questions challenge the theological world today.

An identity is the set of meanings that define who one is. Identity in Indian circles has a peculiar connotation as name, place of birth etc., that identifies one's caste. Caste and patriarchy play a dominant role in determining the status of women in the Indian society. In Indian culture, a name is more than a label that assists the other to refer to a person. It carries with it the identity of one's family and place of birth; in some parts of south India it also indicates one's community or caste. An often-asked question as it is mentioned in the introduction, when one is introduced to another, is the question, 'what is your family name?' It is an indirect way of knowing the total identity of a person. In Indian culture, the family name is much more central to the roots of a person's identity. It indicates birthright, association, location, and caste of a person. In India, to be born in the Brahmin caste is to be on the winning side of life, as that caste identity is superior. One can imagine how in the Indian social hierarchy, caste identity leads either to power and privilege or to powerlessness and an unprivileged life. Hence, the concern of this chapter is to look for theoretical perspectives in search of an identity of Dalit women.

This chapter presents six selected approaches to identity, while offering a brief critique of each approach from a Dalit feminist perspective. The concern is to show how each approach would respond to the questions asked at the beginning of this chapter, such as "Can Identity be lost? If so, is there a possibility to recover that lost identity? What are the alternatives which lead to the process of recovering the lost identity?"

4.2. Definitions and the Nature of the Term Identity

Traditionally, identity as a concept was defined in terms of 'sameness.' However, since 1980s and 1990s it has been theorized and discussed more in terms of difference. Identity is an umbrella term used throughout the social science to describe a people's conception and expression of their individuality or group affiliations.[1] The seventh edition of *Oxford Dictionary* defines 'Identity' as absolute sameness, as individuality, personality, and a condition of being a specified person.[2] The concept identity originated from the Latin term *idem* meaning 'same' and shares effectiveness with the terms 'likeness,' 'oneness,' and *identidem,* meaning 'over and again,' or 'repeatedly.'[3]

The present day definitions of identity are much wider and have moved from Latin concepts of sameness to the concept of differences. The concept of identity portrays a number of issues such as the conceptualization of race, sex, caste, class, ethnicity, culture and how one articulates beliefs in psychology, sociology, religion, theology and other social sciences. Annie Sophie Roalt defines identity as 'those factors of a person's or a group's belief-system, nationality, ethnicity and class, educational background, rural or urban back-ground, gender or sexuality which are highlighted at certain periods of time and in certain places....[4] This definition makes it clear that each human being has multiple identities in multiple contexts.

For David Moshman, an identity 'is a sophisticated conception of oneself...a theory of oneself.'[5] He further explains that there are two characteristics which are relevant in the definition: Firstly, theories are coherent: "To say one's identity is a theory of oneself is to say that it is not just a collection of beliefs about oneself, but rather is organized to generate an integrated conception."[6] Secondly, 'theories are explanatory, to say one's identity is a theory of oneself is to say it is not just a description of oneself; rather it is an attempt to explain oneself.'[7] As Moshman explains, identity is a formation of the self. It is structured in such a way that it develops self-understanding. It is an account of one's beliefs and the way one interprets and explains one's behavior.

J. S. Phinney however defines identity from an ethnic point of view. Her definition is as follows: Identity 'a dynamic, multidimensional construct that refers to one's identity. Or sense of self, in ethnic terms that is in terms of subgroup within a larger context that claims a common ancestry and shares one or more of the following elements: culture, race, religion, language, kinship, or place of origin.'[8]

For Evangeline Anderson-Rajakumar, identity of a person depends on how one understands one's self. Identity can be viewed under two categories; namely subjective identity and objective identity, where the former refers to the way one understands one's own individuality and personality. The latter may be understood as the opinion of an individual or a community. The significance of such a distinction between subjective and objective identity becomes clear in the analysis of individual women's experience. For example, many women are forced to be patient and forgiving in order to save their families. They even give up the thought of quitting situations of violence when they are guided by the opinion of society and its norms.[9]

For Seamon and Kenrick, identity is a constant companion of an individual and it determines how they see themselves and how they feel about themselves. Identity is a stable companion of an individual and it determines how a person sees oneself (self-image) and how the person feels about oneself (self-esteem).[10]

Identity forces people to do various things in relation to others. Identity is the one characteristic of an individual that remains with them forever, whether they are alone or socializing.[11] Each individual has an identity. As field research indicates, Dalit women in SALC have multiple identities. The previous chapter indicates on the one hand that SALC women have acquired new identities that provide them dignity in society. On the other it points out that they have internalized inferior, subordinate and impure identities. On the one hand they admit the fact that they are created in the image of God and on the other they are not comfortable in imaging God in their image. The nature of identity as explained by Seamon and Kenrick has strong implications for explaining the identity of Dalit women. This identity crisis motivates the researcher to explore theological interpretation of identity in the context of Dalit Christian women in order for them to have fuller life. Selected perspectives are therefore discussed in this chapter in the following pages in order to search for Dalit feminist identity.

4.3. Origins of the Concept of Identity

Erikson was one of the earliest psychologists who were extremely interested in the concept of identity. Erikson was the first person to focus both popular and scientific attention on the meaning of identity. His theoretical framework rests upon a distinction and a process between the ego identity or the personal identity and social identity or the cultural identity. He spoke of identity as both a conscious and an unconscious motivation for continuity of individual personality. He used the term 'identity' to refer to that which results from the 'silent doings of ego syntheses and 'that sense of inner solidarity which deals with values of a significant social group.'[12] He affirmed that the development of a strong ego identity leads a person to a stronger sense of identity in general.

4.3.1. Identity Crisis

Erikson has thus coined the term 'identity crisis' to describe generally the crisis that brings about identity problems and specially the shell-shocked condition of the war victims that he treated during the Second World War. He says the dilemma expressed by these patients was that 'they had lost their sense of themselves as having past and future.' Their ego was lost because their sense of ego-identity was severely impaired. Erikson also saw identity confusion associated with ego identity impairment among young people during the war.[13] According to Erikson, identity confusion is manifested in terms of 'contradictory self-images, or aspirations, roles or opportunities or as split of self images, a loss of center and a dispersion.'[14] According to Erikson, 'identity crises may prolong among young adults.' To prove this, Erikson takes Martin Luther as an example. He studies him as a case to point, the prolonged identity crisis of Luther, a crisis stimulated by his experiences with the contradicting practices of the Catholic Church in terms of absolute obedience and selling absolution. Erikson says, Luther resolved his 'identity crisis' by formulating an apparently less contradictory ideology to serve as a 'Protestant' model in order to reform Christianity.[15]

'The identity crisis' begins from their childhood in the lives of Dalit women. In the Indian context, family, church, society and culture play a dominant role in the identity-formation of a Dalit woman. For example, as soon as the baby is born into a Dalit family, based on the historical influences and the present social structure system, it is identified as an outcaste colonized child. If the baby is a girl, one more identity is attached to her at birth. That is, 'minus,' which means boy is a 'plus' for the family and the girl is a minus. The minus identity of the baby is carried all through her life time. These two identities as an 'outcaste colonized and the minus for the family' strongly enters into the psyche of Dalit women. The most affected and influenced are the girl children of that community. A girl often hears the statement that she is a 'minus' in the family. This false identity leads them towards diffusion. Historical, familial, social, cultural and religious factors brand the 'Dalit woman' with a false identity as minus, outcaste, colonized, untouchable, dirty, impure, weak, inferior, subordinate, and sinful. Sangeetha's story that is mentioned in the previous chapter is an obvious clue to the fact that women and men give less importance to girls in their families. In the socialization process, girls learn from their childhood that they are lesser beings. This identity crisis leads to an identity formation in one either for stronger self-esteem or for low self-esteem.

4.3.2. The Identity Formation Process

The identity formation (Who am I?) is rooted in psychoanalytic theory and psychology. This was Erickson's primary research method. According to him, identity formation focuses on three things: the self (Who am I?), acculturation (With whom do I fit in?), and social identity (What does it mean to be part of the group?).[16] James E. Marcia states that at late adolescence, an individual experiences his/her abilities and needs and beliefs within a perceived social context and demands, available alternatives and expectable rewards. These experiences lead to the formation of a new personality structure in a person as 'identity.' This identity provides a sense of continuity with one's past, meaning for one's present and direction for one's future.[17]

Marcia's work on identity status addresses the role of ideological exploration in human maturity and development.[18] From his research, Marcia has come to a conclusion that four identity statuses, such as Identity Diffusion which characterizes low commitment and low exploration, Identity Foreclosure that contains high commitment and low exploration, Identity Moratorium which portrays low commitment and high exploration, and Identity Achievement which characterizes high commitment and high exploration occur. These four identity development statuses are essentially research constructs and every individual is a combination of these statuses.[19]

Among the four statuses, Identity Diffusion is considered as the least mature and least complex status. Identity Foreclosure is thought of as a bit mature status than Identity Diffusion. Marcia suggested that an individual entering into adolescence typically falls into identity-diffused category that has no strong commitment or experience and does not seek for such. Such individuals are satisfied to live day by day and simply see where life takes them. Foreclosure contains some form of commitment. Those commitments have been internalized from parents, society, culture and religion. Foreclosure individuals neither question nor look for other alternatives. For Marcia, it is possible for an individual who is either identity-diffused or foreclosed to move into identity crisis. Those who end up in identity crisis will move on to resolve it. The individual is then likely to resolve his or her identity crisis by entering into a moratorium where the hermeneutics of suspicion is employed. This status will lead an individual to the status of identity achievement with much struggle within oneself.

Identities are therefore constructed on the foundation of various experiences. Some experiences are fixed at birth, such as related to the birth place, to the parental ethos, community, and society environment, and religion, skin color, gender and caste. These experiences are static, and are ascribed. Yet some experiences may be acquired or modified later, such as the language spoken, religion practised, clothing worn, or food eaten. These experiences are not ascribed but acquired. A few identities, then, are based on ascribed status and a few are on shared values.[20] For example, identities such as outcaste, inferior, weak etc., are ascribed to a few communities to legitimize exclusion. Identities such as high caste, superior, strong, dominant etc., ascribed again to legitimize the status quo. An identity such as Dalit is thus an acquired identity.[21]

As it is mentioned in the introductory chapter, in India, roots such as caste, sex, place and religion determine the identity of a person. The work strongly asserts that Dalit women are a combination of the four identity statuses as proposed by Marcia. A number of Dalit women in India in general and SALC in particular have identity diffusion. Most of the rural Dalit women who were interviewed suffer identity diffusion.

However, the research also indicates that SALC women do have achieved identities. 'Who am I' and 'Where am I' are explorative questions from a Dalit feminist perspective. These two questions lead to 'Identity Achievement' as proposed by Marcia.[22] Rooted in Marcia's theory, Phinney has focused her study of ethnic identity on two areas. For her, an individual progresses from an early stage in which one's ethnicity is taken for granted, on the basis of attitudes and opinions of others or of society through a period of exploration into the meaning of implications of one's group membership, to an achieved ethnic identity that reflects a secure, confident self of oneself as a member of a group. Furthermore, an achieved ethnic identity is not necessarily a static end point of development; individuals are likely to re-examine their ethnicity throughout their lives. Phinney identifies three stages: diffuse/foreclosed, in which the issue of ethnic identity is unexplored or still to be addressed; moratorium in which there is active searching for but not a clear acceptance of ethnic identity; and achieved, in which an ethnic identity has been embraced. Acceptance, clear understanding, and a deep sense of belonging to the group characterize the final stage.[23]

Phinney's explanation has strong implications for Dalit women in their search for identity. While discussing the caste identity value, it is imperative to speak of the identity of a Dalit woman although it is not possible to discuss a common identity. This chapter identifies all four statuses proposed by Marcia and Phinney in Dalit women's identity: Caste identity diffusion: It is characterized by a lack of interest, or concern with caste and lack of exploration of caste issues. Typical answers received from field research such as, 'I don't worry about caste,' 'now I am a Christian,' 'Adi Andhra,' 'I have no reason to worry about,' 'my parents had experiences of untouchability but I do not experience it,' 'Why do I bother about?' point to the identity diffusion among Dalit women in SALC. Diffused individuals minimize themselves from making choices about their future, and remain arrested compromising sometimes their lives. Secondly, in identity-foreclosed, Dalit women make commitments that are often conservativist, without questioning them or investigating the alternatives. For example, in the field research, the responses such as, 'The Bible sanctions authority to men to dominate women,' indicate that we need to 'submit' without a question. It is a clear example that Dalit women make commitments to carry on the life in the given context as received by the family, society and religion. The third status, moratorium is the status where individuals in contrast, struggle to accept the given fixed situation and get into a crisis. They keep struggling with this identity crisis. For example, in the field research, one respondent, who is a young widow, kept raising questions, why did God create me? Why should people think of me as inauspicious? It is an identity crisis for her. Many young widows suffer this crisis. The fourth status is identity achieved. The ideal outcome of the identity process is an achieved identity, characterized by a clear, confident sense of one's own Dalit identity. People with an achieved ego identity have resolved uncertainties about their future direction and have made commitments that will guide future action. For example, a respondent from SALC N. Surekha worked on "Liberation beyond Borders: Dalit Feminist Hermeneutics and Four Gospel Women." She says her identity is an achieved identity as Dalit, feminist, Lutheran, Christian woman. She says, "an identity as a Dalit is an honourable one because the term 'Dalit' is an achieved and acquired one, and not imposed. The term 'feminist' is an achieved and acquired identity that looks for a transformation among individuals and the society. Dalit feminist's identity is a recovered identity as 'a confident, powerful, equal, committed, and transformed individual identity." As the Dalit Christian feminist identity is relational 'it commits herself/himself to one's own family, community and church to transform the related people to an achieved identity status.'

4.4. Selected Approaches to Identity

4.4.1. Socio-cultural Approach to Identity

A human being becomes a social being, through the process of socialization. The source of human thoughts and identity are found in the community and social environment in which he or she lives. Human identity is a product of socialization and culture in which she or he grows up. It is through the process of socialization that a person internalizes a world-view and receives orientation of one's identity. Socialization is an evolution, in which 'an individual' becomes a social being within a group and within a given culture.[24] Mead holds a view that an individual's identity is the product of the surrounding social context.[25]

Lev Semyonovich Vygotsky's experiences and interests led him to the general developmental process, those which affect human cognition, emotion and motivation. His developmental perspective is highly challenging for theorizing about how people construct their personal versions of social identities that mediate their behaviour and interpretations of the world. Vygotsky says that semiotic (study of the way in which people communicate through signs and symbols) mediation clarifies the role of culture in the formation of identities. It envisions how actively internalized identities enable a person to control one's behaviour and thus have agency.[26] Vygotsky emphasizes on the role that social, cultural and historical forces play in shaping and influencing the process of identity development. While Erikson defined identity, as a 'subjective sense of invigorating sameness and continuity,' Vygotsky emphasizes on socio-cultural processes into a kind of mediated-action approach to identity formation. Both Vygotsky and Erikson emphasize that social, cultural and historical processes play a very significant role in the formation and transformation of individual identities.[27]

Four aspects of socio-cultural approach which is also called as Vygotskian approach to teamwork are identified: Firstly, all activity is socio-culturally situated. Secondly, the meanings and actions of the participants create the context for their activity. These two principles taken together show that the socio-cultural context and the meanings developed within this context are mutually constitutive. They create, sustain, and transform each other. Thirdly, semiotic mediation an important aspect of the socio-cultural approach, points to the fact that through signs and signals people understand each other and transform each other. Fourthly, cognitive development is inherently connected to social and emotional development.[28]

The socio-cultural approach provides a significant contribution to the understanding of identity. This approach emphasizes that the social context shapes one's identity. The socio-cultural approach is based on the idea that society and culture shapes the understanding of a person. Social customs, beliefs, values, and language play a major role in shaping the person's identity and authenticity. This approach emphasizes that what a person thinks and understands is based on his or her socio-cultural background.

According to this approach, group members within the given social context have access to gain positive values from membership of their group. However, people are not always members of groups which give them a positive social identity, and sometimes it is not possible for them to move to another group. For example, in the Indian context, people who belong to the outcaste social group do not gain positive social identity. The outcaste group reminds the people that those who are born into their group are untouchables and impure. There is no possibility for an outcaste to take up the caste of a Brahmin. It is decided at the birth. Caste plays a major role in religion too. This leads to an identity crisis among Dalit children. It is clear that socio-cultural aspects play a major role in shaping the identity of a person. Shaping can take place both positively and negatively. These socio-cultural influences on Dalit women in India have shaped them and influenced them to think of their identity as inferior, subordinate, untouchable, and unclean. This is very much evident from the field study. For example, a few respondents stated that they are unclean and impure during menstruation. So, they do not touch the Bible and participate in Holt Communion. Women have thus internalized deeply these unclean and impure imposed identities from the time they attain age. Added to that, a few scriptural texts such as Leviticus 15 reinforce this false identity. One respondent, an Upper Primary School Headmistress who is also a Secretary for SALC Women's Maha Samaj shared, "I never touched the Bible and participated in Holy Communion during my menstruation. It is not because someone told me to do so; it is because I feel a kind of guiltiness within me. Our pastor never told us to practice this." From where did she get this feeling of guilt? Why should women internalize this kind of impure or guilt identity? Added to this, caste identity prescribed that they are untouchables. Although, Dalit Christian women who were interviewed responded that they gained new identity as 'Christians' were again very uncomfortable to answer a question, 'to which caste they belong to? Yet again, respondents shared that they do not accept that they are 'untouchables' but it is the society that treats them as untouchables. Hence, they suffer a serious identity crisis.

4.4.2. Historical Approach to Identity

Erikson noted that the concept of identity is located in historical relativity, because identity has become an issue of individual attention, particularly at the point of American history when a new generation of immigrants was struggling for self-definition.[29] This approach provided some important insights into the impact of social change on identity-development for those within a social group. Generally, it is not possible to understand the past without history.

However, an appreciation of historical forces alone is insufficient to account for identity and one's self-definition. Erikson takes two important historical periods to illustrate that historical approach alone is not sufficient in resolving the identity crisis and in forming an identity: The Reformation period and The Indian Independence. Erikson says, both in the lives of Martin Luther and Gandhi, "It was the dynamics of individual psychological struggles of Luther and Gandhi in interaction with critical historical moments that enabled both individual's and social change to occur."[30] Thus, a historical approach alone cannot help one to study identity as problematic in articulating the identity development.

However, for the marginalized and the powerless, historical approach serves as an important theory in searching for one's identity along with personal psychological struggles. For example, along with historical influence, the personal struggles of caste oppression and particularly his experiences of untouchability led B.R. Ambedkar, as a school-going child towards the identity crisis that led him to gain an achieved identity.[31] In the same way, personal and social experiences of Dalit theologians have been led to understand the importance of history for the Dalits. Because of this, various theologians have dealt with the history of Dalits in recent times, especially the history of Dalit Christians. An important aspect of Dalit literature is the question concerning Dalit identity and their roots. They need to affirm that they are enslaved. Ambedkar says, "Tell the slave that he is a slave, he will rise and revolt." The affirmation 'we were no people' proceeds to form the affirmation, 'now we are God's people' as an achievable goal.[32] "The true identity of Dalits must go through a recovery and exposure of the suppressed past..."[33] James Massey, a prominent Dalit theologian captures the wide usage of the term Dalit as follows:

> Dalit is thus not a mere descriptive name or title, but an expression of hope for the recovery of their past identity. The struggle of these

> "outcastes" has given the term Dalit a positive meaning. The very realization of themselves as Dalit, the very acceptance of the state of "Dalitness," is the first step on the way towards their transformation into full and liberated human beings.[34]

It is important therefore for Dalit theologians to establish the identity of Dalits, an identity that can mobilize Dalits for change, as the term 'Dalit' provides an identity.[35] This can be done in the recovery of their past and the memory of their rejection.[36] A few respondents mentioned during the group discussions that the present status cannot be changed as it is historically rooted. A few questions raised were, 'Is there any possibility for Dalits to buy lands and construct houses in the main villages?' 'Is there any possibility to bridge the distance between Dalit colonies (which are treated untouchable areas) and the main villages? Can change be brought about this? Is land possession guarantee for change?

Here comes a place for hermeneutics of reconstruction. Reconstruction of history is essential in recovering the images lost in Dalit women. In combination with socio-cultural approach, historical approach is an important theory for Dalit women to understand the influence of historical roots on them that led them to the present status.

4.4.3. Post-modern Approach to Identity

"'If modern identity is seen as essentialist, postmodern identity may be concerned constructivist.' In other words, post-modernism treats identity as something that is actively constructed on an ongoing basis. It sees identity as fragmented, not unified; multiple, not singular; expansive, not bounded."[37] Interpretative and social constructionist approaches together gave rise to the post-modern approach. This approach is well accepted in cultural studies and feminist scholarship as well.[38] Post-modernist approach critiques the modern institutions because they created a tension between self and society, resulting in identity confusion, alienation, the fragmentation of self and loss of a sense of authenticity among those affected.[39] The post-modernist literature extends these problematic trends to explore new forms of self and identity. This approach recognizes the significance of identities and their connection to political forces. Post-modern theorists maintain that, 'the 'self-identity' is socially constructed, emergent and plural.'[40]

Kumarivadivelu says, "Identity formation is conditioned not merely by inherited traditions such as culture, or by external exigencies such as history, or by ideological constructs such as power, but also by the individual's ability and willingness to exercise independent decision making."[41] The crucial aspect of post-modern identity is the notion of difference. Post-modern identity embraced the idea that identity is fluid, and discontinuous. It is constantly invented and reinvented.[42]

The post-modern approach analyzes the concept of identity from a societal perspective than from a personal level. The strong criticism against post-modern theories is that, 'there are no true identities for postmodern theorists.'[43] They expose a fluid nature of reality. However, while showing that identity is closely tied to social structure and history, they lose sight of the power of people to shape their own identity. For a post-modernist, a transformation of identity is a mere change in image.[44]

For Dalit women, as post-modern approach proposes, change of image is essential in bringing transformation for individuals as well as their community. However, the change of image is a process. It is important for Dalit women to deconstruct modern society which has imposed essentialism. Dalit women have to reconstruct their identity based on transformation. Geetha one of the respondents shares her encounter with caste identity. Geetha, a respondent from Sullur, asserts her image as the child of God. She had a two-year theological training and received a Diploma in "Graduate of Theology." During her training, her world view of a woman and a Dalit has transformed. She realized that she is created in the image of God. This transformative world view helped her to recover her identity as a child of God. She shares her experience how she stood firm in not following the rules laid by the caste people. Geetha says:

> In our village Veerlagunapadu (She is now married and living with her husband) there is a practice in our colony. When the high caste men walk in the streets, Dalit women should not sit on the carts. Even if they want to sit, they have to put the cart upside down and sit. One day it so happened, one high caste man was passing by our street and I was sitting on the cart. My mother-in-law came running, and she asked me to get up or put the cart upside down and sit. I did not listen to her, instead I told her and confronted her gently stating that 'we are the children of God and we need not humiliate ourselves. If he comes to our house, as a mark of respect I can get up. I need not get up while he is walking somewhere.' My mother-in-law was so anxious that this incident may create tension in our village. Fortunately till now nothing has happened.

This kind of assertion is essential in order for Dalit women to recover their lost identities. But it is a long process.

4.4.4. Post-colonial Approach to Identity

Identity is one of the central questions raised by the post-colonial theory. The Post-colonial approach to identities initially arose from the resistance to a prescribed identity imposed by the colonizers and from a need to reformulate and articulate an identity that took shape after the departure of the colonizers. In the process of transformation from a colonial to a postcolonial existence, people who were once victimized, now use their historical suffering to legitimately promote their wounded identities.

The post-modern perspective on identity is shared by post-colonial scholars as well. However, post-colonial scholars provide an additional dimension to the question of difference in relation to identity. The basic argument of the post-colonial approach to identity is that, 'the other identity is imposed by hegemonic power structures.'[45] In this context, Derek Hooks the post-colonial theorist says, "Identity is understood as that set of social and cultural understandings through which we come to know and experience ourselves. These understandings play an important role in constituting who we are – that is, in whom we, and others, understand ourselves to be."[46]

Based on this definition, Hooks brings four aspects of post-colonial approach to identity: identity is social, identity is flexible and mobile, and identity is radically delimited and conditioned by social and material power relations, identity is determined by ideology and by historical patterns of privilege. People have cultural resources too that contribute to the formation of identities.[47] Collins makes it clear that this approach refers to a collection of narratives, values, ideals, and types of knowledge, discourses, social practices and beliefs which are shared, and which maintain a sense of sameness, or continuity, across different contexts within that culture.[48] This approach stresses the ways of talking and ways of making sense of the world. It emphasizes the structural conditions of day-to-day life and stresses the point of material circumstances that define and limit where and how one lives. Given that identity is understood in terms of experience and self-knowledge, this approach views identity which has the potential shifts for negotiation and change. Thus identity can be recovered and achieved. Sugirtharajah espouses the post-colonial approach, which he thinks can best analyze the colonial trappings in biblical texts, offer alternative readings, that address nationalism, identity, ethnicity, and subaltern and feminist concerns as well as interrogate colonial and metropolitan concerns.[49]

Massey expounds four layers of colonization as the fundamental causes for the suffering and the submergence of the identity and culture of the Dalits. They are Aryan, Muslim, British and the high caste internal colonization. This is how he summarizes his position:

> The colonization of the Dalits, which began with their defeat at the hands of the Aryans, was internalized through religious myths and stories and finally by introducing a fixed social order based on a caste system dependent on one's birth. Neither the centuries during which India was successively dominated by Muslims and the British nor the arrival of other religions, including Christianity, succeeded in overcoming the influence of this caste system; indeed, was the effect of Muslim and British colonization to strengthen the status quo. With independence, the rule of the country went back into the hands of the so-called upper caste, the original colonizers of the Dalits.[50]

Dalit consciousness should realize that the ultimate goal of its liberation movement cannot be the 'land flowing with milk and honey.' For Christian Dalit Theology, it cannot be simply the gaining of the rights, the reservation, and the privileges. The goal is the realization of our full humanness or, conversely our full divinity, the ideal of the *Imago Dei,* the image of God in us. To use another biblical metaphor, our goal is the 'glorious liberty of the children of God.'[51] Two hundred years of colonial rule were, indeed, the darkest phase of Indian history, but the internal colonialism that exists after Indian Independence is not less dangerous than the former. The internal colonization has pushed Dalits to the margins such that Dalit women face triple colonization.[52]

4.4.5. Feminist Approach to Identity

Women at some time or the other experience some interaction with the most basic identity-related questions such as 'who am I?' 'Why am I born?' 'Why am I born as woman?' 'Why do I exist?' 'Why should I feel so down?' and 'How long should I live this way?' But, often women do not allow such questions to interrupt their everyday lives; rather they transfer such discussions and interrogations to the background or confine it to sporadic speculations. Some would venture to grasp all these questions together and try to achieve a holistic understanding of their existence of what they are and why they are born. Feminists/womanists fit into this category in exploring the new meaning for their lives. They seek to approach these identity questions from various perspectives such as philosophy, religion, sociology, anthropology etc., to find plausible answers to their questions that are compatible in the present context. In the process, feminists have found that the patriarchal structure of various cultures and religion have played a leading role that led to the present oppressive and exploitative identity of women. Thus, they give extraordinary attention to the lives of women and their multifaceted experiences: their stories, their social roles and relationships, their success and failures in rediscovering their identities.

Human experience serves as both the beginning and the end in searching for feminist identity. Experience includes the experience of the divine, experience of oneself, experience of the community and the experience of the world in an interconnecting dialectic,[53] which is based on practice.

In their theological articulations, feminists have approached the issue of identity in diverse ways. As feminism entered into an era in which differences among women, the multiple identities of women, and identity politics arose at the center of feminist discussions, 'Woman' as a universal identity became no longer practicable for feminist theory and practice. Multiple identities and differences arose to solve the problem of universal claims.[54] For Susan Hekman, identity is defined by two opposites: sameness and difference. She says, "To declare that something or someone has particular identity is to claim simultaneously, that it is identical to the other entities that possess that identity and that, as a particular thing, it possesses unique qualities that are an identity."[55] In other words, it is to say 'you and I' are same and different.

Natalie K.Watson says that Elizabeth Schuzzler Fiorenza's use of spelling 'wo/men' expresses the fragmentation and the particularity of women's lives shaped by structures of class, race, sexual orientation and religion as factors constructing women's social identity.[56] Fiorenza's hermeneutics concentrates on discovering and recovering traditions that challenge culture.[57] Fiorenza in her work, *In Memory of Her*, affirms that even though the Bible is male-oriented, an assessment of the social and historical context will reveal women's historical participation in the earliest Christian communities. She reconstructs the early Christian community as one of egalitarian discipleship.[58] Fiorenza's reconstructions have been very useful in the construction of Indian feminist theology. For example, Pushpa Joseph brings out Fiorenza's egalitarian perspective of the church as a potential dynamic for the liberation of women in India. Pushpa says, "...Fiorenza paves the path for a reconstruction of women's active and creative participation in the construction of religious and social history and offers us tools for the transformation..."[59] Joseph says further, "Individual dialogue is the action by which feminist theology works within religion." Women's identity in India is defined by various issues such as gender, class, caste, and the religious patriarchies which are social constructs. Joseph instructs that it is through the sharing and re-membering of the 'flesh and blood realities of our women' that they are able to claim their identities within Indian society and culture with integrity. The individual sharing of personal stories lays the foundation for the Indian feminist movement to employ 'rigorous systematic critical analysis.'[60] As Joseph suggested, it is important to do serious systematic analysis of the identity of Dalit women in India.

Aniene argues that Ackerman's work in South African context points to a specific theological understanding and interpretation of identity, practice and context within particular historical realities. Her use of identity, practice and context, where the link between her spirituality and the problems of daily life is rooted within the broader framework of practical and feminist theology, is a testimony in search for justice.[61] As a feminist practical theologian, Ackernman has asked critical questions about her place within theology and in the faith community. She is aware that, as a woman, she does theology from a marginalized place, and that her focus on context from a practical perspective is influenced by this marginalized position. Identity issues remain therefore central to her theology, from which she develops a contextual feminist theology of praxis. Her work on identity highlights the following four aspects. 1. Identity is a relational concept 2. Dominant power relations need to be deconstructed 3. Women need to redefine their own identity as part of being equal in relations to others and 4. The private and the public/political identity should not be divided into isolated and closed identities separate from one another.[62]

Kumkum Sangari analyzes the ideology of woman's identity from three different angles: patriarchy, colonialism, and capitalism. In relation to understanding women as agents, she argues that 'notions of femaleness, self or identity' are so tied up with the questions of family, class, religion and other forms of collectivity that they cannot be framed in terms of 'a single unified axis.'[63] She argues that it is necessary to work with the concept of 'multiple identities' that emerge 'through several crises-crossing ideologies rather than a single one,' and that exists in close relation with each other.[64] Enel Dengel-Janic says:

> 'The ideology of ideal womanhood' is constructed in different discourses on women, in which women are positioned, defined, located and images of women are produced that might be diverse and even contradictory, but which nevertheless lead to the effect of dividing societies into the binaries of male and female, the female being the dominated part.[65]

Chandra Talpade Mohanthy advocates post-colonial feminist approach to 'theologizing identity and difference that would proceed from the idea of the oppressions as fundamental to the experience of social and political marginality, the crucial role of hegemonic state in circumscribing women's daily lives and survival struggles, the significance of memory and writing in the creation of oppositional agency, and the differences, conflicts and contradictions internal to Third World women's organizations and communities.'[66] Despite the decolonization of former European colonies, many parts of the world are viewed in this analysis as continuing to experience military, economic and political domination by Western powers and importantly, the ongoing hegemony of Western ideas. Post-colonial feminist approach emphasizes thus identity as relational and historical rather than essential or fixed.

One of the primary tasks of feminist scholarship in India is to deconstruct any given ideological framework in the hermeneutics of suspicion to search for any prevalent elements that destroy/deny/discriminate/dehumanize/distort the identity of women on the basis of their gender and caste. Such elements are present either visibly or invisibly.[67] Kumkum Sangari and Sudesh Vaid argue that underpinning 'every attempt towards identity has been a re-description of women.'[68] One of the practical reasons that motivated Indian feminists to adopt a complex model of women's identity is suggested by Dietrich in her discussion of the impact of the recent rise in communalism on the women's movement. For Dietrich, caste and religion play much stronger roles in the lives of Indian women than gender, at least in situations of communal strife.[69] Dietrich's argument is proved by field research. Women are stronger in their caste identity. Although, caste system is not practiced among SALC people obviously, it is practised during weddings. One respondent shared that she fell in love with a man who does not belong to her sub-caste. She says, "It was my mother who was a strong opponent to our marriage, but my father stood by me and arranged marriage for us." The caste mindset is so deeply imbedded in the psyche of Dalit Christians.

Post-colonial feminism aims at subverting any notions of fixed and universal identities and deconstructs notions of disconnected identities. For a Dalit woman, identity as an outcaste and as a woman, carry double burden and lead to identity crisis. The approach of post-colonial feminism would be appropriate in searching for Dalit feminist identity, as it takes seriously the historical, social, political, cultural, modern and colonial impact of fixing identities that has damaging effects on the image of women.

4.4.6. Narrative Approach to Identity

Since the 1970s narrative theologians have offered various ways of engaging in constructive Christian theology. Narrative theology emerged in North America. Its chief theological precursor was H. Richard Niebhur. He maintains the initiative and involvement of God in History as well as the relative, incomplete nature of all the stories which testify to that. Both stories and general concepts are needed in theology because our lives are reconstituted by time (past, present and future). It means that the narrative is especially appropriate to express the revelation of God's grace and glory in contingent existence.[70] Gabriel Fackre's book, *The Christian Story* with the subtitle 'a narrative interpretation of basic Christian doctrine,' attempts to develop the same in its introduction:

> A category of 'story' that will explain the core meaning of Christian faith. The move to story opens the way to a new means of conceptualizing the divine inspiration while giving place to immanence as well, because its inspiration is the inspiration of story. The brain of narrative theology lies in its declaration that faith requires the connection of our personal stories with the transcendent/ immanent story of a religious community and ultimately with the grand narrative of the divine action in the world. The divine story mediated by the community of faith transcends our individual, finite narratives; yet it is imminent in the history of the world and by faith in the ongoing story of the life of the believer.[71]

With respect to the theological inquiry, narrative thinker Fackre defines 'story' as an 'account of characters and events in a plot moving over time and space through conflict toward resolution.'[72] Fackre rightly says that narrative theology has its base in the connection between the stories of the faith communities of the Bible and the stories of the living faith communities.

John Navone's book, 'Towards a Theology of Story,' points out that 'story theology' provides a link between personal experience and religious symbols.[73] George W. Stroup states:

> One of the strengths of narrative theology has been that it provides a foundation for theology by uniting experience and reflection in a way that other recent forms of systematic theology apparently have been unable to do. Narrative theology is not simply a matter of storytelling. Narrative theology does recognize, however, that Christian faith is rooted in particular historical events which are recounted in the narratives of Christian Scripture and tradition, that these historical narratives are the basis for Christian affirmations about the nature of God and the reality of grace, and that these historical narratives and the faith they spawn are redemptive when they are appropriated at the level of personal identity and existence. Hence, Christian narrative is a primary datum for theological reflection and the appropriate context in which we re-examine the nature of Christian identity...[74]

Christian identity of a person depends on how one understands Christ and one's self. Stroup states further:

> At the centre of Christian faith is the question of identity, a question that is two-sided. On the one hand it is a question about Jesus of Nazareth and the God whom Christians confess to be disclosed in Jesus' life, death, and resurrection. Christian theology is the attempt to think through and understand what faith confesses about the God revealed in Jesus Christ. But, that is only one side of the identity question in Christian faith and only one part of the task of theology. Equally important are the consequences of what it means to confess that Jesus Christ is 'the only begotten Son of God.' Traditionally Christians have claimed that anyone who makes that a confession is led to reconsider what kind of person one is and how one lives in the world. In most cases it is not that confession seem to require a person to 'turn around,' reinterpret personal identity, and live differently in the world. What a person believes about Jesus Christ cannot be separated from how one lives in the world without tearing apart the fabric of Christian faith... The agony of Christian existence in both its personal and its corporate forms is that what one believes and confesses is rarely demonstrated consistently and without distortion in daily life. Sin remains as much a reality for Christians as for non-Christians. Yet the two-sided question of Christian identity – who one understands Jesus of Nazareth to be and what it means to confess him as Lord – stands at the very center of Christian faith.[75]

As Stroup says, the question of Christian identity is central to Christian faith. Christian identity is an issue which is faced by every Christian and the church and particularly in India, in the context of Dalit Christian women; identity is an issue that needs serious attention. As it is mentioned in the introduction of this chapter, the identity of Dalit women is an imposed, distorted identity. This dissertation advocates a repairing and restoring of the broken identity of Dalit women.

Nevertheless, personal identity necessarily assumes the form of a narrative because it is history that is remembered and narrative in turn provides the form and structure in which some events may become the focus for interpreting the meaning of the whole.[76] According to Stanley Hauerwas:

> The category of narrative has been used, among other purposes, to explain human action, to articulate the structures of human consciousness, to depict the identity of agents (whether human or divine), to explain strategies of reading (whether specifically for biblical texts or as a more general hermeneutic), to justify a view of the importance of 'story-telling' (often in religious studies through the language of 'fables' and 'myths'), to account for the historical development of traditions, to provide an alternative to foundationalist and/or other scientific epistemologies, and to develop a means for imposing order on what is otherwise chaos.[77]

Stroup, admitting that Hauerwas offers a sophisticated discussion on 'Why Narratives,' quotes Hauerwas who says a story 'is a narrative account that binds events and agents together in an intelligible pattern.' In so doing Stroup affirms that Hauerwas offers a description and explanation of why things are the way they are.[78] Hauerwas together with L. Gregory Jones quotes James Gustafson's description on 'narrative theology or ethics' in 'Why Narrative?' Gustafson identifies narrative as one of four kinds of moral discourse (the others are prophetic, ethical and policy). He proposes the central thesis of narrative theology and narrative ethics in the following terms:

> Narratives function to sustain the particular moral identity of a religious (or secular) community by rehearsing its history and traditional meanings, as these are portrayed in Scripture and other sources. Narratives shape and sustain those of the community. Through our participation in such a community, the narratives also function to give shape to our moral characters, which in turn deeply affect the way we interpret or construe the world and events and thus affect what we determine to be appropriate action as members of the community. Narratives function to sustain and confirm the religious and moral identity of the Christian community, and evoke and sustain the faithfulness of its member to Jesus Christ.[79]

Harry Nasuti while discussing the importance of narrative says that the biblical law is rooted in the narrative form. This narrative of biblical law forces the reader to ask not only questions relating to one's behaviour, but also questions regarding one's identity, 'Who am I? How am I related to this story?' What does this story say about who I should be?[80] Nasuti focuses on the 'sojourner formula' and the 'slave formula' as examples of this function of the law to specify identity for the reader (Ex. 22:20, 23.9, Lev. 19.34, Deut. 10.19, 23.7).[81] Nasuti points out that those who were former slaves and sojourners, were asked to imitate God in God's identity of love and compassion.[82] Hauerwas has stressed in turn the role of Israel's narrative and legal traditions in shaping Israel's identity. That is, this identity is dependent on both Israel's remembering and Israel's imitating of God's actions on its behalf.[83]

In formulating Dalit Feminist Theological Hermeneutics, storytelling has thus become a powerful method also to communicate divine intervention in the lives of Dalit women to offer them a new life. For a Dalit feminist theologian, 'story telling is an apt method' in describing the personal identities, community identity and religious identities. Melanchthon expresses this intention thus:

> In the act of sharing stories told personally, consciously and politically, women begin to understand themselves and their reality better. From the depths of women's stories of joys and sorrows, triumphs and defeat, we can draw a tapestry of theological exploration and biblical interpretation which is contextual and is based on a community in struggle for humanhood.[84]

As mentioned above, the living experience of Dalit women becomes a strong foundation in this dissertation. Human beings are storytellers. People express their perceptions of reality in terms of myths and stories. Christian education that begins at home with children begins with storytelling. Children as well as adults are interested and enthusiastic in listening to stories. Some of the Bible stories are personal in nature. From ancient times, people have communicated historical events, orally and have written autobiographies and biographies. Tina Beattie while stating that every religious narrative is in some sense concerned with expressing the relationship between transcendence, community, tradition and the individual believer, quotes, Paul Ricoeur who argues that history itself is a narrative fiction, in so far as it is not a series of related events that are factually recounted, but the imposition of order and significance on the past through a process of selective interpretation and story-telling.[85] Tina Beattie further continues to quote Paul Ricoeur who says, we acquire 'narrative identity'[86] by surrendering our subjectivity as 'the author of our own life.'[87]

In the words of Sarojini Nadar, telling stories not only exposes suffering but also the unfairness of the oppression. She asserts that exposing the unfairness of oppression through telling stories forces men (who are not necessarily oppressors) to challenge the unfairness of oppression. She says, "The act of storytelling – of delving into the past – encourages introspection and reflection on our experiences. We begin to see out past in a new light and this consequently makes us read differently. Story-telling shapes and reshapes our identity, recasting the images we have of ourselves as women."[88] She cites Althaus-Reid who speaks of remembering:

> Memories used to relate to the past, to interpret life in the light of faith and past experiences; to the present, to make meaningful an existence with such a deep knowledge of suffering; and to the future, to think about the utopia the reign of God in terms of what is known about the actions of God in recent history.[89]

Listening to the stories of Dalit women as accurately as possible is thus necessary in formulating Dalit feminist hermeneutics. Gnanadasan states:

> By sharing our stories of pain, victimization, and exploitation, feminists attempted to discover a theological dimension in women's search for justice. A new definition of spirituality is women's commitment to justice, to transform economic, political, social and religious institutions to give main concern to the voices of those from whom human dignity is most effectively withheld. The women's movement has brought consciousness to Christian women that their self identity is built on a new foundation of faith which is not patriarchal but faith based identity which demands active participation of women in the transformation of Indian society.[90]

Alice Walker reflects on her mother's story and cultural identity as an African-American woman and on the influence of her mother's stories on her own cultural identity and storytelling. Walker recognizes that her mother's stories have gone unrecorded and that they must be recovered and recorded in her own search for her history and cultural identity. She realizes that her mother's stories and those of other African-American women from generations past have influenced her own cultural identity and are a source of great strength for spirituality, and creativity.[91]

This research falls in line with those theologians who find potential strengths in the narrative theory to approach identity and theology. This research in the context of Dalit community bears in mind the fact that their narrative is in some respect related to the story of salvation and the story of humanity. Jayashree Gokhale's 'From Concessions to Confrontation' is an exciting work on the stories of Dalits. Shankarrao Kharat quoted by Jayashree Gokhale describes the theme of his autobiography thus:

> Along with being my story, this is the story of a community. My autobiography is the story of the emotional, and educational development that an individual, a society, a village has undergone. Most of all, it is the story of the freedom struggle of the untouchables.[92]

In this context, Tina Beattie says: Narrative understanding invites the recognition that we derive our identities and our sense of meaning from the complex cultural narratives within which we are inscribed, with their historical, religious, political and psychological claims upon us.[93] Further to this, Anne Pattel-Gray, in her work on 'Aboriginal Spirituality and Theology' says:

> Story-telling theology embraces traditional and cultural teachings of our people, and continues as the nexus between the ancestral narratives and the Biblical scriptures. Many Aboriginal theologians use this form of theology to teach and maintain the Aboriginal oral tradition, and to enable our people to have greater understanding of theology so they can make it relevant in their daily lives. It is a non-Western, non-intellectualized model of teaching transcendent truths about creation and life. By using ancestral narratives, Aboriginal theologians are able to bring to life the teachings of the Gospel, which may then be sung and danced into life through traditional Aboriginal rituals and ceremonies.[94]

Surekha while writing on the importance of telling stories says in her article titled "A Dalit Women's Voice in Biblical Interpretation: Can She Speak?" emphasizes that the autobiographical element in Dalit women's writings clearly defines narrative authority for Dalit women and encourages them to be forceful in the culture of writing. It helps them to claim their subjectivity which is ignored always and also in Dalit writings. Therefore, Dalit women's autobiographies provide radical space within the literary public in which they can voice out against the caste system and patriarchy. The personal narratives of Dalit women serve as socio-cultural records of their community as well as literary forms of social protest practices.[95] The stories mentioned in this work speak volumes of their identities either as achieved identities or as imposed identities.

In searching for Dalit feminist identity, narrative approach is thus a powerful method to communicate divine intervention in the lives of Dalit women to offer them a new identity.

4.5. Who Should Speak for Dalit Identity?

After discussing various approaches to identity, the question now arises, 'Who should speak for Dalit feminist identity?' It is essential to clarify who is authentic in speaking for Dalit feminist identity. The position that only the subaltern can know the subaltern, or only women can know women or Dalit can know only Dalit and so on, cannot be held as a theoretical presumption.[96]

In this connection, Hooks offers a post-modern critique of identity, challenging the notion of universality. For example, Hooks argues that racism did not have the same impact on everyone. She refers to multiple experiences of identity that ensures diverse cultural productions. She challenges imperialist paradigms of black identity which represents blackness.[97] Sugirtharajah raises the question, if contextual authenticity is based on being in the same cultural tradition, rejecting outsiders, how can one then make authentic propositions about the Bible, a set of documents that originated from a completely different cultural and historical tradition? How does then one know the experiences behind each Bible story? Contextual authenticity makes it impossible to understand the Bible and to identify with it.[98] In the words of Sugirtharajah:

> If contextual authenticity is given credit, only a Jew can then resist anti-Semitism, only a gay can support homosexual rights, only animals can do animal theology and only trees can talk about deforestation: 'Personal experience, cultural affinities and ideological closeness, important though they are, are poor surrogates for understanding and accountability in hermeneutics. Sensing and feeling what is right is sufficient. One does not need to have lived it.[99]

In a multicultural society like India, contextual authenticity will have to be broken down. To claim authenticity is to end conversation. Hence, this chapter proposes that whoever has an empathetic view towards Dalit women's struggles, and who has the commitment to become incarnate into their struggles and identity can talk 'Dalit feminist identity.' Furthermore Dalit feminism should move beyond the borders of the concept of 'insider-outsider' and appreciate the solidarity from neighbouring groups. As the introductory chapter made it clear, Dalit feminist theology will work in collaboration with Dalit theology, feminist theology and other similar contextual theologies.

4.6. In Search of Dalit Feminist Identity

Erikson adopted a psycho-social approach to understand identity by describing the interaction between biology, psychology, and social recognition and response within a historical context. Later theorists emphasized historical, socio-cultural, post-modern, post-colonial and narrative and feminist theoretical frameworks to approach and understand identity. These approaches emphasize the role of history, social and cultural forces in shaping the identity and narrative of one's own life. All these approaches hold their own strengths and limitations.

Hermeneutics is inescapable. One can only 'know' the past within her or his own present world in which she or he lives in. Identity is thus inscribed in socio-cultural practices. As Kobena Mercer remarks: identity only becomes an issue when it is in crisis, when something assumed to be fixed, coherent and stable is displaced by the experience of doubt and uncertainty.[100] People's way of knowing the past must correspond to the multiplicity and difference of identity which is always present in the particularities of race, class, gender and caste. Theological interpretation of identity will be of no value unless it takes on the flesh and blood of transformed social relationships.[101]

The identities of gender and caste are so embodied and visible to the world that our experience of our identities is not merely a concept but the experiences of our bodies is important for our point of Dalit feminist departure. Furthermore not only our bodies affect our experiences of the world, but our bodies as marked by gender and caste also enter the experience of others. Identities of gender and caste function as hermeneutical horizons in searching for Dalit feminist identity. They are the contexts from which Dalit women come to know, understand and reason about the world. Since their identities so strongly affect their interaction with the world, those contexts need to be analyzed, deconstructed and reconstructed in order to recover their identity.

4.6.1. Identity Formation Among Dalit Women

Identity formation focuses on three questions: Who am I? With whom do I fit in? What does it mean to be part of the group? To give definition to the question, 'who am I?' I can define myself only within the relationships I am in. My 'who am I' question is related with 'where I am?' or in other words 'with whom do I fit in,' It is not possible to think of myself apart from the people to whom I am relating in my given context. In the question 'where I am' or 'with whom do I fit in', I have to think about those people in that particular context, how I feel about them, and what is my commitment to them because my identity is all wrapped up in that. I define myself in terms of roles and competencies attached to those roles in relationships.

In this context it is certainly necessary to bring in my identity, the way I understand myself. I present that I have certain identities of mine which play a major role in the way I understand myself and the world I live in and dialogue with. I would like to define my identity as a 'Dalit born into a middle class family, one who has university and theological education, a Lutheran Christian Woman.' Probably, it denotes a significant development and a rise from a low class to a middle class, and my education at both the university and theological college indicates that it is not impossible for Dalit women to rise to a higher level in education. My identity from outcasteness to Dalitness is a recovered identity and not imposed identity. And my final identity as a Lutheran Christian woman signifies that I belong to a community of honour and respect. This definition is unique to me and different from the definition given by the caste men, caste women and Dalit men, as they try to define my identity as secondary, inferior, weak, impure, dirty and untouchable. Swathi Margaret says, "We need to define ourselves otherwise, they will define us for their betterment and for our detriment."[102] My self-perception thus plays a decisive role in building my identity. As the introductory chapter of this study made it very clear, my childhood experiences played a major role in my identity formation.

While the self continues to develop throughout the entire life-time of a human being, it is most vulnerable during childhood and youth, when the most basic elements of self-identity are being constructed. Resistance to abuse and recovery from abuse are always possible. But, in most cases it is not possible either to resist or to bear it. Sometimes it is extremely painful. The field research made it clear that violence in the Dalit families is rampant. Women are beaten up; caste exclusion tells them that they are untouchables. According to field research, Dalit children in schools, particularly in villages face constant discrimination in the name of caste. Violence in the homes and society wounds the self and the psyche of the child and particularly the girl child. They grow in poor self-image and in broken identity. The images that form in their minds would certainly lead them to low self-esteem and low self-image.

Maxine Hong Kingston, a Chinese-American daughter, tells how her family and school played a role in identity-formation. As she grew up, in her own family, her parents would repeat Chinese sayings which told of her female position in Chinese culture and society, such as 'Feeding girls is like feeding cowbirds' . . . 'There's no profit in raising girls. Better to raise geese than girls.' These sayings reflected the reality that Chinese girls were not valued as much as Chinese boys. In Chinese society, girls were expected to marry and to become part of their husband's family, while boys always remained connected with their own families.[103] While Maxine reflects on that situation, she realizes that the silencing of individual voices is also a silencing of the personality (experience of Chinese girls in the school), and she says, "If you don't talk, you can't have a personality." Maxine recognizes the urgency for Chinese-American girls to have a voice in school and in all aspects of their lives.[104]

In the Indian context, caste ideology works in the form of untouchability, impurity and pollution of Dalits (women and men). Similarly, patriarchal ideology works along untouchability, impurity, sinfulness and pollution of women of all castes. Both the ideologies have been causing death and destruction to masses in India. Caste ideology imposed an impure, polluted and untouchable false identity on Dalits,[105] and patriarchal ideology imposed inferior, subordinate, polluted and weak identity on women. Caste ideology has chained the masses in India. Devasahayam states while articulating Dalit theology:

> As a counter caste ideology, Dalit theology seeks to promote values and consciousness that are counter to that of caste values. It seeks to promote values such as liberty, equality, fraternity, freedom, community etc. It maintains the priority of justice over order and seeks to establish community of peace, wellbeing and justice for all.[106]

4.7. Conclusion

This chapter while providing certain definitions and the nature of identity discussed six theoretical approaches to identity while offering a brief critique from a Dalit feminist perspective. The socio-cultural approach sees group's identity as a critical component of the self-concept. The theory further states that individuals attribute value to the group in which they are members and derive their self-esteem from their group. In some cases, a particular group may be subject to discrimination or negative stereotyping, resulting in low self-esteem. In such cases, groups can engage in recovering their identity. Historical approach considers history to be playing a significant role in influencing the identity of a person. However, history alone is insufficient to look for the identity of a person. Post-modern approach emphasizes thus on societal influences than the personal strength of a person. Although, society plays a major role in impacting the identity of a person, each person is bestowed with personal strengths which cannot be ignored. Narrative approach sees the Bible as the story which shows how the individual and community identities are formed, and it enlightens its readers through the narratives, to form one's own identity. Post-colonial approach takes the historical, social, cultural, personal and religious elements in forming the identity of a person. Feminist approach takes all the above said elements into serious consideration in approaching identity. Added to that, the feminist approach emphasizes 'woman's experience' as a hermeneutical key in forming women's identity which is complex, multiple and different in nature.

The field research revealed that a remarkable transformation took place in the status and identity of Dalit women in SALC. However, in spite of the transformation, it is observed that subordinate, inferior and secondary position is maintained by women themselves at various levels. Respondents admit that they are in the 'image of God' but they are not comfortable to 'image God in their image.' They are very comfortable to see the 'image God in the masculine image,' although they say God can be addressed as Mother. In terms of the hierarchical structure as 'man is made in the image of God and the woman is in the image of man,' the assertion that 'man is subordinate to God and woman is to man' remains as a strong opinion in Christian families and churches. Hence re-visiting the 'image of God' from the Dalit feminist perspectives is of paramount importance in this dissertation. The study understands that educational, economic and political status alone cannot recover the lost identity of Dalit women as the image of God. Theological interpretation is essential in order for them to understand that they are created in the image of God and they possess it.

In conclusion, this chapter states that Dalit women need a 'brand new image' which gives an honorable identity to keep up with the times to make a mark in the society. In recovering the new identities for Dalit women, Dalit feminist hermeneutics need to approach identity from the historical, familial, social, cultural, colonial, modern, religious and personal perspectives. This will help in adding more self-value to the identity of Dalit women. However, recovering identities and building an image is a process. It cannot happen overnight and takes a lot of hard work and homework. It also requires employing every available opportunity to build and evoke value to one's professional reputation, and the bottom-line has to be done by oneself. Dalit women therefore need a fresh brand to promote their public image and identity. Chapter V of this work focuses on the 'Image of God' which gives a theoretical framework to re-image God from the perspective of Dalit women in SALC.

End Notes

1. *http://en.wikipedia.org/wiki/Identity_(social_science)* (accessed on 5.7.2010).
2. J. B. Sykes, ed., *The Concise Oxford Dictionary of Current English* (Seventh edition) (Oxford: Clarendon Press, 1982).
3. Colleen Jaurrechette, "Poetry, Prayer and Identity in Finnegans Wake" in *Joys and the Fabrication of Irish Identity*, edited by Michael Pattrick Gillesies and James (Amsterdam: Rodopi, 2000), 71.
4. Annie Sofie Roald, "Who are the Muslims? Questions of Identity, Gender and Culture in Research Methodologies" in *Gender, Religion and Diversity: Cross-Cultural Perspectives,* edited by Ursula King and Tina Beattie (London: Continuum, 2005), 184-185.
5. David Moshman, *Adolescent Psychological Development: Rationality, Morality and Identity* (Mahwah, NJ: Lawrence Erlbaum Associates, 1999), 90.
6. David Moshman, *Adolescent Psychological Development:* 90.
7. David Moshman, *Adolescent Psychological Development:* 90-91.
8. J. S. Phinney, "An Ethnic Identity" in *Encyclopedia of Psychology*, edited by A. E. Kazdin (New York: Oxford University Press, 2000), 254; Cited by Sana Loue, ed, *Sexualities and Identities of Minority Women* (New York: Springer Science & Business Media, LLC. 2009), 4.
9. Evangeline Anderson-Rajakumar, "The Image of God: in the Light of Women's Experiences in an Indian Perspective" *D. Th. Thesis* (Unpublished) (Bangalore: UTC, 1999), 117-118.
10. Evangeline Anderson-Rajakumar, "The Image of God," 117-118.
11. J. G. Seamon and D. T. Kenrick, "Essays on the Nature of Identity, Library of College Term Papers: 2002" in *www.academon.com/Essay-The-Nature-of-Identity/8967* (accessed on 23.7.2010).
12. Jane Kroger, *Identity Development: Adolescence Through Adulthood* (New York: Sage Publications, 2005), 7-8.
13. Erik Erikson, *Identity: Youth and Crisis* (1968). Cited by Cote James E, Charles G. Levine, *Identity Formation, Agency, and Culture: A Social Psychological Synthesis,* (Lawrence Erlbaum Associates, Inc. Publishers. 2002), 91-99.
14. Cote James E, Charles G. Levine, *Identity Formation, Agency, and Culture:* 95.
15. Cote James E, Charles G. Levine, *Identity Formation, Agency, and Culture:* 103.
16. William Gaudelli, *World Class: Teaching and Learning in Global Times* (London: Routledge, 2003), 101.
17. James E. Marcia, "Theory and Measure: The Identity Status Interview" in *Capturing I: Quantitative and Qualitative Methods*, edited by Meike Watzlawik (Aristi Born), 4.
18. James E. Marcia, "Theory and Measure," 4.
19. David Moshman, *Adolescent Psychological Development, Rationality, Morality and Identity*, 83-84.
20. Amin Maalouf, in *The Name of Identity: Violence, and the need to belong* (New York: Arcade Publishing Company, 2000), 10.
21. Down through the centuries, Dalits have been treated as untouchables. They were given different names by the caste people such as Mala, Madiga, Paraya, Pulaya etc., in various states. The British Government called them Scheduled Castes. Mahatma Gandhi called them Harijans. All these names are given by others. Dalits in India are not comfortable with these names. Today, the so called outcastes call themselves "Dalit," a new name they have coined

for themselves. The term Dalit is not a mere name; it is an expression of hope and identity. See for further details, Himansu Charan Sadangi, *Dalit: the Downtrodden of India* (Delhi: Gyan Publishing House, 2008), 61.

22. James E. Marcia, "Theory and Measure: The Identity Status Interview", 4.
23. Jean S. Phinney, "A Three-Stage Model of Ethnic Identity Development in Adolescence" in *Ethnic Identity: Formation and Transmission among Hispanics and other Minorities*, edited by Martha E. Bernal and George P. Night (Albany: New York Press, 1993), 61-80.
24. Constantine M. Mwikamba, "A Search for an African Identity" *African Ecclesial Review* 31 (February, 1981), 97.
25. Robert Lawrence, *Heath, Realism and Relativism* (Macon: Mercer University Press, 1986), 135.
26. Dorothy Holland, and William Lichicotte, JR, Vygotsky and Mead, "The New Socio-cultural Studies of Identity" in *The Cambridge Companion to Vygotsky*, edited by Harry Daniels, Michael Cole and James V. Wertsch (Cambridge: Cambridge University Press, 2007), 109.
27. Mark B. Tappen, "The Cultural Reproduction of Masculinity: A Critical Perspective on Boys Development" in *Cultural and Critical Perspectives on Human Development*, edited by Martin J. Packer and Mark B. Tappen (New York: State University of New York, 2001), 247.
28. Renuka Vithal and John Volmink, "Mathematics, Curriculum Research: Roots, Reforms, Reconciliation and Relevance" in *Researching Mathematics Education in South Africa: Perspectives, Practices*, edited by Renuka Vithal, Jill Adler and Christine Keitel (HSRC Press, 2005), 1987.
29. Jane Kroger, *Identity Development: Adolescence through Adulthood* (Second Edition) (California: Sage Publications, 2007), 13.
30. Jane Kroger, *Identity Development:* 14.
31. B. R. Ambedkar who was born in a poor family struggled all through his life. In his childhood he underwent the agony of rejection at the services offered at barber saloon, drinking water at public places, educational institutions, learning classic languages etc. He is now followed by millions of people throughout the world. After obtaining his doctorate, he came back to India started spreading education among the untouchables. Education alone did not change the status of minorities. Then he tried to deal with economical problems of the minorities. Even economic status did not bring change in the untouchable practices. Then he realized, religion is the basis for untouchable practices. Then he converted into Buddhism and his followers too converted. He was the father of the Indian Constitution. His pen spoke volumes to the world. See for more details, C. D. Nayak, *Thoughts and Philosophy of Dr B. R. Ambedkar* (New Delhi: Sarup & Sons, 2003).
32. V. Devasahayam, *Outside the Camp: Bible Studies in Dalit Perspective (Madras: Gurukul, 1992),* 34.
33. Hans Ucko. *The People and the People of God: Minjung and Dalit Theology in Interaction* (LIT Verlg Munster, 2002), 117-118.
34. James Massey, *Downtrodden: The Struggle of India's Dalits for Identity, Solidarity and Liberation* (Geneva: WCC, 1997), 3. See Walter Fernandez, Ed. *The Emerging Dalit Identity: The Re-Assertion of the Subalterns. (*New Delhi: ISI, 1996).
35 Hans Ucko, *The People and the People of God.* 117-118.
36. See Sharmila Rege, *Writing Caste, Writing Gender: Narrating Dalit Women's Testimonies* (New Delhi: Zubaan, 2006).
37. B. Kumaravadivelu, *Cultural Globalization and Language Education* (Yale University Press, 2008), 143-144.
38. James E. Cote and Charles G. Levin, *Identity Formation, Agency and Culture: A Social Psychological Synthesis* (London: Routledge, 2002), 40.
39. James E. Cote and Charles G Levin, *Identity Formation,* 40.

40. Kathleen Odell Korgen, *From Black to Biracial: Transforming Racial Identity among Americans,* 93.
41. Kumarivadivelu. *Cultural Globalization*, 144.
42. James E. Cote and Charles G Levin, *Identity Formation,* 40.
43. James E. Cote and Charles G Levin, *Identity Formation,* 40.
44. James E. Cote and Charles G Levin, *Identity Formation*, 94.
45. James E. Cote and Charles G Levin, *Identity Formation*. 94.
46. Derek Hook, "Frantz Fanon and Racial Identity in Post-Colonial Contexts" in Norman, Duncan, Derek Hook, Nhlanhla Mkhize, Peace Kiguva and Anthony Collins, Self, *Community and Psychology,* edited by Kopano Ratele (Lansdowne: UCT Press, 2004), 6-1.
47. Derek Hook, "Frantz Fanon and Racial Identity in Post-Colonial Contexts," 6.1-2.
48. Derek Hook, "Frantz Fanon and Racial Identity in Post-Colonial Contexts."
49. See R. S. Sugirtharajah, Ed., *The Postcolonial Biblical Reader* (Malden: Blackwell Publishing Limited, 2006).
50. James Massey, *Down Trodden*, 12-28.
51. James Massey, *Down Trodden*, 27-28.
52. B. N. Singh, "Kushwant Singh's Delhi: A Post-Colonial Novel" in *Writing in a Post-Colonial Space*, edited by Surya Nath Pandey (New Delhi: Atlantic Public Distributors, 1999), 142-143.
53. See Rosemary Radford Ruether, "Feminist Interpretation: A Method of Correlation" in *Feminist Interpretation of the Bible.*
54. Susan J. Hekman, "Introduction" in *Feminism, Identity and Difference*, edited by Susan J. Hekman (Ilford: Frank Cass Publishers, 1999), 1.
55. Susan J. Hekman, "Introduction", 2-4.
56. Elisabeth Schussler Fiorenza, *Critical Theory of Religion: A Feminist Analysis* (Minneapolis Augsburg Fortress, 1995), 24.
57. Elisabeth Schuller Fiorenza, in *Memory of Her: A Feminist Theological Reconstruction of Christian Origins* (New York: Cross Road, 1983), 35.
58. Elisabeth Schuller Fiorenza, in *Memory of Her:* 21, 160-204.
59. Pushpa Joseph, "Trailblazers: Elisabeth Schussler Fiorenza and George M. Sores-Prabhu" in *On Cutting the Edge: The Study of Women in Biblical Worlds: Essays in Honor of Elizabeth Schussler Fiorenza.*, edited by Jane Schaberg, Alice Bach, and Esther Fuchs (New York: Continuum International Publishing Group, 2004), 66.
60. Pushpa Joseph, "Re-visioning Eros for Asian Feminist Theologizing: Some Pointers from Tantric Philosophy," in *Body Sexuality: Theological-pastoral Perspectives of Women in Asia* edited by Agnes M. Brazal and Andrea Lizares Si (Manila: Ateneo De Manila University Press, 2007), 34-57.
61. Aniene Taljaard, "On Belonging and Longing" in *Ragbag Theologies: Essays in Honor of Denise Ackarman,* edited by Miranda N. Pillai, Sarojini Nadar, Clint Le Bruyns and Denise Ackrman (Stellenbosch: SUN Press, 2009), 39-48.
62. Aniene Taljaard, "On Belonging and Longing," 39-48.
63. Kumkum Sangari, "Consent, Agency and the Rhetoric of Incitement," *Economic and Political Weekly*, 1 May (1993), 871.
64. Kumkum Sangari, "Consent, Agency and the Rhetoric of Incitement," 871.
65. Enel Dengel-Janic, "Constructions of Femininity in Cornelia Sorabji's "Greater Love" and Geetha Hariharan's "Revathi" in *Indian Woman's Short Fiction*, edited by Joel Kurotti and Mittapalli Rajeswar (New Delhi: Atlantic, 2007), 2-3.
66. Chandra Talpade Mohanty, "Under Western Eyes: Feminist Scholarship and colonial discourses" Cited by Karina Eileraas, *Third World Women and the Politics of Feminism*, edited by Mohanty Russo and Torres (Bloomington: Indiana University Press, 1991), 10; Karina

Eileraas, *Between Image and Identity: Transnational Fantasy, Symbolic Violence and Feminist Misrecognition* (Lanham: The Rowman and Littlefield Publishing Group. Inc., 2007), xiii.

67. Chandra Talpade Mohanty, Under Western Eyes: 10.
68. Kumkum Sangari and Sudesh Vaid, *Recasting Women: An Introduction* (1990), 9.
69. Gabriel Dietrich, "Women and Religious Identities in India after Ayodhya" in *Against All Odds,* edited by Kamala Basin, Ritu Menon and Nighat Said Khan (Delhi: Kali for Women, 1994), 43-44.
70. See H. Richard Niebhur, "The Story of Our Life," in *The Meaning of Revelation* (New York: MacMillan Publishing Company, 1941), 43-81.
71. Stanley J. Grenz & Roger E. Olson, *20th Century Theology: God & the World in a Transitional Age* (Secunderabad: OM Authentic Books, 1992), 271.
72. Gabriel Fackre, *The Christian Story* (Grand Rapids: Eerdmans, 1984), 5. Cited in Stanley J. Grenz & Roger E. Olson, *20th Century Theology:*10.
73. John Navone, SJ, *Towards a Theology of Story* (Slough, England: St. Paul Publications, 1977).
74. John Navone, SJ, *Towards a Theology of Story,* 17.
75. George W. Stroup, *The Promise of Narrative Theology* (London: SCM Press LTD, 1981), 14-15.
76. George W. Stroup, *The Promise of Narrative Theology,* 112.
77. Stanley Hauerwas and L. Gregory Jones "Introduction: Why Narrative" in *Why Narrative: Readings in Narrative Theology* (Grand Rapids: Michigan, 1989), 2.
78. Stanley Hauerwas, with Richard Bondi and David B. Burrell, *Truthfulness and Tragedy* (Indiana: University of Notre Dame Press, Notre Dame, 1977), 8. See also Stanley Hauerwas and L. Gregory Jones "Introduction: Why Narrative" in *Why Narrative: Readings in Narrative Theology.*
79. James M. Gustafson, *Varieties of Moral Discourse: Prophetic, Narrative, Ethical, and Policy* (Calvin College, The Stob Lectures, 1988,) 19-20, Quoted by Gregory Jones in *Why Narrative: Readings in Narrative Theology.*
80. Harry P. Nasuti, "Identity, Identification, and Imitation: The Narrative Hermeneutics of Biblical Law," *Journal of Law and Religion* 4 (1986): 12.
81. Harry P. Nasuti, Identity, Identification, and Imitation: 12.
82. Harry P. Nasuti, Identity, Identification, and Imitation: 11.
83. Stanley Haurwas, *Peaceable Kingdom: A Primer in Christian Ethics* (Notre Dame, Ind.: University of Notre Dame Press, 1983), 119.
84. Monica Melanchthon, "Indian Dalit Women" in *Gender, Religion and Diversity.* 221.
85. Paul Ricoeur, "Life in Quest of Narrative" in *On Paul Ricoeur: Narrative and Interpretation,* edited by David Wood (London and New York: Routledge, 1991), 33. Cited by Tina Beattie, "Religious Identity and the Ethics of Representation" in *Gender, Religion and Diversity.* 74.
86. Paul Ricoeur, "Life in Quest of Narrative" 33.
87. Paul Ricoeur, "Life in Quest of Narrative" 32.
88. Isabel Apawo Phiri, Devarakshanam Betty Govinden, Sarojini Nadar, "Introduction" in *Her-stories: Hidden Histories of Women of Faith in Africa,* edited by Isabel Apawo Phiri, Devarakshanam Betty Govinden and Sarojini Nadar (Pietermaritzburg: Cluster Publications, 2002), 6.
89. M. Althaus-Reid, "Doing the Theology in Memory: Counting Crosses and Resurrections" in *Life out of Death – The Feminine Spirit of El Salvador,* edited by Best, M. and Huddry, P (London: Catholic Institute of International Relations, 1996), 202.
90. Aruna Gnanadason, "Feminist Theology: An Indian Perspective" in *Readings in Indian Christian Theology* edited by R. S. Sugirtharajah and Cecil Hargreaves (Delhi: ISPCK, 1993) 60-61; Aruna Gnanadason, "Towards an Indian Feminist Theology" in *We Dare to Dream.* 123.

91. See Alice Walker, *In Search of Her Mother's Garden.*
92. Jayashree Gokhale, *From Concessions to Confrontation* (Bombay: Popular Prakashan, 1993), 191. Cited by Arul Thaveedu, *The Relevance of the Social Teachings of Martin Luther for Dalit Liberation* (Madurai: J & D Publications, 1997), 49.
93. Tina Beattie, "Religious Identity and the Ethics of Representation: The Study of Religion and Gender in the Secular Academy" in *Gender, Religion and Diversity,* 74.
94. Anne Pattel-Gray, "Aboriginal Spirituality and Theology" in *Prejudice: Issues in Third World Theologies,* edited by Andreas Nehring (Madras: Gurukul Summer Institute, 1996), 255.
95. Surekha Nelavala, "A Dalit Women's Voice in Biblical Interpretation" in *God's Image,* Vol. 26, No. 3, September, 2007, 51-55.
96. Surekha Nelavala, "A Dalit Women's Voice in Biblical Interpretation" 51-55.
97. B. Hooks, "Postmodern Blackness," in *Post Colonialism: Critical Concepts,* edited by D. Brydon (London: Routledge, 2000), 1306-1313.
98. R. S. Sugirtharajah, *The Bible and the Third World,* 270; *Social Identity and South African Biblical Hermeneutics: A Struggle against Prejudice,* 48-49.
99. R. S. Sugirtharajah, *The Bible and the Third World,* 270.
100. Kobena Mercer, "Welcome to the Jungle: Identity and Diversity in Postmodern Politics," in *Identity: Community, Culture, Difference,* edited by Jonathan Rutherford (London, Lawrence & Wishart, 1990), 43.
101. Kobena Mercer, Welcome to the Jungle:, 178-179.
102. Swathi Margaret, *http://www.sannaduttgu.com/INSIGHT/editorial_swathi_margaret,* (Accessed on 3rd June, 2005).
103. Jennifer Jue cites: "Maxine Hong Kingston's Autobiographical Novel: The Woman Warrior" Jennifer Jue, *Breaking the Silence of Women of Color and Issues of Voice and Cultural Identity,* 458.
104. Jennifer Jue, *Breaking the Silence of Women of Color,* 458.
105. See Mohan Larbeer, "Dalit Identity: A Theological Reflection" in *Frontiers of Dalit Theology,* edited by V. Devasahayam (Madras: Gurukul Summer Institute, 1996), 375-391, "Pollution: A Reality of an Imposed Ideology" in *Frontiers of Dalit Theology,* 392-401.
106. V. Devasahayam, *Frontiers of Dalit Theology,* 281-282.

5

The Image of God
Dalit Feminist Hermeneutical Study Towards The Empowerment of Dalit Women

5.1. Introduction

The previous chapter revealed that Dalit women in SALC through the years have acquired better positions and claim better status in society. Yet, suffer an identity crisis. They claim a poor image for themselves. This was evident from the women interviewed who were familiar with the stories of God from their childhood. Their childhood images of God as the Father and Scripture as the Holy Spirit's inspiration has become rooted deeply in their mind. The most serious observation made was that women had internalized their suffering as it was dictated by God through the Scripture. Although, they admit that they bear God's image in them, they have internalized the 'impure, inferior and subordinate' identities which they claim to be authentic and intended so by God. The concept, 'the image of God' has been used powerfully in the past to legitimate oppression and to perpetuate violence against women. Hence, the image of God has become the most important theological problem for me in doing research from the Dalit women's perspective. Thus, this chapter intends to do a theological exercise in revisiting the image of God from the Dalit feminist perspective. It is chiefly so because the language that is used in the dominant theologies has not adequately responded to the struggles of Dalit women due to its patriarchal ideology. Neither Dalit theology nor feminist theology has taken efforts to address the struggles of Dalit women. Hence, this chapter contributes to the work of constructing a Dalit feminist hermeneutics by focusing on how 'the image of God' functions in empowering faith communities, particularly Dalit women.

I admit the fact that the theological exercise on the image of God in this chapter is not a theoretical/philosophical problem to be debated. But it is primarily a moral issue, which is deeply intertwined with intra-personal relationships, inter-personal relationships and the world which we live in. Thus this chapter focuses on the connections between God's identity and Dalit woman's identity, while giving importance to the concept of the 'image of God,' given the fact that it is misused to oppress and exclude women. This chapter deconstructs, reconstructs and reclaims the image of God using both scriptural and theological resources while drawing attention to the experiences of Dalit women in SALC.

One of the great challenges of any Christian theology and particularly contextual theology is the hermeneutics of the image of God. The overarching question for which I seek biblical and theological help is in answering: How do we know God? In other words how do we know the image of God? What is God's identity? In answer, the feminist reconstruction of the image of God starts by seeking a just and trustful anthropology of the human person.

Some of the responses drawn from both the personal interviews and group discussions are very revealingly biblical, literal and patriarchal: 'God is the Father,' 'Jesus has called God the Father,' 'God is he,' 'Jesus is he,' and 'Holy Spirit is he,' 'therefore we can address God only in male terms,' 'man is created in the image of God,' 'woman is the rib of man,' 'woman is a helper to a man,' 'woman is the cause of sin therefore weak,' 'Paul commanded women to be silent,' 'Jesus' disciples are male therefore women need not be ordained,' and 'Jesus said to Mary at the tomb not to touch him, but he asked Thomas to touch him, so woman is a sinner,' 'women have to cover their heads because the Bible teaches so,' 'women should not take communion and step into the altar during menstruation, because the Bible says they are unclean during that time' and 'women have to obey their husbands.' These responses are the result of their reading of the Bible according to the traditional interpretations. Women are thus the silent spectators of their own oppression, violence and secondary position. They plainly admit that they are impure beings. They have internalized the aspect that they cannot be equal to men because 'man is created in the image of God and woman is created from his rib,' so a woman can never claim equality.

The Bible however contains the story of God with which we are familiar with. It preserves the memory of the past events in such a way that those events still have power for us. The Bible has been misused very often by the dominant to control the powerless and exercise exclusion in the name of gender. This is evident from the field study.

'What is the image of God?' 'What is God's identity?' 'What is the connection between identity and image?' 'Can God's identity reflect God's image?' 'Does the image of God exist in the Dalit woman's being?' 'Or, do the dominant claim that the image of God can survive only in them as it is in the Brahminical ideology which asserts that the outcastes have no part in Brahman's body?' These questions are of serious concern in this chapter.[1]

5.2. Re-visiting the Image of God

Human beings create meanings through inspiration, imagination and metaphor. This study is the result of the inspiration received by the responses of women who challenged the researcher to reclaim the images of God already present in the Scripture and to draw inspiration from them to gain new images and new identities for Dalit women.

Etymologically, the term 'image' is derived from the Latin term *imago* which means image, imitation, copy, likeness, statue, picture, phantom, conception, thought, idea, similitude, semblance, appearance, and shadow, and it contains the same root as *imitari* which means to imitate, copy, depict, replace, be like, act like, and resemble.[2] 'The likeness' refers to the resemblance of that shadow to the figure. The Hebrew term for 'image' is *selem* which means 'shadow.' This word is used five times in the Old Testament while referring to people.[3]

To one's surprise, the term 'image of God' is used only three times in the Hebrew Scriptures and all three uses are found in Genesis, not less than a dozen times in the New Testament and mostly used by Paul. Nevertheless the term 'image of God' exercises a great influence both in the Scripture and in the life of Christians.[4] However, David Carins makes it clear that in the New Testament, the 'image of God' is used in three ways: the term is applied firstly to Christ, then to all believers and to all others.[5] Although, it is affirmed that God is without a body hence without gender, nevertheless God is constantly referred to in male pronouns and characterized in line with the traditional Christian theology as Father-Son and Spirit and all are masculine in Latin upon which western theology is deeply dependent.

People receive God's story through tradition (the time-line) and through the environment (the space line). The story of who we are and of the meaning of our actions has its foundation in biblical narratives.[6] Dalit women draw their strength from biblical narratives to define their identity. Now the question is 'what is God's identity?' In the Hebrew Scriptures, God's identity is predominantly connected with the phrase 'I Am Who I Am,' and the proper name of God that is revealed in Exodus 3:14 discloses an absolute identity of divine being and essence. Moses raises a question of God's identity in Exodus 3:13 "...and if they ask me, 'What is his name?' 'What shall I say to them?' Subsequently God reveals ones own identity to Moses by saying, 'I AM WHO I AM.' This name of God reflects God's relationship with people in the past, present and future. One may say, that the identity-formula of 'I-Am-Who-I Am' signals an undividable communion between God and humans, a commitment to a shared history of 'becoming,' beginning with the emancipation from bondage in Egypt.[7]

In this context, Tjeu Van Knippenberg says, "Identity is the tentative result of the story that people tell about their passage through time and space."[8] Stories help us to imagine certain things that influence our identities. Donald E. Messer while discussing on the 'Art of Imaging' cites John Shea, a story-theologian who argues that 'whenever our biographies are deeply probed, a root metaphor appears, a myth which gives meaning to our lives.'[9] Metaphors are universal and omnipresent in everyday life, language, thought and action. Children learn and construct their world through metaphors from an early age. Most often, religion plays an important role in our imagination by insisting on doctrinal tests, acting as if they have fixed the truth in some particular symbol or dogma.[10] Donald quotes Douglas Bland, who writes about story-telling in connection with the images and metaphors:

> To probe our biographies for root metaphors – those images and incidents that point beyond themselves toward a life-giving myth – and to use storytelling as a way to speak of God is to assume that God is with us to be encountered at the depths of our lives. As long as the biblical witness and our lives are seen as separate entities, all our energy will be spent building bridges over gulfs that do not necessarily exist. If God is really incarnate, the probing for metaphors and telling stories may be the best way to discover and share God.[11]

Thus this chapter reopens the question pertaining to the image of God searching for the life-giving images of God in order to re-assure Dalit women that they are created in the image of God. It is hoped that this work will facilitate Dalit Christian women to discover new identities within them by realizing the image of God that they are born with.

What is God's image? What is the symbol of God? Who is God? What is God? How does God look like? What is God's character? Is God gendered? What kind of God does the church present? Is God relational? If so, what is God's relationship with women? Finding answers to these basic questions are of serious importance to women of SALC. The responses received to the question 'what is the image of God?' are: 'God is a caring father,' 'God is love,' 'God is judge,' and 'God is the creator.' All the respondents admitted the fact that they address God only as father. To the question, 'can we address God as mother?' most of the women responded by saying that they were not comfortable with the term. A few of them answered, "No doubt that God has motherly love, but because 'we have been taught to pray addressing God as father,' it is impossible to address God as mother." God as mother therefore is not part of their imagination. 'What is the image of woman as she is created in the image of God?' 'Does God dwell in them?' 'Is the image 'He' for God adequate in explaining God?' 'Can we replace the image 'She' for God?' 'Can women affirm the image of God that is within them?' These questions need serious attention in finding new identities and new images for Dalit women. As a child I was taught to pray to God the Father and address God as Father. Similar experience was expressed by all the women whom I interviewed. The male image of God 'as man created in God's image' and 'man is the glory of God' and 'woman is the glory of man' has strong effects on women to confirm their position as less than man. I do not claim that re-imaging the image of God is a new thing. Feminist theologians, liberation theologians and Dalit theologians have already begun the process and they have already used different images for God such as Sophia, liberator, redeemer, friend, *shakti*, and so on. The work here uses the resources already available in reclaiming the selected images for God. This is an attempt to reclaim the selected images in order to empower Dalit women.

This chapter argues that the 'image of God' is beyond gender. This argument helps to overcome the over identification of men with God, given the prevalence of masculine imagery for God. The concept 'God is beyond gender' is more problematic in the light of contemporary understandings of how gender is an integral part of identity. What does it mean to be made in the image of God if God does not share such an important part of our identity and self? The theological exercise of this chapter is intended to engage on these lines in reimaging the image of God from Dalit women's context for the sake of the faith community of the Dalit women that continues to speak for God and to God.

Theology as the term implies, begins with God and deals with God's relationship with humanity and creation. The term theology comes from two different terms; *theos* means God and *logos* means Word (reasoning). In a literal sense, theology has to do with the human attempt to speak about God or to explain what we mean by God. In other words, it is the human construction of the conception of God. The task of theology is the analysis, criticism, and reconstruction of the image of God in the context of human relationships and the world as well.[12] Although theology is an academic exercise, God cannot be considered as an object up there to study about. Rather God is a subject of theological inquiry, in relationship with human beings and nature. Theology as a human discipline is not a supernatural one, but it has been handed down from traditions, from particular cultures and the context. As a theological discipline, hermeneutics is 'the science of the interpretative process which begins with determination of the original meaning of a text (exegesis) and leads to elucidation of its sense for modern readers (exposition, paraphrase or sermon).'[13] Urban T. Holmes III while discussing the mystery of God quotes Coleridge who says, 'The exercise of the reasoning and reflecting powers, increasing insight, and enlarging views, are requisite to keep alive the substantial faith of the heart.'[14] Holmes agrees with Coleridge and says that 'the meaning begins with feeling and when it is creative, it moves from there to intuition and on to thinking or rational analysis.'[15] He also quotes Paul Riceour who says, 'The symbol gives rise to the thought.'[16] The nature of religious thought for Holmes is 'grounded in religious experience which is an encounter with the mystery that is God.'[17] Religious experience is not static but dynamic and it differs from individual to individual. When people encounter God in their religious experience, people experience the image of God in diverse ways and it is not one and the same forever. Jesus often used various metaphors for God in his teachings.[18] The art of imaging is at the heart of the Christian gospel.[19] The Bible describes multiple images for God.

Hence, this chapter draws the readers into the discussion on the image of God to propose that the conception of the image of God differs from person to person as Jesus imaged God in various ways that are applicable to the context.[20] The purpose in this research is both academic and practical as it is strongly considered that doing academic theology leads to new discoveries which would promote practical life. The following discussion points out that in the history of both Hebrews and Christians, the concept of the image of God is not constant as it changes according to the context and according to the people's perceptions. Furthermore, one can find a number of images for God both in the Hebrew Scriptures and in the New Testament.

5.2.1. Biblical Images of God: A Brief Overview

5.2.1.1. Images of God in the Hebrew Scriptures

In the Hebrew Scriptures, the primary name that is used for God is Yahweh. The theological circle of the 7th century (BCE) presents Zion as the place where Yahweh dwells and gives the highest place to Yahweh in the story of Hebrews. In early Israel, God was known as Yahweh, along with other names and divine appearances. The name Yahweh meant, 'The one who is with you' (Ex. 3:12).[21] Other terms attached with Yahweh are: 'hosts' mentioned 400 times and *saba* in its plural form, *Elohim* and *Adonai* (I Sam 17:45). Particularly the expression 'Lord of Hosts,' is used nearly 300 times in the Hebrew Scriptures and is common in Isaiah, Jeremiah, Zechariah and Malachi.[22] Yahweh as King always occurs in the Hebrew Scriptures in association with the metaphor Zion as Yahweh's people. Throughout the Hebrew Scriptures, the dominant image that is used for God is King. There can be no doubt that in ancient Israel this was a dominant form in which the people thought of God. The expression 'Yahweh as King' is mostly used by the Psalmist and a few times by other writers.[23] Yahweh as warrior is used in connection with the metaphor king (Ex. 15:3, Dt. 28:7, Num 10:35).[24] The shepherd metaphor is used to express the caring image of Yahweh. The metaphors such as warrior and shepherd were combined often to express and to evoke an image of a powerful but a caring God. Isaiah 49:8-12 combines these two metaphors of a warrior (8), shepherd (9-10) and possibly a parent (8).[25] Yahweh's parental image has been used very often (Deut. 1:31, 32:6, Hos. 11:1, 3-4, Ps.103:13).[26] The metaphor mother too is used for Yahweh (Is. 9:14-16, 46:3-4, 42:14-16).[27] Apart from these, *mil hamaa* (man of war) (Ex. 15.3), *Adon* (Lord) (Josh. 10:1), *Me'od* (Most High, Great One), as a victor, terrible one, still small voice (I Kings 19), shepherd (Is. 40:11), Good (Ps. 136:1), love and mercy (Ps. 103:8),[28] faithful, gentle, pre-existent, eternal, just, righteous, guide, friend, neighbour, wise, creator, shaper, shepherd, saviour, redeemer, king, judge, a lion, shield, a horn of salvation, a rock, a refuge, healer and so on are used to address God. In the Old Testament, God's appearance was found in many forms: awesome, blinding, overwhelming, frightening, full of light, lightning, and terrible in imagery. God is imaged as father in the Hebrew Scripture (Ex. 4:22-23, Deut. 4:32, 14:1, Is. 63:16, 64:8) although not very often but plainly and in several places. God's work is compared with that of a parent, mother or father or both (Deut. 32:18). The social meaning for 'father' in Israel was related with authority, care, discipline, protection and dignity. When God's work is compared to that of a parent, the language that is used is warm, gentle, affectionate, nurturing, and caring. God is addressed in the image of father predominantly in the texts which deal with creation, affection and leading. 'Father' was a social assumption, part of the social and cultural mould into which the faith of the Hebrew Scriptures was poured.[29] Most strikingly the father image is used only in 20 places in the Hebrew Scriptures.[30]

A brief examination of the Hebrew Scriptures makes it clear that most terms, images and expressions that are used for God are derived from human experience and from nature. Although, most of the images used for God does not present God as male and only in male terms in the Old Testament, for centuries, exclusive male language was used in the traditional interpretation to articulate theology. The diversity of views in the Hebrew Scriptures which arose from the people over the course of at least nine centuries makes it clear that there cannot be one accord on the images of God.[31]

4.2.1.2. New Testament Images of God: A Synopsis

The Hebrew Scriptures uses the proper name Yahweh for God. More surprisingly, the term Yahweh is completely absent in the New Testament. The New Testament writers did not borrow much from the language of Hellenistic Judaism. For example, Paul's usage of God is 'God.' In Romans he uses the term God 146 times.[32] He uses the term 'Father' a few times in Romans. Twice he referred to it in association with Jesus Christ (see Romans 1: 7, 15:7). In Ephesians, Paul used slightly a different language. The term God is found twenty three times in the six chapters and the pronoun 'he' is often used for God and the term 'Creator' is found. In contrast to Romans, the term Father is used for God frequently in Ephesians.

On the other hand, Mark as an earliest Gospel writer refers to 'God' as simply God.[33] The term 'Father' is referred twice in Mark. Luke uses the term God 122 times and in Acts 168 times. Although Luke mentions the term 'Father,' 'Father Language' is not dominant in Luke. Luke refers twice as 'my father' and thrice as 'your father' and four times in other terminology. Matthew and John elevate the title 'Father' for God. Matthew uses the term God 51 times and father over 40 times. In Matthew's Gospel, God is assigned hegemonic masculine roles, such as father or master of the house. Of the 63 instances of *pater* in Matthew, not less than 44 times they refer to God and all the references are found on the lips of Jesus. John uses the term God 83 times and Father 108 times.[34]

The Hebrew Scriptures gave much importance to the metaphor 'King' for God. However, uncompromisingly Jesus during his life time fought against this understanding of God. He taught in the Lord's Prayer, "Thy Kingdom come," but there was no king in God's kingdom. Mammen Varkey says, 'The 'Kingdom' does not have a king! The 'Kingdom' does have only a Father! We can say, as well, a Mother, the God, whom Jesus told us about and witnessed to, is 'Parent – God.' Not 'imperial' God."[35]

Mammen Varkey clearly declares that Jesus broke the authoritarian image of God as King but recovered the parental image of God as Father as well as Mother. However on the whole, God is referred as God and that image is dominant in the New Testament and each writer has his own expressions of God. As feminist theologians point out, the Bible is the product of males and so reflects the male imagery very often.[36] Very few times one can find female imagery for God. The Father-Son analogy to image God is dominant in the New Testament. It communicates that God is personal. God and Christ are equal. The relationship between God and Son are just as human fathers and sons as the male was considered the active force in producing new life.[37]

However, patriarchal teachings which emphasized only the male imagery of God have had damaging effects on the psyche of women. Hence, hermeneutics of reconstruction of the image of God is essential in the context of women and Dalit women in particular. The Bible contains no fixed image for God. The Bible does not accept unconditionally a fixed dwelling place for God either. It is because God is the living God (*el'hay*) in permanent and dynamic activity who cannot be grasped in a static conception since God's revelation is never concluded. Yahweh is a God who places One-self alongside human beings, closely concerned with their lives and behaviour, and who makes the demands of God's will felt in their actual history. This will of God demands submission to God, to one another and to a community. What is the will of God in the context of Dalit women who use scriptural texts to claim their identity as 'impure and inferior' in spite of their acquired identities? How can a Dalit feminist hermeneutical study contribute to realize the will of God in the context of Dalit women? Is it God's will that women should suffer disadvantages due to patriarchal teachings of God? Is it God's will to box God only in particular form that assumes God in a masculine image? This 'male image box' however for God is deeply fixed in the minds of women and hence the need here is to revisit the image of God to dismantle 'patriarchal male image box' for God in order that Dalit women realize the will of God in their lives to establish a new relationship with God in owning God's image in them reflecting God's image in them. Hence, the following section is an attempt to depatriarchalize the male image God.

5.3. The Image of God: Depatriarchalization

According to Gordon D. Kaufman, 'The symbols of God have been built up in order that they can serve as the ultimate point of reference for understanding and interpreting all of experience, life and the world."[38] The image of God is a human construct like all symbols. The traditional construction of the image of God draws heavily on human metaphors and models such as father, lord, judge, master etc.[39] Although the term 'image of God' is applied to all believers irrespective of gender, it is taken for granted that the image of God means 'man.' However the term has been used in different ways by different people in ways that lead to conflicts, contradictions, exploitation, oppression, dehumanization, and idol worship. The patriarchal traditional interpretations of God instruct that 'God is in the image of man,' and 'God created man in God's image.' Prejudiced male physical imagery for God has been thus explored in the traditional theology. On the one hand, Christianity believes that God is beyond gender and on the other attributes male gender to God. Traditional theologies failed to a larger extent to study what is the image of God which dwells in each and every human being.

Feminist theologies reject the notion of male gendered God and also the images of God which are authoritarian and disciplinarian.[40] They argue that the male gendered God has damaging effects on the image of women. The traditional theological interpretations have neglected the female imagery for God, and eventually neglected the female aspect. The male imagery of God has legitimized the subordination of women and reinforced women's internalized inferiority. Although systematic theologians maintain that God transcends sexuality,[41] in practice only male symbols are used to address God in the liturgies and prayers that reinforces patriarchal ideologies which are crippling women. Feminist theologians argue that the effects of such patriarchal God-language have deeply wounded the psyche of women. When God is spoken of only in male terms, this has severe psychological and sociological effects upon women's sense of identity and psychological well-being as well.[42] The exclusive male God-language theologically idolizes certain understandings of God and limits the scope of divine self-disclosure.[43] Torah is clear in its teaching that God is neither male nor female nor neutral. God is to be thought of in terms of eminence and a pleasant experience and not in terms of physical body in a literal sense.[44]

Athalya Brenner raises questions on the statement that, 'God created male and female in God's image (Genesis 1:26-28),' "Does that actually mean that the Hebrew God embodies both M and F principles? Or is God genderless" Or is God beyond gender or bi-gender?"[45] Mary Daly is right in her statement, "If God is male then male is God."[46] Traditional interpretations thus reinforce the attitude that men are gods. For example in Augustinian views, a woman is secondary to and subject to a man's will, while both are subjects to God's will. As souls, man and woman are equal in the eyes of God. But as bodies, man is made in the image of God.[47]

According to Augustine, the woman's body is not made in the image of God. Augustinian polemic understanding of human being divides thus body and soul and as soul-mates man and woman are in the image of God and as body-mates only man is in the image of God. Augustine's image of God in body form is highly questionable as the scriptures clearly disclose, God is beyond physical body. Augustinian view has had profound influence on later theologies. Susan Rockozy cites Thomas Aquinas who says, the girl child as a defective human being as the result of an accident to the male sperm. The sperm was to contain the complete human being and to reproduce its likeness, that is, another male. Using Augustine's thought, Aquinas says that the male possesses the image of God in a different way from woman and that his image is superior to that of woman. The woman in her sexuality involves a weaker and more imperfect body and she is subordinate.[48]

Philo speaks of God as beyond visibility. Peter Frick says, "Throughout his writings, Philo maintains that God's essence is completely concealed and unknowable to the human mind. God can be known and apprehended only through the activity of the powers in the works that follow him..."[49] However Philo conceives of an undifferentiated and incorporeal God. He also makes it clear that he understands God to be masculine as he frequently associates God with maleness in a metaphorical manner.[50] Bultmann on the other hand considers it as immaterial whether God is viewed adequately or inadequately, whether we speak of God in anthropomorphic terms or not. The question for him is: What does God mean for a human being?[51]

For Bultmann then, hermeneutics is centered on the question what is the meaning of God-talk? In this vein, the relation between revelation and experience occupied him throughout his demythologizing venture. His concern was to help the modern human mind to understand and experience God. He says, to speak of God's activity is at the same time to speak of one's own existence.[52]

Bultmann expresses God in relationship with human beings either in some form or not in any form. It does not matter to him. But for Paul Riceour, it is necessary to destroy the idolatrous father image of God. Paul Riceour is not against the conception of God as Father. He suggests depatriarchalization to break the father idol as is in Radford Ruether Rosemary's thought. According to him, the image of the father can be recovered as a symbol in the process of reconstruction. An idol must die so that a symbol of being may begin to speak. He points out that depatriarchalization is already found in the biblical Scripture; God who has been pictured as king and ruler in the covenant relationship has been moved into a loving husband like father in the prophetic teachings and finally into the form of Messiah. It is therefore important to recognize the depatriarchalization process that is already present in the biblical texts.[53] Rachel Adler cites, Mordecai Kaplan, who understands God to be the power or process in the universe that supports human fulfillment.[54] Alter Waltmann writes in his 'Methodology of Latin American Liberation Theology and a Contextual Re-reading of Luther,' the question of God is raised differently, according to the various cultural, socio-economic and political contexts. In the Latin American context, the question is not one which deals with the existence or non-existence of God. The question is whom do we refer to when we talk of God.[55] While dealing with the question of God, he quotes Luther's definition of God which is extremely challenging in reconstructing the image of God. In his Large Catechism, Luther declares:

> A God means that from which we are to expect all good and in which we are to take refuge in all distress. So, to have a God is nothing other than trusting and believing Him with the heart. I have often said that the confidence and faith of the heart alone make both God and an idol. If your faith and trust is right, then your God is also true. On the other hand, if your trust is false and wrong, then you do not have the true God. For these two belong together, faith and God (Hebrews 11:6). Now, I say that whatever you set your heart on and put your trust in is truly your God.[56]

Luther's definition of God gives much hope as one can find someone or something in whom or in which we place our trust, but not a God who is boxed in a male image. The World Council of Churches concludes that 'the doctrine of God's image (imago Dei) has by tradition been a source of oppression and discrimination against women.'[57]

Returning to feminist theological critique of the male imagery for God, Susan Brooks Thistlewaite asserts that the use of Father Language in reference to God is particularly the 'key affix' for white Western patriarchy. She rejects the father language for God from her perceptions as a child of a violent father who exercised violence against her mother and herself.[58] Aruna Gnanadason declares, "In Western Christianity most of the images of God are male – king, father, lord, master – because it is based on the social norms and gender role specified in that culture's national ecclesiastical, business and family level."[59]

While there is a strong resentment against the male images of God among feminist theologians, Diane Tennis raises a question, "Is God the Only Reliable Father?" and she answers, "Women need the Father God because the 'biblical God' is 'reliable,' whereas earthly fathers are often not reliable."[60] But Tennis' thesis sounds a superficial interpretation as black women's use of Father Language for God is due to the unreliability of real black fathers.[61] It is the male images that have been used exclusively,[62] literally[63] and patriarchally.[64] Hence, feminist theologians had a great deal of struggle with the biblical stories which are androcentric in nature. Reformist theologians believe that the same tradition that oppressed and excluded women is capable of liberating. Feminist theologians have deconstructed the male image of God and reconstructed new images. In the hermeneutics of reconstruction, the doctrine of God is no longer a doctrine of male-God. God is re-imaged both in female and male forms. Rose Mary Ruether's prophetic critical principle of feminist hermeneutics is the promotion of the full humanity of women. "Whatever denies, diminishes, or distorts the full humanity of women is therefore, appraised as not redemptive."[65] The male imagery that has the damaging effects on the lives of women is not perceived as promoting the full humanity of women. Though Ruether's critical principle sounds negative, it has positive elements in it. Whatever promotes the full humanity of women is considered Holy and reflects the Divine.[66] The female images of God which are obvious in the biblical texts have been reconstructed from the experiences of women which promote full humanity of women. However, Ruether points out "Humanity can be reconciled with God only if God is converted from 'His' patriarchalism to become the ground of reciprocity in creation."[67] For Philis Trible, the re-appropriation of the forgotten, suppressed and hidden feminine images of God present in the biblical tradition such as God as mother, midwife, nurse, lover, Sophia etc., is essential. Somen Das brings out an interesting exposition of the feminine images of God which are found in the Hebrew Scriptures. He says:

> 'Compassion' or 'Mercy' is a translation of the Hebrew word, *recham* and its plural, *rechamim.* It literally means 'womb' in Hebrew. Isaiah 49 passage compares God to a nursing mother, who sustains us all and will never forget us. 'Blessings of the breasts and the womb' (Gen. 49:25) is one of the blessings of God. Isaiah 42 compares divine judgment to a baby gestating in the womb of God. Similarly, God's *hesed* (love) is described in prophet Hosea in a feminist style. The Hebrew word for 'womb' is from the same root as the *ruah,* meaning spirit/breath mentioned in the creation narratives. Womb is the affirmation of creation or the creative process, which involves both pain and joy.....[68]

Somen Das is clear in his explanation that God cannot be attributed only with fatherhood apart from motherhood and that metaphor cannot be taken in a literal sense. For him, the metaphor of fatherhood and motherhood of God affirms the intimate, personal, and immediate relationship between God and humanity. He further says, "Therefore, God the Father is not to be understood in any ontological/metaphysical and physical sense but as a symbol of divine creativity or productivity."[69]

The patriarchal box that wrapped God in male image, according to Elizabeth Johnson, is a 'Divine mystery cramped into a fixed, petrified image.' Mcfague names it idolatry and Ruether calls it blasphemy.[70] Evangeline Anderson Rajkumar states that the 'patriarchal God is a false God.'[71] For Aruna Gnanadason, the father model becomes an idol, as father becomes God's name and patriarchy becomes the proper description of governing relationship at many levels.[72] R. A. Norris Says, "To ascribe sex to God is to subject the infinite in its own being too created limitations and thus to substitute an idol for God."[73] R. L. Hnuni discussing on the same line says:

> The exclusive use of male pronouns and male terms and symbols for God has projected and perpetuated the ideology that God is male and

> that it is not possible to address God or understand God in other ways. Maleness is seen as essential to the nature of God and male leaders are God's representatives of God on earth; because God is regarded as a father...[74]

Hnuni expresses that Western, Jewish and Christian theology used a discriminatory and sexist language. They used only male imagery for God and project God in various male pictures.[75] The patriarchal box that imaged God in particular male form needs to be broken, unlocked and unwrapped. According to Mary Daly, women who are the victims of archaic God-projections should bring this process of creativity into a new phase. She says, "This involves iconoclasm – the breaking of idols."[76] Breaking of idols should begin at the level of internalized image of God as male. Thus God can be meaningfully related as God-self to people in their own context. Thus it is essential to discover or recover or reclaim new images for God in order that individuals and community can as well worship God expressively.

5.4. The Image of God: Reconstructions

For traditional theology, God is male. For feminist theology, God is also female. However, Dalit theology looks at God as a Dalit. Black theology explains God as black. A central conflict underlying God-language debate in feminist theologies, and in fact in all contextual theologies, concerns whether personality should be ascribed to God. Reconstructionist theology asserts that God is an impersonal dynamic rather than a personality. Therefore, Judith Plaskow asserts that the parental images of God are problematic in relation to the experience of women and the problem of selfhood.[77] The problem thus of imagining God is not solved by adding a feminine image to God, although to image God as female, to think of God as 'She' may be to speak of empowering women. In the Indian context, people worship goddesses. But, the women are not liberated.[78] But, the father image of God has been imposed to exclude women in the monotheistic religions. Thus Peter C. Hodgson states, "An appropriate strategy for our time, in my view, would be to give up the father figure, not attempting to repossess it after its dispossession." And he suggests that attributing the name God to God is simple and appropriate. The Hebrew word for God is *Elohim*, which is simply translated *theos* in Greek, and *Gottor* in German.[79] Attributing to God male or female image or any image leads to idolatry and to the fixation of God. Marcia Falk accuses the anthropomorphic language of liturgy and prayer as 'liturgical idolatry':

> It is not just the exclusive maleness of our God-language that needs correction, but its anthropocentrism in all its ramifications. For as long as we image divinity exclusively as a person, whether female or male, we tend to forget that human beings are not the sole, not even the 'primary' life-bearing creatures on the planet. We allow our

> intelligence and our unique linguistic capabilities to deceive us into believing that we are 'godlier' than the rest of creation.[80]

The vision at the burning bush, in which God gives the name for God-self, 'I am who I am' does not convey God either as male or female. This revelation of the name, writes Paul Ricoeur, 'signifies the annulment of all anthropomorphic conceptions, all forms and shapes, including the form of the father.'[81] The name stands against the idol. The feminine use of 'she' for God is highly appropriate for liturgical and for political purposes, but it too is metaphorical and anthropomorphical. The feminist interpretations of God's image as female are once again not adequate. Walter Altmann in his article, 'Methodology of Latin American Liberation Theology and a Contextual Re-reading of Luther' quotes Ludwig Feuerbach who says, in 'The Essence of Christianism' that 'not God created the human being in his own image, but the human being created God in his own image.'[82] Walter Altmann affirms that Luther was well aware of this thought. According to Walter Altmann, for Luther, 'human beings affirm themselves, thus annihilating God. And they do it by creating a god who is adjusted to their own desires, their private interests, and their ideologies – an idol.'[83]

Children are taught to believe that God is male. Sunday schools teach them to address God as father. These patriarchal teachings stay firm in the mind of a child as she or he grows. Deborah Van Deusen Hunsinger in her work on 'Theology and Pastoral Counseling' while bringing out an analytical description on how one internalizes and develops an unconscious image of God from a psychoanalytic perspective quotes Ana Maria Rizzuto,[84] who locates the source of an individual's private image of God in the relationship to person's primary objects, especially person's parents. Rizzuto argues:

> A child creatively pieces 'God' together out of fantasies about and experience with these emotionally significant people. An internal psychic image or representation of God is formed from the *prima materia* of a child's hopes, fears, and longings, as they are imaginatively interwoven with some of the actual characteristics of those in the family of origin. Such a God representation is used throughout life to provide psychological stability and equilibrium, a minimum of relatedness to others, particularly those people who contributed to the formation of the God image, and a sense of self-esteem and hope.[85]

Rizzuto finds in her investigation that 'God' was seen to be a creation of the human mind, an illusory image created by the child out of the 'simple warp and woof of everyday life.'[86] While Sigmund Freud refers to the father as the prototype for one's picture of God, Rizzuto found that the mother and sometimes grandparents and siblings were just as consistently used as sources of the God representation. Indeed, her study showed that frequently the mother, not the father, was the primary source for God's image. She disagrees with Freud's contention that one's God image is fixed, it stays forever, fixed at one stage. She argues that the individuals frequently rework and re-elaborate their God images throughout life, particularly in time of crisis in personal psychological development.[87] Hence, the metaphoric language cannot be fixed for ever. It depends on the moods of the people, and on the experiences. People can image God according to each one's understanding, perceptions and experiences as both the Old and New Testament writers used. But, no symbols or metaphors or images are completely authoritative images of God. They are just symbols or metaphors. God cannot be boxed in any symbol or form or image. The task of Dalit feminist theology is therefore to search for resources within the biblical, theological and intellectual traditions to recover and reclaim the images for God.

Some feminist theologians express a dire need for female images of God to provide the loving and nurturing aspects of God. The patriarchal nature of traditional theology has made God an idol with a male image and boxed God. The same patriarchal ideology has boxed women with subordination. Yet other feminist theologians stress that God is beyond gender and consider it idolatrous to think of God as literally male, female, or even human.

While patriarchal theology boxes God in a male image, feminist theology should go further in not only depatriarchalizing God but also in attempting at a reconfiguration of God who is beyond sex, gender, position, class, race, colour, creed, religion and caste. Hence, it is an imperative to expand our images of God to include all aspects of transforming goodness in a way that can help both men and women to lead a life in fullness. It is a mandate for Dalit feminist theology to break the box that contains an idolatrous image for God and liberate both God and women from the boxes. The primary task of Dalit feminist theology is to deconstruct the image of God as male, female and neutral and reconstruct the image of God in God's personality.

Having said that the image of God is neither female nor male nor neutral, nor a particular image at this moment, what image can we prescribe to God in proclaiming the Gospel and administering the Word? What image can we ascribe to God in our prayers, praises and worship? In the context of Indian Dalit women, the aspiration for new images of God which is not authoritative and oppressive, but life-enhancing is imperative. Attributing a particular gender to God makes God too small. The equal relationship that exists between the patriarchal image of God and the male positions of power in church and society has negative effects on the lives of women. It should be overcome in theological discourses. The divine must be understood in the categories of relationships. God cannot be attributed any form, however we can speak only symbolically about God, every symbol that sets itself up as absolute must be relativized. We cannot live without symbols, but the symbols we use must be relativized and go beyond idolatry. God in fact transcends only when we do not lock God into prisons of symbols. Feminist theology does not deny that father is one symbol among many symbols for God, but if one makes it 'the only symbol,' then it is not acceptable because it boxes both God and women. The inclusive language used for imaging God will be beneficial to women and men. It will serve to stress the fact that not only man but also woman is the image of God. It also stresses the nobility of the motherhood of God. But, the inclusive images of God need to be used with much care in a symbolic way.

5.5. Reclaiming the Selected Biblical Images of God

For Virginia Fabella, "Without women's perspective and their contribution to theology, God, Jesus Christ, Holy Spirit, Salvation, Church and mission will be only half understood."[88] Women's contribution to theology is a particular exercise of how hermeneutics can influence our perception of God's revelation and God's image.[89] God is relational to each and every human being in one's own context. Biblical Scriptures present God in various images in various contexts. God related God self in the Scripture to various people in various ways. Hence, God cannot be wrapped up in one particular image. However it is impossible to discuss all those images in this chapter and so a few selected images of God are reclaimed which are present in the biblical texts for continuing our theological discourse. As the Bible was written by men in the context of patriarchal cultures, the central norm of Christian faith cannot be just the Bible itself, but also the experience of women and all human beings for that matter. As Monica Melanchthon precisely declares:

> The Bible was shaped in a male-dominated world, councils of men determined the canon itself, and over the centuries, male theologians and scholars interpreted texts that were considered to subordinate women. It is therefore a difficult and complex task to reconsider those texts from the perspective of women and bring to the fore an interpretation that reveals God's concern for the whole humanity.[90]

Though the Bible is encompassed by male domination and stamped by patriarchal oppression, it is still called the Word of God in the entire world and it stands firm as authoritative. It is evident from field research that the Bible takes the highest place in the life of Dalit Christian women. They regard the Bible as the one that speaks guides, corrects and transforms them. Therefore, it is necessary to re-interpret the Scriptures if they have to be meaningful and relevant in a particular context. The Bible is rich in resources which enhance the liberation and transformation of the marginalized communities. God is imaged in a variety of ways in the Bible which are highly empowering and life-giving. As explained by Deborah, God's image is functional whenever it provides the individual with a source of self-esteem, love and security.[91] A question was raised in the beginning of this chapter with regard to God's identity. In the process it is understood that God's image is not single, it is not static either but a relational personality with multiple identities. Thus selected images of God are re-claimed below to discover and recover the connections between the image of God and the image of Dalit women.

5.5.1. God as Life: Towards a Theology of Fullness

In one of the group discussions, respondents were sharing that unfortunately, when a child is born in India, a different code language is used to express the gender of the child. Mathematical symbols such as minus for girls and plus for boys are often used in Andhra Pradesh when a baby is born. Respondents shared that parents have to pay dowry for girls so they are equated with minus and parents receive dowry for boys so they are equated with a plus code. Women expressed this with deeply wounded hearts. It is fun in the families to crack a joke that minus is born. Of course, the baby cannot listen to these assertions; however these assertions play a damaging role in the lives of young girls when they listen to them. They suffer serious identity crisis. Thus there are very few people who really celebrate the birth of a girl in India. However, God is believed to be the source of life of a child. People celebrate the continuing creative act of God as the source of life. People believe that God is life and God gives life. In life-experiences such as birth, growth, awakening of senses, feeling of the sense of warmth, and so on, people believe that God is life and God helps life to grow. Life is forever specific and not constant and never general. Life is different and plural. Life is the gift of God to both men and women. Life is the image of God that is present in the personalities of both women and men. Revisiting God's image as life is a strength for Dalit women to draw on and to begin to image themselves as the life given by God to live a life of fullness. God is the source of life and women posses that life. Dalit women need to reclaim their life as God's image. Letty Russell's interpretative key emerges from her life story and from her pastoral experiences. For her:

> Bible opens up possibilities of new life as we comprehend visions of God's partnership at work in both the biblical story and in our own lives. Authority in partnership grows in a community when people take time to be partners with one another. And join God in working to repair the groaning creation in all its parts.[92]

Women and men need to become partners with God in repairing the broken world. Russell further explains:

> God's act of renewing creation, women and men are set free to develop new ways of relating to one another, to the world and to God. This work of mending includes designing ways to do theology that can include the input of those struggling against patriarchy towards a new vision of partnership. This experience of faith and struggle leads to spiral of action/reflection. Thus we gain new insights and questions.

> In the spiral again and again we move out and come again with the gained experience that is the experience of women's faith and struggle.[93]

The creation story makes it clear that God is Life and Life proceeds from God. God created human beings in God's image as female and male, in the combination of Adam (the dust of the ground) and Eve (the life). They became living beings with the image of God in them that is Life.[94] Charles Nyamiti cites G. Von Rod, to say, the full meaning of 'man' in the creation story does not only mean male but also female. It is man and woman as completing each other that frames the authentic 'image of God.' The perfection of God reflects both in man and woman in their own way.[95]

The Hebrew Scriptures are clear that the Spirit (*ruach*) is the breath of God's life. God creates everything through the Spirit. The image of God in human beings is life.[96] What is life for Dalit women in India? In fact, only a few enjoy life and a majority does not. Dalit women in India struggle for life. Kumari's story which is mentioned in the second chapter of this work is an indication that Dalit women are living in broken identities. Her expression that she could not give her child milk when the child was hungry and she gave warm water with sugar is not only an issue of poverty. It is also an issue of male violence in the family. It is also an issue of Christian Ethics. How does God work in such situations? What is the message of the church (theological language of the church) to such women who undergo violence? Are these women created in order to live miserable lives? What is the point of being in a Christian community? How does God identify Godself with these women?

In this faith struggle, God is discovered as life. God wants humanity to live life in fullness. The mystery of God's love can be seen in God's action of liberation. God is the life giver, when that life is destroyed; when that life is threatened, God liberates them out of God's love. When God revealed God's name to Moses, for the first time, it was in connection with commissioning Moses for the historic mission of liberation.[97] Jurgen Moltmann while asserting the Holy Spirit as source of life says:

> In the experiences of the Spirit, God is felt as primal and all-embracing presence; God is no longer an aloof counterpart in heaven. In the experiences of the Spirit we perceive a much more intimate relationship than the relation of Creator to creature, more intimate even than the relation between father or mother and child. It is the intimate fellowship of mutual indwelling: God is in us in a divine way, and we are in him in a human way (I Jn. 4.16). In the fellowship of the Holy Spirit the eternal God comes to share in our mortal, sick and disabled life and we have a share in the eternal life of God. This mutual fellowship is for us an inexhaustible well-spring of strength.[98]

Susan Rokoczy states on the same lines:

> The Spirit's whole movement in hearts and communities is to create LIFE in the midst of despair, mediocrity, apathy and the denial of life. The promise of Jesus is the fullness of life: 'I have come that they may have life, and have it in abundance' (Jn. 10:10). This is life which begins here, in the days given to us, and continues for ever.[99]

But, patriarchy and caste system have not only snatched away life from women but also they have stolen hope from them. For women, the need to experience the power of the life of the Risen Lord in and through the Spirit is the need of the hour so that they would live life in fullness. This fullness of life is given to each one through the Holy Spirit of God. The fullness of life is described by John in beautiful images: as the bread of life (Jn 6), the light of life (Jn 8.12), the life of resurrection (Jn 11.25), the way, the truth and the life (Jn 4.6). The Gospel is proclaimed and written so that we might believe and have life in Christ Jesus (Jn 20.31).[100] As Susan puts it, the fullness of life which Jesus promises does begin here, but it does not come to completion here. Every taste of new life makes us hungry for yet more, for the bread of life who is Jesus can never be exhausted as we share it among ourselves.[101]

Yahweh is conceived as the 'living God,' not only God lives, but by definition possesses an inexhaustible life, which is the source of all life.[102] The faith of Israel emphasizes the fact that wherever there is life, Yahweh provides the benefits of nature (Hos. 2, Jer. 31:10-14 Ps. 104), living with Yahweh means prosperity and abundance of good for Israel (Deut. 7:9-15, 8:7-10, 2:1-14). Ronald Munoz states further:

> The God of Israel is not 'spiritual' in an abstract sense, as if relating to Yahweh involves only the inner life of an individual; on the contrary, Israel sees God wherever there is abundance, salvation and joy shared among friends. As the spiritual and physical spheres are not opposed, and still less mutually exclusive, in Hebraic thought, the Hebrew prophets have imaged God not only in physical image but also in terms of all dimensions of human life.[103]

This interpretation of Ronald Munoz helps us to an understanding that the worship of God does not imply a spiritual sphere alone but also life in its entirety. This means, God is related with human beings not only when they worship God as a community in the church but in all the spheres of life. *Somen Das states:*

> God is conceived as life-producing or life-giving and enhancing. This becomes quite evident in the creation narrative, when God affirms 'very good' after he/she had created everything including woman. The word 'Eve' comes from the Hebrew word, meaning life. Jesus reaffirms

this fundamental character of God, "I have come that they may have life, and have it in its fullness" (Jn. 10:10).[104]

5.5.2. God as Freedom: Towards Svathanthra

Freedom is the state of not being a prisoner. Freedom is associated with one's rights. For some, freedom means to live without constraint; for others, with restraint. For some, freedom is the right to give full expression of one's powers; for others it is the unchecked right to impose one's power upon others. For Paul Tillich, freedom is overcoming authority; for St. Paul freedom means being 'a slave of Christ.'[105] For feminist theologians freedom is wholeness. Wholeness or freedom has several dimensions. It is the elimination of the interlocking system of oppression of any kind; it implies that the society is united in the struggle for life; it means that individual women and men confront the ways in which societal oppression has made life less than whole. It is also working with a particular vision, a vision of liberation.'[106]

Jesus' key proclamation, "You shall know the Truth, and the Truth will make you free" (John 8:31), has attracted Mahatma Gandhi to train himself to struggle for Independence. Gandhi introduced the concept of *Satyagraha* as a non-violent moral force against the British to achieve *svathantra* (Independence). The presupposition of Gandhi's practice of Satyagraha is that the change of behaviour can affect the change of character or structure. Truth was very central in Gandhi's thought and life. Harvey J. Sindima writes that Gandhi once wrote: "To me God is truth and love...He is long suffering."[107] So Harvey says, "Since God is truth, the seeker is drawn into a community of love and sacrifice."[108] A true *Satyagrahi* is the one who has learnt the Truth – God. Satyagraha is based on the fundamental conviction that human nature is basically good and is capable of being changed and the change can take place by self-suffering. For Gandhi, the law of love is the law of life. In the concept of *satyagraha,* the attack is on evil and not on evildoers. When evil is separated from the evildoer, the doer is transformed and a new harmonious relationship is established within the person and between the parties involved.[109] For Gandhi, Truth is God and God-realization is to be activated through service to the afflicted. And this is what *Sarvodaya* (the welfare of all) stands for and which he aimed at and for which Jesus died for.[110] Both for Gandhi and Christ, God is Truth.

Svathanthra means freedom. Freedom is an important subject in Lutheran theology. The church has insisted on God's freedom in creating human beings and the world. The underlying theological starting point for a Christian in general and marginalized in particular in India is to ask what does 'freedom' mean to the oppressed communities in the context of restrictions and discriminations in the name of religion, gender, and caste? [111]

5.5.2.1. Concept of Svathanthra (freedom) in the Bible

The Hebrew term that is used for freedom is *hupsa* and in Greek, *eleutheria*. The Bible considers freedom as liberty which is opposed to slavery.[112] In the Old Testament, freedom mostly referred to a social state. The 'Year of Freedom' (Lev 25:10) and the concession of freedom to slaves (Ex 21: 2-26, Deut. 15:12ff, Lev 19:20) is a theological subject[113] of liberation as the fact remains that 'Israel had been a slave in the land of Egypt,' and Yahweh had 'freed her from the house of slavery' (Deut 15:15). In the New Testament, freedom was often referred to the ultimate relationship between the believer and Christ. Paul emphasized freedom as a spontaneous loyalty and obedience to God in Christ.

God exercises freedom to pour out God's love and to establish justice through reconciliation in Jesus. The freedom of God in God-self represents the sum of the gospel and includes all the liberating activities of Jesus – his teaching, his mighty acts of healing, his deliverance of captives from oppressive structures of sin and death through his own death and resurrection. Jesus in his freedom and self-sacrifice brought reconciliation between God and humanity and between one another. God is free to relate God-self to people most intimately. God is free to become human in Jesus Christ. Human liberation is the purpose of God's freedom. Unless freedom is achieved, reconciliation is unattainable. God cannot be boxed into any categories, for God is God. 'I am who I am' is the expression to create, to love, to liberate, to deliver and to free people from any bondage.[114] The affirmation of God as creator does not mean just to refer to past events of creation but to a continuous involvement of God to sustain it.[115] For V. Devasahayam the biblical God is free. He says, this God is free, absolutely free to hear the cry against the powerful; God cannot be domesticated. God expresses God's solidarity with the victims of society because they are voiceless, defenseless and look to God for their defense.[116]

Dalit theologians claim that the gospel of freedom and equality for building up egalitarian communities (Gal. 5. 12) is the need of the hour in the Indian context. Therefore, the defence of the gospel for the sake of the people stands justified (Gal. 5. 13).[117] Richard H. Bliese says while quoting biblical text from the epistle to Galatians, "For you were called for freedom, brother" (5:13) and 'For Freedom Christ has set us free; so stand firm and do not submit again to the yoke of slavery' (5:1), 'God's freedom always emerges out of God's order and, it is freedom in Christ that transforms all orders and established a new creation.'[118] Richard H. Bliese further states:

> According to the Bible, then, freedom and God's mission in Christ are connected. God's triune mission arises out of God's freedom in terms of creation, redemption and sanctification....Human freedom comes from God's love. Love is the basis for freedom and, consequently, for a lot of disorder. This freedom is a gift of God.[119]

5.5.2.2. Theological Understanding of Freedom

Theology is not merely the acceptance of beliefs about God but a personal commitment to God – a commitment that interprets experience and thus gives meaning to life.[120] The Gospel of Christ is a Word that liberates. When theology is applied to human concerns, it refers to the human face of God, to God's solidarity with humanity. The freedom of God is an absolute necessity for any theology which attempts to address the human concern. In general, in our theological articulations, worship and programmes of the church, God is identified with our own interests and commitments. Thus the Christian community has the confidence, hope and faith that God alone can give freedom because God is Truth and God can set people free. For Karl Barth, God always takes the stand unconditionally and passionately against the oppressor on behalf of the lowly, and against those who already enjoy rights and privileges on behalf of those who are denied and deprived.[121] Karl Barth understands the image of God as love and freedom. Since Truth in Godself is love and freedom, God is able to be the same in relation to us.[122] Deborah van Deusen Hunsinger says, "The concept of God's freedom is Barth's primary way of designating the divinity of God, in other words, that which makes God to be God."[123]

Irenaeus, a second century bishop and theologian, identified God's image in human beings with human reason and moral freedom. He emphasized that, even at the fall, God's image (human reason and moral freedom) is not lost.[124] God's transcendence means God's radical freedom from all human systems of sin and God's immanence means God's liberating presence in us. These two are ultimately the same; that is, God is liberating as the one who is radically free from our systems of sin.[125] The patriarchal God, the God who is masculine-mind-externality, by excluding the feminine-body-internality, lacks authentic transcendence. Such a God is the creature of human ideologies and systems of power that justify the dominance of men over women, the powerful over the powerless. Martin Luther affirms the view that human beings create God in their own image. It is the sinful alternative to the true God. Human beings create God who is adjustable to their own desire, their private interests, their ideologies which Luther calls an idol.[126] God is understood in feminist theology as the one who is radically free and the source of freedom from all systems of sin. For P. Arockiadoss:

> Freedom is, positively, the capacity to act as a human person or a community, by free choice and deliberate decisions in a responsible way for the good and growth of oneself along with others. Negatively, freedom consists in being liberated from enslaving forces, both internal and external, from enslaving oppressive socio-political structures, exploitative economic relations, and dehumanizing cultural orientations.[127]

The New Testament declaration, 'Where the Spirit of the Lord is, there is freedom' (2 Cor. 3:17)[128] affirms and confirms that God is freedom and human beings as God's creation bear the image of God as freedom. Dwight N. Hopkins says:

> ...the anointing of 'the spirit of the Lord' commissions us to proclaim the good news of freedom. God's loving freedom has become our freedom because Jesus' victory over oppression has opened up a new world where everlasting life begins now (John 3:16). This spirit calls on theology to speak with, for and to those who have no voices. It calls on theology to say the gospel of freedom ....[129]

For Gandhi nothing exists, except Truth (God); Truth is *Saccidananda* (God).[130] Only through *satyagraha* one can achieve *svathanthra.* For Gandhi, *svathanthra* (freedom) consists of three things: freedom from control of others – self-reverence; freedom from any tendency to control others – self-knowledge; and freedom from being driven by one's own desires – self-control.[131] Where there is freedom there *purna swaraj* (one's own complete kingdom) exists. For Gandhi, *purna swaraj* means harmony, freedom from aggression from within and without, and a progressive improvement in the economic conditions of the masses.[132] The one who has *svathantra* can have one's own *swaraj* in which *sarvodaya* can take place and in the concept of *sarvodaya* there is no place for *himsa* (violence) and Gandhi opted for *ahimsa* (non-violence). The message of democracy is the message of freedom and equality. It is chiefly a spiritual message though it finds expression in political or social garbs. For Gandhi, Truth is God, and God-realization is to be activated through service to the afflicted. And this is what *Sarvodaya* stands for.[133]

Gandhi's identity crisis in South Africa led him to choose Jesus' concept of *Satyagraha* (knowing the Truth) to liberate India from British bondage. In the same vein, Christians in India and particularly Dalit Christians opted for conversion from Hinduism to liberate themselves from all kinds of bondages and particularly idolatry. How far can they claim that they are free? Can they claim that they know the Truth? Gandhian freedom is two-fold: one, becoming free by knowing the Truth; and two, freeing others. The nature of his freedom of self-rule denotes freedom from control by others, freedom from any tendency to control others and freedom from being driven by one's own desires. In other words, freedom rests in self-reverence, self-knowledge and self-control. The Dalit Christian's freedom and especially Dalit woman's freedom in India is under siege from divisive elements within the country, based on religion, community, class, caste, language, gender, socio-economic disparities, corrupt and corrupting political power rivalries. The image of God (Truth) as Freedom is a powerful image to liberate women and to transform them.

5.5.3. God as Shakti (Power): Towards Empowerment of Dalit Women

The term *Shakti* comes from Sanskrit word shak *which* means 'to be able,' meaning sacred force or empowerment. *Shakti* is the primordial cosmic energy and represents the dynamic forces that move through the entire universe. *Shakti* is the concept, or personification, of divine feminine creative power, sometimes referred to as 'The Great Divine Mother' in Hinduism. Not only is *Shakti* responsible for creation, but it is also the agent of all change. *Shakti* is cosmic existence as well as liberation. *Shakti* exists in a state of *svatantra*, dependence on no-one, being inter-dependent with the entire universe.[134]

The Bible uses the term power – *Shakti* for God. Most remarkably the term power is associated with the Holy Spirit, or the Spirit of God. Indian Christian theologians like Chenchiah, Chekkarai and others have already used the term *Shakti* to explain the power of the Holy Spirit. Indian feminist and eco-feminist theologians have extensively used the term *Shakti* to refer to the image of God that is present in women. Hence, this chapter draws insights using their framework in order to empower Dalit women.

People in reality use different kinds of power. People execute power at every step of their life. They delight in the supreme or partial use of power over others: parents over children, husbands over wives, teachers over students, employers over employees, pastors over congregations, castes over out-castes, men over women and first world over third world and so on. Some handle power brutally, cruelly and arrogantly to make sure submission and oppression rather than liberation. The aptitude of power is extended to: spiritual, religious, moral, kingly, administrative, community-oriented, professional, family and personal. Power struggles are rife in the material world. One has to realize that every human being has power within oneself. The only power that lasts a lifetime is the hidden power within the inner world. One needs to realize this power that has control over one's own words and actions.[135] The nature of power depends on how it is used and that gives a moral dimension to it. Feminist interventions in the debate of power have transformed and enriched its meaning.[136] Otto Maduro avoids reducing power only to the idea of 'power over others' which in fact would be only one modality of social power, which is identified with the words 'domination,' 'oppression,' and 'exploitation.'[137] Otto Maduro, explains power in a sociological sense:

> As the capacity of a group (or an individual) to define its (his or her) interests and goals and attain the latter, including vis-à-vis other groups and persons. In this sense, nobody enjoys absolute power: our power is always partially defined in relation to and limited by the power of those with whom we interact as well as our finite faculties and restricted resources. Conversely, nobody lacks power entirely: while we are alive, while we are still able to somehow move and communicate, we can influence even if minimally – some of the processes affect

> our existence. In this sense, we might understand social power as something simultaneously relational, gradational, and unstable....[138]

As Otto Maduro explains, the power in the new liberated community leads to empowerment. The power of God gives life to the dry bones and makes it a new nation (Ezek. 37). In the words of M. M. Thomas:

> For in 'the new humanity in Christ which is being renewed in knowledge after the image of its maker,' the distinction of nature, history, culture and religion are not absolutized but transcended in the awareness of solidarity with all mankind and common participation in the new humanity of Christ. 'Here there cannot be Greek and Jew, circumcised and uncircumcised, barbarian, Scythian, slave, freeman, but Christ is all.' Through Jesus Christ a new communion of the Spirit, based on mutual forgiveness and gratitude to the divine Forgiveness received in Christ, building up tissues of love, comes into being among the communities of the world, producing the spiritual ferment of their renewal and humanization (Col. 3.10-18).[139]

5.5.3.1. 'Power' in the Scripture

Various Hebrew words are used for the term 'power' in the Old Testament. *Hayil, koah* and *oz* are the main words. The true power rests in God alone according to the Old Testament (Ps. 62:11). The Power of God is visible in creation (Ps. 148:5). The Power of God which is active in Creation is also active in sustaining that Creation (Ps. 65:5-8). The Power of God is shared with human beings (Gen 1:26-28, Ps. 8:5-8, 115:16). God's Power is also active in liberating God's people from bondage (Ex.15:6).[140] God's *shakti* is perfectly exhibited in the stories of creation and liberation. In the New Testament, the terms *dynamis* and *exousia* are often used to refer to power which means the right to do something (Mt. 21:23-27). *Dynamis* also means ability (2 Cor. 8:3), or strength (Ep. 3:16), or it may mean a powerful act (Acts 2:22), or a powerful spirit (Rom. 8:38). Jesus ministered in the power (*dynamis*) of the Spirit (Lk 4:14).[141] Samuel Rayan, in his liberation pneumatology sees 'the Holy Spirit, the Spirit of God and of Jesus Christ' as the 'heart of the Christian gospel.' Drawing on the *shakti* tradition, he portrays the Spirit as the 'breath of fire,' who comes 'to enable us to re-create our earth, not to put us to sleep,' and is present 'not in ethereal euphoria, but in committed historical action.'[142]

5.5.3.2. God as Shakti: Theological Explorations

Robin Boyd observes that pneumatology emerges as the 'corner-stone' of Indian Christian Theology. God's dealings with the word are seen primarily in terms of the Spirit.[143] For Chenchiah, the Holy Spirit is 'the new cosmic energy.' For this new cosmic energy, Chenchiah uses the word *Mahashakti* that literally means 'great power.' In Hinduism, *Shakti* is often personified as the goddess of power. He feels that the Indian understanding of *Shakti* as personalized divine energy is in a good position for developing and deepening the meaning of the Christian life in terms of yoga of the Spirit. For Chenchiah, Christian life will be meaningful only if it searches for the source of God's power and conscious submission to that power and to the use of power. And that power is found only in and through the Holy Spirit.[144] Indian feminist theologians have used the term *Shakti* for God. Stella Baltazar says that the transcended Christ can be imagined as the embodiment of the feminine principle, the *shakti*, the energizer and vitalizer.[145] Vandana Shiva an Indian eco-feminist condemns modern science as a male project and development programmes as the brain children of Western patriarchy, which is leading to the death of feminine principle. She says feminine principle or *shakti* is characterized by harmonious relationship between humans and nature and between men and women and the respect for diversity and the sharing of resources.[146] Aruna Gnandason takes a thought from Hinduism and images God in the form of *Shakti* which is the Power.[147] She discovers God in her new spirituality as *Shakti* (Power) which has a feminine dimension.[148] She explains the meaning of *Shakti* as:

> The dynamic energy, which is the source and substance of all things, pervading everything. The manifestation of this primordial energy is called *prakrithi* (nature). This nature, both animate and inanimate, is thus an expression of *Shakti*, is feminine and creative principle of cosmos; in conjunction with the masculine principle (*Purusha*) *Prakrithi* creates the world.[149]

Aruna attributes the image *Shakti* for God and *Shakti* means power. *Shakti* is a spiritual energy, which is the essence of great religious traditions of Asia. It is an energy that is at the source of all things. In the re-emergence of *shakti*, Aruna discovers an affirmation of a new community in Christ. She builds on Rosemary Radford Ruether's 'communal personhood.' In that community women find their dignity and selfhood, and reclaim their right to define what their womanhood is, what their femininity means and all that in community. Secondly in *shakti*, women will be critically involved in liberation struggles.[150] *Shakti* also means *svatantra*, hence *shakti* and *svatantra* complement each other. Pushpa Joseph, in articulating '*shakti* theology' says:

> *Shakti* theology deconstructs and reconstructs the Scriptures in order to unleash its empowering aspects. *Shakti* theology is critical and imaginative in reclaiming and re-articulation of women's silences through the use of new metaphors. A *Shakti* theology, which considers power as 'power for,' will transform knowledge from an instrument of power to a means of emancipation. Especially for the poor and

> marginalized most of whom are women and children, *Shakti* theology can mediate a mode of governance, which allows room for individuals and collectives for self-determination. Fostering an inclusive approach a *Shakti* theology which emerges from the life stories of Indian women will be contextual.[151]

According to Pushpa, energy as *Shakti* is also viewed as a merging of powers originating from each person. In popular worship in Hinduism, *Shakti* has several names such as Kali, Durga and Parvathi, who are considered as incarnations or avatars of *Shakti.*[152] *Shaki* is worshipped as a power that can lead to spiritual liberation.[153] Pushpa Joseph associates the creative powers of Eros with the divine energy of *Shakti*. She proposes a *Shakti* Theology, which with its rousing of the entire energies one can discover in one's body, emotions and mind, is an alternative to the excessive intellectualism of patriarchal theologies. Based on an egalitarian foundation, *Shakti* theology with powerful connectedness and distinct identity, advocates 'power with' as opposed to patriarchal 'power over' relationships.[154] Interestingly, Pushpa explores that Shatki is present behind the creation. In addition to it, there is neither creation nor destruction of energy, only transformations. This reality has no beginning and no end. It is eternal, self-luminous and dynamic.[155] Pushpa gives a new twist to feminist thought in the model of Siva-Shakti. She says, Siva is sentient and luminous and Shakti is dynamic, free and produces livingness, which gives rise to the awareness of one's own self. This awareness of one's own self is a form of Siva, but Siva is also the inseparable part of Shakti. She finds harmony and oneness in Siva-Shakti relationship,[156] which is the best model to maintain the relationship between man and woman in upholding the equality.

5.6. God as Life, *Svathanthra,* and *Shakti*; Implications for the Empowerment of Dalit Women

5.6.1. God's Identity as Life: Towards Inclusive Identity of Dalit Women

In working out Dalit feminist hermeneutics, discovering a new definition of spirituality is essential in order for Dalit women to recover their identity as God's children. Arvind P. Nirmal says in his article, 'Towards a Christian Dalit Theology' that 'the ideal of Imago Dei in us leads us to the question of God.'[157] He further declares:

> The Dalit Consciousness should realize that the ultimate goal of its liberation movement cannot be the 'land flowing with milk and honey.' For a Christian Dalit Theology cannot be simply gaining of the rights, the reservations and privileges. The goal is the realization of our full humanness or conversely, our full divinity, the ideal of the

> Imago Dei, the image of God in us. To use another biblical metaphor, our goal is the 'glorious liberty of the children of God.'[158]

'Life' as the Image of God is a powerful conception which leads to liberation of Dalit women. Liberation happens at physical, personal, social, political and spiritual level. For Dalit women, liberation means fullness of life, it begins with survival and security. It means the basic needs to sustain physical life. Dalit women bristle with the quest for life in its fullness. Life is not only related with physical needs but also has to do with knowledge, feelings and emotions which are also dependent on the physical being just as the evaluative functions of the mind and that plays a significant role in forming the identity in the community. As such, the very existence of Dalit women stands threatened in India. Both the church and Dalit community have to play a role in helping Dalit women to recover their identity as created in God's image. Excluding Dalit women from the mainstream either in the family, church and community at large is to ignore their existence. This study seriously challenges such ignorance and names it a 'sin.' This study calls for repentance on the part of the perpetrators for committing sin of ignoring God's life that is fully present in Dalit women and thereby destroying their identity. This study encourages and empowers Dalit women to name themselves as embodied selves of God's life. They are the co-workers with God in nurturing the lives and nature on earth. This study affirms Dalit women as co-workers in God's Kingdom.

5.6.2. God as Svathanthra: Towards the Liberation of Dalit Women

Jesus' words, 'Know the Truth and the Truth will set you free,' are powerful not only to empower Gandhi to attain freedom for himself and his nation but also to Dalit women to empower themselves. Christians in general claim that their God liberated them from the bondage of sin through Jesus Christ. If that claim is true, how many are really liberated from the sin of gender and caste bias? Is the church free from the oppressive, suppressive, violent and sinful structures of patriarchy and caste system? As of today, caste hierarchy and patriarchal hierarchy continue to oppress Dalit women in the church.

To live in India as a woman in general and a Dalit woman in particular is a disgrace because of the restrictions placed on her. However, women in the Indian church have considerable freedom to pray, to sing songs, to conduct family visits, to raise funds, to visit hospitals, to conduct women's fellowships, to cultivate income-generating programmes, to support churches, to become self-sufficient in the field of economics, to give religious teaching to children and youth and to clean church premises. Along with the said freedom, do they have freedom to participate in decision-making body of the church? Do they have their due place in the church? Where is the self-identity of women? The Constitution of India assures freedom (religious freedom to practise and to propagate and to participate as full members) to all its citizens – legally and theoretically, however, not in practice. What does freedom and liberation mean to women of different castes in the context of violence perpetuated by the caste system and patriarchy in the church?

The image God as freedom is powerful in empowering Christian Lutheran women in India. Whoever knows the Truth will be free because Truth (God) is freedom. The need for women to realize the Truth that 'the Truth will make them free' is a powerful challenge in their context, in order to strengthen themselves and their community.

Restricted by caste, Dalit women are treated as untouchables in India. Constrained by patriarchy, Dalit women have limited opportunities. Dalit women are chained in various ways. The freedom that they exercise in the family, community and church at large is partial freedom. They need a complete liberation from all kinds of bondages. This study invites Dalit women to come to a complete realization of God the Truth so that they will be set free. But the theological language of the Indian church needs much revision in widening her perspectives in self-analysis to see God's image of Freedom in every human being and particularly in Dalit women.

5.6.3. God as Shakti: Towards Dalit Women's Empowerment

To the powerless category, Dalit women, the powerful image of God as *Shakti* is an empowering image as they have internalized the concept of powerlessness within them. The power of Jesus to empower others is the best paradigm for Dalit women. An empowerment took place in the life of the woman with the flow of blood (Matt. 9:20-22, Mk. 5:25-34, Lk. 8:43-48). Jesus had the inner power to liberate others, to free others from all kinds of sufferings, to produce self-esteem in others and to give a sense of belongingness to others. The call for power and power-sharing led to empowerment instantly in the biblical story. This story of the woman with the flow of blood helps Dalit women to be empowered in calling for power. Shared power and values would lead to the success of Dalit women.[159] The vision and goal of Jesus is to free the people from all the bondages that lead to stress. While the present socio-political-economic-cultural reality forces Dalit women and men to internalize and believe and feel ashamed of their skin, body and blood, and to think of themselves as impure and dirty, and polluted, a new Dalit feminist hermeneutics should affirm that the bodies and the blood of Dalit women and men are equal, life-giving, in all aspects of their lives. Their bodies and blood have equal share in the body of Christ to release power and to receive power in order to bring transformation in the lives of Dalit women. M. E. Prabhakar while discussing 'Dalit Power'[160] quotes A. Alan Boesak who says, "The affirmation of selfhood or personhood is a powerful act that constitutes a farewell to innocence."[161] Prabhakar adapting the thought from A. Alan Boesak says:

> The focus on dalitness affirms their Dalit Power not only for self-definition and theologizing but also for their involvement in social

> change. Dalit Power is a clear critique of and a force for fundamental change of systems and patterns in society which oppress or give to the oppression of Dalit people.[162]

K. P. Aleaz observes that the Holy Spirit the Shakti 'in Dalit perspective will be the Spirit which revives the dry bones of Dalits, gives them life, unifies and empowers them (Ezekiel 37) for the liberation struggle.'[163] While observing that the anointing Holy Spirit is power and active in building up new humanity, Aleaz continues to say, the Dalits in the power of the Spirit speak up and denounce vehemently the evils of the caste system. They condemn the sin of untouchability. They expose the falsehood and spiritual bankruptcy of the existing religions which either justify caste or accept it uncritically.[164]

This study extends a call to the community of Dalit women as a renewed and liberated community to discover within themselves the strength and power that they were created with. God's image as Power in Dalit women will help them to form new identities for them in order that they attribute more self-value to their lives. However, building an image is a process. It cannot happen overnight and takes a lot of hard work and homework. It also requires employing every available opportunity to build and evoke value to build up their life.

5.7. Conclusion

This work affirms that the redemptive reality of which the Christian faith speaks is not something apart from the daily realities of Dalit women; it is part of their daily living. It impacts the situations they face day in and day out. The way of life Dalit women embrace must lead to radical changes in the oppressive and exclusive practices of society. Theology-in-action must in the first place, be firmly rooted in the daily experiences. Secondly, it should be concrete and should be connected to actual places, spaces, situations and moments. It should strive forward for the radical changes in small and big, immediate, and successive ways in the way we think and act in different areas of our lives. It is a process of conscientization and concretization that helps us to become moral agents and subjects of our own history. Donald Messer pointing out that images affect human behaviour at a deeper and subliminal level cites Susan Brooks Thistlethwaite who says:

> Metaphor is thought in action. Metaphor reveals the deepest experiences of human beings and impels them to act in new ways. Metaphor has frequently been employed by Christians in the history of the church both to describe their communal experience and to motivate themselves to repentance and change.[165]

An imposed outcaste, impure, dirty, and polluted identity carries dishonour whereas caste people are comfortable with their caste brand. For example, during the field research I have come across a few women belonging to the high caste. They mentioned their 'caste name' in 15 minutes dialogue, and expressed the dislike of their family members on embracing the God of Malas, while they were at ease in using the term Mala persistently. In case of Dalits, it is very hard to name the caste, as the image 'Low Caste Women' carries emotional pain and humiliation. This chapter affirms that the image of God exists in the various metaphors in the being of Dalit women. But, God's image in the Dalit women is boxed under the sinful structures of patriarchy and caste system. The box needs to be broken so that God's image will be visible in them.

In the depths of one's psyche a positive image of oneself is essential in forming one's identity. As argued in this thesis, Dalit women on one hand acquired identities and on the other, suffer broken identities. For instance, as it is already mentioned, four women have been ordained in SALC in January 2011. I witnessed a celebration of acquired identities of these women who were ordained. All four ordained women were invited to serve Holy Communion in the dedication service of a newly constructed church at Rapur. The researcher was one among them. Among them two ordained women were present in the service with their husbands who are also ordained. The church gave opportunity to these couples to serve Holy Communion together, while the wife was distributing bread, the husband distributed the wine. It was a joyful celebration of acquired identities of Dalit women. But, only four among thousands of women could acquire these new identities. A majority of them suffer disadvantages of low self-esteem due to their deep fixed imposed identities. Unfortunately a majority of women think that they are impure during menstruation and they forget that it is through this menstruation cycle life is produced. This life giving image of God is powerful and relevant for women to image God in their thinking as the life producing conception.

Hence, re-claiming the biblical images of God as Life, *Svathanthra* and *Shakti* as meaningful and relevant images in the context of Dalit women is a serious concern in this chapter. Re-claiming God's images as Life, *Svathanthra* and Shakti can trigger powerful feelings that may explode into new aspirations and actions for women in SALC. This chapter brings firm connections between God's identity and Dalit women's identity and God's image and Dalit women's image as Life, *Svathanthra* (freedom) and Shakti. These images are relational, powerful and transforming.

End Notes

1. Part of this chapter is published. See Prasuna N. "Towards Dalit Feminist Theology: Re-Visiting the Image of God" in *Ecumenical Horizon Journal*, Vol. 2/No.1 (December 2008-January 2009).
2. Yoshida, Megumi, "Imaging" as Theological Methodology: From Logo-centric to Holistic Approach" in *God's Image*, Vol. 28, No. 4 (December 2009), 43.
3. C. Barnabas, *Basic Christian Doctrines* (Trichy: IIICS Study Book Series, 2003), 172.
4. Frederic Greeves, *Theology and the Cure of Souls: An Introduction to Pastoral Theology* (Manhasset, New York: Channel Press, INC, 1962), 110.
5. Cited in David Cairns, *The Image of God in Man*, 110.

6. Tjeu Van Knippenberg, "Transcendence and Personal Histories/Life stories" in *The Human Image of God,* edited by Hans-George Ziebertz, Frederick Schweitzer, Hermann Haring and Don Browning (Leiden: Brill, 2001), 268.
7. Richard Kearney "The God Who May Be," in *Questioning God,* edited by John D. Caputo, Mark Dooley and Michael J. Scanlon (Bloomington: Indiana University Press, 2001), 161.
8. Tjeu Van Knippenberg, "Transcendence and Personal Histories/Life stories" Op. Cit. 264.
9. John Shea, *Stories of God: An Unauthorized Biography* (Chicago: Thomas More, 1978), 56.
10. Donald E. Messer, *Contemporary Imagery of Christian Ministry* (Nashville: Abingdon Press, 1989), 20-24.
11. Douglas Bland, "Story Telling as Grief Ministry." *The Christian Century* (September 1982), 33, Cited by Donald E. Messer in *Contemporary Imagery of Christian Ministry.* 20-24.
12. Gorden D. Kaufman, *God – Mystery – Diversity: Christian Theology in a Pluralist World* (Augsburg: Fortress Press, 1996), 43.
13. Lewis S. Mudge "Hermeneutics" in *A New Dictionary of Christian Theology,* edited by Alan Richardson & John Bowden (London: SCM Press, 1983), 250.
14. Urban T. Holmes III cited The Completed Works of Samuel Taylor Coleridge, Edited by Professor Shedd, Vol. 1 (New York: Harper & Brothers, 1853), 122 in Ministry and Imagination (New York: The Seabury Press, 1981), 69.
15. Urban T. Holmes III cited The Completed Works of Samuel Taylor Coleridge, Edited by Professor Shedd, Vol. 1 (New York: Harper & Brothers, 1853), 122 in *Ministry and Imagination* (New York: The Seabury Press, 1981), 69.
16. Paul Riceour, *The Symbolism of Evil* (Trans. Emerson Buchmann) (New York: Harper & Row, 1967), 352.
17. Urban T. Holmes III. *Ministry and Imagination.* 70.
18. For example, Luke 15 reflects the metaphors of God in different ways. God is pictured by Jesus as the Shepherd, the Woman and the Father.
19. Donald E. Messer, *Contemporary Imagery of Christian Ministry,* 31.
20. For example, Jesus used the images of Shepherd, the Woman and the Father in Luke: 15.
21. Wesly J. Furest, "How Israel Conceived of and Addressed God" in *Our Naming of God: Problems and Prospects of God-Talk Today,* edited by Carl E. Braten (Minneapolis: Fortress Press, 1989), 61-66.
22. J. D. Douglas et. al. Ed., *New Bible Dictionary* (Second Edition) (Secunderabad: OM Books, 1962), 495.
23. Eliya Mohol, "Metaphors of Zion Tradition and their Relevance for Missions in India" in *UBS Journal,* Vol. 5 No.1, March (2007), 87-88. See Ps, 24:8-10, 44:4, 47:2-3, 46:1, 48:15, 96:10, 99:1-2, 132:7, Num 23:21, 1 Sam 12:12, Is. 32:22, Ezek, 20:33.
24. Eliya Mohol, "Metaphors of Zion Tradition and their Relevance for Missions in India", 89.
25. Eliya Mohol, "Metaphors of Zion Tradition and their Relevance for Missions in India", 90-91.
26. Eliya Mohol, "Metaphors of Zion Tradition and their Relevance for Missions in India", 92.
27. Eliya Mohol, "Metaphors of Zion Tradition and their Relevance for Missions in India", 93.
28. Furest, J Wesley. "How Israel Conceived of and Addressed God", 61-66.
29. J. D. Douglas et. al. Ed., *New Bible Dictionary* (Second Edition), Secunderabad: OM Books, 1962), 428.30 Joachim Jeremiahs, *The Prayers of Jesus* (Philadelphia: Fortress Press, 1978), 12.
31. Genesis 1 & 2 present God as the creator, Exodus presents God as Liberator, Prophets present God as just, Psalmist present God as just, liberator and as advocate of the poor and so on. Robert Kysar, *Called to Care: Biblical Images for Social Ministry* (Minneapolis: Fortress Press, 1991), 24.
32. Paul speaks of God as a comforter in Romans (15:5), Peace (15:33), Hope (15:13) and so on.

33. Mark refers to God in association with other terms such as 'Son of God,' 'the house of God, 'the will of God' and so on. He also uses other expressions like 'the Heavens, 'the Blessed,' 'the Power' and so on.
34. See for more details Edgar M. Krentz, "God in the New Testament" in *Our Names of God.* 75-90, Janice Capel Anderson and Stephen D. Moore, "Matthew and Masculinity" in *New Testament Masculinities,* edited by Stephen D Moore and Janice Capel (Atlanta: SBL, 2003), 75-76.
35. Mammen Varkey, "Church as People's Movement" in *Religion & Society*, Vol. 55 No. 1& 2, March/June (2010), 82.
36. Patriarchy is treated as idolatry by feminist theologians as it excludes women. Emily Cheney, *She can Read: Feminist Reading Strategies for Biblical Narrative* (Pennsylvania: Trinity Press International, 1996), 133, Elizabeth Schussler Fiorenza, *Bread Not Stone: The Challenge of Feminist Biblical Interpretation* (Boston: Beacon Press, 1984), 10-13; Monica Melanchthon, "Indian Dalit Women and the Bible: Hermeneutical and Methodological Reflections" in *Gender, Religion and Diversity*, edited by Ursula King and Tina Beattie (London: Continuum, 2005), 221; Letty M Russell, *Church in the Round: Feminist Interpretation of the Church* (Louisville: Westminster/John Knox Press, 1993), 170; See Rosemary Radford Ruether, *Sexism and God-Talk.*
37. Catherine Mowry Lacugna, "The Trinitarian Mystery of God" in *Systematic Theology: Roman Catholic Perspectives*, edited by Francis Schussler Fiorenza & John P. Calvin Vol. 1, (Minneapolis: Fortress Press, 1991), 180.
38. Gorden D. Kaufman, *God – Mystery – Diversity: Christian Theology in a Pluralist World* (Augsburg: Fortress Press, 1996), 46.
39. God is depicted as a metaphorical being who is steadfast, loving, caring and responsible husband in the Hebrew Bible. Hosea 1-3, Isaiah 49:14-23, 50, 17-23, 54, 62:4-5. 'Feminine imagery' ascribed to the community of Israel in the Covenant relationship. Within the context of Isaiah 49-66, the imagery of God as husband is as frequent as the imagery of God as father. Naomi Goldenberg, *The Changing of the Gods* (Boston: Beacon Press, 1978); Gail Ramshaw, "Naming the Trinity: Orthodoxy and Inclusivity" in *Worship,* 60 (1986), 491-498; Salle McFague, calls those western metaphors as imperialist and triumphalist. Salle McFague, *Models of God: Theology for an Ecological, Nuclear Age.* Ix.
40. Alice Miller finds God the Father of the Hebrews is the one who is "easily offended, jealous, and basically insecure; He therefore demands obedience and conformity in the expression of ideas, tolerates no graven images and – since 'graven images' included works of art for the Hebrew God – no creativity either." Alice Miller, *Thou Shalt Not Be Aware: Society's Betrayal of the Child* (New York: Farrar, Straus and Giroux, 1984), 221.
41. Paul Ricoeur, "Religion, Atheism, and Faith" and "Fatherhood: From Phantasm to Symbol," in *The Conflict of Interpretations: Essays in Hermeneutics,* edited by Don Ihde (Evanston III.: Northwestern University Press, 1974) 440-67, 441, 467, 481-97.
42. Elizabeth Johnson, "God" in *Dictionary of Feminist Theologies,* edited by Letty M. Russell and J. Shannon Clarkson (Louisville: Westminster John Knox Press, 1996), 129.
43. Gail Ramshaw, "The Gender of God" in *Feminist Theology: a Reader*, edited by Ann Loades (Great Britain: SPCK, 1990), 169. See also Deut. 14:15-19.
44. magining God's image in male form leads to more complications. Ascribing white male body to image God (western, patriarchal model), Rosemary Radford Ruether, 'Eco-feminism: First and Third World Women" in *Women Resisting Violence: Spirituality for Life,* edited by Mary John Mananzan (Orbis Books,1996) ascribing Brahman male body which inhumanly divides people into castes, and ascribing rapist male image to God and endless questions arise, and these questions question the divinity and integrity and credibility of God's character if we ascribe the male image to God.

45. M and F are referred to male and female gender. Athalya Brenner, "The Hebrew God and His female Complements" in *Oxford Reading in Feminism: Feminism and Theology,* edited by Janet Martin Soskice and Dian Lipton (Oxford: Oxford University Press, 2003), 156.
46. Mary Daly, *Beyond God the Father: Toward a Philosophy of Women's Liberation* (Boston: Beacon Press, 1973), 19.
47. Augustine accepts woman and man as the image of God. But his hierarchical ideas exhibit deep rooted androcentrism. Cited by Tina Beattie, *New Catholic Feminism: Theology and Theory* (London and New York: Routledge, 2006) 121; see cited Susan Rakoczy IHM, *In Her Name: Women Doing Theology* (Pietermaritzburg: Cluster Publications, 2004), 34.
48. Cf. *The Summa Theologica of St. Thomas Aquinas*, Part II, Second Part (translated by the Fathers of the English Dominican Province) (London: Burns, Oates & Washbourne Ltd, 1929), 270. See for further information Cited Susan Rakoczy IHM, *In Her Name*, 3.
49. Peter Frick, *Divine Providence in Philo of Alexandria* (Tubingen: Mohr Siebeck, 1999), 35.
50. Colleen Conway, "Gender and Divine Relativity in Philo of Alexandria" Journal *for the Study of Judaism*, Vol. 34, Number 4. 2003. 389.
51 H. C. Van Der Nolle, "Bultmann's vision of God's revelation in Creation" in *Theology Digest,* Vol. 26 (2) 1978, 161.
52 H. C. Van Der Nolle, "Bultmann's vision of God's revelation in Creation" 161.
53. Paul Ricoeur, "Religion, Atheism, and Faith" and "Fatherhood: From Phantasm to Symbol," in *The Conflict of Interpretations: Essays in Hermeneutics*, 440-67, 441, 467, 481-97.
54. Mordecai Kaplan, *Judaism as a Civilization: Toward a Reconstruction of American Jewish Life* (New York: Schocken, 1967), 391-405.
55. Alter Waltmann, (1996), 106.
56 Martin Luther "The Large Catechism" in *Concordia: The Lutheran Confession* (Second Edition) (Saint Louis: Concordia Publishing House, 2005), 358.
57. Susan Rackozy, *In Her Name,* 36.
58. Susan Rackozy, *In Her Name*, 112.
59. Aruna Gnanadason, "Feminist Theology: An Indian Perspective" in *Readings in Indian Christian Theology,* edited by R. S. Sugirtharajah & Cecil Hargreaves Volume 1 (New Delhi: ISPCK, 1993), 67.
60. Diane Tennis, *Is God the Only Reliable Father?* (Philadelphia: Westminster, 1985), 9.
61. Susan Brooks Thistle Waite, *Sex, Race, and God: Christian Feminism in Black and White* (London: Geoffrey Chapman, 1990), 110-111.
62. Male images have been used for God exclusively, in Jewish thought and Christian theology, until recently to exclude female imagery and in fact any other imagery such as animals, or creation. Susan Brooks Thistle Waite, *Sex, Race, and God:* 26.
63. Although it is officially denied that God-language is exclusively masculine, it functions literally or at least subconsciously. In literal sense of treating God in male terms leads to a danger of idolatry. Susan Brooks Thistle Waite, *Sex, Race, and God:* 27.
64. Elizabeth Johnson, *She Who Is: The Imagery of God in Feminist Theological Discourse* (New York: Crossroad, 1992), 5. The male images those used for God which cluster together into one dominant patriarchal model of male ruling power that dominates the Christian tradition and it is a pyramid form of structure which has God on top and follows by man, woman, children and nature. See also Karen Bloomquist, "Let God be God': The Theological Necessity of Depatriarchalizing God" in *Our Naming of God: Problems and Prospects of God-Talk Today* (Minneapolis: Fortress Press, 1989), 45-60; Carl E. Braten, "The Problem of God-Language Today," 26-27, 11-33.
65. Rosemary Radford Reuther, *Sexism and God-Talk: Towards a Feminist Theology* (London: SCM Press Ltd., 1983), 19.
66. Rosemary Radford Reuther, *Sexism and God-Talk:* 19.

67. Cited Rosemary Radford Ruether, "Christology and Feminism: Can a Male Saviour Help Women?" (an occasional paper issued by the United Methodist Board of Higher Education and Ministry as Vol. 1, No. 13, (December 1976), 9. *To Change the World: Christology and Cultural Criticism* (New York: Crossroad, 1981), 53; Paul R. Sponheim, *God – The Question and The Quest: Toward Conversation Concerning Christian Faith* (Philadelphia: Fortress Press, 1985), 161-162.
68. Somen Das, "Trying to be a Feminist Man" in *We Paint the Colors of Shanti,* edited by Moumita Biswas & Sushma Ramswami (Delhi: NCCI-COT-AICCW/ISPCK, 2006), 142.
69. Somen Das, "Trying to be a Feminist Man" 143.
70. Elizabeth Johnson, *She Who Is: The Imagery of God in Feminist Theological Discourse.* 39; Also see for further details, Sallie Mcfague, *Metaphorical Theology: Models of God in Religious Language* (London: SCM Press LTD., 1983) and *Models of God: Theology for Ecological, Nuclear Age* (Philadelphia: Fortress Press, 1987); Rosemary Radford Ruether, *Sexism and God-Talk* (London: SCM Press LTD., 1983); *Faith and Feminism*, 25-28; Linda A Mercadante, *Gender, Doctrine & God: The Shakers and Contemporary Theology* (Nashville: Abingdon Press, 1990), 10-20; Mary Daly, *Gyn/Ecology: The Metaethics of Radical Feminism* (Boston: Beacon Press, 1978).
71. Evangeline Anderson-Rajkumar, "Through her Life: A Comment on Engendering Theological Education" in *Mission with the Marginalized,* edited by Samuel W. Meshack (Tiruvalla: Christava Sahitya Samithi, 2007), 564.
72. Aruna Gnanadason, "Feminist Theology: An Indian Perspective", 67.
73. R. A. Norris. Jr., "On the Maleness of Christ" in *Theology Digest,* Vol. 25 (1), 1977. 13.11-14.
74. R. L. Hnuni, *Vision for Women in India: Perspectives from the Bible, Church and Society* (Bangalore: Asian Trading Corporation), 2009), 37.
75. R. L.Hnuni, *Vision for Women in India:* 35-37.
76. Mary Daly, "Beyond God the Father" 42. 41-46.
77. The problem of imaging God is not solved by adding feminine image to God, although to image God as female, to think of God as 'she' may be to speak of empowering women. In the Indian context, people pray to Goddesses. But the experience of women is not liberated. See Judith Plaskow, *Sex, Sin and Grace: Women's Experience in the Theologies of Reinhold Neibuhr and Paul Tillich* (Washington, D. C.: University Press of America, 1980), 162-167.
78. See Judith Plaskow, *Sex, Sin and Grace: Women's Experience in the Theologies of Reinhold Neibuhr and Paul Tillich* (Washington, D C: University Press of America, 1980), 162-167.
79 Peter C. Hodgson, *God in History: Shapes of Freedom* (Nashville: Abingdon Press, 1989), 102-103.
80. Marcia Falk, "Notes on Composing New Blessings," in *Weaving the Visions: New Patterns in Feminist Spirituality,* edited by Judith Plaskow and Carol P Christ (San Francisco: Harper & Row, 1989), 132.
81. Dorothee Soellee, *Theology of Skeptics: Reflections on God* (Translated by Joyce L. Irwin) (Minneapolis: Fortress Press, 1992), 22-23.
82. Alter Waltmann, "Methodology of Latin American Liberation Theology and a Contextual Re-reading of Luther" in *Prejudice: Issues in Third World Theologies,* edited by Andreas Nehring (Madras: Gurukul Summer Institute, 1996), 114.
83. Alter Waltmann, "Methodology of Latin American Liberation Theology," 115.
84. Ana Maria Rizzuto, a psychiatrist with expertise in object-relations psychology is a Roman Catholic woman. Cf. Deborah Van Deusen Hunsinger, *Theology & Pastoral Counseling: A New Interdisciplinary Approach* (First Indian Edition) (Secunderabad: OM Books, 1999), 105-106.
85. Ana Maria Rizzuto, *The Birth of the Living God: A Psychoanalytic Study* (Chicago: University of Chicago Press, 1979), 89, 99 & 202.
86. Ana Maria Rizzuto, *The Birth of the Living God,* 5.

87. Deborah Van Deusen Hunsinger, *Theology & Pastoral Counseling*, 108.
88. Virginia Fabella, "A Common Methodology for Diverse Christologies" in *With Passion and Compassion,* edited by Virginia Fabella and Mercy Amba Oduyoye (New York: Maryknoll, 1988), 117, 108-117.
89. Philip Gibbs, *The Word in the Third World Divine Revelation in the Theology of Jean-Marc Ela, Aloysius Pieris and Gustavo Gutierriez* (Italy: Gregorian University Press, 1995), 84.
90. Monica Melanchthon, "Indian Dalit Women and the Bible: Hermeneutical and Methodical Reflections" in *Gender, Religion and Diversity: Cross-Cultural Perspectives*, 212.
91. Deborah Van Deusen Hunsinger, *Theology and Pastoral Counseling,* 129.
92. Letty M Russell, "Good House Keeping" in *Feminist Theology: A Reader*, 230-231.
93. Letty M. Russel, "Reflections on White Feminist Theology in the United States" in *Women's Visions,* 106.
94. Somen Das, "Trying to be a Feminist Man," 144.
95. Charles Nyamiti, "The Doctrine of God" in *A Reader in African Christian Theology,* edited by John Parrat (London: SPCK, 1987), 65, 58-68.
96. See Jorgen Moltmann, *The Source of Life: The Holy Spirit and the Theology of Life* (London: SCM Press LTD., 1997).
97. Jorgen Moltmann, *The Source of Life,* 258.
98. Jorgen Moltmann, *The Source of Life,* 68-69.
99. Susan Rakoczy, "The Transforming Power of the Spirit" in *Becoming a Creative Local Church,* edited by Patrick J. Hartin, Paul B. Deacock, & Bernard F Connor (Pietermaritzburg: Cluster Publications, 1991), 274-276.
100. Susan Rakoczy, "The Transforming Power of the Spirit" 274-276.
101. Susan Rakoczy, "The Transforming Power of the Spirit" 274-276.
102. Ronaldo Munoz, *The God of Christians* (Trans. Paul Burns) (Great Britain: Burns & Oates, 1991), 128, See Jer. 2:13, 17:13, Deut. 30:20, Ps. 36:10.
103. Ronaldo Munoz, *The God of Christians,* 128-129.
104. Somen Das, "Trying to be a Feminist Man," 144.
105. Alexander J. Mckelway, The *Freedom of God and Human Liberation* (London: SCM Press, 1990), 88.
106. Letty M. Russell and J. Shannon Clarkson, Eds., *Dictionary of Feminist Theology,* (Louisville: Westminster John Knox Press, 1996), 121-122.
107. Harvey J Sindima, *The Gospel According to the Marginalized* (New York: Peter Lang Publishing, 2008), 128.
108. Harvey J Sindima, *The Gospel According to the Marginalized*, 128.
109. Mohammad Taghi Karo, *Just or Unjust War: International Law and Unilateral use of armed force by states at the turn of the 20th Century* (Burlington, Ashgate Publishing Company, 2004), 51.
110. Karuna Chanana, "Social Change or Social Reform: The Education of Women in Pre-Independence India," in *Social Structure and Change,* edited A. M Shah (New Delhi: Sage Publications (1996), 120-121, 145.
111. Part of this chapter was published in *in God's Image*. See Prasuna, Gnana, "Gandhian Struggles in the Freedom Struggle: Towards Theology of Reconciliation" in *God's Image,* Vol. 27, No. 3, September. (2008), 49-57.
112. David Noel Freedman, Ed., *The Anchor Bible Dictionary* (London: Doubleday, 1992), 855.
113. David Noel Freedman, Ed., *The Anchor Bible Dictionary,* 855.
114. Carter Heyward, *Our Passion for Justice: Images of Power, Sexuality and Liberation* (New York: The Pilgrim Press, 1988), 28.
115. J. Russell Chandran, "I Believe in God" in *Aikyatha,* (April-May 1991): 8-10.
116. V. Devasahayam, *Outside the Camp: Bible Studies in Dalit Perspective* (Madras: Gurukul, 1992), 11.

117. James Massey, ed., *Dalit Bible Commentary: New Testament*, Vol. 2, (New Delhi: Centre for Dalit/Subaltern Studies, 2010), 420.
118. Richard H. Bliese, "The New Missiology: The Call to Freedom" in *Gurukul Journal of Theological Studies*, Vol XII, No. 1 & 2, (2003), 25.
119. Richard H. Bliese, The New Missiology: 26.
120. Hielke T. Wolters, *Prophetic Participation: M.M. Thomas' Concept of Salvation and Collective Struggle for Fuller Humanity in India* (Delhi: ISPCK/UTC, 1996), 22-23.
121. Alexander J. Mckelway. *The Freedom of God and Human Liberation*, 2.
122. Deborah Van Deusen Hunsinger, *Theology & Pastoral Counseling*, 117.
123. Deborah Van Deusen Hunsinger, *Theology & Pastoral Counseling*, 118.
124. Of course Iraneus identifies 'likeness' with original righteousness which human being received from God that which is lost at the time of fall. C. Barnabas, *Basic Christian Doctrines*, 173.
125. C. Barnabas, *Basic Christian Doctrines*, 173.
126. Walter Altmann, "Methodology of Latin American Liberation Theology" 114-115.
127. P. Arockiadoss, S. J. "The Spirit of New Creation an Exploration into Dalit Pneumatology" in *Frontiers of Dalit Theology*, 449.
128. C. Barnabas, *Basic Christian Doctrines*, 173.
129. Dwight N. Hopkins, "Keeping the Dream Alive" in *Gurukul Journal of Theological Studies*, Vol. XVI. No. 1&2, January & July (2005), 114.
130. *Brahma* (God) as *Saccidananda* (Sat-truth, Cit-knowledge, and Ananda-bliss) is a famous definition which was first expounded by Keshub Chandra Sen to explain the concept of Trinity in Indian terms and many Indian thinkers used the term. See Robin Boyd, *An Introduction to Indian Christian Theology* (Delhi: ISPCK, 1969), 34.
131. George Pattery, S. J. *Gandhi – the Believer: An Indian Christian Perspective*, 59.
132. George Pattery, S. J. *Gandhi – the Believer:* 110.
133. Karuna Chanana, "Social Change or Social Reform: The Education of Women in Pre-Independence India," in *Social Structure and Change*, edited by A. M. Shah, B. S. Baviskar, E. A. Ramaswamy (New Delhi: Sage Publications, 1996), 120-121, 145.
134. *en.wikipedia.org/wiki/Shakti* (accessed on 3.5.2010).
135. Mini Krishnan and Malini Seshadri, "From Power to Empowerment" in *Hindu, Young World*, August 10, 2007.
136. See Ada Maria Isasi-Diaz and Yolanda Tarango Eds., *Hispanic Women, Prophetic Voice in the Church: Toward a Hispanic Women's Liberation Theology* (Minneapolis: Fortress Press, 1993), Cited in Otto Maduro, "Notes toward a Sociology of Latina/o Religious Empowerment" in *Hispanic/Latino Theology: Challenge and Promise*, edited by Ada Maria Isasi-Diaz and Fernando F. Segovia (Minneapolis: Fortress Press, 153.
137. Otto Maduro, "Notes toward Sociology of Latina/o Religious Empowerment" in *Hispanic Latino Theology: Challenge and Promise*, 153.
138. Otto Maduro, "Notes toward Sociology of Latina/o Religious Empowerment" 153-154.
139. M. M. Thomas, "The Secular Ideologies of India and the Secular Meaning of Christ" in *Readings in Indian Christian Theology*, edited by R. S. Sugirtharajah and Cecil Hargreaves Vol. 1 (Delhi: ISPCK, 1993), 98.
140. J. D. Douglas et. al. Ed., *New Bible Dictionary* (Second Edition) (Secunderabad: OM Books, 1982), 956.
141. J. D. Douglas et. al. Ed., *New Bible Dictionary*, 956.
142. Samuel Rayan, *Breath of Fire – The Holy Spirit: Heart of the Christian Gospel* (London: Geoffrey Chapman, 1979), vii.
143. Robin Boyd, *Introduction to Indian Christian Theology*, 241.
144. Robin Boyd, *Introduction to Indian Christian Theology*, 241.

145. Stella Baltazar, "Domestic Violence in Indian Perspective" in *Women Resisting Violence: Spirituality for Life,* edited by Mary John Mananzan (Mary Knoll, N.Y: Orbis Books, 1996), 64 , Pui-lan Kwok, *Postcolonial Imagination and Feminist Theology* (Westminster: John Knox Press, 2005), 179, *trn.sagepub.com/cgi/reprint/23/1/30.pdf* (accessed on 8.5.2010).
146. See, Vandana Shiva, *Staying Alive: Women, Ecology and Development* (London: Zed Books Ltd., 1988), 38-41.
147. Aruna Gnanadason, "Feminist Theology: An Indian Perspective", 67.
148. Aruna Gnanadason, "Women and Spirituality in Asia", 351-360.
149. Aruna Gnanadason, "A Church in Solidarity with Women: Utopia or Symbol of Faithfulness?" *Councilium* 1 (1996), 96.
150. Aruna Gnanadason, *A Church in Solidarity with Women*, 96.
151. Pushpa Joseph, "Re-visioning Eros for Asian Feminist Theologizing: Some Pointers from Tantric Philosophy" in *www.geocities.com/ecclesiaofwomen/jan2005/pushpa,* (accessed on 1.2.09).
152. Pushpa Joseph, "Re-visioning Eros for Asian Feminist Theologizing: Some Pointers from Tantric Philosophy" in *Body and Sexuality: Theological-Pastoral Perspectives of Women in Asia,* edited by Agnes M. Brazal and Andreas Lizeras Si (Manila: Ateneo De Manila University Press, 2007), 39.
153. Pushpa Joseph, "Re-visioning Eros for Asian Feminist Theologizing: Some Pointers from Tantric Philosophy" 39.
154. *ecclesiaofwomen.ning.com/.../ewa-2-homepage-body-and* (accessed on 5.4.2010).
155. Pushpa Joseph, "Re-visioning Eros for Asian Feminist Theologizing" 42.
156. Pushpa Joseph, "Re-visioning Eros for Asian Feminist Theologizing: Some Pointers from Tantric Philosophy" 43.
157. Arvind P. Nirmal, "Towards a Christian Dalit Theology" in *Indigenous People: Dalits,* edited by James Massey (New Delhi: ISPCK, (1993), 222.
158. Arvind P. Nirmal, "Towards a Christian Dalit Theology," 222.
159. See Prasuna Gnana Nelavala, "Caste Branding, bleeding body, building Dalit womanhood, Touchability of Jesus" in *Dalit Theology in Twenty-first Century: Discordant Voices, discerning pathways,* Ed. Sathi Clark et.al. (Oxford: Oxford University Press, 2010), 266-276.
160. The term Dalit Power is borrowed from the Black Panthers of the USA by the Dalit Panthers of our country and became popular during the 1970s. M. E. Prabhakar, "The Search for a Dalit Theology" in *Indigenous People: Dalits,* 211.
161. A. Alan Boesak, *Black Theology – Black Power,* (Mowbrays: London and Oxford, 1978), Cp. Introduction, 1& 4.
162. A. Alan Boesak, *Black Theology – Black Power, 1&4.*
163. K. P. Aleaz, "In Quest of Dalit Theology" in *Religion and Society,* Vol. 49, Nos. 2&3, June - September (2004), 79.
164. K. P. Aleaz, "In Quest of Dalit Theology" 79.
165. Susan Brooks Thistlethwaite, *Metaphors of the Contemporary Church* (New York: The Pilgrim Press, 1983) 18, see Donald E. Messer, *Contemporary Images of Christian Ministry*, 24-25.

Appendix 1

Questionnaire

1. General Information

1.1. Age:

1.2.

1.3. Marital Status:

( ) Unmarried ( ) Married ( ) Separated
( ) Divorced ( ) Widowed

1.4. Family Details: Total No. of Members
( ) No. of daughters ( ) No. of sons

1.5. Educational Status:

a. Respondent: ( ) Illiterate ( ) Primary
( ) Secondary ( ) Hr. Secondary
( ) Degree/Diploma ( ) Any other

b. Husband:
( ) Illiterate ( ) Primary ( ) Secondary
( ) Hr. Secondary ( ) Degree/Diploma ( ) Any other

c. Children:
( ) Illiterate ( ) Primary ( ) Secondary
( ) Hr. Secondary ( ) Degree/Diploma ( ) Any other

1.6. Status of the Employment:

a. Respondent:

b. Husband:

c. Total income of the family:

d. What type of property does your family own?
( ) Land ( ) House ( ) Shop
( ) Estate ( ) Company ( ) Business
( ) Vehicles ( ) Any other

1.7. Women's Status in the Family:

a. Women are treated subordinate in the family?
( ) I strongly disagree ( ) I disagree ( ) I agree
( ) I strongly agree ( ) Any other

b. Who takes decisions in your family?
( ) I decide ( ) My husband ( ) Both of us
( ) My father ( ) Any other

c. Do you have any experience of wife battering?
( ) Yes ( ) No

d. If yes, you can describe
....
....
....

e. D you have economic freedom?
( ) Yes ( ) No

f. Is there a preference for boy child in your community?
( ) Yes ( ) No

g. Which child do you like to educate more?
( ) Female ( ) Male ( ) Both ( ) None

h. Do men in your family involve in cooking?
( ) Yes ( ) No

i. Are you treated equally in your family?
( ) Yes ( ) No

1.8. Status in the Church:

a. Women are treated equally in the church: What is your opinion?
( ) I strongly disagree ( ) I disagree ( ) I agree
( ) I strongly agree ( ) Any other

b. What is your involvement in church activities?
( ) Praying ( ) Singing ( ) Sunday school
( ) Youth Fellowship ( ) Cleaning the church
( ) Fund raising ( ) Any other

c. Women are treated impure during menstruation
( ) I strongly disagree ( ) I disagree ( ) I agree
( ) I strongly agree ( ) Any other

d. What is your opinion on menstruation?
( ) A humiliation and a curse

( ) An impurity abomination
( ) An aspect of Divine creativity
( ) Don't know

e. What is your opinion on women participating in Communion during menstruation?
( ) Cannot take part ( ) After taking bath they can take part
( ) Can take part ( ) Don't know

f. What about women's involvement in church administration?
( ) Should not be involved ( ) Should be involved
( ) Don't know ( ) Any other

g. Personally, what is your approach to political involvement in the church?
( ) I don't like to be involved ( ) Like to be involved
( ) any other view

h. What is your opinion on woman's ordination for church ministry?
( ) Should not be ordained ( ) Should be ordained
( ) Don't know

1.9. Women and the Bible:

a. How often do you read the Bible?
( ) I can't read ( ) I don't read
( ) Whenever I find time ( ) Twice a day
( ) Any other

b. Do you understand when you read the Bible?
( ) Yes ( ) No
( ) Sometimes I need help

c. How do you value the Bible? Describe in three sentences

1.10. The Image of God and You

a. Both woman and man created in God's image: Do you agree?
( ) I agree ( ) I don't agree ( ) Any other view

b. Do you bear God's image in you?
( ) Yes ( ) No ( ) I don't know

c. Do you think God is in your image?
( ) Yes ( ) No ( ) I don't know

d. How do you address God?
( ) God ( ) Lord ( ) Father
( ) Mother ( ) Any other

e. In whom you find the image of God?\
( ) Mother ( ) Father ( ) Both
( ) None ( ) Any other

2. Caste System

a. What is your caste?
b. What do you know about the term Dalit?
c. Have you experienced caste discrimination and humiliation in your life?
( ) Never ( ) In the village
( ) In the town ( ) Educational institution
( ) Work place ( ) Any other place
d. Describe if you have any humiliating experience briefly
e. How do you feel when people ask what is your caste?
( ) Neither uncomfortable nor comfortable
( ) Uncomfortable/humiliated
( ) Comfortable ( ) Any other view
f. Do so called high caste people participate in your family functions?
( ) Never ( ) Sometimes ( ) Always
g. Do you find caste discrimination in the church/Christianity?
( ) Never ( ) Sometimes ( ) Always
h. What is your approach to inter-caste marriages?
( ) I will not allow ( ) I will allow

3. Violence

3.1. Dowry Related Violence
a. Is there dowry practice in your community?
( ) Yes ( ) No
b. Did you give/take dowry?
( ) Gave ( ) Give
( ) Take ( ) I will not give/take
c. Is there dowry related violence in your community?
( ) Yes ( ) No

3.2. Violence Related Alcoholism
a. Do you have experience with alcoholic addicts?
( ) Never ( ) Sometimes ( ) Regularly
b. Is there alcoholic addict in your family?
( ) Father ( ) Mother ( ) Husband
( ) Son ( ) Daughter ( ) None
c. Describe the violence related alcoholism if you have encountered?

3.3. Violence Related to Forced Widowhood
a. What is your option on widow remarriage?
( ) Can get married ( ) can't get married
b. What is your opinion on forced widowhood?
( ) Inhuman ( ) It is good
( ) It should not be practiced

c. In your area/caste, widow remarriage is…
( ) Restricted ( ) Sometimes allowed
( ) Freely allowed

d. How are widows treated in your area?
( ) With respect
( ) Excluded especially in auspicious occasions
( ) inauspicious

e. Describe yours/your relatives' experience of enforced widowhood

3.4. Wife Battering

a. Do you have experience of wife battering?
( ) Yes ( ) No

b. If yes, describe

4. Missionaries Intervention and Conversion

a. What do you know about missionaries

b. Mention the names of women missionaries you know and you heard about

c. What is the contribution of women missionaries to the development of SALC?

d. Do you have any personal story to share about the missionaries?

e. Are you a convert?
( ) Yes ( ) No

f. If yes, what made you to choose Christianity?

g. If you are a traditional Christian, which generation you belong to?
( ) My parents ( ) My grandparents
( ) My great grandparents

h. Describe the reasons for their conversions.

Bibliography

Abbasayulu, Y. B. *Scheduled Caste Elite: A Study of Scheduled Caste Elite in Andhra Pradesh*. Hyderabad: Osmania University, 1978.

Aleaz, K.P. "In Quest of Dalit Theology." *Religion and Society*, Vol. 9, Nos. 2&3 (June & September 2004): 75-97.

Ambassadors for Christ in India, Gurukul Archives: 1980.

Anderson, Janice Capel and Moore, Stephen D., "Matthew and Masculinity." *New Testament Masculinities.* Edited by Stephen D Moore and Janice Capel. Atlanta: SBL, 2003.

Anderson-Rajkumar, Evangeline. "Through her Life: A Comment on Engendering Theological Education." *Mission with the Marginalized.* Edited by Samuel W. Meshack. Tiruvalla: Christava Sahitya Samithi, 2007.

___________. "Dalit Body: A Subversive Tool for Theologizing in Context" in *God's Image*, Vol. 26, No. 3, (September 2007): 40-43.

___________. "Skin, Body, Blood: Explorations for Dalit Hermeneutics" *www.womenutc.com/07womenrsrcsindia_art04evangeline.htm - 29k* (5th September 2008).

___________. *The Image of God: In The Light of Women's Experiences in an Indian Perspective* (D.Th. Dissertation). United Theological College, 1999.

Arles, Nalini. "Pandita Ramabai: An Appraisal from Feminist Perspective." *Bangalore Theological Forum*, Vol. XXXI, and No.1 (July 1999): 64-86.

Arul Raja, A. Maria. "Perspectives of Dalit Hermeneutics." *Gurukul Journal of Theological Studies,* Vol. XVI No. 1&2, (January & July 2005): 23-30.

___________. "A Dialogue between Dalits and Bible: Certain Indicators for Interpretation." *Journal of Dharma.* No. 1, XXIV (1999), 40-50.

___________. "Some Reflections on a Dalit Reading of the Bible" in *Frontiers of Dalit Theology*. Edited by *V. Devasahayam.* Madras: Gurukul Summer Institute, (1996), 336-355.

___________. "New Exorcism and Dalit Assertion" in *Frontiers in Dalit Hermeneutics.* Edited by James Massey & Samson Prabhakar. New Delhi: BTESSC/SATHRI & CDSS, 2005.

Aruldoss, Thaveedu. *The Relevance of the Social Teachings of Martin Luther for Dalit Liberation.* Madurai: J&D Publications, 1997.

Ayrookuzhiel, A. M. Abraham, Ed. *The Dalit Desiyata: The Kerala Experience in Development and Class Struggle.* New Delhi: ISPCK, 1990.

Baltazar, Stella. "Hermeneutics of Subaltern Praxis: With Special Reference to Dalit Women" in *Frontiers in Dalit Hermeneutics.* Edited by James Massey & Samson Prabhakar. New Delhi: BTESSC/SATHRI & CDSS, 2005: 29-33.

Barbara R. Joshi. *Untouchables: Voices of the Dalit Liberation Movement.* London: Zed Books, 1986.

Barnabas, C. *Basic Christian Doctrines.* Trichy: IIICS Study Book Series, 2003.

Beattie, Tina. *New Catholic Feminism: Theology and Theory.* London and New York: Routledge, 2006.

___________. "Religious Identity and the Ethics of Representation: The Study of Religion and Gender in the Secular Academy." *Gender, Religion and Diversity: Cross-Cultural Perspectives.* Edited by Ursula King & Tina Beattie. London: Continuum, 2005: 65-78.

Bhai, Nirmala. P. *Harijan Women in Independent India.* New Delhi: B.R. Publishing Corporation, 1986.

Bhasin, Kamala and Said Nighat Khan. "Some Questions on Feminism and Its Relevance in South Asia." *Feminism in India.* Edited by. Chaudhuri Maitrayee. New Delhi: Kali for Women and Women Unlimited, 2004: 3-7.

Bhave, Sumitra. *Pan on Fire: Eight Women Tell Their Story*. Indian Social Institute, Delhi: 1988.

Bliese, Richard H. "The New Missiology: The Call to Freedom." *Gurukul Journal of Theological Studies*, Vol. XII, No. 1 & 2, (2003): 17-33.

Bloomquist, Karen. "'Let God be God': The Theological Necessity of Depatriarchalizing God." *Our Naming of God: Problems and Prospects of God-Talk Today.* Edited by Carel E. Bratten. Minneapolis: Fortress Press, (1989), 45-60.

Boesak, A. Alan. *Black Theology – Black Power*. Mowbrays: London and Oxford, 1978.

Boff, Leonardo. *Faith on the Edge.* San Francisco: Harper & Row, 1989.

Boyd, Robin. *An Introduction to Indian Christian Theology.* Delhi: ISPCK, 1969.

Brazal, Agnes M. and Si, Andreas Lizers, Eds. *Body and Sexuality: Theological-Pastoral Perspectives of Women in Asia.* Manila: Ateneo De Manila University Press, 2007.

Braden, Carl E. Ed. *Our Naming of God: Problems and Prospects of God-Talk Today.* Minneapolis: Fortress Press, 1989.

Brenner, Athalya. "The Hebrew God and His/female Complements." *Oxford Reading in Feminism: Feminism and Theology.* Edited by Janet Martin Soskice and Dian Lipton. Oxford: Oxford University Press, 2003: 155-174.

Burgess S. Andrew, Ed. *Lutheran World Missions.* Minneapolis: Augsburg Publishing House, 1954.

Cairns, David, *The Image of God in Man.* London: Collins, 1973.

Caputo, John D, Mark Dooley, & Michael J. Scanlon, Ed. *Questioning God.* Bloomington: Indiana University Press, 2001.

Carmody, L. Devise. *Feminism and Christianity.* Abingdon: Nashville, 1982.

Carr, Dhyanchnad. "Dalit Theology is Biblical and it Makes the Gospel." *A Reader in Dalit Theology.* Edited by Arvind P. Nirmal and V. Devasahayam. Madras: Gurukul Lutheran Theological College, 1985: 71-84.

Catherine, LAcugna Mowry. "The Trinitarian Mystery of God." *Systematic Theology: Roman Catholic Perspectives.* Vol. 1 Edited by Francis Schussler Fiorenza & John P. Calvin. Minneapolis: Fortress Press, 1991: 151-192.

Centennial Souvenir, South Andhra Lutheran Church, 1865-1965.

Chaudhuri, Maitrayee, Ed. *Feminism in India.* New Delhi: Kali for Women and Women Unlimited, 2004.

Chanana, Karuna. "Social Change or Social Reform: The Education of Women in Pre-Independence India." *Social Structure and Change.* Edited by A. M. Shah, B. S. Baviskar and E. A. Ramaswamy. New Delhi: Sage Publications, 1996: 113-148.

Chandran, J Russell. "I Believe in God." *Aikyatha.* (April-May 1991): 8-10.

Chandy, Thomas. "Where are the children in the elections? All Political parties must make investing in children a national priority." *The Hindu.* (15 April 2009).

Cheney, Emily. *She can Read: Feminist Reading Strategies for Biblical Narrative.* Pennsylvania: Trinity Press International, 1996.

Clark, Sathinathan. "Transforming Identities, De-textualizing Interpretation, and Re-modalizing Representation: Scriptures and subaltern Subjectivity in India." *Theorizing Scriptures: New Critical Orientations to a Cultural Phenomenon.* Edited by Vincent L Wimush. New Jersey: Rutgers University Press, 2008: 95-104.

Coggins, J. R. & J. L. Houlden, L. J. Eds. *A Dictionary of Biblical Interpretation.* London: SCM Press, 1990.

Coleridge, Taylor Samuel. Ed. *The Complete Works*, Vol. 1, New York: Harper & Brothers, 1853.

Cone, James H. and Gayraud, S. Ed. *Black Theology: A Documentary History.* Vol. II, 1980-1992, Maryknoll, N. Y.: Orbis Books, 1993: 257-351.

Conway, Colleen. "Gender and Divine Relativity in Philo of Alexandria" *Journal for the Study of Judaism*, Vol. 34, No. 4 (2003): 471-491.

Daly, Mary. *Beyond God the Father: Toward a Philosophy of Women's Liberation.* Boston: Beacon Press, 1973.

__________. *Gyn/Ecology: The Metaethics of Radical Feminism.* Boston: Beacon Press, 1978.

Das, Somen. "Trying to be a Feminist Man." *We Paint the Colors of Shanti.* Edited by Moumita Biswas & Sushma Ramswami. Delhi: NCCI-COT-AICCW/ ISPCK, 2006: 138-148.

Dengel-Janic, Enel. Constructions of Femininity in Cornelia Sorabji's "Greater Love" and Geetha Hariharan's "Revathi." *Indian Woman's Short Fiction.* Edited by Joel Kurotti, Mittapalli Rajeswar, and New Delhi: ATLANTIC, 2007: 1-15.

De Oliveira, Rosangela Soares. "Feminist Theology in Brazil." *Women's Visions.* Edited by Ofelia Ortega. Geneva: WCC Publications, 1995: 65-76.

Derek Hook, "Frantz Fanon and Racial Identity in Post-Colonial Contexts." *Self, Community and Psychology.* Edited by Kopano Ratele, Norman, Duncan, Derek Hook, Nhlanhla Mkhize, Peace Kiguva and Anthony Collins. Lansdowne: UCT Press: 2004, 6.1-22.

Devasahayam, V. *Doing Dalit Theology in Biblical Key.* Chennai: ISPCK/Gurukul, 1997.

Devasahayam, V. Ed. *Dalits and Women: Quest for Humanity.* Madras: Gurukul Summer Institute, 1992.

__________. *Frontiers of Dalit Theology.* Madras: Gurukul Summer Institute, 1996.

__________. "Doing Dalit Theology: Basic Assumptions." Frontiers *of Dalit Theology.* Edited by V. Devasahayam. Madras: Gurukul Summer Institute, 1996: 270-282.

__________. "Dimensions of Dalit Dilemma." *Prejudice: Issues in Third World Theologies.* Edited by Andreas Nehring. Madras: Gurukul Summer Institute, 1996: 273-301.

Dietrich, Gabriele. "Emerging Dalit Feminism" *in In God's Image* Vol. 26, No. 3 (September 2007): 32-39.

Dietrich, Gabriele, Ed. *A New Thing on Earth.* Delhi: ISPCK, 2001.

Douglas, J.D., et. al., Ed. *New Bible Dictionary.* (Second Edition). Secunderabad: OM Books, 1962.

Dube, Musa W. *Other Ways of Reading: African Women and Bible.* Atlanta/Geneva, Society of Biblical Literature/WCC Publications, 2001.

Dubey, S. N. *Administration of Social Welfare Programmes in India* Bombay: Somaiya Publication Pvt. Ltd., 1970.

Dyrness, William A. and Veli-Matti Karakainnen, Eds. *A Global Dictionary of Theology: A Resource for Worldwide Church,* Downers Grove: Intervarsity Press, 2008: 419-421.

Eileraas, Karina. *Between Image and Identity: Transnational Fantasy, Symbolic Violence and Feminist Misrecognition.* Lanham: The Rowman and Littlefield Publishing Group. Inc., 2007.

Fabella, Virginia. "A Common Methodology for Diverse Christologies" With *Passion and Compassion: Third World Women Doing Theology.* Edited by Virginia Fabella and M. A. Oduyoye. New York: Maryknoll, 1988: 108-117.

Fabella, Virginia and Mercy Amba Oduyoye, Eds. *With Passion and Compassion: Third World Women Doing Theology.* New York: Maryknoll, 1988.

Fackre, Gabriel. *The Christian Story.* Grand Rapids: Eerdmans, 1984.

Fernandez, Walter. *The Emerging Dalit Identity: The Re-Assertion of the Subalterns.* New Delhi: ISI, 1996.

Fiorenza, Elizabeth Schussler. *In Memory of Her: A Feminist Theological Reconstruction of Christian Origins.* New York: Cross Road, 1983.

___________. *Bread Not Stone: The Challenge of Feminist Biblical Interpretation.* Boston: Beacon Press, 1984.

___________. "For the Sake of the Truth dwelling among us: Emerging Issues in Feminist Biblical Interpretation." *Christian Feminism: Visions of New Humanity.* Edited by Judith Weidman. New York: Harper and Row, 1984: 33-54.

___________. "Foreword" in Gabriele Dietrich, *a New Thing on Earth.* Edited by Gabriele Dietrich. Delhi: ISPCK, 2001.

___________. "The will to choose or to reject." *Feminist Interpretation of the Bible.* Edited by Letty M Russel. Philadelphia: The Westminster's Press, 1985: 125-136.

___________. *But She Said: Feminist Practices of Biblical Interpretations.* Boston: Beacon, 1992.

___________. *Critical Theory of Religion: A Feminist Analysis.* Minneapolis: Augsburg Fortress, 1995.

Fiorenza, Schussler Francis & P. John Calvin, Eds. *Systematic Theology: Roman Catholic Perspectives.* Vol. 1, Minneapolis: Fortress Press, 1991.

Freedman, David Noel, ed. *The Anchor Bible Dictionary*, London: Doubleday, 1992.

Frick, Peter. *Divine Providence in Philo of Alexandria.* Tubingen: Mohr Siebeck, 1999.

Furest, J Wesley. "How Israel Conceived of and Addressed God." *Our Naming of God: Problems and Prospects of God-Talk Today.* Edited by Carl E. Braten. Minneapolis: Fortress Press, 1989: 61-74.

Gaudelli, William. *World class: Teaching and Learning in Global Times.* London: Routledge, 2003.

Ghurye, G. S. *Caste and Race in India.* Bombay: Popular Prakasham, 2005.

Gibbs, Philip. *The Word in the Third World Divine Revelation in the Theology of Jean-Marc Ela, Aloysius Pieris and Gustavo Gutierriez.* Italy: Gregorian University Press, 1995.

Gnanadason, Aruna. "Women….Where are You? Women in the Protestant Churches." *The Emerging Christian Woman.* Edited by S. Faria et al., Pune: Satprakashan Samachar Kendra/Ishvani, 1984: 169-180.

___________. "Women's Oppression: A Sinful Situation." *With Passion and Compassion: Third World Women Doing Theology.* Edited by Virginia Fabella & Mercy Amba Oduyoye. Mary knoll, NY: Orbis, 1988: 69-76.

___________. "Feminist Theology: An Indian Perspective." *Readings in Indian Christian Theology.* Edited by R. S. Sugirtharajah & Cecil Hargreaves. Volume 1. New Delhi: ISPCK, 1993: 59-72.

___________. "A Church in Solidarity with Women: Utopia or Symbol of Faithfulness?" *Councilium* 1 (1996), 74.

___________. "Dalit Women: The Dalit of the Dalit" in *A Reader in Dalit Theology.* Edited by Arvind P. Nirmal, and V. Devasahayam (Madras: Gurukul Lutheran Theological College and Research Institute, 1985).

Gnanavaram, M. "Dalit Theology and the Parable of the Good Samaritan." *JSNT50.* (1993): 59-83.

Gokhale, Jayashree. *From Concessions to Confrontation.* Bombay: Popular Prakasham, 1993.

Goldenberg, Naomi. *The Changing of the Gods.* Boston: Beacon Press, 1978.

Gorhe, Neelam. "Social Development and Dalit Women." *Dalit Women in India: Issues and Perspectives.* Edited by P. G. Jogdanad. New Delhi: Gyan Publishing House, 1995: 146-156.

Grant, Jacquelyn. *White Woman's Christ and Black Woman's Jesus.* Atlanta: Scholars Press, 1989.

Greeves, Frederic. *Theology and the Cure of Souls: An Introduction to Pastoral Theology.* Manhasset, New York: Channel Press, INC, 1962.

Grenz, J Stanley et.al. ed. *20th Century Theology: God & the World in a Transitional Age.* Secunderabad: OM Authentic Books, 1992.

Grey, Mare. "Dalit Women and the Struggle for Justice in a World of Global Capitalism." *Feminist Theology,* Vol. 14, No.1, (2005): 127-149.

Gustafson, M. James. *Varieties of Moral Discourse: Prophetic, Narrative, Ethical, and Policy,* Calvin College, The Stob Lectures, 1988: 19-20.

Gutierrez, Gustavo. *A Theology of Liberation.* Maryknoll, N.Y.: Orbis Books, 1973.

Hauerwas, Stanley, Richard Bondi and David Burrell B, eds. *Truthfulness and Tragedy.* Indiana: University of Notre Dame Press, 1977.

Haurewas, Stanley. *Peaceable Kingdom: A Primer in Christian Ethics.* Notre Dame, Ind.: University of Notre Dame Press, 1983.

Hauerwas Stanley and Gregory L. Jones, Eds. *Why Narrative? Readings in Narrative Theology.* Grand Rapids: Michigan, 1989.

Heath, Robert Lawrence. *Realism and Relativism.* Macon: Mercer University Press, 1986.

Hekman. Susan J, Ed. "Introduction." *Feminism, Identity and Difference.* Ilford: Frank Cass Publishers, 1999: 2-4.

Heyward, Carter. *Our Passion for Justice: Images of Power, Sexuality and Liberation.* New York: The Pilgrim Press, 1988.

Hodgson, Peter C. *God in History: Shapes of Freedom.* Nashville: Abingdon Press, 1989.

Holmes III, T Urban. *Ministry and Imagination.* New York: The Seabury Press, 1981.

Holland, Dorothy et.al. "The New Socio-cultural Studies of Identity" in *The Cambridge Companion to Vygotsky.* Edited by Harry Daniels et.al.. Cambridge: Cambridge University Press, 2007: 101-135.

Hooks, Bell. "Postmodern blackness." *Post Colonialism. Critical Concepts.* Edited by D. Brydon. London: Routledge, 2000: 1306-1313.

Hopkins, Dwight N. "Keeping the Dream Alive" in *Gurukul Journal of Theological Studies,* Vol. XVI. No. 1&2 (January & July 2005): 109-118.

Hnuni, R. L. *Vision for Women in India: Perspectives from the Bible, Church and Society.* Bangalore: Asian Trading Corporation, 2009.

Hunsinger, Deborah Van Deusen. *Theology & Pastoral Counseling: A New Interdisciplinary Approach.* First Indian Edition. Secunderabad: OM Books, 1999.

Ihde, Don, Ed. *The Conflict of Interpretations: Essays in Hermeneutics.* Evanston III: Northwestern University Press, 1974.

Ilaiah, Kancha. "Why I am not a Hindu." *Gender & Caste: Issues in Contemporary Indian Feminism.* Edited by Anupama Rao. New Delhi: Kali for Women & Women Unlimited, 2003: 86-89.

Irudayaraj, Xavier S. J. *Emerging Dalit Theology.* Madras: Jesuit Theological Secretariat, 1990.

Isaiah, G. "Homiletics." *UBS Journal,* Vol. 2, No. 1 (March 2004): 58-69.

Isasi-Diaz, Ada Maria and Yolanda Tarango, Eds. *Hispanic Women, Prophetic Voice in the Church: Toward a Hispanic Women's Liberation Theology.* Minneapolis: Fortress Press, 1993.

James, E. Cote and Levine, G. Charles. *Identity Formation, Agency, and Culture: A Social Psychological Synthesis.* Lawrence Erlbaum Associates, Inc. Publishers, 2002.

James. M. V. "An Analysis of the Impact of Socio-Cultural factors on the Health of the Respondents of North Chennai." M. Phil Thesis, Annamalai University Archives, 2008.

Jaurrechette, Colleen. "Poetry, Prayer and Identity in Finnegans Wake." *Joys and the Fabrication of Irish Identity.* Edited Michael Pattrick Gillesies, James. Amsterdam: Rodopi, 2001: 71-110.

Jayakumar, Samuel. *Dalit Consciousness and Christian Conversion: Historical Resources for a Contemporary Debate.* Chennai: Mission Educational Books, 1999.

Jesuratnam K. "Towards a Dalit Liberative Hermeneutic: Re-reading the Psalms of Lament." *Bangalore Theological Forum.* Vol. XXXIV, No.1 (June 2002): 1-34.

Jeremiahs, Joachim. *The Prayers of Jesus.* Philadelphia: Fortress Press, 1978.

Jogdand, G. P. *Dalit Women in India: Issues and Perspectives.* New Delhi: Gyan Publishing House, 1995.

Johnson, Elizabeth A. *She Who is: The Imagery of God in Feminist Theological Discourse.* New York: Crossroad, 1992.

__________. "God." *Dictionary of Feminist Theologies.* Edited by Letty M. Russell and J. Shannon Clarkson. Louisville: Westminster John Knox Press, 1996.

Jones, Serene. *Feminist Theory and Christian Theology: Cartographies of Grace.* Minneapolis: Fortress Press, 2000.

Joseph, Pushpa. "Women theologians in India are reclaiming space" *National Catholic Report, NCR online.org.*

__________. *Indian Feminist Hermeneutics: A Contextual Analysis of Reconstructionist Model of Elizabeth Schussler Fiorenza.* (Ph. D. Dissertation) University of Madras, 2002.

__________. "Trailblazers: Elisabeth Schussler Fiorenza and George M. Sores-Prabhu." *On Cutting the Edge: The Study of Women in Biblical World.* Edited by Jane Schaberg, Alice Bach, and Esther Fuchs. New York: Continuum International Publishing Group, 2004: 53-68.

__________. "Re-visioning Eros for Asian Feminist Theologizing: Some Pointers from Tantric Philosophy." *Body and Sexuality: Theological-Pastoral Perspectives of Women in Asia,* Edited by Agnes M. Brazal and Andreas Lizeras Si. Manila: Ateneo De Manila University Press, 2007: 34 -57.

Jue, J. "Breaking the Silence of Women of Color and Issues of Voice and Cultural-Identity" *Religious Education,* 88 (3) (1993), 451-563.

Kaplan, Mordecai. *Judaism as a Civilization: Toward a Reconstruction of American Jewish Life.* New York: Schocken, 1967.

Karo, Mohammad Taghi. *Just or Unjust War: International Law and Unilateral use of armed force by states at the turn of the 20th Century*, Farnham: Ashgate Publishing Company, 2004.

Kaufman, Gorden D. *God – Mystery – Diversity: Christian Theology in a Pluralist World.* Augsburg: Fortress Press, 1996.

Kearney, Richard, "The God Who May Be." *Questioning God,* Edited by John D. Caputo, Mark Dooley, & Michael J. Scanlon. Bloomington: Indiana University Press, 2001: 153-185.

King, Urusula and Tina Beattie. *Gender, Religion and Diversity: Cross-Cultural Perspectives.* London: Continnum, 2005.

Kishwar. Madhu. "A Horror of 'Isms': Why I do not Call Myself a Feminist." *Feminism in India.* Edited by Chaudhuri Maitrayee. New Delhi: Women Unlimited, 2004: 26-51.

Knippenberg, Tjew Van. "Transcendence and Personal Histories/Life stories." *The Human Image of God.* Edited by Hans-George Ziebertz, Frederick Schweitzer, Hermann Haring and Don Browning. Leiden: Brill, 2001: 263-284.

Korgen, Kathleen Odell. *From Black to Biracial: Transforming Racial Identity among Americans.* Westport, Conn.: Praeger, 1998.

Krentz, Edgar M. "God in the New Testament" *Our Naming of God: Problems and Prospects of God-Talk Today. Edited by* Carl E. Bratten. Minneapolis: Fortress Press, 1989: 75-90.

Krishnan, Mini and Melina Sephardic. "From Power to Empowerment." *The Hindu, Young World. (Chennai)* August 10, 2007.

Kroger, Jane. *Identity Development: Adolescence through Adulthood.* New York: Sage Publications, 2005.

kumaravadivelu, B. *Cultural Globalization and Language Education.* London: Yale University Press, 2008.

Kumari, Prasanna, Ed. *A Reader in Feminist Theology.* Madras: Gurukul, 1993.

Kwok, Pui-lan. *Postcolonial Imagination and Feminist Theology.* Louisville: Westminster/John Knox Press, 2005.

Kysar, Robert. *Called to Care: Biblical Images for Social Ministry.* Minneapolis: Fortress Press, 1991.

Larbeer, Mohan. "Dalit Identity: A Theological Reflection." Frontiers *of Dalit Theology.* Edited by V. Devasahayam. Madras: Gurukul Summer Institute, 1996: 375-391.

___________. "Pollution: A Reality of an Imposed Ideology." Frontiers *of Dalit Theology.* Edited by V. Devasahayam. Madras: Gurukul Summer Institute, 1996: 392-401.

Loue, Sana, Ed. *Sexualities and Identities of Minority Women.* New York: Springer Science & Business Media, LLC. 2009.

Luther, Martin. "The Large Catechism." *Concordia: The Lutheran Confession.* Second Edition. Saint Louis: Concordia Publishing House, 2005.

Maalouf, Amin. *In the Name of Identity: Violence, and the need to belong.* New York: Arcade Publishing Company, 2000.

Maduro, Otto. "Notes Toward Sociology of Latina/o Religious Empowerment." *Hispanic/Latino Theology: Challenge and Promise.* Edited by Ada Maria Isasi-Diaz and Fernando F. Segovia. Minneapolis: Fortress Press: 151-166.

Maitrayee, Maitrayee, Ed. *Feminism in India.* New Delhi: Women Unlimited, 2004.

Malik, Suneila. *Social Integration of Scheduled Castes.* New Delhi: Anubhav Publications, 1979.

Mananzan, Mary John, et.al. Ed. *Women Resisting Violence: Spirituality for Life.* Mary Knoll: N.Y: Orbis Books, 1996.

Marcia, James. E. "Theory and Measure: The Identity Status Interview" in *Capturing Identity: Quantitative and Wualitative Methods.* Edited by Meike Watzlawik, Aristi Born. Maryland: University Press of America, 2007: 1-14.

Massey, James and M. E. Prabhakar, Eds. *Towards Dalit Theology.* Delhi: CISRS/ ISPCK, 1988.

Massey, James. "Scheduled Caste: A Special Reference to Scheduled Caste Origin." *Religion and Society* Vol. XXXXVIII, No.3 (March, 1991): 30-38.

____________. *Towards Dalit Hermeneutics: Rereading the Text, History and the Literature.* Delhi: ISPCK, 1994.

____________, ed. *Indigenous People: Dalits - Issues in Today's Theological Debate.* New Delhi: ISPCK, 1994.

____________. *Roots: A Concise History of Dalits.* New Delhi: ISPCK. 1994.

____________. *Dalits in India: Religion as a Source of Bondage or Liberation with Special Reference to Christians.* New Delhi: Manohar, 1995.

____________. *Down Trodden: the Struggle of India's Dalits for Identity, Solidarity and Liberation.* Geneva: WCC, 1997.

____________. *Dalit Bible Commentary: New Testament.* Vol. 1 New Delhi: Centre for Dalit/Subaltern Studies, 2010.

Massey, James and Samson Prabhakar, Eds. *Frontiers in Dalit Hermeneutics.* Bangalore: BTESSC/SATHRI & Delhi: CDSS, 2005.

Mayell, Hillery. "India's Untouchables face Violence and Discrimination." *news.nationalgeographic.com/news/2003/06/0602_030602_untouchables.html,* National Geographic News, 2003, (10th October 2008).

McFague, Sallie. *Models of God: Theology for an Ecological,* Nuclear Age. Philadelphia: Fortress Press, 1987.

____________. *Metaphorical Theology: Models of God in Religious Language.* London: SCM Press Ltd., 1983.

Mckelway, Alexander J. *The Freedom of God and Human Liberation*. London: SCM Press, 1990.

Megumi, Yoshida. "Imaging as Theological Methodology: From Logo-centric to Holistic Approach." In *God's Image,* Vol. 28, and No. 4 (December 2009): 365-48.

Melanchthon, Monica. "Indian Dalit Women and the Bible: Hermeneutical and Methodological Reflections." *Gender, Religion and Diversity.* Edited by Ursula King and Tina Beattie. London: Continuum, 2005: 212-224.

Melanchthon, Jothsna Monica. "Dalit Readers of the Word: The Quest for Hermeneutics and Method." Frontiers *in Dalit Hermeneutics.* Edited by James Massey and Samson Prabhakar. Bangalore: BTESSC/SATHRI & Delhi: CDSS, 2005: 45-64.

Menon, Nivedita. "Nation, Identity, And Citizenship: Feminist Critique in Contemporary India" in Political *Ideas in Modern India: Thematic Explorations.* Edited by Vrajendra Raja Mehta, Thomas Pantham. New Delhi: Sage Publications, 2006: 340-366.

Mercadante, A. Linda. *Gender, Doctrine & God: The Shakers and Contemporary Theology.* Nashville: Abingdon Press, 1990.

Mercer, Kobena. "Welcome to the Jungle: Identity and Diversity in Postmodern Politics" in Identity*: Community, Culture, and Difference.* Edited by Jonathan Rutherford. London: Lawrence & Wishart, 1990: 43-71.

Meshack, Samuel W. ed., *Mission with the Marginalized.* Tiruvalla: Christava Sahitya Samithi, 2007.

Messer, Donald E. *Contemporary Imagery of Christian Ministry*. Nashville: Abingdon Press, 1989.

Miller, Alice. *Thou Shalt Not Be Aware: Society's Betrayal of the Child.* New York: Farrar, Straus and Giroux, 1984.

Mitchem, Y. S. *Introducing Womanist Theology*. New York: Orbis Books, 2002.

Mohanty, Chandra Talpade. "Under Western Eyes: Feminist Scholarship and Colonial Discourses." *Third World Women and the Politics of Feminism*. Edited by Chandra Talpade Mohanty Ann Russo and Lourdes Torres. Bloomington: Indiana University Press, 1991: 51-80.

Mohol, Eliya. "Metaphors of Zion Tradition and their Relevance for Missions in India" in UBS Journal, Vol. 5 o.1 (March 2007): 85-98.

Moltmann, Jurgen. *The Source of Life: The Holy Spirit and the Theology of Life:* London: SCM Press LTD., 1997.

Moore, Stephen D. and Janice Capel Anderson, Eds. *New Testament Masculinities.* Atlanta: SBL, 2003.

Moore, Stephen D. and Janice Capel Anderson, Eds. "Mathew and Masculinity." *New Testament Masculinities.* Edited by Stephen D Moore and Janice Capel Anderson. Atlanta: SBL, 2003: 75-76.

Moshman, David. *Adolescent Psychological Development: Rationality, Morality and Identity*. New Jersey: Lawrence Erlbaum Associates, 1999.

Mukharjee, Ila. *Social Status of North Indian Women*:1576-1701 AD Agra: Shivalal Agarwala & Company, 1972.

Munoz, Ronaldo. *The God of Christians.* Trans. Paul Burns. Great Britain: Burns & Oates, 1991.

Muthumary, J. "Dalit Women in India," *www.asiasource.org/asip/dalits.cfm - 62k* (10th April 2009).

Mwikamba, Constantine M. "A Search for an African Identity" in *African Ecclesial Review* 31, (September, 1989), 91-107.

Nadar, Sarojini. "Subverting Gender and Ethnic Assumptions in Biblical Narrative: Exploring the Narrative Voice of Ruth." *Journal of Constructive Theology,* 6 (2) (2000): 67-83.

__________. "A South African Indian Womanist Reading of the Character of Ruth." *Other Ways of Reading: African Women and Bible.* Edited by Musa W. Dube. Atlanta/Geneva, Society of Biblical Literature/WCC Publications, 2001: 159-175.

Nasuti, Harry P. P. "Identity, Identification, and Imitation: The Narrative Hermeneutics of Biblical Law," *Journal of Law and Religion* 4 (1986): 9-23.

Nayak, C. D. *Thoughts and Philosophy of Dr. B. R. Ambedkar.* New Delhi: Sarup & Sons, 2003.

Nehring, Andreas. Prejudice: Issues in Third World Theologies. Madras: Gurukul Summer Institute, 1996.

Nicholls, Bruce, "Is the Kingdom Coming?" in *Third Way*. Vol. 4, No. 7, July-August (1980), 16-31.

Niebhur, Richard H. "The Story of Life." in *The Meaning of Revelation.* New York: MacMillan Publishing Company, 1941.

Nirmal, Arvind P. "Towards a Christian Dalit Theology." *Indigenous People: Dalits.* Edited by James Massey, New Delhi: ISPCK, 1994: 214-230.

__________. *Heuristic Explorations.* Madras: The Christian Literature Society, 1990.

__________. "Towards a Christian Dalit Theology." *A Reader in Dalit Theology.* Edited by A. P. Nirmal and V. Devasahayam, Madras: Gurukul Lutheran Theological College, 1985: 65-69.

Nirmal, A. P. and V. Devasahayam, Eds. *A Reader in Dalit Theology.* Madras: Gurukul Lutheran Theological College, 1985.

Nolle, Van der H.-Chr. "Bultmann's Vision of God's Revelation in Creation." *Theology Digest*, Vol. 26, 2 (1978): 160-164.

Norris. R. A. "On the Maleness of Christ." *Theology Digest*, Vol. 25, 1, (1977): 11-14.

Nyamiti, Charles. "The Doctrine of God." *A Reader in African Christian Theology.* Edited by John Parrat, London: SPCK, 1987: 58-68.

Omvedt, Gail. Dalits and the Democratic Revolution: Dr. Ambedkar and the Dalit Movement in Colonial India. New Delhi: Sage Publications India Pvt. Limited, 2004.

Ortega, Ofelia. *Women's Visions.* Geneva: WCC Publications, 1995.

Pande, Rekha. "Solidarity, Patriarchy and Empowerment: Women's Struggles against Arrack in India." *Feminist Politics, Activism and Vision: Local and Global Challenges.* Edited by Luciana Ricciutelli, Angela Miles and Margaret M Mcfadden, New York: ZED Publications, 2005: 212-226.

Paswan, Sanjay and Paramanshi Jaideva, Eds. Encyclopedia of Dalits in India: Human Rights: Dimension in Dalit Problems. Delhi: Kalpaz Publications, 2003.

Patnaik, *N. Caste and Social Change: An Anthropological Study of Three Villages.* (Hyderabad: National Institute of Community Development, 1969).

Pattel-Gray, Anne. "Aboriginal Spirituality and Theology." *Prejudice: Issues in Third World Theologies.* Edited by Andreas Nehring, Madras: Gurukul Summer Institute, 1996: 219-272.

Pawade, Kumud. "The Life of a Dalit Woman." Dalit Women in India: Issues and Perspectives. Edited by P. G. Jogdanad, New Delhi: Gyan Publishing House, 1995: 157-168.

Periannan, Sebastian S. *Social Research Methodology: An Introduction.* Chennai: Department of Christian Studies, University of Madras: Reprint 2010.

Phinney, J. S. "An Ethnic Identity." *Encyclopedia of Psychology.* Edited by A. E. Kazdin, New York: Oxford University Press, 2000: 254-259.

Phinney, J. S. "A Three-Stage Model of Ethnic Identity Development in Adolescence." *Ethnic Identity: Formation and Transmission among Hispanics and other Minorities.* Edited by Martha E. Bernal and George P. Night, Albany: New York Press, 1993: 61-80.

Plaskow, Judith. *Sex, Sin and Grace: Women's Experience in the Theologies of Reinhold Neibuhr and Paul Tillich.* Washington, D. C.: University Press of America, 1980.

Plaskow, Judith and Carol P. Christ, eds. *Weaving the Visions: New Patterns in Feminist Spirituality.* San Francisco: Harper & Row, 1989.

Prabhakar, M. E. "The Search for a Dalit Theology." *Indigenous People: Dalits, Issues in Today's Theological Debate.* Edited by James Massey, New Delhi: ISPCK, 1994: 201-213.

Prasuna, N. G. "The Dalit Woman." *Frontiers of Dalit Theology* Edited by V. Devasahayam. Madras: Gurukul Summer Institute, 1996: 100-116.

___________. *A Study of Feminist Hermeneutics and its Impact for the Liberation of Dalit Women,* (M. Th. Thesis), Madras, Gurukul Lutheran Theological College & Research Institute, 1997.

Prasuna, Gnana. "Gandhian Struggles in the Freedom Struggle: Towards Theology of Reconciliation" in *In God's Image,* Vol. 27, and No. 3 (September 2008): 49-57.

___________. "Towards Dalit Feminist Theology: Re-visiting the Image of God" in *Ecumenical Horizon,* Vol. 2 No.1 (December 2008-January 2009), 17-24.

Pui-lan Kwok. *Postcolonial Imagination and Feminist Theology.* Louisville: Westminster John Knox Press, 2005.

Rajasekar, J. Paul. "Lutheranism in Asia and the Indian Sub-continent." *The Future of Lutheranism in a Global Context.* Edited by Arland Dean Jacobson and James Aageson. Augsburg Fortress, 2007: 61-76.

Rajawat, Mamata. et.al. *Encyclopedia of Dalits in India,* Vol. 1, New Delhi: Anmol Publications PVT. LTD., 2004.

Raj, Anjali. "Lifted from the Funeral Pure but Left in the Cremation Ground: Aruttu-Kattatha Widows of Kulthalai Taluk." *In God's Image.* Vol. 26, No. 3, (September 2007): 13-21.

Raj, C. M. *Dalitology: The Book of the Dalits.* Tumkur: Ambedkar Resource Centre/Rural Education for Development Society, 2001.

Rajkumar, Evangeline. *The Image of God: in the Light of Women's Experiences in an Indian Perspective* (D. Th. Thesis), Bangalore: UTC Archives, 1999.

Rakoczy, IHM Susan. *In Her Name: Women Doing Theology.* Pietermaritzburg: Cluster Publications, 2004.

Ramshaw, Gail. "Naming the Trinity: Orthodoxy and Inclusivity." *Worship.* 60 (1986): 491-498.

___________. "The Gender of God." *Feminist Theology: A Reader.* Edited by Ann Loades, Great Britain: SPCK, 1990: 168-180.

Rao, Anupama, Ed. *Gender & Caste: Issues in Contemporary Indian Feminism.* New Delhi: Kali for Women & Women Unlimited, 2003.

Rayan, Samuel. *Breath of Fire – The Holy Spirit: Heart of the Christian Gospel.* London: Geoffrey Chapman, 1979.

Rege, Sharmila. *Writing Caste, Writing Gender: Narrating Dalit Women's Testimonios.* New Delhi: Zubaan, 2006.

Reinard, C. John. *Introduction to Communication Research.* Madison: WCB Brown & Benchmark Publishers, 1994.

Richardson, Alan and John Bowden, Eds. A New Dictionary of Christian Theology. London: SCM Press, 1983.

Ricciutelli, Luciana, Angela Miles and Margaret H Mcfadden, Eds. *Feminist Politics, Activism and Vision: Local and Global Challenges.* Toronto/London: Inanna/ZED Books LTD., 2004.

Ricoeur, Paul. *The Symbolism of Evil.* Trans. Emerson Buchmann. New York: Harper & Row, 1967.

___________. "Life in Quest of Narrative." On *Paul Ricoeur: Narrative and Interpretation.* Edited by David C. Wood, London and New York: Routledge, 1991: 20-33.

___________. "Religion, Atheism, and Faith" in *The Conflict of Interpretations: Essays in Hermeneutics.* Edited by Don Ihde, Evanston: Northwestern University Press, 1974: 440-67.

___________. "Fatherhood: From Phantasm to Symbol" in *The Conflict of Interpretations: Essays in Hermeneutics.* Edited by Don Ihde, Evanston: Northwestern University Press, 1974: 468-497.

Roald, Anne Sofie. "Who are the Muslims? Questions of Identity, Gender and Culture in Research Methodologies." *Gender, Religion and Diversity: Cross-Cultural Perspectives.* Edited by Ursula King and Tina Beattie, London: Continuum, 2005: 179-189.

Ruether, Rosemary Radford. "Christology and Feminism: Can a Male Savior Help Women?" (an occasional paper issued by the United Methodist Board of Higher Education and Ministry as Vol. 1, No. 13, December 25,1976.

___________. *To Change the World: Christology and Cultural Criticism.* New York: Crossroad, 1981.

___________. *Sexism and God-Talk: Towards a Feminist Theology.* London: SCM Press Ltd., 1983.

___________. 'Eco-feminism: First and Third World Women." *Women Resisting Violence: Spirituality for Life.* Edited by Mary John Mananzan, New York: Orbis Books, 1996: 27-35.

Russell, Letty M. *Church in the Round: Feminist Interpretation of the Church.* Louisville: Westminster/John Knox Press, 1993.

___________. "Authority and the Challenge of Feminist Interpretation." *Feminist Interpretation of the Bible.* Edited by Letty M Russell. Philadelphia: The Westminster's Press, 1985: 137-146.

___________. "Good House Keeping." *Feminist Theology: A Reader.* Edited by Ann Loades. London: SPCK, 1990: 225-238.

___________. "Reflections on White feminist Theology in the United States." *Women's Visions. Edited by Ofelia Ortega,* Geneva: WCC Publications, 1995. 102-111.

Russell, M. Letty, Ed. *Feminist Interpretation of the Bible.* Philadelphia: The Westminster's Press, 1985.

Russell, M. Letty and J. Shanon Clarkson, eds. *Dictionary of Feminist Theology,* Louisville: Westminster John Knox Press, 1996.

Russo, Mohanthy and Torres, Eds. *Third World Women and the Politics of Feminism.* Bloomington: Indiana University Press, 1991.

Sadangi, Charan Himansu. *Dalit: The Downtrodden of India.* Delhi: Gyan Publishing House, 2008.

Sakenfeld, Katherin Doob. "Feminist Uses of Biblical Material" *Feminist Interpretation of the Bible.* Edited by Letty M Russell, Philadelphia: The Westminster's Press, 1985: 55-64.

Sangari, Kumkum and Vaid, Sudesh. *Recasting Women: an Introduction.* New Delhi: Kali for Women, 1990.

Sangari, Kumkum. Consent, "Agency and the Rhetorics of Incitement," *Economic and Political Weekly,* 1 May (1993), 867-882.

Saravanavel. P. *Research Methodology.* Allahabad: Kitab Mahal Agenices, 2005.

Schaberg, Jane, Alice Bach, and Esther Fuchs, Eds. *On Cutting the Edge: The Study of Women in Biblical World.* New York: Continuum International Publishing Group, 2004.

Selvi, Kamala Raja M. "The Dalit Woman-The Fourth Class Citizen." *Frontiers of Dalit Theology.* Edited by V. Devasahayam, Madras: Gurukul Summer Institute, 1996: 117-129.

S. J. Arokiadoss A. "The Spirit of New Creation an Exploration into Dalit Pneumatology" in *Frontiers of Dalit Theology.* Edited by V. Devasahayam, Madras: Gurukul Summer Institute, 1996: 433-456.

S. J. George Pattery. *Gandhi – the Believer: An Indian Christian Perspective.* Delhi: ISPCK, 1996.

S. J. Navone, John. *Towards a Theology of Story.* Slough, U.K.: St. Paul Publications, 1977.

Sequeira, Leo. "Human Response to Dalit Women Today" in *Dalit Women in India: Issues and Perspectives,* Edited by P. G. Jogdand, New Delhi: Gyan Publishing House, 1995: 122-134.

Shah, A. M., B. S Baviskar, & E. A. Ramaswamy, Eds. *Social Structure and Change: Women in Indian Society,* Vol. 2. New Delhi: Sage Publications, 1996.

Shea, John. *Stories of God: An Unauthorized Biography.* Chicago: Thomas More, 1978.

Shiva, Vandana. *Staying Alive: Women, Ecology and Development.* London: Zed Books Ltd., 1988.

Shinde, Kumar Pande, Ed. *Dalits and Human Rights: Dalits: Security and Rights Implications.* New Delhi: Isha Books, 2005.

Sindima, J. Harvey. *The Gospel According to the Marginalized.* New York: Peter Lang Publishing, 2008.

Singh, Buta. *The Dalits and Dalit awakening in India.* New Delhi: Gyan Publishing House, 2004.

Singh, B. N. "Kushwant Singh's Delhi: A Post-Colonial Novel" in *Writing in a Post-Colonial Space.* Edited by Surya Nath Pandey, New Delhi: Atlantic Public Distributers, 1999: 141-153.

Soares-Prabhu, George. "The Table Fellowship of Jesus: Its Significance for Dalit Christians in India Today." *Jeevadhara.* XXII (1992): 140-159.

Soellee, Dorothee. *Theology of Skeptics: Reflections on God,* Translated by Joyce L. Irwin. Minneapolis: Fortress Press, 1992.

Soskiceand, Martin and Dian Lipton, Eds. *Oxford Reading in Feminism: Feminism and Theology,* Oxford: Oxford University Press, 2003.

Sponheim, Paul R. *God – The Question and The Quest: Toward Conversation Concerning Christian Faith.* Philadelphia: Fortress Press, 1985.

Spivak, Gayathri Chakravorty. *Outside in the Teaching Machine.* New York: Routledge, 1993.

Stroup. George W. *The Promise of Narrative Theology.* London: SCM Press LTD, 1981.

Sugirtharajah, S.R. *Vernacular Hermeneutics.* Sheffield: Sheffield Academic Press, 1999.

____________. *The Bible and the Third World: Pre-colonial, Colonial and Post-colonial Encounter.* Cambridge: Cambridge University Press, 2001.

Sugirtharajah S. R. and Cecil Hargreaves, Eds. *Readings in Indian Christian Theology.* Vol.1. Delhi: ISPCK, 1993.

Sugirtharajah R. S., Ed. *The Postcolonial Biblical Reader.* Malden: Blackwell Publishing Limited, 2006.

____________. Asian Biblical Hermeneutics and Post Colonialism: Contesting the Interpretations, London: Continuum International Publishing Group, 1999.

Sumitra, Sunand. *Christian Theologies from an Indian Perspective.* Bangalore: Theological Book Trust, 1995.

Surekha, N. *Liberation Beyond Borders: Dalit Feminist Hermeneutics and Four Gospel Women* (Doctoral Thesis) New Jersey: Drew University, 2008.

____________. "A Dalit Women's Voice in Biblical Interpretation" in *God's Image,* Vol. 26, and No. 3 (September 2007): 51-55.

Sujatha, Surepally. "The Status of Dalits", *International Humanist News www.iheu.org/node/1813* (8th October 2008).

Sykes J. B, Ed. *The Concise Oxford Dictionary of Current English* (Seventh edition) Oxford: Clarendon Press, 1982.

Taljaard, Aniene. "On Belonging and Longing" in *Theologies: Essays in Honor of Denise Ackarman.* Edited by Miranda. N. Pillai, Sarojini Nadar, Clint Le Bruyns, Denise Ackrman, Stellonbosch: SUN Press, 2009: 39-48.

Tappen, Mark B. "The Cultural Reproduction of Masculinity: A Critical Perspective on Boys Development" in *Cultural and Critical Perspectives on Human Development.* Edited by Martin J. Packer, Mark B. Tappen New York: State University of New York, 2001: 241-260.

Tennis, Diane. *Is God the Only Reliable Father?* Philadelphia: Westminster, 1985.

Thaveedu, Aruldoss. *The Relevance of the Social Teachings of Martin Luther for Dalit Liberation.* Madurai: J & D Publications, 1997.

"The Autobiography and Family History of Gertruth Kettener," *Women's Missionary Outlook*, (Chennai: Archives, Gurukul).

"The Lutheran Enterprise in India: Hermannsburg and Ohio in India, Rev. C. W. Oberdorfer, Gudur" in *Gospel Witness.* Vol. XXXIV, No. 3 (November 1938).

Thistle Waite, Brooks Susan. *Sex, Race, and God: Christian Feminism in Black and White.* London: Geoffrey Chapman, 1990.

Thomas, Linda. "Womanist Theology, Epistemology, and a New Anthropological Paradigm", *www.crosscurrents.org/thomas.htm.* (13th September 2008).

Thomas, M. M. "The Secular Ideologies of India and the Secular Meaning of Christ" in *Readings in Indian Christian Theology.* Vol. 1 Edited by R. S. Sugirtharajah and Cecil Hargreaves, Delhi: ISPCK, 1993: 93-101.

Tolbert, Ann Mary. "Defining the Problem: The Bible and Feminist Hermeneutics" in *Semeia: An Experimental Journal For Biblical Criticism. 28* Chicago: Scholars Press, 1983: 3-27.

Trible, Philis. *God and the Rhetoric of Sexuality.* Philadelphia: Fortress Press, 1978.

Trivedi, R. Harshad. *Scheduled Caste Women: Studies in Exploitation.* Delhi: Concept Publishing Company, 1977.

Turner J. C. and H. Giles. *Intergroup Behavior.* Oxford: Blackwell, 1981.

Ucko, Hans. *The People and he People of God: Minjung and Dalit Theology in Interaction.* Munster: LIT, 2002.

Van Der Nolle, H. C., "Bultmann's vision of God's revelation in Creation" in *Theology Digest,* Vol. 26 (2) (1978) 160-164.

Varkey, Mammen. "Church as People's Movement." *Religion & Society*, Vol. 55 No. 1& 2 (March/June 2010): 61-66.

Virginia, Fabella and Mercy Amba Oduyoye, Eds. *With Passion and Compassion: Third World Women Doing Theology.* New York: Orbis Books, 1989.

Vithal, Renuka and Volmink, John. "Mathematics, Curriculum Research: Roots, Reforms, Reconciliation and Relevance" in *Researching Mathematics Education in South Africa: Perspectives, Practices*. Edited by Renuka Vithal, Jill Adler and Christine Keitel, HSRC Press, 2005: 2-26.

Walker, Alice. *In Search of our Mothers' Gardens: Womanist Prose*. London: The Women's Press, 1984.

Waltmann, Alter. "Methodology of Latin American Liberation Theology and a Contextual Re-reading of Luther" in *Prejudice: Issues in Third World Theologies*. Edited by Andreas Nehring, Madras: Gurukul Summer Institute, 1996: 102-119.

Watson, Annie Rajula. *A Christian Understanding of Land Ethics*. Delhi: ISPCK, 2004.

Weidmann, Judith. *Christian Faith*. New York: Harper and Row, 1984.

Webster, C. B. John. et.al. Ed. *From Role to Identity: Dalit Christian Women in Transition,* Delhi: ISPCK, 1997.

Wilfred, Felix. *Asian Dreams and Christian Hope: At the Dawn of the Millennium*. Delhi: ISPCK, 2000.

Williams, S. Delores. *Sisters in the Wilderness: The Challenge of Womanist God-Talk*. New York: Orbis Books, 1993.

____________. "Womanist Theology." *Women's Visions*. Edited by Ofelia Ortega. Geneva: WCC Publications, 1995: 112-126.

____________. "Womanist Theology: Black Women's Voice" in *Black Theology: A Documentary History*. Vol. II Edited by James H. Cone and Gayraud S. Wilmore, N.Y: Orbits Books, 1993: 265-272.

Walters, T. Heike. *Prophetic Participation: M.M. Thomas' Concept of Salvation and Collective Struggle for Fuller Humanity in India*. Delhi: ISPCK/UTC, 1996.

Wood, C. David, Ed. *On Paul Ricoeur: Narrative and Interpretation*. London and New York: Routledge, 1991.

Webliography

dictionary.reference.com/browse/status (accessed on 23.9.2010).

http://en.wikipedia.org/wiki/Identity_(social_science) (accessed on 5.7.2010).

Joseph, Pushpa. __________. *www.geocities.com/ecclesiaofwomen/jan2005/pushpa,* (1st February 2009).

Joseph, Pushpa. __________. *ecclesiaofwomen.ning.com/.../ewa-2-homepage-body-and* (5th April 2010).

Margaret, Swathi. *http://www.sannaduttgu.com/INSIGHT/editorial_swathi_margaret* (3rd June 2005).

Massey, James. "Need of Dalit Theology." *CTC Bulletin*. *www.cca.org.hk/resources/ctc/ctc01-04i.htm* (2nd November 2008).

www.uelci.org/member-churches.asp (accessed on 23.6.2009).

dalitstudies.org.in/.../Report_on_the_Dalit_Women_Conference_Mar_2010.pdf (accessed on 20.9.2010).

www.dalitchristians.com/Html/dalittheology.doc (2nd October 2008).

Archives

SALC 125th Anniversary, *Souvenir*, (1991).

Souvenir of the Centennial (1865-1965): Celebrated by the South Andhra Lutheran Church and Her Founding Missions at Tirupati, Chittor District Andhra Pradesh. Madras: Diocesan Press, 1966.

"50 Years History of Harmannsburg Evangelical Lutheran Mission of South Andhra Lutheran Church from 1865-1915" (Chennai: Archives: Gurukul).